STONES OF THE NEW CONSCIOUSNESS

ALSO BY ROBERT SIMMONS:

The Book of Stones: Who They Are & What They Teach (with Naisha Ahsian)
Moldavite: Starborn Stone of Transformation (with Kathy Warner)
Earthfire

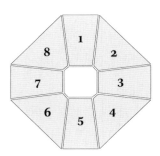

1. Moldavite 2. Phenacite 3. Rosophia 4. Blue Celestite
5. Azeztulite 6. Morganite 7. Agni Gold Danburite 8. Cryolite

STONES
OF THE NEW
CONSCIOUSNESS

Healing, Awakening & Co-creating
with Crystals, Mineral & Gems

ROBERT SIMMONS
Introduction by Robert Sardello

HEAVEN & EARTH PUBLISHING LLC
EAST MONTPELIER, VERMONT

North Atlantic Books
Berkeley, California

Published by
Heaven and Earth Publications LLC
PO BOX 249
East Montpelier, Vermont 05651
and
North Atlantic Books
PO BOX 12327
Berkeley, California 94712

Cover photos by John Goodman and Jeff Scovil
Cover design by Pat Gaudreault and Margery Cantor
Book design by Margery Cantor

Scenes of the Passion, detail of the Universe by Antonio Campi on page 69. Photo by Jean Schormans. Photo credit: Réunion des Musées Nationaux/ Art Resource, NY.

"A Chunk of Amethyst" used by permission from Robert Bly.

Photo credits
    All photographs by John Goodman, except as noted below.
    Jeff Scovil 122, 129 (x2), 196, 225, 226
    Rob Lavinsky 157, 195, 384
    Mae Won Ho, ISIS Foundation 30
    NASA 68
    Robert Sardello 73

Collages by Kathy Helen Warner xx, 2, 42

Printed in Canada

Stones of the New Consciousness: Healing, Awakening and Co-creating with Crystals, Minerals and Gems is sponsored by the Society for the Study of Native Arts and Sciences, a nonprofit educational corporation whose goals are to develop an educational and cross-cultural perspective linking various scientific, social, and artistic fields; to nurture a holistic view of arts, sciences, humanities, and healing; and to publish and distribute literature on the relationship of mind, body, and nature.

North Atlantic Books' publications are available through most bookstores. For further information, visit our Web site at www.northatlanticbooks.com or call 800-733-3000.

Heaven and Earth Publications' books are widely available. For further information call 800-942-9423 or visit our Web site at www.heavenandearthjewelry.com.

Library of Congress Cataloging-in-Publication Data

Simmons, Robert, 1951-
  Stones of the new consciousness : healing, awakening, and co-creating with
crystals, minerals, and gems / Robert Simmons ; foreword by Robert Sardello.
      p. cm.
  Includes bibliographical references and index.
  ISBN-13: 978-1-55643-811-0
  ISBN-10: 1-55643-811-7
  1. Crystals—Miscellanea. 2. Minerals—Miscellanea. 3.
Gems—Miscellanea. 4. Precious stones—Miscellanea. 5. Spiritual healing.
I. Title.
  BF1442.C78S559 2009
  133'.2548—dc22
                        2009026398

1 2 3 4 5 6 7 8 9 Transcontinental 14 13 12 11 10 09

To the Stone Beings, and to the One who dwells within my heart, and every heart.

The author with two of his favorite Azeztulites.

ACKNOWLEDGMENTS

My heart calls out in gratitude to my friend Robert Sardello, who encouraged me in every possible way, helping me to reimagine the stones and our relationship with them. Robert, your ideas have inspired and awakened me, and they have led me to many treasured things. I stand beside you as a friend of Sophia.

To Cheryl Sardello, I offer deepest thanks for your friendship and openness, and your attention to the many details of running the School of Spiritual Psychology. You have made your home a welcoming place for me and for hundreds of people seeking the path of soul.

I am grateful to my friend and co-author of *The Book of Stones,* Naisha Ahsian. You have taught me, amazed me, tolerated me and made me laugh on numerous occasions. I know I am your brother, whatever planet that happened on.

Mr. Daniel Deardorff, a man on speaking terms with the Stone People, thanks for saving my life and holding me in your heart, as well as teaching me a thing or two about the living world and life outside the Wall.

To Margery Cantor, our dear friend and book designer, my deepest appreciation for fun times and Buddhism, for the beauty of your work and the loveliness of your soul. To my pal Dr. Bill Warnock, thanks for helping me with health and poetry, which belong together. To Hisae Matsuda and Kathy Glass, who contributed immeasurably to getting this monster to press, I bequeath a pair of first-class tickets to Valhalla, or the Divine realm of your choice. To Richard Grossinger and Lindy Hough, thanks for being my friends, and for running a publishing house in a way that makes me proud to know you. To the staff of our company, Heaven and Earth, whose work, spirit and sense of humor make my life possible, more gratitude than I can say in words. You are all in my heart. For photographer and buddy John Goodman, my salute to a hero who is insufficiently sung. No one reading this book will be able to tell which pictures you took from the roof of the Nerd Center.

To everyone who reads my work, or who loves the stones, I extend my heartfelt appreciation. You are the pioneers of the New Consciousness.

I admit to having saved the best for last. To my beloved wife Kathy Helen Warner, I offer my all, forever. You have shared your life with me. You hugged me, helped me, healed me, consoled and encouraged me. You taught me truth by being true. You taught me love by loving. You are my best friend, my inspiration and my treasure.

—Robert Simmons

CONTENTS

INTRODUCTION

Dear readers, you are about to be amazed, moved, challenged and quite possibly radically transformed! The content of this book will do that if you allow it to. But, it is not the force of the content alone that will surge through you, prompting pleasurable inner upheaval and a rearrangement of who you are, placing you within the conscious possibility of experiencing much more vividly who you are intended to be as a spiritual human being. The internal fire of Robert Simmons warms this writing—or, I should say, fires it up, so that you can see your lives in a new light and feel a new kind of love ignited.

At last count, the number of books on what crystals can do for you was beyond count. They pretty much all follow the same format—a listing of minerals and crystals along with the characteristics they inspire. No one, NO ONE, until this book, had developed a clear and persuasive framework for understanding why one would desire to work meditatively with crystals and minerals for other than what finally amounts to personal desire for improvement, healing or receiving qualities that one feels in need of. Spiritually seen, we have to say that a strong element of egotism follows the existing crystal path. Now, thanks to this writing, we are able to see that those many compendiums of stones and all the effort that so many people have put into working with stones has been a preparation for what is described in this writing—the potential for inner work with stones to be world-transformative! It is a matter of *utilizing* the ground we stand on to *change* the ground we stand on.

The title of this book carries two meanings. It promises that there is a grouping of stones that can be of assistance in initiating a different and advanced mode of consciousness. This promise means that working with the stones described cannot be seen as another "add-on" to who you are. Spiritual interests often carry the assumption that, after all, we are pretty good and effective and important the way we are, but it would be nice to be able to be even more that way, and crystals can help fill in the gaps. Working that way with stones will not produce a new consciousness.

A second way of hearing the title is that the writing itself is exemplary of the new consciousness. This book could not have the title *Stones of the New Consciousness* while the writing is itself an example of old consciousness; that is, if the very tenor of the writing of this book were typical and usual, that would be a cause for some degree of suspicion on the part of the reader. The form of this writing does not disappoint, and thus it requires a degree of openness to enter fully into the flow, a willingness to release any concern of wondering where it might be going and, most importantly, the capacity to notice what is occurring inwardly as you read.

Of course, the title immediately brings up the question of what counts as "old" and what counts as "new." The terms here are not about time *per se*. It is not so much a matter of what came earlier and what came later; in fact, one is urged to be cautious of that way of reading, for consciousness is always whole, and thus "old" and "new" cannot primarily be thought of linearly. If something is promised to be new as a consciousness, that means that the Whole has reconfigured. Thus, the writing itself is within this reconfiguration and is not merely a "journalistic" report *about* it. When you complete this book you will notice an ongoing reverberation, as if your consciousness, down to your toes, "hums" a "new tune," one never heard nor felt before, but one that has been longed for without knowing what the longing was about.

The way into this book is to keep in mind that the author has been through everything that he speaks of within the writing. The authoritative voice herein comes from someone who has undergone radical transfiguration of being through work with stones. This transfiguration occurred without a road map. He did not know where he was in the process, for how can one foresee where the road is to come to at least a provisional stopping place if the road is not even there until being made, step by step by the inner practices described in this writing? Still, something of the nature of "new consciousness" did come to our author when he woke one morning to a voice that said that the new consciousness is "blessing." This active word "blessing," which is both a doing and a way of being as well as the very most intimate gesture of the world toward us, constitutes the path of this book.

Does "blessing" mean that we are blessed by stones? Does it mean that we approach stones within a blessing mode of consciousness and being? Neither of these alternatives would be "new consciousness." In our more usual consciousness, those who are intrigued and interested in stones typically carry the notion that somehow the stones themselves have special, maybe magical properties that are available to us merely by being in proximity to a stone with given attributes. That is "blessing" in the old sense. Similarly, if one thinks that it takes someone with a particular gift to convey the power of stones, that understanding of "blessing" is also old. What is new and transformative here is the very experience of "blessing" as the "between," the overlap between our consciousness and the stone's consciousness. This is the transfigurational "space" where we can, at last, be relieved of our intrepid egotism, get out of ourselves and dwell within qualities so large and vast and deep and unending and so active and all-encompassing that not only are we changed, but currents of change then reverberate into the world.

Robert Simmons was not content with the appearance of "blessing" as a "message" heard upon waking one morning. To stop there would be incommunicable—it would not help others in the quest, and stopping with inward satisfaction would have the result of taking the new consciousness as something merely personal, not for the whole of humanity and the Earth. The comparison might be exaggerated, but I am reminded of the great mystic Jacob Boehme. He was polishing a pewter dish one day when he suddenly saw into the light on the dish, and the whole of creation opened to him. This vision lasted a very short time. He then spent the rest of his life writing huge volumes trying to convey the vision. Boehme was willing to engage in this life work because he knew he saw something for the whole of the world. This story is a helpful analogy in reading the present book. There is a moment of a real vision, the words spoken by an unknown presence: "The New Consciousness is Blessing." The whole of this book is an unfolding of what those words really say.

You have before you the writing of a stone initiate. Do not, then, take this writing as another popular book on stones and maybe wonder why it seems considerably more complex than the others. This writing contains perhaps the deepest mysteries of the Earth—and of the Cosmos (as we know them so far). Thus, the chapters form a complex interweaving of myths, stories, biography, alchemy, science, description, experiences, dreams, meditations and practices—all oriented toward providing an invitation for us to enter into this new spiritual path that has as yet been singularly tread by this author. Imagine what it is like to set out where consciousness has never turned its light, and imagine the great gifts offered in this book—gifts of understanding, ideas, descriptions and tools to set us on that path.

Robert Simmons establishes a reasonable theory that adequately accounts for his initiatory experiences with stones. I am using the term "theory" here in its original sense rather than in its more restricted scientific sense. The term originally meant a "seeing," as when, for example, Greek heroes left the community to explore the unknown, going through innumerable trials to finally come to a "vision" or a theory, which is then brought back to spiritually advance the community. What Simmons sees is brought back in multiple forms. Science is one of the forms.

Why the science in this book on entering a new consciousness? Science is first of all a mode of consciousness rather than a body of knowledge gained by means of a certain method, as we typically understand it. It is a *way* of knowing, primarily of knowing the material world. While there are "social sciences," they follow the lead and methods of the physical sciences. The key here, though, is the interest in the physical world, in matter. The new consciousness resolves the false and illusory split between matter and consciousness. The whole of this writing is based on the dissolution of that split. It is thus possible, and is brilliantly done here, to read the findings of scientific research of a physical sort for its contribution to understanding not only consciousness but also future-consciousness. Indeed, one of the great spiritual tasks of our time is to work with the findings of science to hear them resound metaphorically, imagistically and symbolically within the soul. Such a practice, beautifully exemplified in this writing, saves us from the deadly literalism and materialism of the findings of science that sit there waiting for their completion within us as soul realities.

The science part of this book consists of Simmons' careful reading of research that he interprets as showing integral relationships between the human body and the realms of crystals and minerals. The intriguing research on the liquid crystal within the body, the research showing the emission of light by DNA, the now-large body of research on the thinking, feeling and capacity of consciousness exhibited by the heart, and the coherence of this body of research with some of the stones described in this book all make an important bridge between science, body, consciousness and world. The key dimension is the connection made between the research and the properties of stones such as the various forms of Azeztulite (with their relation to the "Nameless Light") and Moldavite and Rosophia (with their intimate connections to the heart and the imagination of a world-of-the-future, which is here now).

The most significant aspect of scientific discoveries reported by our author is his interpretation of the research that provides a feeling for how it is possible for the human body to perceive emanations of power from crystals and minerals. Simmons intuits an age-old truth concerning any kind or form of knowing: we cannot know anything of the outer world except through the existence of the known, in some form, as it exists within us. For example, we can see because the eye not only receives the light, but because a subtle form of light, etheric light, is emitted by the eye itself. We see not only because light comes into the eye, but because light goes out to meet the light. Something of this same sort applies to being able to sense the currents of stones. We feel the substantial qualities of stones, Simmons shows, because of the liquid crystal dimension of the human body. This research is significant in the context of this writing because Simmons has entered into a dimension of non-duality with the spiritual quality of "blessing." That same region of overlap, the process that exists between ourselves and the stone—not coming from here alone, not coming from there alone—Simmons is convinced should show up in the findings of science; and he found it with what is being called the " Liquid Crystal Body Matrix." The crystal within resonates with the crystal without, in the overlap of vibrations. Thus, we enter an entirely different kind of spirituality—one that does not separate spirit and matter. It is a spirituality that matches the very essence of stones as simultaneously spirit and matter, and of the human body partaking of that same unity.

In the research into scientific "evidence" for how crystals could possibly affect the human being, we have more than a search for verification from the present-day arbiter of what counts as real. One more link is provided that prevents such a hasty conclusion. That link is Simmons' report of research showing that meditative practices induce long-term changes in the body. This research provides the needed vision that allows us the insight that crystals do not only affect the body; working meditatively with crystals can elevate the vibratory qualities of the body to a higher state of coherence matching that of certain stones.

"To what end?" you may be asking. And you may be thinking, "I want to get something from crystals; I don't want to become a crystal." This is the point at which you are challenged to inwardly separate using crystals for your purposes only and crossing a threshold to enter into dimensions that are beyond our personal selves and are our deep soul and spirit participation with the Earth and the Cosmos and its intentions. Work with stones, though, is not quite such an either/or proposition; it is a matter of seeing and feeling that even when we utilize stones for our own purposes, the currents—because they occur "between"—are also world-shaping.

It is perfectly possible to read and derive much from this book without entering these very deep dimensions. An invitation, not a demand, is issued. There is plenty, heaps, loads in this book for those who have and are quite satisfied with a bit less serious relationship with stones. In fact, some may need to stay with simply experiencing the stones for a good long while. The time to enter these deeper dimensions will be felt as an inner pull. This is not a book designed for a one-time reading, but rather one of those rare writings that changes each time you read it, encompassing a great deal and existing simultaneously on different levels.

A number of sections in this book refer to and describe meditative practices that center in the region of the heart, while emphasizing the centrality of the heart rather than the mind in working with many of the stones of the new consciousness. The qualities occurring "between" the one working with stones and the stones themselves—the region of overlap—can only be recognized from within heart-consciousness. This locus also provides further clarity concerning exactly what is meant by "new consciousness." Simmons' heart approach is congruent with the research of Joseph Chilton Pearce, as well as the meditative heart practices of the School of Spiritual Psychology and the Heartmath organization. Working with stones, particularly those listed in the Stones section of this volume, not only assist one in developing capacities of heart-consciousness but also strongly suggest that the new consciousness *is* heart-consciousness.

Heart-consciousness first entails feeling. Feeling, not emotion. Feeling belongs to the heart and is the heart's capacity to, in effect, go beyond itself and come into connection—with anything, anywhere—and it is a form of knowing unlike any other kind of knowing. Thus, the word "feeling" is understood in exactly the way it functions as a word: a reaching-out to touch another, to feel the immediate presence of another, even when the other may be at a far distance or may be a spiritual being. Feeling is an act, just as when I reach out my hand and feel/touch the presence of another person. It is not an emotional reaction. The outer boundaries of the feeling heart are unknown. The new consciousness is not space- and time-bound. In addition, heart-consciousness is inherently creative consciousness. In the overlap that exists between the one working with a stone and the stone itself—a region that exists for the heart prior to the separation between the person and the stone—a particular and new mode of consciousness can be experienced, a mode of consciousness with its own laws. For example, the laws of cause-effect are suspended and we enter the lawfulness of simultaneity, instantaneity and synchronicity.

While this kind of creative consciousness is new to most if not all of us, it has its precedents. The Grail myth is once such precedent, and the integral practices of Sri Aurobindo and the Mother are another. Our author delves into both of these sources to amplify the creative nature of the new consciousness. How heart creates is somewhat different than how we typically understand creativity. We generally take "creativity" to mean that we produce something out of our imagination, something not pre-thought but more spontaneous and unknown. Heart-consciousness works like this too—with one great and wonderful addition: we are completely conscious within the process of the creating. Working with stones, Simmons shows, can enhance and further develop this new kind of creativity, not only for us individually but as something that can be brought into the world.

In this book the word "heart" most often refers to the organ of the heart. When "heart chakra" is intended, that term is always specified. Something exquisitely interesting happens when the capacity to enter into heart-consciousness is developed. We are fully conscious, and fully ourselves—in fact, we are ourselves in the way we are spiritually intended to be. We are our true "I." In ordinary and usual consciousness, our sense of "I" is that of a "me"—a me that is distinct and separate from others and from the world, and is completely oriented toward its own interests and survival. When we are within the heart, we are uniquely "us," and we also recognize from within, as a kind of moment of oscillation, that others are (like us) completely unique, and yet we are not separated from them but rather in intimate union with them. Others are as intimately with us as our jugular vein. And the world, too, as well as the Earth and the spiritual worlds, from within the heart, are uniquely themselves while at the same time a perfect unity of ourselves and these others exists. Both are coming into existence at each moment. This is the new consciousness. The Grail stories tell us the path of Parsifal toward this new way of being. Sri Aurobindo, the Mother and the creative telling of their story and furthering of it by Satprem give us a picture of a mighty exploration of this creative domain. Robert Simmons shows how working with stones can help develop and intensify the creative capacities of the new consciousness of the heart.

The heart that is the center of heart-consciousness is and is not the physiological organ of the heart: a conundrum for the mind, for sure. An analogy may help. Imagine a being whose lower part lives and is immersed in the water, and whose upper part lives within the air and earth environment. Further, imagine that the part living below the water is solid, substance, physical, while the part that lives above, in the air, is also of substance but diaphanous, subtle and visible only to those who have undergone a practice to see in new ways. This unity is a kind of picture of the heart and of heart-consciousness described in this book. The heart spoken of in this writing is the physical heart, which is also simultaneously a spiritual organ of perception that can, in its own ways, feelingly think and feelingly will.

This kind of soul, spirit and matter unity also characterizes the Light Body that working with stones can assist in building up. Heart-consciousness reconfigures the body into the Light Body. A human potential begins to be an actuality through stone assistance. With the Light Body, it becomes possible to perceive the Light Body of the Earth and to see that Earth herself is in a process of evolution, of spiritual evolution that is intimately interwoven with the spiritual evolution of the human being. One cannot occur without the other, as this writing confirms.

Simmons gives a very detailed meditative stone practice for experiencing the Light Body, a practice consisting of a stone layout on the body. It is an amazing practice utilizing the most important stones of the new consciousness. Such stone layouts are often utilized for healing; here it is used for body transfiguration. When done, no intellectual questions concerning the nature of the Light Body will remain. Experience resolves the inevitable doubting of the mind. It also resolves the doubting of the cells of the body themselves.

One of the most fascinating sections of this book, a point of intensification of the whole of the book, concerns the new consciousness and immortality. The word is terribly confusing and makes us think either of angels or Frankenstein. The thought that working with stones might result in immortality could well bring you to a heavy pause in reading. Immortality should not be approached as a mental question. Our mentality is not up to it. Experience the stone layout for the Light Body. Within the consciousness of that layout there is simply the absence of being a transient organism. Something bodily occurs, and this occurrence is not the result of a dimming of consciousness into a trance state or a suggestive state, or a delirious state of ecstasy. The change occurs in the opposite direction. We find ourselves more intensely as well as more widely conscious, more vividly present, more here than ever, and it is immediately inwardly given that being a Light Body is our true nature.

Why does this state not persist? Is it due to the habit-nature of the cells, as Simmons suggests based upon the research of the Mother? Perhaps. Habit is our way of inhabiting the past every moment instead of living within the coming-to-be. Habit is the abode of security, one that we cannot simply discard, as it is deeply inscribed into every dimension of our being. It would seem, then, that with every movement into the unknown we are condemned to meet only a version of what we have already been. The way through this enclosure formed the central research of the Mother in India (with somewhat mixed results). Now, with this new work with stones, the question has been re-opened.

In order to enter the question of immortality from the point of view framed by Robert Simmons, and in order to enter it not cautiously but rightly, it is important to notice and inwardly work with the sections of this writing having to do with the Soul of the World, She who in the esoteric tradition is called Sophia. Simmons has done an amazing job of interweaving science and spiritual practice. In addition, he skillfully incorporates the necessary dimension of soul. Soul concerns interiority as it exists individually but also as the interior animating dimension of everything. The reason why it is not yet possible to enter into the Body of Light and for it to persist is that the cosmic and personal dimensions of soul can and do separate from its (better said, Her) unity with spirit. It is a necessary and nonetheless tragic separation, one that theologies of the spirit have pondered endlessly. Through soul separating from its unity with spirit (for example, the Gnostic myth of the fall of Sophia tells this story), longing for spirit becomes unfilled desire that holds fast to past experiences, either to avoid future difficult and painful experiences or to try to endlessly savor the pleasurable ones. At the same time, soul gives the gift of experiencing interiority, along with the dimension of freedom. If we were only spirit, our spiritual practices would make us into automatons of the good. Much existing work with crystals would in fact unwittingly make us into such automatons who, having this or that crystal, are magically transformed into our higher selves. The pinnacle of the innumerable contributions of Robert Simmons in these pages is to be found in his artful inclusion of the soul dimensions and stories of the World Soul and Sophia in a work of spiritual meditation with stones.

Working with stones by way of the many practices detailed in this book, particularly always starting such practices with the one titled "Heart Alignment," will ensure that a re-orientation of the soul toward the spirit occurs with every occasion of working with stones. Such work changes desire that is only personal and often disguised as selfless (when it is actually self-centered) into longing. The shift from desire into longing alleviates the press of feeling that we have to get something for ourselves, for the "me" in this work with crystals and minerals. As long as spiritual work with stones is "me"-centered, it can be of no real assistance to the needs of the world, though it may assist our conceptions of what we might think the world needs. Spirit is always impulsive. It explodes out, tries to get to the goal without going through the thickness of the world. The Grail story tells of the dangers of the manic spirit and the necessary detour through the world's interiority in order to arrive at the goal, the Grail, which is immortality properly understood. By "properly understood" I mean that it is not literalized immortality as spirit without soul would conceive of it, and neither is it bound to the desire for immortality as soul would conceive of it without spirit. Parsifal, the main character of the Grail story, is a name that means "through the middle"; the "middle" resonates with the place of the heart as the middle between mind and will, thinking and doing, and it also resonates as the path through the thickness of the interiority of the world, between the mania of the heights and the depression of the depths. Following the trail of what a true sense of immortality might mean and the role of stones in coming to such an experience is one of the most exiting aspects of what Robert has given us.

If you begin to find an inner feeling of mania while you read, then slow down—the soul quality of the writing is being missed. The soul quality occurs between the words, and in the gulps and pauses, and in the seemingly irresolvable questions, and in the holding of the whole of this writing in its unity. In the many practices described, a very special soul dimension is to be discovered; when you enter into it you enter into the nameless, so it is mostly without words and close to impossible to describe.

Sophia is certainly mentioned, many times, in this writing and in relation to this concrete experience of intimations of immortality. It is not so easy, though, to have a real sense of the Sophia, and even more difficult to enter into relationship with her. There is a tendency to place her among the goddesses, to make a cult of her. Such inclinations are radical mis-directions, for she is the source of all the goddesses without herself being a goddess alongside them. It is as much of a mistake to think of her as a Goddess as it is to think of God as a old man with a beard; that is, she cannot be personified, though she is the source of all personifications of spiritual and soul beings. Perhaps a brief picture will help. This picture comes from the visionary spirituality of Jacob Boehme, whom I mentioned before.

A central aspect of Boehme's visionary state concerned the moment of creation. It is a moment that is happening all the time, not some time in the distant past. He first describes God as the simultaneity of pure interiority and all-concentration and as pure expansiveness: concentration inward and expansion outward, simultaneously. This simultaneity, however, creates nothing. It becomes only a vortex of motion, for a vortex is precisely this same simultaneity, now in a form approaching creating but not in itself able to create anything. And, within this vortex of concentration and expansion exists desire and imagination. It is not an empty void. Boehme includes nature within the deity. An incredible move. But, God is only potential, there is no created, only creating, which by itself is only potential. There is another element present. It is described by Boehme as a kind of Mirroring—a vast Mirroring, as vast and without end as the creating vortex itself. This Mirroring is Pure Receptivity; it is Sophia, Wisdom, who by Her active radical receptivity brings about the patterning of all of the created. Upon "seeing" the presence of Sophia, She who is present from the beginning, a lightning flash of untold proportions happens (today we call this the Big Bang), and creation takes place. As creation takes place, however, the Soul of the World, Sophia, becomes detached from its original unity with the One. This process of increasing detachment is called the Aeons by the Gnostic tradition. It is, in the words of the Russian Sophiologist, Bulgagov, the task of the divine humanity to reorient individual and World Soul toward the spirit. When we are within the heart we are within our divine humanity.

Robert Simmons intuits—that is, inhabits—the very essence of this myth, this truth that never happened but is always happening. His devotion to Soul, and to the Soul of the World, will not allow him to put forth a theory of crystals, of stones, that manically flies off to a projected goal, leaving the whole of the world behind and unrecognized in its soul being. His devotion to Soul, further, will not allow him to bypass the meaning of his night dreams, soul's language, as informative of the way of stones, nor does he bypass the details of what he experiences, felt interiorly. It is this devotion to Soul that leads him to the heart and makes the heart the leader of this new discipline, this new path, this new consciousness.

Large portions of this book are dedicated to describing practices with stones, various "tools" for working with stones, how stones heal, and the vital compendium of stones of the new consciousness. These chapters are integral with the whole of the book, and letting this writing live deeply within the soul means being able to integrate these sections within the fullness of the context of the book. They are as much a part of the thinking of the whole as the thinking chapters are aspects of the doing. It is helpful, for example, to do some of the practices and then go back and read sections of the book that might have at first seemed abstract. Those sections change considerably once experience with the stones takes place.

The compendium of stones of the new consciousness, the descriptions of what the stones facilitate and the descriptions by Simmons of his experiences with the stones are invaluable. For example, the descriptions are written in such a manner that we are led into being able to notice things beyond what strikes us in our usual consciousness as important—that is, beyond our personal desires. He speaks very specifically of the flow of felt-currents through the body. These felt-currents differ in quality and form of movement for different stones. Noticing these currents gradually awakens body-awareness.

Development of the new consciousness demands awakening to body-awareness. Body-awareness is something very different than awareness of our body. The latter takes our body to be the material, physical, physiological, anatomical thing—perhaps with meridians and chakras inserted which we can, through practice, become aware of. That is old consciousness. It is our ingrained thoughts and ideas about the body that are then filled in, mostly in illusory ways, by what we might experience with stone meditations. We find the way out of that constructed view of the body into immediate body-awareness, first by being able to notice body sensations in conjunction with stone meditations. More importantly, transformations of body are occurring with the stone practices, and the "trails" of those invisible transformations are what can be experienced in body-awareness. The various currents do not "mean" anything; that is, they are really not intended to be interpreted as meaning something other than what they are—the flow of forces through the body that are loosening, transforming, subtlizing body, changing body from an abstract noun we live and have no real connection with except through sympathizing with our desires and having antipathy for what we don't like, into the continual creative act of bodying. Instead of carrying around something like an anatomical corpse, filling it either with abstractions or lofty ideals, we begin to feel the complete unity of body, soul and spirit. The differences of our trinity of being are differences of function, not differences of being. We are one, unified, unfinished, always bodily unfolding, feeling interiority within the folds of our flesh; and we are living substance on the way to becoming consciously spiritualized, but never disembodied.

A further and crucial dimension of working with the particular stones listed in the compendium concerns the loosening of the habits of the cells of the body and the re-orientation of soul from the desire to satisfy the "me" to the longing for the divine characterizing the creative

"I"—a longing that includes world-longing and Earth-longing to be, once again, included within the Whole of creation rather than separated off for utilitarian use and pleasure. Working with the stones, feeling their working on you bodily, is a process of catharsis. Catharsis means purification, the purification of the soul, the shifting of soul from darkness to luminous darkness. There is no opposition here between the Light and the Dark. Rather, there is the realization that there are two kinds of darkness. There is the abysmal darkness, darkness without the eternal Light, where we know who we are only in the smallest sense of ourselves, given through the turbulence of our desires and their satisfaction and the fleeing from unpleasantness. That is living in the dark. Then, there is another kind of dark, the kind we enter through working with the stones of the new consciousness. This is illuminated or luminous darkness—the Light beyond the Light is the way the esoteric Sufi tradition described this lighted darkness.

The purpose of this writing is to invite us into a process without end. A new way of living. There are other ways to enter into this process, but they are often tortuously difficult or filled even more with personal intentions than we have to confront when working with stones. For, with stones, we have the Silence of the stones that meets and beckons us—something which, by its very nature, removes us some from our own inner chatter and takes us out and beyond our usual selves. We need give only the slightest attention to a stone and we find the Silence, the deepest Silence imaginable, which is the entry into a new world. If we had to achieve this Silence on our own, we would almost immediately convert it into something that we want for ourselves, blessed solitude. But the stones, well, they are everywhere, and they are in and of the world, the Silent spiritual world of matter, the very matrix of our being. This matter is not the same matter known by physics. The last time such holy matter was known was during the time of the Vedas. Now, it is being rediscovered with this work with stones.

Just quietly holding one of the stones of the new consciousness puts us into resonance with the Truth. The Truth, though, is not something that one has and can possess. For example, in experiencing the Body of Light through the assistance of stones, if one takes the experience of the Light Body as an illumined body, there was not sufficient and careful enough attention, and one might feel that at last one has the Truth of the Light Body. One has not actually become the Light Body but has instead identified with one's thought of the Light Body. The actual Light Body concerns the much more invisible experience of the source of the Lighting, physically embodied, rather than what is lit up—a vast difference, and one that the stones themselves direct us toward if we but attend to them.

There are many and multiple ways of working with stones. A list of those ways is given in one of the chapters—wearing them, meditation, shamanic journeying, receiving messages, body layouts, healing grids, crystal acupuncture and many other practices. It is crucial, however, to know that working with crystals not only provides information but shapes the information provided. These methods may or may not result in an entry into the new consciousness, because the methods themselves shape what one is able to experience. For example, the shamanic world, real and powerful in its own right, is something very different than the world one enters through the heart. It is not a matter of excluding one in favor of another. Simmons displays a wonderfully open eclecticism at the very same time that he tries with all his might to orient us toward the magnificence of a particular direction. Active engagement, though, is first, and anything that will bring that about opens the possibility of finding this path that is particularly suited to this stage of the evolution of consciousness, the stage Rudolf Steiner spoke of as the age of the spiritual soul. And this path is suited to the mighty challenges and tasks of this time.

Robert Simmons' journey, remember, begins with Moldavite and then continues with Azeztulite. Rosophia is a stone of particular heart significance These are perhaps the prototypal stones of the new consciousness, with the rest serving as necessary reflectors, aspects of development, cleansing, healing, clearing and purification, in the particular ways needed for what is coming into being in the world—the entry of humanity into the guidance of the Feminine. The chapter on Azeztulite and its connection with the Great Central Sun points to this very significance. The Great Central Sun is a reference to the center of our galaxy. On December 21, 2012, the Earth will line up with the Sun and the center of the galaxy. In ancient Egypt the center of the galaxy was called Isis, the one who is also called Sophia. The Sun is the son of Isis and Osiris, Horus. A temple inscription has her saying: "*I, Isis, am all that has been, that is, or shall be. The fruit that I have brought forth is the Sun.*" And the Earth is us.

The Great Central Sun has been occluded for centuries and is thus esoterically known as the Black Sun, the Sun behind the Sun; or Sophia is known as the Black Madonna. The center of our galaxy shines a thousand times brighter than any other part of the galactic body, yet this presence lies hidden to our view. It is not likely that on December 21, 2012, the center of the galaxy will suddenly become visible. The moment marks the entry into the new time of the Feminine. Robert Simmons says that in a microcosmic way, Azeztulite is the stone of the Great Central Sun. The alignment begins the process of Her continual giving birth to a new consciousness, a new body and a new Earth. She may have prepared the way by installing this new stone, Azeztulite, into the Earth.

By being in alignment inwardly with our perfect nature (the Sun of the heart), and by surrendering our usual earthly ego to the heart, we come into connection with the purified spiritual Soul (the purified individual soul and the Soul of the World). The alignment of 2012 will be a new resonance of the human being, the resonance of the *spiritual human being,* who is humanity in a new form, something entirely different than human beings who do spiritual things. We begin our working partnership with the gods, or we could begin it at that time. The latter part of this book with its essays on the stones—their qualities and properties when worked with inwardly—is a training manual for learning the ways of this new, conscious partnership in the work of creating.

It is utterly amazing how Robert Simmons has been working these many years, intuitively and yet with great knowledge and even greater persistence, to prepare us for this moment. True originality and genius operates like that. It is not a matter of pre-knowledge and then working out the details. It is working totally from the pull of the heart, each trial, each practice discovered, revealing a little more. Proceeding in this manner is certainly something more than trial and error. Only a true friend of Sophia would be able to follow such a path so tirelessly. Robert Simmons, we are filled with gratitude that you have so honored this friendship!

—Robert Sardello, PhD
Co-director, the School of Spiritual Psychology
Benson, North Carolina

CHAPTER ONE

A New Crystal Vision

"The seat of the soul is where the inner world and the outer world meet. Where they overlap, it is in every point of the overlap."

—NOVALIS

I began my journey into the world of stones as a boy, way back in the 1960s. I recall going to a rock and mineral show with my Cub Scout group and purchasing a tumbled stone, an orange piece of Carnelian or Sardonyx. In the following months, that stone became my talisman—my favorite treasure—kept in the wooden box with the hidden latch that my aunt brought back for me from China. I didn't know why, but it was my most prized possession, more than any toy or book. I used to take it out of the box and look at it on my bed—a blaze of fiery, swirling color with a glossy, smooth skin, a heavy miniature world that lit up inside when I held it to the lamp. It was more precious and more mysterious than my exotic stamps, or the foreign bills and coins my aunt gave me, and much more valuable than my penny collection. I wondered where it came from, how long it had waited underground to be discovered and brought to my hands. We seemed to have a secret connection between us.

A year or two later, moving from the Midwest to Utah, my mother and I stopped at a tourist shop along the highway in Wyoming, where I saw a little medicine bottle of agates for sale for one dollar. She granted my excited request, and I now had a few dozen more magical shining stones, including one that was bright red. In our new home, I frequently spilled my whole horde out on the kitchen table to examine and arrange them. All of them were treasure, but the big orange orb remained King.

We meet the world through our senses and our imagination. That is how I met the stones. As the above quote from the nineteenth-century Romantic poet Novalis states, the meeting of the inner and outer world is the location of the soul. The soul is not within our body. The body is within the soul. Stones offer us one of the paths to the meeting of inner and outer, and they themselves have their own inner and outer qualities. Meeting the stones via the senses and the imagination is our path to engaging with *their* worlds, their souls. In that meeting, we may find a mutual capacity for enrichment, liberation and even love. On this path, we seek stones not so much for what they can do for us in terms of our "getting" prosperity, health, love or any other such concept. It is more a matter of pursuing the reward of the mutual pleasure of loving relationship, and the freeing of one another, and our shared overlap. The qualities of the stones that we perceive and identify exist in their *potential*. When we greet and encourage the stone beings, their qualities are freed into the world, for the benefit of the world. Because we are in the world, we share in that bounty. But just as importantly, the world is nourished. Approaching the stones as I did all those years ago, as children do instinctively, is a beginning step on this sacred path.

I again want to quote the poet Novalis. In regard to spiritual development, he wrote, "The first step is to look within, the discriminating contemplation of the self. He who remains at this point only half develops. The second step must be a telling look without—independent, sustained contemplation of the external world." Here is a place where the spiritual work we can do in partnership with stones goes beyond what is attempted on many spiritual paths. Work that emphasizes meditation and "retreat" from the distracting or unpleasant influences of life, or work that focuses primarily on mental or even emotional balance within oneself, can be helpful, but it isn't enough. One can and must do such inner healing work—the examination and re-working of one's patterns, wounds and habits. However, if the focus remains centered only on "me"—on "my" healing, "my" problems, even "my" happiness—things will not go well. If we leave out our relationship with the world, we end up isolated, alienated and afraid of life. As soon as we leave the meditation room, those pesky "outside" events upset our precarious inner "balance," and we are again frustrated. We are not separate from the world, and until we find our feet and claim the world as our home—our beloved living partner in life and evolution—our inner work will be unsustainable.

So where do the stones come in and join us? How can crystals help us establish conscious relationship with the world? There is much to say about that, and we can begin with the recommendation of Novalis. If the seat of the soul is where the inner and outer worlds meet, then there are innumerable opportunities for such meetings. Every moment of perception is just such an opportunity. However, since our focus here is on the stones, let's go into that: A stone is a part of the "outer" world, yet, as most readers of this book know from experience, it evokes inner qualities or feeling currents within us, if we open ourselves to the stone. Some of us are so eager to get to that surprising, rewarding inner experience that we don't give much focused attention to the outer traits of a stone. Others love the stones for what we call their beauty, or their amazing form, without realizing that the sense of beauty or amazement is an inner response to the outer expression of the stone itself. Why, we could ask, are gems precious to us anyway? Is it more than the colors and light reflections that meet the eye? If that were all, we would be satisfied with cut glass!

One way of practicing awareness of the outer qualities of stones, as they lead us into inner experience, involves what is called *phenomenology*. This word means "the study of what happens." That sounds either rather Zen or completely obvious, and it *is* both subtle and simple. For our admission into the realms of the stones, we have to pay a price—we have to pay *attention*—to what is present, and to what happens, both without and within. In so doing we develop the *capacity* of attention. A greater capacity of attention is a very genuine expansion of awareness. It may sound a little boring in comparison to our fantasies of great cosmic illuminations, but the capacity of attention is what makes us available to receive cosmic (and earthly) illuminations, both great and small. Engaging the stones to help us develop this capacity can make it both much easier and much more fun.

A POET PAYS ATTENTION

The poet Robert Bly has written a number of phenomenological prose poems. He calls them "object poems," and in them he focuses his inner and outer attention simultaneously on everything that happens as he observes an object. He has written one such poem about his experience with a crystal. The poem is called "A Chunk of Amethyst." We'll go through it together. As you read, notice how the poet is paying attention to what his senses tell him, and how the senses weave inward into his intuitive feeling.

"A Chunk of Amethyst"

Held up to the windowlight, the amethyst has elegant corridors that give and take light. The discipline of its many planes suggests that there is no use in trying to live forever. Its exterior is jagged, but in the inner house all is in order. Its corridors become ledges, solidified thoughts that pass each other.

This chunk of amethyst is a cool thing, hard as a dragon's tongue. The sleeping times of the whole human race lie hidden there. When the fingers fold the chunk into the palm, the palm hears organ music, the low notes that make the sins of the whole congregation resonate, and catch the criminal five miles away with a tinge of doubt.

With all its planes, it turns four or five faces toward us at once, and four or five meanings enter the mind. The exhilaration we felt as children returns. . . . We feel the wind on the face as we go downhill, the sled's speed increasing . . .

Having my own sense of the physical characteristics and spiritual properties of stones from years of working with them, I love seeing how Bly has come to meet the stone, and how he has actually felt its qualities. As he begins, he notices the way the crystal has grown, with its *elegant corridors* of light. He sees their regularity and calls it *discipline,* and indeed it is this regularity that defines crystallinity itself. He senses the stone's durability, in comparison with human frailty, saying that the crystal's discipline tells us *there is no use in trying to live forever.* He recognizes that the interior form of the crystal is orderly, whether its outer form is regular or not. Then he goes a little more inward, noticing the consciousness within the stone as *solidified thoughts.*

Holding the stone has by this time awakened the poet's imagination more deeply. Its physical qualities of coolness and hardness bring him into mythic, imaginal associations—*hard as a dragon's tongue.* Intuition becomes involved, and he senses the stone as what we might call a "record keeper": *the sleeping times of the whole human race lie hidden there.* He then begins to sense the stone's spiritual qualities, as *organ music* that brings doubt to one's *criminal* side. Amethyst is known metaphysically as a stone of spiritual purity and truth, aiding one in letting go of addictions and bad habits. This is resonant with the poet's intuitions, though he speaks them more colorfully.

In the last section, Bly encounters the stone as a being. He meets it. He mentions *four or five faces* turning toward him. He describes the enhancement of consciousness the stone brings to the encounter, as *four or five meanings enter the mind.* He then describes the thrill of recognition that comes when we realize that the stone is, in its own way, vibrantly alive—*The exhilaration we felt as children returns. . . . We feel the wind on the face as we go downhill, the sled's speed increasing.*

My own moments of meeting the stones as spiritual/soul beings have been moments of just such exhilaration. Many readers know what I mean. My belief is that it is possible for all of us. When we utilize that clear external observation, linked to inner willingness to be led by intuition and imagination, we will experience the opening of the doors to the many mansions of the crystal realms.

WHO ARE THE STONES?

Robert Sardello, my friend and contributor of the foreword of this book, has written:

> There is an unmistakable presence, a Who, that accompanies every stone with which we establish a relationship. And the connection is spiritual while being completely within matter. Here, by working in depth with stones, the age-old false division between spirit and matter is demonstrated as wrong, each moment we really take time to notice what is happening while holding a stone. Matter's spirit and soul reveals itself to us in utmost particularity. Sometimes we are shocked and thrown into tears with the overwhelming recognition of the soul of matter. . . .
>
> The range of the felt-sense of a relationship with a stone simultaneously spans the whole of the outer cosmos and the whole of the inner worlds, which are, after all, one. Stones, in other words, are the perfect tool in all the universe for simultaneous world and self-understanding. Scientific explanations are a metaphor for the outer dimension of the relationship, and magical explanations are a metaphor for the inner dimensions.

So Who, or what, are these crystals? One dictionary definition says a crystal is: "The regular form which a substance tends to assume in solidifying, through *the inherent power of cohesive attraction.* It is bounded by plane surfaces, *symmetrically arranged,* and each *species* of crystal has fixed axial ratios." [author's italics]

It is interesting to see that even this abstract dictionary definition resorts to terms that indicate intelligence, and even life. The *power of cohesive attraction* is not explained, though it sounds rather like the organizing intelligence that calls together and animates the substance of our own bodies. The phrase *symmetrically arranged* implies something or someone responsible for the arrangement, order and harmony that make a crystal what it is. And again, each type of crystal is a member of a *species,* just like all living organisms are. The unspoken sense that crystals are a sort of mineral version of life permeates even our science.

The word "crystal" derives from the Greek word *krystallos,* which means "ice." The ancients believed that quartz was actually water from the heavens frozen into eternal ice by the gods.

Consider that crystals were thought to be frozen *heavenly* water. Heavenly water, in the metaphorical sense commonly used in myth, would be the spiritual life-principle, just as physical water is the life-essence substance in the world of matter. So, for the ancients to say that quartz is frozen water from heaven is to say that the life-substance of heaven is, in the material world, eternally frozen—and eternally present in crystals, quartz in particular.

This sense of the living qualities of crystals was noticed by the genius of electricity, Nikola Tesla, who wrote, "In a Crystal we have the clear evidence of the existence of a formative life principle, and though we cannot understand the life of a crystal, it is nonetheless a living being."

Rudolf Steiner, another visionary who contributed greatly to the realm of science, offered the following:

> For us the crystal is an expression or the manifestation of an entire world. We look at many crystals, each of which encloses a world in itself. And here we stand on earth and say to ourselves: in the earth element we encounter the deeds of many worlds. And when we human beings on earth think and act, the thinking and doing of manifold *beings* flows together into our thinking and doing. We see in the immeasurably diverse crystal forms the revelation of *a great abundance of beings* living out their existence in spatial and mathematical figures. *In the crystals we are looking at the gods.*

In another lecture Steiner said:

> Our sense organs are therefore perceiving with, but do not perceive themselves. The same applies to the angels and the mineral world. Their sense organs are to be found in the mineral physical world. *Our precious stones are the angels' sense organs!* Precious stones are the secret instrument with which angels perceive.

Here we have a number of amazing ideas, which are not altogether unfamiliar to spiritual explorers who love crystals. The delight that enters us as we behold and engage with a lovely stone is easier to understand if we are encountering not only an interesting lifeless object but a living spiritual entity. We can imagine that this being has expressed itself in the material realm in a form that can transmit its essential qualities as well as receive impressions from other beings within the world. Let's assume that Tesla and Steiner are correct, that crystals are the expression of a life principle or angelic intelligence. In other words, the physical stone is the material component of a multi-dimensional being, and as such it is an inseparable expression of the nature of that being. For us, our bodies are the physical expression of our own essential nature. We can "meet" a stone in a way similar to the way we might meet a person, or an angel. And, as with a person from another country or an angel from another realm, we need to learn how to communicate, or commune, with the being behind the outer appearance.

How can we evaluate the suggestion that crystals are "angels among us"? What is the essential pattern or gesture of an angel? An angel is traditionally said to be a faithful messenger, carrying the Divine word, message or pattern of expression into this world. Faithfulness is one of the most clearly observable qualities of crystals as we already know them. Clocks are made with quartz crystals because of their unwavering fidelity to specific frequencies to which we attune them. Computers utilize silicon (quartz) chips for memory because they hold and retrieve information with utter dependability. Crystals are used in maintaining broadcasting frequencies, in microphones, in radios and other electronic equipment because they are such faithful *messengers,* just like the angels of our spiritual mythologies. Crystals are synonymous with inner harmony and order, just as the poet Robert Bly perceived in his meditation with the amethyst.

We know that crystals can and will hold the patterns and frequencies we ask them to carry for us, but what patterns do natural crystals hold? What have these angelic messengers brought into this world from the spiritual realms? These patterns are what authors like me and millions of stone lovers have called the stones' "spiritual properties." These properties or qualities are what we sense when we meditate with a crystal long enough, and carefully enough, to enter the realm of its nature. When we meet the spirit of a stone and discover its qualities, we have gone part of the way. The next, essential activity is to open inwardly to embody, through our own free will, those qualities. In this gesture we "accept the offer" from the spirit of the stone, and we make our own offer: to bring the potentials encouraged by the stone-spirit out of potential and into expression through our own being. By taking in and then expressing the properties offered by the spiritual realms—through the faithful angelic messengers, the stones—we "free" those qualities, which exist in the stones only as possibilities. What makes the miracle real is the overlap of ourselves as soul/spirit beings with the soul/spirit beings behind the stones. As I mentioned earlier, this is primarily a gift to the world, though the benefit of this blesses all.

Later in the book we will delve into the qualities of various stones, the ones that seem to me to be the most significant for the co-evolution of human beings and the Earth at this critical time. For now, I want to plant this seed about the new orientation toward our work with stones. Through this new outlook we can begin to recognize that our goal is not so much to achieve or gain anything but to offer ourselves wholeheartedly into the love relationship we already have with the Soul of the World. In this relationship, we will find ourselves within the New Consciousness, which can transform everything and allow us to live our highest destiny.

CRYSTALS IN MYTHS AND LEGENDS

Crystals and gems are associated with magic and supernatural qualities in the myths and lore of many cultures. According to the creation myths of the ancient Japanese, quartz materialized through the breath of the venerated White Dragon. As such, quartz was regarded as the perfect jewel and came to symbolize perfection or the pursuit thereof.

The Australian Aborigines used quartz crystals to invoke rain, as did certain Native American tribes. In Australian Aboriginal mythology, quartz is the most common substance identified with their mystical substance called maban, the material from which wise men (called karadjis) are said to obtain their magical powers. The Australian sky god, Daramulun, was long portrayed through art and sculpture as having a mouth full of quartz. Could a "mouth full of quartz" mean that the god "spoke" through the crystals?

Oceanic and Australian shamans also spoke of quartz as "a stone of light broken off from the celestial throne." (This recalls the ancient Greek image of quartz as eternally frozen heavenly water.) Ancient Chinese myths asserted that the heavens were like the roof of a cave, and stones were actually stalactites that had broken off and fallen to Earth. Stones such as the Black Stone of Cybele, the Palladium of Troy, and the omphalos at Delphi were considered prophets, or used as aids to divination. Some were believed to speak but others gave their oracles by rocking or, like the Roman Lapis lineus, changing colors.

In many countries, people (particularly heroes or the first humans) were said to have been born from stones. Usually these mother-stones had fallen from the sky. All stones were called the "bones of Mother Earth" in Greco-Roman and Native American traditions. Greek mythology explained the repopulation of the Earth after the Flood by claiming that the two survivors, Deucalion and Pyrrha, tossed the "bones of Mother Earth" over their shoulders and these then sprang up as members of a new human race.

In researching this book, I discovered that the name of Mani, the founder of Manichaeism and an important figure in the stream of Rudolf Steiner's work and that of Robert Sardello's spiritual psychology, is the Sanskrit word for "jewel" or gemstone. Mani's name was not from his family but was almost surely a chosen name or one given in initiation. Why that name? Mani was a third-century follower of Jesus. He was a Christian mystic who wanted to unite all religions, and he considered himself to be an incarnation of the Paraclete, or Divine Comforter. To take a name that means "gemstone" suggests that Mani, and others around him, associated gems with Divine qualities.

Following the thread of Mani, I came upon the legend of the Chintamani, or wish-fulfilling jewel of Tibetan and Hindu lore. For the Hindus, the mystical gem was involved with the myth of Ganesha, the elephant god who was said to grant wishes and remove obstacles. For the Tibetans, the Chintamani was *a sacred gem fallen from heaven,* kept in the fabled land of Shambhala. The mystic painter and world peace activist Nicholas Roerich, who lived and worked in the early twentieth century, believed the Tibetan and Hindu legends that the Chintamani stone truly existed, and he is reported to have made a pilgrimage to Tibet to retrieve a piece of the stone, which was used in an ultimately failed attempt to create a world government based on peace and tolerance.

Author Mark Amaru Pinkam has written the following:

When Nicholas Roerich was touring Tibet and Mongolia he constantly heard cries among the Buddhist monks of "It is the time of Shambhala!" According to the monks, the King of the World would soon sweep down from Shambhala with a huge army to destroy all evil upon the Earth before declaring himself our planet's eternal ruler. Supporting his inevitable rule was destined to be the Chintamani Stone, which currently resides in the King's Tower in the very center of Shambhala. Roerich and his mentors within the Great White Brotherhood and the Theosophical Society founded by Madam Blavatsky maintain that the army of the King of the World is, in truth, a power emanating from Shambhala that continually raises the frequency of our planet. It was, for example, this power that fueled WWII and, ultimately, led to the fall of the Third Reich, even after the Nazis attempted to harness it for their own self-serving purposes. Eventually this transformative power will destroy all energetic blockages that exist at a lower frequency than itself (i.e., negativity, greed, control, etc.) while simultaneously accelerating the evolution of all life forms on Earth. Once it has completed its pre-destined goal, state the Theosophists, a planetary civilization based upon love and equality will finally emerge. Perhaps then the King of the World and his Chintamani Stone will make their presence known universally to all.

One of the key stones we will discuss in this book is Moldavite, the meteoric gemstone that has long been compared to the Chintamani stone and similarly likened to the Philosopher's Stone and the Stone of the Holy Grail.

Following the thread of the Sanskrit word for gemstone, *mani,* I discovered yet another association of jewels and spiritual enlightenment, contained within the well-known Buddhist mantra *Om mani padme hum.* Here are the Dalai Lama's teachings regarding this phrase:

It is very good to recite the mantra *Om mani padme hum,* but while you are doing it, you should be thinking on its meaning, for the meaning of the six syllables is great and vast. . . . The first, *Om,* symbolizes the practitioner's impure body, speech, and mind; they also symbolize the pure exalted body, speech, and mind of a Buddha. The path is indicated by the next four syllables. *Mani,* meaning jewel, symbolizes the factors of method—the altruistic intention to become enlightened, compassion, and love. The two syllables *padme,* meaning lotus, symbolize wisdom. Purity must be achieved by an indivisible unity of method and wisdom, symbolized by the final syllable *hum,* which indicates indivisibility.

The usual translation of *Om mani padme hum* is "The jewel is in the lotus." Or we could make a sentence using the Dalai Lama's meanings: *The body, the gemstone, and wisdom are inseparable.* One could say that *Om mani padme hum* tells us that wisdom (which we will later define as the essential nature of the World Soul, or Sophia), the gemstones (those angelic presences carrying the patterns or messages of the heavenly realms), and our bodies are indivisibly one. This turns out to be literally true, since our physical bodies are, in fact, crystals.

THE CRYSTAL NATURE OF HUMANS

We are crystalline in two ways—through the liquid crystal nature of our tissues and cell structures, and in the crystal molecule of our DNA. We will look at each of these aspects in turn.

Molecular biologist Mae Wan Ho, a pioneer researcher into the liquid crystal nature of living organisms, has written:

> There is a dynamic, liquid crystalline continuum of connective tissues and extracellular matrix linking directly into the equally liquid crystalline interior of every single cell in the body. Liquid crystallinity gives organisms their characteristic flexibility, exquisite sensitivity and responsiveness, thus optimizing the rapid, noiseless intercommunication that enables the organism to function as a coherent, coordinated whole. In addition, the liquid crystalline continuum provides subtle electrical interconnections which are sensitive to changes in pressure and other physicochemical conditions; in other words, it is also able to register "tissue memory." Thus, the liquid crystalline continuum possesses all the qualities of a highly sensitive "body consciousness" that can respond to all forms of subtle energy medicines.

With this insight and these words, Mae Wan Ho offers a vision of our own physical bodies that makes us akin to and potentially resonant with all the other types of crystals. If the "body consciousness" is not dependent on neurons and electrical signals, then it is easier to imagine other consciousnesses that do not even require nervous systems. She also implies an answer to the questions posed by modalities such as acupuncture and other subtle energy medicines such as reiki and other types of hands-on healing, as well as homeopathy. All of these may be operating on the resonance of well-being within the entire liquid crystalline organism. This sort of view opens up our self-perceptions greatly. We are not prisoners within a mechanism. It is more like being a center of harmonious activity within a greater harmony.

Mae Wan Ho continues:

> The living body is a grand jazz concert in which every single cell, every single molecule is performing and improvising from moment to moment. And yet each molecule, each cell is so sensitive and responsive that it keeps fully in step and in tune with the whole system in evolution . . . [and] works in tandem with, and independently of the nervous system.

All she has said so far concerns the physical body and its measurable activities within matter. Does she offer us a bridge between the body and the spirit? This question is important in understanding the stones as beings, and our potential for relationship with them. And Mae Wan Ho does present us with just such a bridge:

> With our new view of the coherent organism, think of each organism as an entity that is not really confined within the solid body we see. The visible body just happens to be where the wave *function* of the organism is most dense. Invisible quantum waves are spreading out from each one of us and permeating into all other organisms. At the same time, each of us has the waves of every other organism entangled within our own make-up. We are participants in the creation drama that is constantly unfolding. We are constantly *co-creating and re-creating ourselves and other organisms in the universe,* shaping our common futures, making our dreams come true, and realizing our potentials and ideals.

If Mae Wan Ho's view is correct, then a particular mental stumbling block begins to dissolve, allowing us to take seriously the idea that we can "relate" with stones. We are not confined to the envelope of our body, she says. In fact, we extend far beyond the perimeter of our skin, into a gracefully entangled web of being that involves all other organisms. And what, in this vision, constitutes an organism? A crystal. Liquid in our case, solid in the case of stones. But in both instances the so-called physical body is merely the location where the activity of our being is most dense. Suddenly the difference between solid-state and liquid-state crystalline beings diminishes. We know we have consciousness, or we are consciousness. When we experience mysterious, wordless engagement with what appear to us as soul/spirit beings whose location of greatest density happens to be within stones . . . well, that doesn't seem like such a great leap.

At this point, we have figuratively jumped out of our skin, expanding our awareness of ourselves into the net of all being, and in doing so we find ourselves easily embracing our mineral kin. Now, in revealing our own crystalline nature, let's dive into our microscopic selves, discovering the crystal that gives us the pattern of our body and the seed of our self-awareness—the crystalline molecule known as DNA.

There is a mind-boggling book called *The Cosmic Serpent: DNA and the Origins of Knowledge* by a fine author named Jeremy Narby. We will look briefly here at some of the relevant implications of his work.

The DNA molecule found in the nucleus of every cell in all living organisms is itself a hexagonal crystal. It is an almost immeasurably thin ten atoms wide and would, if stretched out rather than remaining intricately folded (as it is within the cell nucleus), extend lengthwise about six feet. Think of that. Every cell in your body has one of these astonishingly long, thin, perfectly folded crystalline molecules at its core, and that crystal molecule carries the pattern of information that dictates your body's species, form, sex, eye and hair color, size, and to some extent your intelligence, talents, gifts, vulnerability to disease and likely longevity. All in that tiny crystal, or in the patterns it faithfully holds.

Another correspondence between mineral crystals and DNA is the fact that both quartz and DNA emit light under certain conditions. In the case of quartz, applying mechanical force to a crystal by pressing or twisting it causes the crystal to acquire an electrical charge and to emit electromagnetic radiation, or light. This capacity of quartz to transduce mechanical energy into electromagnetic energy is called the piezoelectric effect. The DNA molecule is known to emit biophotons of visible-spectrum light on a periodic basis, so regularly that it has been compared to an ultra-weak laser. The fact that both quartz and DNA are hexagonal crystals that can emit visible light suggests a deeper resonance between the mineral and living realms, which is verified by the myths and spiritual practices of indigenous cultures.

In his book, Narby recounts his experiences with South American shamanic practitioners and their intimate familiarity with the properties of curative, poisonous and hallucinogenic plants. He notes that the shamans claim their knowledge comes directly from the plant spirits, who speak with them during altered states of consciousness. Much of this knowledge is offered by the Cosmic Serpents, progenitors of life, which appear in many of these visions. Narby's revolutionary idea is that the Cosmic Serpent is a metaphoric representation of the twisting, serpentine DNA molecule, and that DNA is itself a conscious being, a kind of mind-at-large of the living world. Once again, we are approaching crystal consciousness, this time as the soul/spirit being of all life. This is not so different from the entangled quantum net of all living organisms suggested by Mae Wan Ho.

Narby's search for the DNA connections took him deeply into the mythologies of indigenous cultures around the world. Peruvian shamans say that *maninkari* (teacher beings who instruct them about the uses of medicinal plants and other patterns in nature) are present in plants and crystals. In one of the most exciting correspondences in his book, Narby reports that both the Desani of South America and the Australian Aborigines envision the Cosmic Serpent, progenitor of all life, as having been *led by a quartz crystal* in the development of the multiplicity of forms of life on the Earth. "Leading the Cosmic Serpent" can easily be interpreted as *providing the seed pattern* that led to the evolution of all life. If this idea is in some sense true, then humans and all other living things are intimately involved with the quartz that makes up the bulk of the Earth's crust. To say that the Cosmic Serpent (DNA) was led by quartz may be to say that the life spirit in the world was introduced to the Earth from the spiritual realms through quartz. Just as a crystal radio can receive electromagnetic waves transmitted through the air from a broadcast tower, transducing them into sound waves, quartz within the Earth's crust may have received, transduced and broadcast the patterns of life from the spiritual realms into the material world, where they began organizing into RNA, DNA and the multitude of wonders we now call life. Such a tale might explain the appearance of life on Earth better than either random-chance materialist explanations or the religious dogmas of creationism.

Quartz crystals *are* apparently older, though perhaps not greatly older, than life on this planet, with datable specimens about 3.5 billion years old. So it is at least temporally possible for the Desani/Aborigine myths to ring true. If crystals formed at the same time or shortly before life began, the idea of DNA or the Cosmic Serpent being led into existence by quartz becomes that much more plausible. And if there is a link on as basic a level as the pattern of life itself, it's less surprising that we might also find links between our consciousness and the currents or influences of crystals. In fact, if the history of life's evolution is rooted in the influence of crystals, it makes sense that the opportunities now for conscious, self-directed evolution by human beings would be involved again with guidance from the spiritual realms, communicated via the beings we know as the stones.

I want to hearken back a little farther in this chapter to my mention of crystals as the bodily densities of the beings we call angels. Angels, like the quartz crystal that purportedly led the Cosmic Serpent, carry the divine Word, the message, the pattern from the spiritual worlds into the material realm. In our old stories, angels, like the Peruvian *maninkari* teacher-beings, bring humankind the beneficial truth from the Divine to help us in our lives and growth. And if DNA is itself a minded being, as Narby suggests—or if, as Mae Wan Ho has said, we are entangled with all of life—then each of us participates in the consciousness of the entire biosphere and most likely the mineral realm as well, since, as we have seen, the boundaries between them are far more porous than we may ever have imagined. And the opportunities provided by our willing, conscious relationship with the angels of the crystal kingdom are perhaps greater than we *can* imagine.

CHAPTER TWO

The New Consciousness & the Soul of the World

"In all ages and in all places, an unending partnership of the human, the divine and the world has been declared, proclaimed and protected through the presence of the Sophia. Her creating and mediating activity—under such names as Isis, Sophia, Wisdom, Shekinah, Achamoth, World Soul, Athena, Alchymia, Spenta Armati, Black Virgin, Mary, Eternal Feminine—has always looked toward the future birth of creation into the cosmos of love. The present time, I believe, signals the genesis of this birth."

—ROBERT SARDELLO, *Love and the Soul*

In late 2004, while I was working on *The Book of Stones,* my wife Kathy introduced me to a book that would change my life. It was *Love and the Soul* by Robert Sardello. At the time I was in the midst of coping with a long, difficult illness, and I was spending some months with Kathy in the Florida Keys, hoping to gain some vitality from exposure to the sun. Surprisingly, it was not the sun but Sardello's book that set me on the path of healing.

The full tale of that discovery is told elsewhere, and I recommend that all my readers and friends discover Sardello's work. However, the reason for mentioning it here is that this book of Sardello's introduced me to a Being. She has been known by many names, but Robert Sardello calls her Sophia, after the Greek goddess of Wisdom. As he says, this being is more than a goddess—she is in a sense the One who gives rise to all goddesses. She is the Soul of the World, and her presence is not visible in any thing, yet it is She who we can glimpse through the beauty and harmony that the things, creatures and activities of the world express. She is not the waterfall, but the way the water froths and curls and eddies. She is not the deer, but the grace with which it runs. She is not the crystal, but the radiance of its light and the order of its planes. She expresses herself through the all-permeating love, sorrow, longing, courage and joy of the world.

Why do I bring her into *Stones of the New Consciousness*? I do it because the New Consciousness, in my vision of it, is one of conscious co-creation in partnership with Sophia. We do not "create our own reality" through our self-willed visualizations, as some popular books attest. But neither are we passive passengers—in the world but not of it. Although we are largely unaware of Sophia, we have the opportunity to join with her in a delicate and beautiful co-creative dance, an ongoing activity of creating the world in each moment. That dance has always been going on, but our mental habits, which turn the world into a set of "outside" objects, have kept us from participating consciously.

Our evolution, as Sardello teaches, has always been *with* the world, and our destiny is a joint destiny. The stones can be seen, from a certain viewpoint, as expressions of Sophia, of the living wisdom of the World Soul. It is easy to notice Sophia in some stones' beauty and symmetry, their opulence of color. We can feel her life currents in the stones' vibrations. We can sense her sweetness in the love we feel emanating from them. (And the fact that we *can* feel the spiritual currents of the stones is one of our most promising doorways into this essential relationship!) Even stones we might not describe as beautiful still participate in the harmony of structure and the calm stability that one might ascribe to Sophia. For that matter, we ourselves are expressions of Sophia, since we are very much of the world, our bodies composed of astonishing internal harmonies of structure and activity, as we saw in the previous chapter. The Soul of the World and we ourselves as soul beings are utterly intertwined.

So, because we are entwined with the crystals, and because (I believe) our relationships with them are crucial for realizing our partnered destiny of conscious, co-creative evolution, we must recognize the presence of Sophia. As the Mother of all, she is feminine in tone. Her mode of being is intimacy. She is unlike many of our ideas of God, far away in some heaven. She is more likely to be noticed when a bird at the feeder looks at you with obvious awareness, or when an utterly "impossible" synchronicity occurs, which could only mean something to *you*. She is closer than the air I breathe as I type these words, or the breath you take as you read them. Amazingly, it is clear to me, after working with Sardello's books and after a few years of paying attention to subtle clues, that Sophia—who is so embedded in every detail of the world that she is invisible within it—somehow knows and offers her love to every being *individually*. That's how intimate she is.

Writing about Sophia can begin to sound circular, because the relatively straight lines of sentences don't work well for pointing to someone who is both invisible and present every-where. So instead of saying more about her, I will offer a story in which she appears. It is help-ful, too, that a few beings from the crystal realm show up in it. Actually I have two little tales to relate, and Sophia does not arrive until the second one, although I think she is the source of both.

In the summer of 2008, I spent several weeks preparing to give a talk at the Seventh Sophia Conference, sponsored by Robert and Cheryl Sardello's School of Spiritual Psychology. The title of the conference was "A New Heaven and a New Earth: The Birth of a New Body, a New Earth and a New Consciousness." I was invited to speak about Stones of the New Consciousness. (Yes, that is where the title of this book originated!) As I prepared, I realized that although I believed that a new consciousness was coming and that stones were involved in it, I had no idea what to say the new consciousness is to be. So I went to sleep one night, hoping to get help by means of a practice Robert Sardello taught me. It is called "Last Thought—First Thought." The practice is to repeat in one's mind immediately prior to going to sleep a question for which one seeks insight. During sleep, the soul travels to the spiritual realms (as it always does), and when it returns, the first conscious thought one has is the answer. Sometimes the answer is clear, and sometimes it seems obscure. On occasion, the answer comes as a dream.

On this particular night I went to sleep repeating the question, "What is the new conscious-ness?" Around five AM, I was awakened by a voice inside me announcing loud and clear, "The new consciousness is an activity of blessing." I told myself to remember this and write it down later. Then I fell back to sleep. (This was a bit dangerous, because I often forget.) Twenty minutes later I woke again with the identical message. Again I fell asleep. The third time, at six o'clock, I woke with the same words echoing within: "The new consciousness is an activity of blessing!" This time I managed to write them down in my journal before nodding off. When I awoke later, I began puzzling over what seemed to me to be an enigmatic, if insistent, message. As my day went on, I started to sense the truth of those words and their ramifications.

I think of a blessing I might receive from another person as an act of generosity from his or her heart, a gift, something offered without any thought of return, a well-wishing with the flavor of love in it. So how might that become an activity, something ongoing, giving rise to a new consciousness?

I looked first within myself, reasoning that consciousness is "inside." I remembered my wife's credo for dealing with difficult encounters or any problematic moment of life: "Observe, without judgment; pause; drop attention to your heart; ask your heart how to respond; pay attention to the immediate impulse; follow that urge without question." Could there be some-thing akin to this in the activity of blessing?

What would blessing be, within one's own heart-brain or heart-mind system? I thought of that generous sense of well-wishing. I attempted to feel it inwardly, sitting down to meditate (with a Moldavite and three Azeztulite stones). I tried sending a blessing, an expression of love and appreciation, from my head to my heart: "I am so grateful for your presence in me." Immediately I felt a sort of shining back from my heart, a love impulse. Receiving that (in my head), I reflected it back again. Once more I felt the "shining upward" from the heart. Soon there was a sort of circular feedback loop going between my head and my heart, an ascent/descent of sweet-feeling currents. Some carried images or little echoes of thoughts; others felt like pure, nameless currents. By giving attention and a small nudge from my will, I could keep the process going. I was sure that with practice, it could become a way of being, an ongoing "activity of blessing." (The stones made my hands and forearms tingle with a pleasurable current during the meditation, reinforcing the effects of my intention.) Perhaps this interior circulation of love/blessing was the feeling of the new consciousness arising.

I considered that, on the bodily level, the formation and repetition of such activity as a new pattern within the nervous system might strengthen the neural pathways between the heart and the prefrontal cortex of the brain (the most recently evolved and "highest" brain area), as well as the limbic brain, seat of emotional awareness. If this pattern of heart-to-brain-to-heart circulation became the new "normal" consciousness, it might de-emphasize the old predominance of the amygdala and the rest of the reptile brain. These relatively primitive brain structures are designed to protect us by recalling past experiences of danger and setting off defense mechanisms to avoid or confront any similarly threatening situation. However, our culture, being so deeply entangled in patterns of guilt, shame and coercion—plus television, with its synthetic shocks and violent images—have overloaded these systems such that we unconsciously feel threatened much of the time. This has created a situation in which the most primitive parts of our brain reign like political tyrants in the name of survival, so that our "normal" state is one of unconscious alienation and defensiveness. This defensive posture even has a hand in implanting the view of the world as a collection of "outside" things, rather than a whole within which we are supported. We don't even realize how separated we are from the world, because we don't know there is any other possibility. This pattern is the bedrock of the old consciousness, out of which we are trying to evolve before we "survive" ourselves to death. If the practice of interior blessing could strengthen the pathways between the heart and the higher parts of the brain, perhaps the negative old-brain patterns would atrophy. And there is more to this than what is physical, as we shall see.

Coming out of my first meditative experiment with the "activity of blessing," I felt a soft buzz in my forehead and a warm, liquid glow in my chest. When I saw my wife, I was filled with love and gentleness toward her. The feeling of blessing I had initiated in myself wanted to extend itself to her, and I felt it reaching out to the world as well. Looking toward the trees and grass in the yard, the birds outside the window, even my car in the driveway, I sensed an extension of self-giving, gratitude and love permeating my perceptions. If I were to maintain this, if others were to practice it, we would live in a different world. It felt almost too simple, and it felt totally real.

This new pattern of conscious, heartfelt engagement with the world gives one new eyes, a whole new set of senses. One is present to each moment, because the activity of blessing is a kind of attention. In order to bless each perception one has to be present, noticing and inwardly praising each sight, sound, smell, taste and touch. It is something we choose, something we will, and it can be what we will ourselves to will, so that it becomes a way of being.

An interesting and essential quality of the new consciousness as this activity of blessing is something Robert Sardello calls "interiority." In reaching out from our heart to embrace and bless the world through each perception (and our perceptions are not actually separate—they flow in a continuum), we bring the world into our heart. All people whom we bless, by extending our appreciation and wishing them well, enter our heart. We carry them there. The same is true when we "bless" the world while we are perceiving it. We begin to experience the felt sense of the whole world, including ourselves, within the interior feeling of the heart. Everything shines within a love which we have initially "offered," and which we and the world are now somehow together "inside." It is easy enough to understand this when we think of someone with whom we are or have been "in love" (i.e., within love). Practicing the activity of blessing allows one to be in love—within love—with the world. We find our soul inseparably conjoined with the soul qualities of the world, as lovers are with one another, as children are with parents, in a way that runs even deeper than most of our human relationships.

In alchemy, the conjunction (the complete love-entwinement) of the Sun and Moon is said to form the Philosopher's Stone, the magical object capable of transmuting lead to gold and conveying immortality. In some traditions there are two or more levels of Conjunction, just as we see resonant patterns in the returning spiral of one's spiritual path. I want to say that inside our bodies, Conjunction is this flowing dynamic of the mind-heart (or brain-heart) engagement. Spiritually, the heart is the seat of the Divine within us—so says numerous spiritual traditions. The Philosopher's Stone may, on one level of resonance, be the complete integration of these two centers of consciousness into a single whole—brain/mind and heart—the human and Divine as one. In the Gnostic Gospel of Thomas, Jesus says, "When you make the two one, and you make the inner as the outer and the outer as the inner and the above as the below . . . then shall you enter the Kingdom."

If we follow the Sun/Moon imagery, the heart represents the Sun. It is the source of our inner radiance and the seat of the Divine—the seat of Love in us. The Moon reflects the Sun's radiance, and the Sun delights in the beauty of the Moon. In old consciousness, the impulses of the heart are overridden by the dictates of our mental patterns, fears and habits. If the mind, as a center of consciousness, turns away from the heart, the heart, as the seat of the Divine (or Love) within us, can never impose itself. If it did, it would no longer be love. Its nature is to offer and to wait, respectful of the will and sovereignty of the other. Love, and our heart, will wait a whole lifetime and longer for the impoverished everyday self to turn toward Home. And like the Prodigal Son, it is welcomed without blame. It is blessed. I saw this in that first meditation when I turned to my heart in gratitude.

When the mind, or our Prodigal Self, turns toward the heart in appreciation—in recognition, for there can be no real appreciation without recognition—the conscious activity of blessing can begin. We could say that the Moon at last reflects what the Sun has always offered. Within us, the Heart/Sun feels the return of its love and is filled with joy, enlivened, nourished. Instantly it shines back, and the mind is illumined. When the flow is not interrupted, this continues ceaselessly, in an ever-increasing looping intensity, until there is no more separation between call and answer, between love given and love received. All is one. It is Conjunction, and the formation of the Philosopher's Stone, the marriage of Heaven and Earth. Within the individual, it is coming into true wholeness. In an interior alchemy, our leaden, fragmented self is transmuted into gold, its true nature and highest expression. Whether we then are immortal, as the alchemists predicted, is a mystery beyond my knowing. But in the Gospel of Thomas, Jesus did say, "Whoever finds the explanation of these words will not taste death."

I have spoken here of alchemy and the Philosopher's Stone only in a passing way, but we will return to them later. There are other resonances to explore, such as the actual, material stones that appear to facilitate the inner experience of transmutation I have been trying to describe. Those stones, too, can be seen as aspects of the Philosopher's Stone, and they can help us to achieve the goal of the Great Work of the alchemists.

I'll make one more attempt here to describe how profoundly the simple little gesture of continual blessing transforms one's experience of the world. The poet Novalis, whose quotation opens this book, wrote, "Every beloved object is the center of a Paradise." Consider this statement. What is Paradise but the realm where love prevails? When all objects are beloved—the fulfillment of our ongoing activity of blessing—all the world becomes Paradise, because all the world exists, for us, within love. We too are within that love, within the world as Paradise.

I have one more story to tell, and then we'll return to the crystals, and perhaps we will discover that we have unsuspected friends and allies who wish us well and offer their help on our journey toward wholeness.

BREATHING WITH SOPHIA

During the same few weeks while I was preparing my talk for the Sophia Conference, I had a remarkable dream. As it began, my wife and I were sitting together in a room within a big farmhouse. I knew somehow that this farm was new, that a lot of people were working cooperatively there, and that "new crops," which had never been grown before, were being planted. There was an air of quiet excitement, and a lot of hustle and bustle as new arrivals came in and found their places. Kathy and I were in our room. She was sitting in her bathrobe, writing checks to "pay off our debts."

I was worried that someone would come in and see us before we were fully dressed. I said to Kathy, "Hurry up. Someone could walk in here at any moment." The next thing I knew, someone did enter. He was a man, almost seven feet tall, thin and lanky like Abraham Lincoln. He looked like a normal person, except for his head, which was made *entirely out of amethyst*! His features were anything but smooth—he had hundreds of pointed crystals sticking out all over his head. His huge jaw was a hinged thing like a steam shovel, made from more deep-purple amethyst crystals. He was wearing sunglasses, also made of amethyst, and the sides of them were shaped like fish. He said something to me but I couldn't understand him. I answered with a sort of sideways comment on his sunglasses: "Wow! Are those fish?" (Why I didn't say "Wow, your head is made of amethyst," I will never know!)

The Amethyst man muttered something else and stepped aside. Then I noticed that standing behind him were three more beings, so strange-looking they made the Amethyst man look normal. This trio was completely non-human, with straight, rigid white bodies, short, stumpy arms and legs, and faces embedded in their trunks. They wore no clothes, had no necks, and the tops of their "heads" came to a point. In my dream, I was shocked and said to myself, "Whoa! Are those demons?" But a voice within me immediately reassured me, "No, they just look alien to you because you've never seen anything like them before." As I gazed upon the three odd fellows, they began to chant, and they repeated jovially, "Dance or die, dance or die!" Then they began to dance around, in a comical stump-legged way, in complete unison with one another.

Before my astonishment had time to subside, another character appeared. This one was a human, a young woman or girl, looking about sixteen or seventeen years old. She wore a simple white tunic, like something from ancient Greece. She was lovely and radiant, and she smiled playfully, though her eyes were serious and intent. She walked toward me where I sat and bent forward, bringing her face ten or twelve inches from mine. I felt that some important moment had come, that I was supposed to understand something, but that neither she nor I was allowed to speak.

She looked into my eyes with great seriousness, and then she blew her breath, gently but purposefully, onto my face. She continued looking, as if to assess whether I understood. When I didn't respond, she blew her breath on me again, and again she waited. I worried. I didn't know what to think or do, but I didn't want to fail in whatever was hoped for or expected from me. Again, she blew her breath. This time, not knowing what else to do, I blew mine back.

As I exhaled, she inhaled, taking my breath into her body. Then, when she exhaled, I inhaled. Feeling her breath move into me was like inhaling ambrosia, the nectar of the Divine. We exchanged our breaths, back and forth like that, perhaps ten or twelve times. I was filled with delicious life each time I inhaled, and my exhalations were full of appreciation and loving intent. She, too, seemed to be nourished by the exchange. When we had completed our silent ritual, the corners of her mouth twitched upward in a mischievous smile, and she broke the "rules," saying two words to me. Though I can share this story, I am not supposed to repeat those words.

Then I woke up.

I awoke in a state of wonder, and a good measure of joy. Though I had worked with stones for more than twenty years, this was the first time any of the mineral-realm beings had appeared in my dreams. It was clear to me that not only Amethyst man but also the pointy-headed white fellows were crystals, or the soul beings of crystals. (I later suspected that the chanting dancers were the Azez, the guardians of Azeztulite, but we'll come to that later.) The young girl, however, was someone else, someone I was sure I recognized. She was a manifestation of Sophia, the Intimate One. She had offered me a teaching, and a blessing, and she had shown me in a gesture the nature of our human relationship with her.

The activity of blessing—the new consciousness, as I imagine it now—is not confined to our bodies, or our separate selves. It is not even a gift we give to the world. It is a living relationship, a mutual blessing between ourselves and the Soul of the World. It is the gesture from the dream—she breathes life into us, and we breathe life into her! Because she is so essentially love, the Sophia figure in my dream (How marvelous that this vast, ancient Divine Feminine being would appear in my dream as a fresh, radiant young girl!) could not *tell* me to breathe back to her. She could only hint very gently, offering her breath, waiting to see if I would understand, and if I would choose to return her gesture. Love can only offer—it never compels. Her breath felt like pure life as it entered me, and it seemed that my breath, my blessing, was (amazingly!) nourishing to her.

Yet she is not usually as easy to see as she was in my dream, and our relationship with her is more subtle, at least in the beginning, as we start trying to notice her. If the dream was a true teaching, how are we to "breathe out" to Sophia? I believe that our outbreath is the gesture of appreciation, of loving, of blessing the world by reaching out to greet and praise each moment of perception. The nourishing inbreath in which we receive her life force can be felt as the experience of beauty, of gratitude, of recognition of the ongoing miracle of the world and our life. If we passively experience the world only as whatever makes it through the screen of our habitual sensing, we miss all of that magic, and we do not exhale to her. We give her nothing to breathe. It is in the activity of creative sensing and blessing, which is a *conscious, willed* activity, that we uphold our end of the astonishing partnership between ourselves as soul beings and the Soul of the World.

Genuine love is always an amazing, humbling gift. To realize that something, or someone, as vast as the being we call Sophia not only loves us but needs and desires our love is so wonderful that it is hard to take in. To feel it all the time would be to live in Paradise, which is where, I believe, we are destined, though not guaranteed, to live. As Novalis said, every beloved object is the center of a Paradise. Now imagine that we are not the only source offering love and thereby creating Paradise. Envision that we are the Beloveds of the Soul of the World, and that through our love relationship with her, we have the chance to co-create, to re-create the World as Paradise. We don't have to do it alone, and what we can do together with her is far better than anything we could imagine alone! The new consciousness, when it is fulfilled, may be a shared consciousness, something we experience in a kind of unity with the world. Though this path is a stepping every moment into the unknown, I am certain that each step will open us to greater joy.

When I finally came to the Sophia Conference in Santa Fe in August of 2008, I had the outline of a talk as outlandish as this chapter has been, and as wildly hopeful. I felt sure that the vision animating my thinking was a true one, but I was uncertain whether I could get it across. When I arrived with Kathy at the Retreat Center, we were shown to our room. On the shelf, as soon as we walked into the room, I saw a stone. It was a rather rough, reddish rock, about the size of a grapefruit. I picked it up and instinctively held it to my chest. Within moments, sweet currents undulated in and around my heart. Kathy felt them just as clearly. This stone brought out the loveliest heart-feeling I had ever experienced with a stone, but I didn't know what it was. I found out later that it was native to the area, and I actually discovered more pieces in a nearby canyon. Amazingly to me, no one else had apparently noticed this type of stone before, at least not its currents and its soul qualities. Not knowing what it was called, we gave it a name that seemed appropriate—Rosophia, the Rose of Sophia. It is one of the primary stones of the new consciousness, and it has its own section later in this book. Finding it, in that place, at the moment of our arrival at a conference honoring Sophia, seemed clearly to be one of her gestures—an outbreath, a blessing.

About a week after the conference, I returned to Santa Fe and the surrounding area with a friend, Justin, who helped me seek and gather a supply of Rosophia stones so we could make them available to other rock lovers. The fact that we were able to find and gather as many as we did, in such a short time, was itself an amazing, sustained synchronicity. After a couple of days we drove north through the Rocky Mountains to Denver, where a gem and mineral show was to be held.

On that day, driving amid the beauty of the mountain meadows and pristine rivers, we practiced sending our blessings out with our perceptions. It was easy, immersed in such grandeur, to appreciate the presence of the Soul of the World, shining out of every vista. Yet we knew that she is everywhere, so we made a point of appreciating the humblest things we noticed as well as the greatest. Tufts of brown weeds received our silent praise, as did the clouds, the scent of sage on the wind, and the light glistening off the dew-laden grass. Even the asphalt highway and the road signs were included as beloved objects in our imaginal Paradise. It is an enjoyable way to drive along, and it costs nothing though it rewards us greatly to take the world, just as it is, into our heart. As Justin and I drove, we were surprised by the steady upwelling of happiness that we both felt. Eventually happiness turned to joy, and silent rapture. We agreed not to talk for a while, and as we drove along, the silence itself seemed to be alive. The world was no longer a "thing" to us—it was a living being, intimately aware of us and present with us in our silent Paradise. Each mile, each moment was its own perfect, ever-changing eternity. That was our initiation into "breathing with Sophia" as an activity of *mutual* blessing. It is the way I aspire to meet each experience of life; and it is the key, I believe, to a new and wonderful way of meeting the stones. Each of them can become, through love, "the center of a Paradise," as can we.

CHAPTER THREE

What's Going On Here?

"The first life forms were perhaps crystals."

—A.G. CAIRNS-SMITH, *Genetic Takeover and the Mineral Origins of Life*

"Crystals, then, may be considered frozen music holding the proportions of musical intervals in the relationships of their corners, edges and faces. The forms of nature configure as visual music . . . The simple beauty of a crystal is, in part, its strict mathematical order . . . Now we can begin to see how the world virgin is fertilized, swirls into archetypal patterns, gives birth to the world mother, and then nourishes and clothes the geometric patterns with substance, the four ancient 'elements,' manifesting as atoms in configured patterns we can sense."

—MICHAEL S. SCHNEIDER, *A Beginner's Guide to Constructing the Universe*

"The most beautiful thing we can experience is the mysterious. It is the source of all true art and science."

—ALBERT EINSTEIN

So far, this book has made some strong assertions. The stones are the physical aspects of angels or benevolent spiritual beings. The qualities of the stones are pure, but frozen in the stones, and through relationship with us the qualities can be freed into the world. The stones' beings and we ourselves are individualized emanations of the Soul of the World, Sophia, and through conscious, loving relationship with her, we can engage in a dance of joyful co-creation that can remake the world into a Paradise. We are called, at this dire and propitious moment, to open ourselves to voluntary, willed evolution, in partnership with Sophia and with the soul beings of the crystals and stones.

By saying these things at the beginning I have, in a sense, begun with my conclusions. I think it was important to do so, because the idea of the New Consciousness is central to everything else in the book; and what I have said about it so far is meant to provide a frame of reference through which to view the chapters on the individual stones and their stories. Still, I imagine many readers will wonder, "Who is this fellow, and what brought him to the point of saying all this?"

I want to say less about my own history and more about the events that brought me here, because I think that will be more helpful (and the first part of *The Book of Stones* tells enough). It's true that I was always attracted to stones, and as a child I really loved them. But education played its role of sophisticating much of the early passions out of me, and I reached adulthood, like most people, intending to build a career. I had started my own business, a handcrafts gallery, right after college; and the twists and turns of that brought me back to stones, this time in the form of gems, as I learned to make jewelry.

By 1985, I was a full-time jewelry designer, and through that I met Kathy Warner. I had just stumbled upon the mysterious meteoric gemstone, Moldavite, and was trying to come up with some cosmic jewelry designs. She was pursuing dual careers in engineering and crystal healing. As I fell in love with Kathy, the world of crystals and their healing properties began to open my skeptical eyes. Kathy knew immediately that Moldavite was a stone of great spiritual importance for the Earth, and that people working with Moldavite could "ground a lot of Light" for the healing of the planet—and our own healing as well. I wanted to believe her, but I didn't have any personal spiritual experiences with stones other than the thrill I felt upon discovering the existence of Moldavite. When Kathy and I opened Heaven and Earth, our crystal and jewelry shop, the day after we got married, I could tell that other people were having powerful spiritual experiences with stones. I wanted to have such experiences myself, but wanting them didn't make them happen. I felt oddly on the outside of my own work. Then something amazing happened, on a very ordinary day.

TRIP TO THE GREAT CENTRAL SUN

It had been about a year since we opened our store. I was still struggling with the fact that I didn't "feel" the stone energies our customers were so excited about. I knew that Kathy did, and so did many of our friends, so I was not a disbeliever. I guess I was an interested agnostic. During the first months we were together I tried really hard, meditating with each hand in a small bucket full of Moldavite. My theory went like this: if I was a little deaf to this music, I would turn up the volume. But the only results I had to show for my efforts were scratched hands and an appreciation of the calming effects of meditation. Eventually I gave up on the buckets of stones and settled for holding my own Moldavite raw piece in my right hand during my morning sit. I often listened to music during these sessions, and this increased my capacity for relaxation, which helped during our long days in the shop with customers and tourists.

One day in May or June of 1987, I sat with my stone, eyes closed, while flute music played in the background. On this day, I remembered something Kathy had told me when I explained to her that I didn't like creative visualization. "How will I know whether I'm making it up?" I asked.

"Imagination is the doorway into spiritual experience," she asserted. "It gets you to the door, but once you enter, things go their own way."

Given the fact that little if anything of a visionary nature ever happened in my meditations, I decided that a little fantasy was permissible. I would pretend that I was rising up out of my body, looking down at myself and the room. So I imagined that scenario, inwardly viewing myself and my surroundings. As the music played and seemed to lift, like a bird in flight, I decided to rise a little higher. I let my point of view go up through the roof of the house. I could see the neighborhood, the other houses, the park across the street and the sea extending into the horizon. I felt a bit surprised at the vividness of my inner "sight."

Around that time, my vision took on a life of its own. Without any prompting or intention, my viewpoint flew up higher and higher into the sky. The altitude and speed at which I seemed to lift were dizzying. I could see the coastline of our town, then the whole of New England, and soon the curve of the Earth, which was becoming increasingly spherical. In a matter of moments I was looking at the whole Earth, watching it become ever smaller in my sight. Surrounding me, bright stars appeared in ever greater numbers.

Although I could still hear the music playing in the room, my attention was captured by this interior vision of space. I felt myself flying among brilliant star fields, the Earth now far behind me. I wondered where I was going, although it seemed not to matter. Eventually my attention was drawn to a golden star off to my left, so I turned toward it. I flew closer and closer, until the star became a sun, filling the space around it with rich gold light. I went nearer, and I noticed that I was not the only one orbiting this star. There were many transparent beings circling this sun, each having a small golden orb within it, circling together, all in the same direction in the same horizontal plane, at varying distances. It was a grand procession of beings, loving and honoring this golden Sun. Next I noticed that each being was linked to the Sun by a thin golden thread of light that extended from the Sun itself into the center of the orb within each being. Somehow I sensed that the orbs were the hearts of these beings, shining through their transparent bodies.

At that moment, it occurred to me to look at my own "body," whatever it might be in this inner universe. As I did, I was astonished to see that I too was transparent, with a golden orb in my chest linked to the great Sun by a thread of gold. In the instant of that vision, I heard an interior voice say aloud, "The light you seek without is identical to the Light within." A wave of joy coursed through me.

Then, back in the room, I felt an intense sizzle of energy from the Moldavite in my right hand. I was so surprised that I opened my eyes, finding myself back in the living room. But the energy coursing into me from the stone did not stop. It traveled up my arm and went straight into my heart. From there it moved simultaneously upward to the top of my head and downward to the base of my spine. Along the way, all of the fabled "chakras" or energy centers along the spine opened like interior flowers of light. There was no subtlety in any of this. I felt as if warm, pleasurable electricity were pulsing through me, lighting me up from within. As each chakra opened, an intense wave of pleasure and ecstasy rippled through me. The room itself seemed to be filled with light. My breath came in huge, deep gasps.

As she was getting ready for work upstairs, Kathy, who had always been psychically sensitive, felt something unusual going on with me, so she came down to the living room. When she opened the door, she took a look and me and said, "Bob, you're full of light!"

All I could manage to say was "I know!"

Over the next hour, as we talked about it, the intensity of the experience began to fade. Eventually I decided that I wanted to go into the shop with Kathy, that I was feeling relatively normal and capable of working. I was, of course, hugely excited by what had happened, and when I touched my Moldavite, I could still feel an echo of its tingling electricity.

When we got to the shop, I went straight to a big tray of crystals. I was amazed. I could feel the individual tingle of each stone, and each type of stone, and every one was different! I spent almost the entire day playing with them, astonished and yet quite at home. Now, at last, I knew what all those people had been so excited about. From that day forward I have been able to feel the stones. Sometimes the level of sensitivity varies, and it has probably never been as strong as it was that day, but it has never gone away.

That story tells a part of how I got here, into the middle of this puzzling and wonderful realm of the stones. But there was even more to it all than I realized. The journey of that day, initiated by imagination and carried forward by I knew not what, offered me my first glimpse of something that was to reverberate through the story of my life, weaving in and out over more than twenty years. During that time, I have come to believe that the golden Sun I saw in my vision was not any star in the outer "familiar" universe, and not a mere phantom of fantasy. I feel now that it is the source of inner Light, known by various names, among them the Great Central Sun.

My reason for associating Moldavite with the Great Central Sun begins with the story I have just told. Since that time I have come upon references in the Grail stories and the literature of alchemy that deepen this connection. (See the Moldavite section in the "Individual Stones" part of this book.) Some years after my initial Moldavite experience, the stone Azeztulite arrived. It was an unusual, rather humble-looking form of Quartz, with currents more powerful than those of any Quartz I had ever touched. This stone's entrance was presaged by telepathic communications received by my friend and co-author of *The Book of Stones,* Naisha Ahsian. She reported that she had linked inwardly with angelic beings, going by the name Azez, who were spiritually engineering an earthly stone to carry the current of the Nameless Light emanated by the Great Central Sun. This newly awakened stone was to seed a rapid evolution among human beings, triggering cellular rejuvenation and transfiguring us into our true form as beings of Light. It was also foretold that this stone would facilitate the healing and awakening of the Earth. (Chapter Ten, "The Tale of the Azez.")

From these two stories, as well as many others that are told throughout this book, I have concluded that the Great Central Sun is pivotal in regard to the spiritual openings that the stones are encouraging and helping us to make. But what do we mean by those words? Where is this Sun, and what is it? Have others come upon it, and under what circumstances?

The Great Central Sun in Alchemy

Author Leonard Lee in his article "A General Look at Alchemy" writes that the origins of alchemy date back to the Egyptian sage Hermes Trismegistes, and he traces its lineage through Moses, Jesus, Zoroaster and the Mystery Schools of antiquity. The Emerald Tablet of Hermes, an alchemical text purported in legend to have been inscribed upon a huge Emerald, recalls the supernatural Grail Stone (the Emerald from the sky, perhaps akin to Moldavite) that was said to convey the goals of alchemy—immortality and awakening to enlightened awareness. These goals were not confined to the alchemists of Egypt and Greece but were also sought by the Oriental Taoist alchemists as well as the Hindu alchemists of India. The Hindu stream was descended from the still more ancient Vedic tradition. Lee reports that alchemy's widespread practice in the ancient world, in which travel and communications were limited, suggests a single and surprising origin:

> . . . the parallel growth of alchemy in the Orient and the regions of the Fertile Crescent suggested to some Esoteric historians that alchemy may have had a common origin in that sunken continent Atlan, or Atlantis, as it is more generally known. Esoteric Tradition declares that a handful of the Atlantean Root Race survived the submergence of the land and transmigrated to Egypt, China and the Americas. It is reasonable to assume that they brought with them their sciences, art and culture, which influenced the inhabitants indigenous to the regions where they settled. This would explain the similarities in the traditions and beliefs of native cultures to be found both East and West.

Those of us involved in spiritual work with crystals may perk up our ears at the mention of Atlantis, which has long been considered to be a lost civilization in which the use (and perhaps the abuse) of crystal energies loomed large. But let us go now to where Lee mentions the alchemical view of the Sun:

> Alchemy is defined as an art of transmutation and precipitation—the changing of base metals into gold. The work of alchemical transmutation is designated as "the Labor of the Sun." This "Eye of Ra" symbolically represents the perfection with which nature is gradually unfolding in her creations. At the physical level the Sun of Perfection is represented by gold. Alchemy is the science and art which hasten the creations of Nature to attain perfection at their own respective level. Gold is the perfection attained by metals and minerals. Minerals, however, are also following another line of perfection—that of its ability to sustain life and consciousness. And Man, the acme of organic life, is evolving to the state where he acquires perfection in Divine Self-Awareness. . . .
>
> . . . *[picking up later in Lee's text:]* There is a higher source of the life-essence that is rayed from the Great Central Sun directly to the Monad and down to the Atma of man, and this is associated with the flame of life residing in the physical heart. Daily devotions to the flame within and to the "Father who art in heaven" cause a descent of the essences of life, of the Atmic fire, into the quaternary vehicles of Egoic expression and results in a regeneration of the whole psychobiological system. . . . Man, the Monad, is a spark of Fire from the Great Central Sun; all of Man's principles are fire in lesser manifestation and intensity. A spark of the Monad lies hidden in Man's heart. Fueling this flame with daily devotions of Right Action, Right Thought, Right Speech, meditation and prayer increases the power, wisdom and love of the divine nature of Man—this is spiritually represented by the threefold nature of the heart-flame, the fleur-de-lis.

Although the vocabulary Lee uses is rather specialized, he is writing about something very like what was rendered by Naisha in the words of the Azez. The stone Azeztulite is said by them to carry the currents of the Great Central Sun, for the transmutation of human beings and the world. This closely resembles the goals of alchemy—to change the "leaden" everyday self into the "gold" of the Divine human being. According to the Azez, this takes place through the infusion of the Nameless Light into the cells. Here is Naisha's recounting of their words:

> Disease on your planet is the result of certain frequencies of light. You block cellularly these light waves through thought-form shields and contracting emotional patterns. Your cellular consciousnesses are therefore unable to properly learn and expand, resulting in disease. Azeztulite carries energies and frequencies of Light that help release the shields and blocks, healing disease and aiding in cellular rejuvenation and expansion.

This sounds virtually identical to Lee's depiction of the life-essence descending from the same Great Central Sun invoked by the Azez, and the results, in Lee's words, are "regeneration of the whole psychobiological system." It is interesting as well to note Lee's mention that the spark of the Central Sun burns in the human heart—that is precisely what I experienced in my original visionary journey to the Central Sun.

The Heart and the Sun

I mentioned earlier that synchronicities are to me gestures from Sophia, the Soul of the World, with whom we are called into ongoing co-creative activity, giving birth in each moment to the New World. We are not yet to that point in our story, but as I was researching the Central Sun and its links to us, I unexpectedly received in the mail, at exactly the right moment, a magazine published by students of Rudolf Steiner, the great clairvoyant seer and teacher of the last century, who viewed stones as "the Gods" and the "sense organs of angels." Immediately my eye was caught by an article entitled "The Mystery of Heart and Sun." It offered several key ideas from Steiner that built upon what I had read in Lee's book. There was even an alchemical connection:

> The Alchemist Agrippa of Nettlesheim (1486–1535) gave prominence to the heart in reference tables, designating it "the first living and the last dying" and having a relation to the Sun, whereas the brain stood in relation to the Moon. In addition, the heart was understood as bearing a relationship to the Son principle of the threefold Deity. Agrippa of Nettlesheim held that "the breast, where the heart is, is the seat of life, answering to the celestial world."

There were three quotes from Steiner on the spiritual nature of the heart: (1) "The human heart is composed of the gold which lives everywhere in light; this pours down from the universe and actually forms the human heart. Light is full of gold [in homeopathic form] which lives and moves within it, and during a person's earthly life his heart . . . is made . . . from the light of the whole universe." (2) "In the heart, as far as the universe is concerned, you have a cosmos gathered up into a center . . . the substance of the whole cosmos is contained within him; it is drawn together in his heart, in the etheric body of his heart." (3) "The heart is organically the place where through the instrument of the blood, the real 'I' of the human being as it manifests in our consciousness comes into being. . . . The real 'I' consciousness of man does not take place in the brain, but in the heart."

To me these words of Steiner's evoke first the image of the golden Sun I saw within my chest in the Moldavite journey, as well as the way Azeztulite is experienced first in the heart by many of those who work with it (often triggering spontaneous tears). As in my vision imagery, the heart as described by Steiner is intimately linked to the "light of the whole universe" (aka the Great Central Sun). The heart, where this light is focused in the body, is also, as Lee proposed, the center of the true self, which Lee calls "the Atma of man." That was my felt experience when the inner Sun from my journey literally lit up within my physical chest. There was an unmistakable sense of being (at last) identified with my true self, a much greater self, and yet a humbler one than my everyday ego.

These personal observations are not presented to make any claims of being enlightened or evolved. (I fall prey to the snares of the "lower self" as much as anyone!) But I do want to show the threads by which ideas such as these can link into one's personal life, because it seems to me that we are called to enact our *real* evolution, both spiritual and physical. I want to show how this all weaves right into life, if we offer ourselves to it and pay attention to what happens.

THE BODY OF LIGHT

Let's consider for a moment some of the threads we have been weaving. We have our body, which is liquid crystal in its activity and structure. We have the light-emitting DNA crystalline molecule, the coded intelligence of life, at the core of every cell. (Recent scientific research indicates that healthy cells emit biophotons of organic light in a highly coherent fashion, while cancer cells emit light much more chaotically.) We have the legends saying that life, in the form of the Cosmic Serpent, was led into existence by a Quartz crystal (which can also emit light); and we have our subjective experiences, in which we feel the currents of the stones interacting with our body and our consciousness. Often these currents are "seen" inwardly as light, and we speak of crystals and the "rays" that they carry. We have the legends of the Stone of the Holy Grail and the alchemical Philosopher's Stone, both of which are said to convey enlightenment (seeing and being the Light within) and immortality. We have the ancient legends of magical stones that fulfill wishes, heal the body and carry the spirits of angels or spirit helpers. We have the image—from experience, from alchemy and from other sources—of the Great Central Sun, which seems to be located at the spiritual core of the Universe and in the center of the human heart. The stone Azeztulite is said to carry the Nameless Light from that Inner Sun.

Add to that the enduring idea, carried forward by multiple spiritual traditions, that the Divine presence is frequently signified by inner or outer spiritual Light. One has only to look at the artistic renderings of holy people and supernatural beings to see that images of radiant light surround the innumerable depictions of those beings. If we are to evolve into the next manifestation that is calling us, it is reasonable to assume that this will involve an increase in our radiance. As we become the next species, or the spiritual human being, we are likely to shine with greater Light. Perhaps it will come from a new alignment or excitement of our DNA. Perhaps the Great Central Sun in our hearts will awaken, as it did in me years ago, when I sat holding my Moldavite. Many contemporary spiritual books mention the Light Body. Let us now look for more clues about our potential evolution into or awakening as what my friend and *The Book of Stones* co-author Naisha called "the beings that we truly are—beings of Light." The idea of this has inspired human beings for many centuries. We can imagine that the truth of it would be considerably more powerful.

THE INTELLIGENCE OF THE HEART

Our hearts are constantly emanating light, electromagnetic energies that are beyond the normal visible spectrum. In fact the heart seems, in one sense, to work a bit like an electric motor, rotating the ionically charged blood through its circulating vortex-generating chambers. The electromagnetic field around the heart is a torus—a donut- shaped field extending outward in all directions with a central axis. It is much more powerful than the field generated by the brain—so powerful that it is possible to take an electrocardiogram with sensors as much as three feet away from the body. And the heart's field is holographic: it is possible to gather information about the heart's activity from *any point* in the field.

Joseph Chilton Pearce's book *The Biology of Transcendence* is a good place to look for information about the heart and its intelligence. That is where I learned that the heart is much more than a pump—it is an organ of perception and intelligence, not only spiritually, as I already believed, but physically. Pearce asserts that the heart contains more neurons (the sort of cells that compose the brain and nervous system) than muscle cells—that the heart is actually as much as sixty percent neurons. This would give a material basis for the contention, held since ancient times, that the heart is where the soul (or the sort of intelligence and perceptive capacities we associate with soul) resides. The heart is in numerous traditions the seat of our most trustworthy perceptions. The mind *thinks,* but the heart *knows.* The old phrase "I know it in my heart" is apparently more than a metaphor.

If the heart perceives, and perceives truth more readily than the brain, I believe that its perceptions must be mediated not through the traditional five senses but directly through the field it generates, and the interaction of its field with all the other fields overlapping from the various things and beings in the world. (Or perhaps the field of our heart resonates holistically with the entire world!) In sensory perception, the brain takes the nerve impulses coming in from the sense organs and generates our picture of the world out of those impulses. It is amazing to realize that we never actually see the light from the sun, stars, moon or any outside source. We see the images of light that our brain generates from neural impulses from the eyes. Sight, sound, taste, smell and even touch are literally "all in our head." The heart's perceptions through its field would be much more direct, giving us a true awareness of the way the world feels to the heart. Such perceptions are more like intuitions than sights or sounds, and often our "heart knowing" is in the feeling mode. But because our heart feels the world as it is and does not generate hypothetical situations, it is our best "compass" in regard to pointing ourselves toward what is true. On the spiritual level, the ideas we touched upon regarding the Heart and the Sun as well as our subjective sense of how we feel toward our own heart all support the view of the heart as an organ of consciousness. It also seems that our heart harbors a special sort of awareness, the capacity to feel the future coming into being.

Robert Sardello speaks of Sophia, the Soul of the World, as She who is always coming to be. She is the source or the very nature of what he calls the "time stream from the future." In this discussion, the future is not pre-determined but is being created in each moment, between ourselves and Sophia. It is reminiscent of, though much more intimate-feeling than, what quantum physicists describe as the collapse of the quantum wave potential through the act of observation. It is when possibilities become actualities. Sophia dances always on the leading edge where the potential is manifesting. She is neither the unmanifested potential nor the manifested fact. She is in between. And since she is wisdom, beauty, harmony and love, even at her most disorderly, she is what makes the world into something that lives. Our way of engaging with Sophia is through our heart. It is easy to feel this. The heart is where we know beauty, harmony, wisdom and love. And the heart is where we get a good or a bad feeling about what we can expect in the future, from a person or a situation. An interesting confirmation of this idea of the heart comes from Joseph Chilton Pearce's discussion of a peculiar experiment.

An organization called Heartmath has done great work in recognizing that the heart has its own intelligence, and that getting the heart and the brain into "coherence" with each other can make a person happier, calmer, more compassionate and more productive. Joseph Chilton Pearce relates a Heartmath experiment that produced some astonishing results. Subjects who were trained to reach a state of heart/brain coherence sat before a computer screen and were told to press a button when they were ready to view an image. (Monitors kept track of the heart/brain coherence.) After the button was pushed, there was a ten-second delay, after which a randomized program chose one of fifty images and flashed it on the screen. Ten of the fifty images were very unpleasant or disturbing, while the other forty were benign. Subjects viewed a number of successive images in this way.

As one might expect, viewing the upsetting images broke down the heart/brain coherence. However, the astonishing result was that the heart tended to go out of coherence four to seven seconds *before* a negative image was selected by the random program! The brain followed the heart out of coherence a fraction of a second later. But these results seemed to show that the heart could somehow feel the negative images coming before they were chosen, and since neither human being nor computer knew what image would be selected, *the heart had some way of feeling the future coming,* beyond the confines of space and time!

This is an almost exact corroboration of Sardello's assertion of our meeting Sophia, who is what is coming-to-be, through the heart. This also links to Mae Wan Ho's suggestion that the human body is simply the location where the quantum waves of ourselves are most dense, and that we extend through quantum entanglement (which takes place beyond the traditional parameters of space/time) with all things and all beings in the universe. The torus, the donut-shaped energy field of the heart, echoes the shape of the electromagnetic fields of the Earth, the Sun, our galaxy and even the whole of the universe, as well as smaller energy fields surrounding objects perhaps as tiny as atoms. If all of these fields act upon and blend into one another, perhaps that is why we can simply "know" something in the heart, without having to prove or defend it in the brain.

My sense is that our usual mental consciousness (which was, by the way, unaware that either the heart or the brain had lost coherence before the negative images arrived in the experiment) is focused mostly on the past, with endless strategies to predict and control the future. The heart, and what I want to begin imagining as the crystalline consciousness of the cells, is engaged each moment with what is coming to be. I want to suggest that the liquid crystal "body consciousness" of the cells is interactive with the heart's field, and that both are more directly aware of the world than we can be through the mental veil. Bringing the cells into fuller self-awareness and making the heart the center of our being may be the path toward the evolutionary goal of a new human being. At least that was the direction championed by three extraordinary spiritual pioneers. (Bear with me, Oh Reader, and we will come again to the doorstep of the stones!)

SRI AUROBINDO, THE MOTHER & SATPREM

It would be easy to write an entire book about any of these three extraordinary people. Indeed, there are numerous volumes written by and about all of them. To do them justice would take us far from our objectives here, so we will only dip our toes into this water.

Sri Aurobindo was a man born in India and educated in Great Britain, who experienced spiritual enlightenment while awaiting his execution in an Indian jail cell, a situation resulting from his anti-British revolutionary political activities. His sentence was unexpectedly commuted, and after his release he remained in the awakened state, devoting the rest of his life to a more profound revolution, the revolution of human evolution. Sri Aurobindo found in the ancient Vedas the corroboration of his intuitive understanding that human beings, as we are now, are not the final stage of evolution. "Man is a transitional being," he said. The rishis, who sang the Vedic Hymns five thousand to seven thousand years ago, seem to have devoted themselves to the Divine Fire, or Agni. (The agni mani, or Gem of Fire, has also been compared to Moldavite.) Aurobindo worked throughout his life to find the way of evolution into the New Human Being, and his greatest work of writing was the epic poem Hymns to the Mystic Fire. Aurobindo believed that the fulfillment of our evolution would also entail the overthrow of death.

The Mother was Sri Aurobindo's companion, disciple and confidante. She was of French and Turkish descent, gifted with great psychic capacities. After meeting Aurobindo, she foreswore delving into the occult and devoted herself to Aurobindo's project of self-chosen evolution, or "the willed mutation of our species." The Mother, as she became known at Aurobindo's ashram, attempted to initiate an age of what she called "the divine materialism," meaning a spiritual awakening—not in the evanescent realms of spirit, but here, in the world of matter. The Mother believed that the "Mind of the Cells" must be awakened and educated to open itself to the Divine physical life, rather than repeating the pattern of death.

Satprem (whose name means "one who loves truly") was the Mother's disciple and confidant. After Aurobindo's departure from the physical world, Satprem encouraged and supported the Mother in her great adventure of attempting to teach the cells to reattune to the Divine vibration of immortality. He recorded thousands of hours of conversation with the Mother and wrote numerous books about her work, and Sri Aurobindo's.

None of these committed spiritual seekers had anything to do with crystals, so why do I bring them up? I do so because of their deep work with the body, in particular with the cells. We have already learned, through Jeremy Narby and Mae Wan Ho, about the crystalline qualities of the body, which are found in the interior of the cells and in the intercellular structures, and about their light-emitting qualities—something that Aurobindo, the Mother and Satprem may have known only inwardly. And there is reason to believe that they did. Here is a quote from Satprem's book *On the Way to Supermanhood:*

> Man has a self of fire in the center of his being, a little flame, a pure cry of being under the ruins of the machine. This fire is the one that clarifies. This fire is the one that sees. For it is a fire of truth in the center of the being, and there is one and the same Fire everywhere, in all beings and all things and all movements of the world and the stars, in this pebble beside the path and that winged seed wafted by the wind. Five thousand years ago, the Vedic *rishis* were already singing its praises: "O Fire, that splendor of thine, which is in heaven and which

is in the earth and in its growths and its waters . . . is a brilliant ocean of light in which is divine vision. . . .". The *rishis* had discovered that fire five thousand years before the scientists—they had found it even in water. They called it "the third fire," the one that is neither in flame nor in lightning: *saura agni,* the solar fire, the "sun in darkness." It is this fire which is the power of the worlds, the original igniter of evolution, the force in the rock, the force in the seed. . . . No species, even pushed to the extreme of efficiency and intelligence and light, has the power to transcend its own limits by the power of its improved chromosomes alone. It is only this fire that can.

In his passionate and poetic language, Satprem speaks on themes we can recognize from the sources we have already examined. Most notably, he tells us that the holy Fire that both he and the *rishis* (as well as Sri Aurobindo and the Mother) saw at the heart of matter, at the center of our own being, is a *solar* fire. The *saura agni* of the Vedas, which is the impetus behind life, behind evolution, behind all being, is none other than the Great Central Sun. Let us recall what Leonard Lee wrote in his treatise on alchemy:

> There is a higher source of the life-essence that is rayed from the Great Central Sun directly to the Monad and down to the Atma of man, and this is associated with the flame of life residing in the physical heart. Daily devotions to the flame within . . . result in a regeneration of the whole psychobiological system. . . . Man, the Monad, is a spark of Fire from the Great Central Sun; all of Man's principles are fire in lesser manifestation and intensity. A spark of the Monad lies hidden in Man's heart.

Lee also reminds us that the Vedic hymns and wisdom are descended from the even more ancient alchemical tradition that may have been rooted in Atlantis.

Another detail worth noting is Satprem's recognition that the same solar fire is both "the force in the rock" and "the force in the seed." Certain legends tell us that Atlantis was destroyed because of the misuse of crystal energies, while Rudolf Steiner has written that the Atlanteans improperly harnessed the life force present in seeds. If we follow Satprem, this was, in both cases, the power of the Great Central Sun, the *saura agni.*

Now backtrack with me once more to the story of Azeztulite, which is quartz—quartz awakened by a certain stream of angelic beings, the Azez, to carry the currents of the Great Central Sun. Naisha, my *Book of Stones* co-author, knew nothing about any of the esoteric traditions and authors we have quoted here when she began to communicate with these beings inwardly, yet the information she received fits precisely with what these historical sources tell us. Where Lee speaks of the capacity of the currents of the Great Central Sun for *regeneration of the whole psychobiological system,* the Azez, speaking through Naisha, proclaim that the currents of the Nameless Light of the Great Central Sun (carried by Azeztulite) aid in *healing disease and in cellular rejuvenation and expansion.*

As we try to wrap our imagination around all of these parallels and possibilities, let us recall that current science informs us that the DNA in every cell emits light, measurable physical light. We have been discussing inner light, spiritual light, in regard to the Great Central Sun, the *saura agni,* the holy Fire of Satprem and the *rishis.* Where are these two lights intertwined? I propose that the crossroads of these inner and outer streams is the heart.

As we have seen, the heart is the center of our being. It is neurologically equipped to "think." It generates a field that extends beyond the body for direct perception of the world. That field may provide the organizing pattern, or at least the primary pattern that informs the "body consciousness" of our liquid crystal selves. Rudolf Steiner tells us: "The human heart is composed of the gold which lives everywhere in light . . . and during a person's earthly life his heart . . . is made . . . from the light of the whole universe." That "light of the whole universe" radiated in brilliant golden beams from the great Sun of my first inner Moldavite journey, and its resonant likeness was present in my heart and the hearts of the other beings orbiting/worshipping that Sun. Yet that light was also kindled in my body back in the living room, and my wife could see it shining through me when she came in. Satprem wrote: "Man has a self of fire in the center of his being, a little flame, a pure cry of being . . . a fire of truth in the center of the being, and there is one and the same Fire everywhere, in all beings and all things and all movements of the world and the stars." And Leonard Lee tells us: "A spark of the Monad lies hidden in Man's heart." The experiment from Heartmath demonstrates that the heart has a mysterious capacity to feel the future coming—an awareness beyond space and time. From all of this, and from the other sources we have touched upon, and more than anything else from my own experience, I conclude that the heart is the junction of spirit and matter within each of us. It is our compass of truth, the fount of our love, our wellspring of blessing. It is where we meet Sophia. It is through the heart that we can find our way into the worlds of the crystal beings, and it is through the heart that we can find the path to the New Consciousness, the New Body and the New Earth.

AN IMMORTAL BODY?

Sri Aurobindo, the Mother and Satprem all saw the possibility that the goal of human evolution, in both the spiritual and physical aspects, involves transmutation of the body and liberation from death. This is scarcely imaginable to us, and what we can imagine is either not attractive to us, or it is attractive for the wrong reasons. Although we all try to live as long as we can, most people reject immortality as impossible, or they say it would be horrible to be trapped in one's body forever. Others imagine that they would desire immortality, but for egotistic reasons. Some say we are already immortal through reincarnation. (Satprem would answer that reincarnation is a stage of our evolution, but not its goal.) Yet it was not only these three pioneers who responded to this dream. The twin goals of alchemy have always been transmutation of matter (from "lead" to "gold") and immortality. Christianity too has held out the prospect of eternal life (in heaven rather than on Earth) as the Divine promise. And there is much more teaching about the victory over death in the Gnostic gospels. In the Gospel of Thomas, Jesus says, "Whosoever finds the explanation of these words shall not taste death." The Stone of the Holy Grail was also said to convey regeneration of the body and indefinite prolongation of life.

We have been touching on the idea of the Light Body, and many current metaphysical books mention it. As I consider the implications of the infusion of the Light or Fire of the Great Central Sun, centered in the heart, transmuting the patterns of the liquid crystal matrix of blood and cells, it seems clear that it is possible for us to embody more spiritual Light, and to radiate light. We already do radiate light through our DNA.

Satprem and the Mother used the inner chant *Om Namo Bhagavate* (I salute/surrender/ offer myself to the Supreme Divine) to replace the habits of fear, contraction, degeneration and death in all levels of themselves, all the way to the mind of the cells. They reasoned that the habit of death could not simply be removed; it had to be replaced with a new habit of pure life. Their mantra was an opening or offer to that which does not die, the Supreme Divine. If that new pattern could reach all the way through to the cells, they hoped, the old patterns would change, and the body would be open to transmutation. Yet, as Satprem said, no species can transcend itself by its own will alone. We must be met by a greater power or being. That power was what Aurobindo called the Supramental Force, or the *saura agni,* or what we might call the Great Central Sun. Satprem's reports of his own initial stages of transmutation by that force indicate that a New Body seems to have been awakened within the old body, or superimposed upon it. He was awed by the power of the spiritual force he had invoked. (Sri Aurobindo said it was "harder than diamond, yet more fluid than gas.") The idea of the superimposed New Body as the achievement of our spiritual destiny is echoed in the Gospel of Thomas: "When you make eyes in the place of an eye, and a hand in the place of a hand, and a foot in the place of a foot, and an image in the place of an image, then shall you enter the Kingdom."

I want to propose that this metamorphosis is real, and that it is the transmutation of the body as we have known it into the Body of Light. I do not know how this will come about, or what the New Body will be like, or when it can happen. I do not think it will be an abandonment of the body we know but a transfiguration of it, like caterpillar to butterfly, only greater. I feel sure that it entails a deeper opening to the *saura agni,* the solar fire, the Nameless Light of the Great Central Sun.

We who are working spiritually with the stones have in some ways an easier course to follow than pioneers like Satprem, because our helpers are all around us, embodied as the stones. By now it must be clear that, from my own perspective at least, Azeztulite is a direct ally in this venture, carrying the currents of the Nameless Light. And, if Robert Sardello is correct, as our Light Bodies awaken, so will the Light Body of the Earth. This is precisely in line with the plans of the Azez to attune all the Quartz on Earth to the currents of the Nameless Light. In such a case, it's easy to imagine ourselves and the Earth moving through a mutual transmutation.

And there is more to the story than Azeztulite. Each crystal or mineral embodies different qualities, patterns or potential expressions of the Divine language, the silent words of Sophia. Legends of Sophia tell us that she was trapped in the world's matter, and that when offered the opportunity to escape, she remained here, as her free act of love, until individual beings—ourselves—choose to enter into relationship with her, freeing both her and us. The crystals and stones can be viewed as parts of her body, or as angels or gods "trapped" in matter. All of these concepts together can be held, but there is surely more to the story. As wild and grand as my imagination and perceptions have made this tale, I'm sure it isn't wild and grand enough to fit the truth. Yet these possibilities fill me with wonder, and they teach me that "knowing the answers" is mostly a trap. My message to my fellow adventurers, seekers and servers of the crystal realms is: Open your heart to the stones and follow the paths that appear. Develop the capacities that will begin to emerge as you repeat the practices. Allow yourself to evolve new practices. Let the essays presented here about the stones be your invitation to learn for yourself rather than to accept concepts in lieu of experience. Refuse to put limits on what is possible. We really don't know if there are any.

The Philosopher's Stone, the elixir of life, the magical talisman able to turn lead to gold and convey immortality, was said in legend to be so common and humble-looking that many of those seeking it would step right over it or kick it aside. I want to suggest that most of what we have imagined thus far about crystals and minerals is inadequate to encompass their potential, and ours. We may well have in our hands, under our noses, the Treasure of the World, the Chintamani, the Holy Grail, the stones. Yet they are no more, and perhaps no less, a treasure for us than we are for them. Relationship, love, blessing, partnership, service, friendship—focusing on these will be of far more benefit, and bring forth truer treasures, than any goodies we might ever dream of getting for ourselves.

I'll end this chapter, so filled with potential and dreams, with this mysterious promise, attributed to Jesus in the Gospel of Thomas: "If you become disciples to me and hear my words, these stones will minister to you."

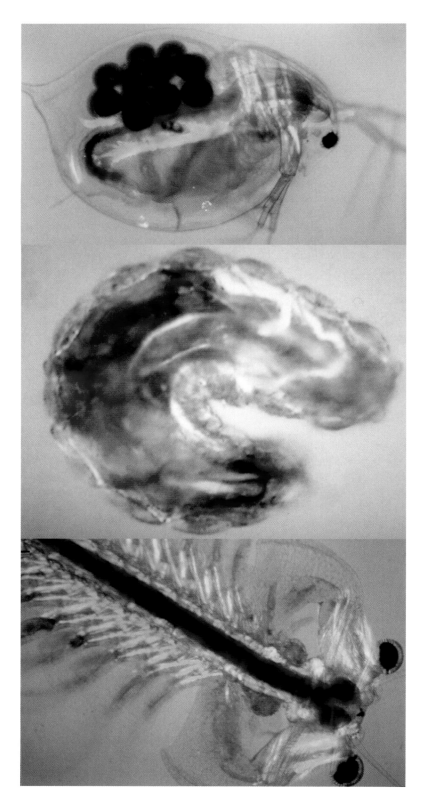

Images of tiny organisms filmed under polarized light conditions display their liquid crystal qualities. Organisms are (top to bottom) daphnia (water flea), drosophila (fruit fly larva) and artemia (brine shrimp). Images courtesy of Mae Wan Ho, Institute of Science in Society (ISIS).

CHAPTER FOUR

The Liquid Crystal Body Matrix

"[T]he ability of biological organisms to form fluid structures of some rigidity in an aqueous environment is central to the existence of life on this planet."

—PROFESSOR PETER J. COLLINGS, *Liquid Crystals: Nature's Delicate Phase of Matter*

"The human body is a sophisticated, multi-faceted antenna system comprised of a crystalline matrix that is constantly transmitting and receiving (transceiving) all manner of informed energies. . . . James L. Oschman, who authored Energy Medicine: The Scientific Basis, *echoes this sentiment by stating, 'crystalline arrangements are the rule, not the exception, in living systems.' He goes on to suggest that energy and body workers who use quartz, shells and stones, which are also crystalline materials, create resonant interactions with the liquid crystal structures found in tissue. He states that, 'Crystalline components of the living matrix act as a coherent molecular antenna, radiating and receiving signals.'*

"The way to tune this antenna is through the repetition of such practices as yoga, martial arts or even playing an instrument. These disciplines also involve entrainment, which is mindfulness of breathing and heartbeat rhythms that bring the body and brainwave activity into a synchronous, harmonious state. Entrainment of the crystalline matrix in this way brings the entire being into a state of coherence. In other words, the whole being becomes one big, resonant antenna."

—MAANNA STEVENSON, "The Body's Crystal Matrix"

In the early chapters and throughout this book, I refer to the Liquid Crystal Body Matrix. In this chapter I want to delve more deeply into the meaning of this term, and into the evidence that has convinced me that liquid crystallinity is a fundamental property of our bodies. I also hope to show something about how the development of greater coherence in our Liquid Crystal Body Matrix can enhance our path of spiritual/physical evolution, and why I believe this development can be greatly aided by working with the stones. Throughout this chapter, I will quote the writings of biologist Mae Wan Ho, as well as an exceptional article by Lian Sidirov entitled "Control Systems, Transduction Arrays and Psi Healing: An Experimental Basis for Human Potential Science" (see bibliography).

THE LIQUID CRYSTAL BODY MATRIX

Living organisms are highly organized. In fact, organization could be said to be what makes an organism. As human beings, we have a nervous system that appears to act as the seat of mental consciousness, sensory awareness and the regulation of numerous functions of our organs and their systems. It is linked to all parts of the body through a neuronal net, and we know that electrochemical impulses travel along our neural wiring, bringing information to the brain and receiving instructions from it. Most of this goes on below our level of conscious awareness, as does much brain activity. Our language, our mathematics, our work and nearly all of our activities are governed consciously through the brain and nervous system. For example, I am using my brain to write this book, and you are using yours to read it.

The heart seems to have another sort of awareness, and its activities and perceptions are less well-understood. Books such as *The Biology of Transcendence* by Joseph Chilton Pearce describe the heart's unique intelligence and its generation of an electromagnetic field via which it is able to perceive. Through the heart's field (which I believe to be profoundly more than electromagnetic), we have a second way of sensing the condition of other people, our environment and our world milieu. Lian Sidirov recounts an experiment conducted using a Heartmath heart/brain entrainment technique in which "heart energy"—a focus of deep love—was able to significantly increase or decrease denaturation of DNA solution samples, either held by the subjects or kept in a laboratory half a mile away. Other Heartmath experiments seem to indicate that the heart's awareness can even feel the wave of future events before they occur! (See Chapter Three for more on this study.)

Whatever we mean by "love," its natural point of origin in us seems to be the heart, and whatever we mean by the Divine also makes the heart its home within us. This has been understood intuitively by spiritual cultures through the centuries, in which everyone knew that the chest, the heart, was the seat of the soul. Today this idea is both remembered and forgotten—we give away paper hearts on Valentine's Day, but the insistence of old-paradigm science that consciousness is generated exclusively in the brain makes our symbolism appear quaint and sentimental. The relationship between the heart and brain is a vital one for the fulfillment and well-being of every individual, and for the whole of our species and world. However, in our current culture, the predominance of mental consciousness has tended to isolate us from our hearts and made us largely unaware of the heart's perceptions and communications. I feel that this heart/mind disconnection is one of the fundamental aspects of the fragmentation that creates the many imbalances in the human world.

We also have a third consciousness, underlying those of the brain and heart, and this consciousness has only recently been rediscovered by science. It is a body-consciousness arising out of a liquid crystalline continuum, extending from intracellular molecules to the cytoplasm, extracellular matrix and connective tissues. This consciousness is our body-knowing, involving awareness of our physical self as a whole and as all of its parts. Here is a key quote from biologist Mae Wan Ho, in an article describing how liquid crystallinity of our bodies can explain the efficacy of subtle energy medicines such as acupuncture:

> There is a dynamic, liquid crystalline continuum of connective tissues and extracellular matrix linking directly into the equally liquid crystalline cytoplasm in the interior of every single cell in the body. Liquid crystallinity gives organisms their characteristic flexibility, exquisite sensitivity and responsiveness, thus optimizing the rapid, noiseless intercommunication that enables the organism to function as a coherent, coordinated whole. In addition, the liquid crystalline continuum provides subtle electrical interconnections which are sensitive to changes in pressure, pH and other physiochemical conditions; in other words, it is also able to register "tissue memory." Thus, the liquid crystalline continuum possesses all the qualities of a "body consciousness" that may indeed be sensitive to all forms of subtle energy medicines including acupuncture.

We can surmise that a body consciousness sensitive to acupuncture is likely to be sensitive to other subtle energies such as the currents of crystals. When I meditate with a stone, I often sense the infusion of its currents as tingling in various parts of the body—my hands, forehead or heart—sometimes followed by a "wave" of sensation through the entire body, especially if I "invite" the currents in. Without delving into questions about the consciousness of the stones as beings, or what it means for them to seemingly respond to our invitations, I am sure that the awareness within me initially feels the stone currents in the liquid crystal body consciousness. As Mae Wan Ho has indicated, the entire body consciousness participates almost instantaneously in whatever a part of the organism experiences. I have called this body consciousness the Liquid Crystal Body Matrix.

Lian Sidirov states, "The lipids in cellular membranes, the cytoskeletal and muscle proteins, collagen and other connective tissue macromolecules, as well as the DNA in chromosomes—all these essential and ubiquitous molecules of living systems are liquid crystals. Consequently, the organism may be seen as a solid state possessing many of the physical characteristics of these highly interesting materials." Among those characteristics are semiconduction and piezo-electric properties, which living organisms (such as us) share with certain minerals (such as quartz). This is one highly suggestive point of correspondence that may indicate how and why our bodies can find beneficial resonances with the currents of stones.

The lines of communication and centers of energy in the Liquid Crystal Body Matrix seem to correspond to the meridians as mapped by acupuncture, and also to the chakras, which we know from numerous spiritual systems. These may or may not be features of the body *per se* as much as they are points of correspondence where the Liquid Crystal Body Matrix aligns with aspects of our non-physical nature, such as the astral and etheric bodies. This begs the central question of what we mean by "body" and where its boundaries, if any, exist. The scientific papers about liquid crystallinity do not directly address these non-physical attributes, although some of them are beginning to approach these questions. In regard to acupuncture, Mae Wan Ho states, "Aligned collagen fibres in connective [liquid crystal] tissues provide oriented channels for electrical intercommunication, and are strongly reminiscent of acupuncture meridians in traditional Chinese medicine." This is one means of explaining, for instance, how a needle in one's toe can affect vision in one's left eye. The acupuncture meridians most likely have their corporeal aspect in the collagen channels of the Liquid Crystal Body Matrix rather than the neurons.

Crystallinity, whether liquid or solid, is distinguished by its orderly structural arrangements. Liquid crystals are fluid, but they are not chaotic like a gas or a non-organized liquid. Sidirov states, "Liquid crystals are mesophases—states of matter between solid and liquid phase. While they possess long-range orientational order, they are highly mobile and responsive . . . Liquid crystals can convert information about minute changes in pressure, temperature and light into electrical currents." The liquid crystal matrix of our bodies exhibits changeable but orderly structures and alignments that account for both tissue memory and adaptability. Our bodies know and act out the many patterns required for the expression of life, and they can do this in a magnificently coordinated fashion because of liquid crystallinity.

But just how flexible are we? Are the parameters of life fixed for everyone? The variability of human talents and sensitivities suggests that they are not. At the frontiers of human capacities lie spiritual abilities and *psi* talents that seem to cross the borders of physicality, at least as we know them. Even the sensitivity to crystals is on that border. Although many of the readers of this book can feel the currents of the stones, we all know people who don't. Could such differences have something to do with our Liquid Crystal Body Matrix?

In his brilliant article, Lian Sidirov discusses how we may actually be able to *increase* the degree of our internal coherence, or liquid crystallinity, through focusing our conscious intention in certain spiritual practices. In the abstract for his article, he writes:

> The central hypothesis is that practices such as *qigong* and yoga induce long-term structural and physiological changes in the body's semiconducting liquid crystal matrix, which maintain the system in a higher-than-average state of coherence, hence optimizing energy utilization, sensitivity and regulatory DC current feedback loops, which in turn control the expression of DNA and the "tuning" of sensory transduction arrays.

Simply stated, Sidirov suggests that *qigong* and other practices can increase the degree of one's liquid crystallinity, which increases the well-being and special capacities of the individual. These increases can involve extraordinary abilities such as healing, remote viewing and even the ability to live without food.

This is an exciting link between the mind and the Liquid Crystal Body Matrix. If focusing one's intention on meditative practices can affect the physical substance of the body and its liquid crystallinity, that gives us an important avenue for individual development, and perhaps even collective evolution. If we can learn to make ourselves more coherent—more crystalline— we could conceivably have found the physical substrate for spiritual development, perhaps even the hardware for awakening to the New Consciousness.

My intuition and experience with the stones tell me that through working with them we have found another way of increasing our coherence. As we know from experience and can intuit from what we learn about the qualities of the stones, solid crystals are very coherent, both in their structure and in the currents we feel from them. I have observed now for decades how Moldavite makes people feel warmth in their body, how Phenacite causes foreheads to tingle, and how Rosophia creates sweet swirls around the heart. Many people who have no prior knowledge or experience of these stones describe the resulting currents in these exact ways. Similar commonality of experience applies to all of the stones written about in my books. And when we return to these or other stones, the nature of their currents is consistent, even though they may initiate processes within us that go through a variety of stages. Different authors may disagree about the *properties* of the stones, but the *felt experience,* before one begins to draw conclusions about it, is quite similar.

I want to suggest once again that this felt experience occurs in the Liquid Crystal Body Matrix, and that this experience is delivered to mental consciousness. I have noticed in myself that the first "wave" of an encounter with a stone is a full-body one, although it may "enter" through the portals of one or more chakras. Next I often see an inner image, and almost immediately after that my mental consciousness starts interpreting the image. I believe that the image is generated by the heart as the result of a feeling impression of the stone currents. (There are important spiritual traditions like Sufism, as well as modern scientific investigators such as the Heartmath team, which maintain that the heart "thinks" in images.) For years, this happened so quickly that I failed to notice the arising images, although I always noticed the bodily currents. As I have worked more carefully with the stones, I have come to see these three ways of sensing them (bodily, heart and mental) as distinct albeit integrated modes.

I want to suggest that, over time, although not necessarily a very long time, meditative work with stones can facilitate the development of many capacities that are either dormant or minimal. In my own case, I have witnessed my sensitivities, both to stone currents and to other subtle phenomena, increasing a great deal. As one example, I have over the past five to ten years discovered and consequently nurtured a very great increase of awareness and sensitivity within my heart. (Twenty years ago, I was mostly "dead from the neck down"!) The ability to feel and direct currents through my third eye chakra has also been enhanced through repeated work with the stones. Now I can often distinguish different stones from one another by the kinds of currents I feel in my forehead when I touch them there. And there is nothing special about me, except for my high level of interest and years of practice.

However, simple exposure may be almost as helpful as practice. At my company, Heaven and Earth, we all spend our days among thousands of stones, many of which are high-vibration varieties. Over the years we have noticed that new employees seem to take two to four weeks to adjust to the high-energy environment. During that time they may feel light-headed, fatigued, nauseous, emotionally hypersensitive, giddy or any number of other unusual states. After that they are usually fine, and they do not feel overwhelmed by the energies. In my opinion, the Liquid Crystal Body Matrix in each of them has worked its way into harmony with the building full of stone currents into which it was suddenly immersed. I believe that this attunement must entail an increase in the degree of bodily coherence—an increase of liquid crystallinity—just as Sidirov suggested in qigong and yoga practitioners. One piece of evidence for this is the fact that after some weeks or months in the building, new employees often spontaneously develop the capacity to feel crystal energies, even if they never sit down to meditate with a stone, and even though they never previously had such an experience.

One of the patterns of nature is that like resonates with like, and in this case I think we are seeing the influence of the highly coherent structures and currents of the mineral crystals bringing the more fluid liquid crystals of our human bodies into resonant alignment with them. My sense that this crystal-enhanced environment is beneficial is supported by a number of cases in which we have seen individuals in our workplace evolve spiritually, with more frequent psychic experiences, increased incidence of synchronicities, improved health and more heart-based relationships. All of this happens without any focused meditative practice, and I believe that it provides anecdotal evidence of increased inner coherence (liquid crystallinity) due to daily exposure to a large quantity of high-vibration stones.

One final note on this idea that the body consciousness is enlivened by exposure to the stones: In our workplace, we sometimes have visitors who are crystal lovers, already accustomed to stone energies. They almost invariably comment on how good they feel in our crystalline environment. Even those who find it a bit too intense tend to call it "a little too much of a good thing." I think that both responses come directly from the body consciousness of the person's Liquid Crystal Body Matrix. The body *likes* to become more coherent, more crystalline. This is felt as a high vibration of inner harmony. The sense of "too much of a good thing" is probably coming from the body's being unaccustomed to the higher vibrational state and its felt need for time to integrate a shift of that magnitude.

If the body is crystalline, with a consciousness of its own, could it be capable of more than we now know? What might we be able to "teach" the body, and what could we learn about our own extraordinary capacities? If we keep one eye on science and the other on our experience, we will begin to glimpse some of the patterns of our potential.

TANGLING WITH ENTANGLEMENT

Both Mae Wan Ho and Lian Sidirov bring the concept of quantum entanglement into their writings. I first encountered this idea under synchronistic circumstances. On the morning of the second Crystal Conference, I was making the last notes on my outline before going to the ballroom to present my talk. One of the attendees had sent a news clipping up to my room with the note, "I think you might be interested in this." The clipping was a short article about laboratory experiments involving something called entanglement theory. In the experiment described in the article, scientists had constructed an apparatus that could send a pair of photons through a crystal together. After emerging from the crystal, the photons were in a state of mutual "entanglement" on the quantum level. The amazing result of entanglement was that the photons were now permanently bonded to one another in such a way that anything an experimenter did to affect one of the photons would instantly affect the other in a coordinated way. For instance, changing the spin of one photon immediately changed the spin of the other. This effect would happen instantaneously, regardless of whether the photons were separated by one inch or a hundred thousand light years! In the world of physics, this is big stuff, because it seems to imply that such instant "action at a distance" violates the speed-of-light limit on signal transmission.

I took the article's arrival as an omen of sorts. The idea that crystals have the capacity to "entangle" photons with one another might also apply to us. The bond of the photons reminded me of human bonds, like friendship and love, in which what happens to one partner affects the other, sometimes instantaneously. Considering the event that was about to begin, I imagined that the relationships we were all going to form might be more powerfully bonded than usual, since we were in the conference's crystalline environment. When I began my talk, before mentioning the article, I asked the audience members to turn to the persons to the left and right of them as well as in front and behind them, and to declare, "I am entangled with you!" It made for a jovial moment and was a good ice-breaker. Beyond that, I believe there *was* some potent entanglement that made the conference atmosphere very coherent. The weekend was filled with synchronicities, and the group became amazingly cohesive. Each day we all felt that we were "getting high" on the energetic atmosphere that we and the thousands of stones in the hotel were generating together. It was like a highly amplified version of the workplace atmosphere I described above.

I mention all this because both Mae Wan Ho and Sidirov hypothesize that entanglement works for people as well as photons, though it is harder to test in a lab. As we go into this, let's remain mindful of the fact that laboratory entanglement of photons was accomplished by sending them through a *crystal,* presumably to bring them into a coherent, coordinated state by pulsing them through the highly organized crystal lattice. Since our own bodies are liquid crystalline, it may be a natural function for us to become entangled *by choice* with other people, objects, processes, spiritual beings and who-knows-what. It may also be that it is relatively easy and powerfully beneficial for us to entangle ourselves with the stones, because of our mutual crystalline nature.

Sidirov is proposing in his article a paradigm for understanding how certain *psi* functions such as remote viewing and distant healing might operate, and he looks for the physical correlates of such capacities. Because considerable study has been done on the healing and psi capabilities of *qigong* practitioners, he places particular focus on these people. He notes that *qigong* practitioners have been able, through willed focus of *qi* energy, to slow the growth rate of cancer cells and in some cases to have profound healing effects on late-stage cancer patients. Some gifted individuals have been shown to be able to influence DNA and RNA samples in laboratory experiments. Many have the capacity to literally "send light" out of their hands. The best of these have been measured to produce biophoton outputs up to one hundred times that of control subjects.

Sidirov writes that one of the most striking effects of *qigong* practice is the *Bigu* state, in which practitioners engage in normal activities while consuming only three hundred calories per day. This state typically can last for weeks or even months. Rather than undergoing any physical or mental deterioration, the practitioners report that they do not experience hunger and that their energy levels as well as physical and mental competency are enhanced during this period. The state is said to occur naturally, when the accumulated *qi* reaches a certain level. Some researchers maintain that the bodies of these individuals enter into a "super-efficient state," like a car suddenly getting eighty miles per gallon rather than fifteen. The *Bigu* state is traditionally referred to as "feeding on light." Although most scientists would balk at taking such a phrase at face value, it apparently describes the felt sense of those who experience the state. There are numerous esoteric reports of people who have learned to stop consuming food and to "live on light." Some mystics have foreseen the potential of human beings to develop a Body of Light. Certainly a nourishing-feeling flood of inner light is among the experiences people have reported during meditation with crystals, and it is one I have undergone myself. Sidirov states, " . . . the role of light in biosystems is much farther-reaching than previously assumed."

Sidirov suggests that the discipline of *qigong* may lead to physiological changes, in which the liquid crystallinity of the body increases due to the repeated practice of attuning to the ambient universal *qi*. He indicates that such changes may also result from other spiritual practices. I quote below one of the key sections of the article for our purposes:

> One of the major challenges facing us is to understand why and how certain training techniques lead to an enhancement in psi function—in other words, why the interface between the physical and cognitive dimensions becomes more permeable with certain meditation practices. It is well known that *siddhis* [psychic powers] (spontaneous or specifically cultivated) characterize advanced practice stages in many spiritual traditions. Swann (1996a) emphasized that the primary goal of yoga (as described by Patanjali's and other ancient sutras) was an overall expansion of sensory awareness—and that as a result of this expansion, other mechanisms also became activated, accounting for what we would today call psychic powers. . . . The evidence also suggests that these advanced stages are not merely a matter of "know-how," but involve long-term/permanent changes in the practitioner's physiology.
>
> What we propose is that *qigong* and other meditative techniques work by progressively increasing the overall coherence ("qi flow"?) of the electromagnetic/liquid crystal continuum via conscious mental driving, in a way not dissimilar to laser pumping or the gradual orientation of ferromagnetic particles in an EM field. Meditation frequencies engage the thalamic silent periods and possibly other frequency-window pacemakers, and thus "drive" the configurational states that the body naturally cycles through, to sensitize its liquid crystal matrix to particular frequencies. The semiconductor nature of living tissues suggests that, with repeated passage of an electromagnetic current through them, their sensitivity to subsequent signals should increase—a property which, we believe, is critical to the understanding of long-term physiological changes seen in *qigong* practitioners. This "kindling" effect of meditation would, in our model, lead to both a gradual increase in tissue liquid crystallinity (hence greater perceptual sensitivity, energy efficiency and ability to absorb stresses as per Ho's model of frequency delocalization); and to more efficient coupling between intent (electromagnetic signal modulation) and its physical transducers—be they

DNA molecules regulating the body's physiological responses or other, yet-unknown elements which may be instrumental in anomalous cognition and psychokinesis.

In the above quote, Sidirov suggests that "practice makes perfect" in regard to developing sensitivities to subtle frequencies and enhancing non-ordinary perceptual capacities, because the practice itself brings about permanent physiological changes that correspond to the improved capacities. These allow the individual to direct his or her attention and intention to tasks such as remote viewing, healing and other *"siddhis"* or psi functions, with an increasing tendency for success. The physiological changes involve an increase in our inner coherence—our liquid crystallinity.

Now, back to entanglement. Sidirov indicates that the capacity of *qigong* practitioners to heal from a distance is an example of willed entanglement. He suggests that "the '*qi* state' can be seen as an entanglement between the healer and surrounding ('universal *qi*') spacetime sheets, as a result of which surrounding energy becomes available via magnetic bridges and can be subsequently transferred to the target."

I admit that I don't understand much about the magnetic bridges and spacetime sheets, but I have observed enough healing to get the gist the idea he is proposing. When my wife Kathy does a hands-on healing, she meditatively attunes herself to a frequency of gold-white light, which is for her the healing current. She asks to be a conduit for the healing and highest good of the person receiving the treatment. She then allows the current to run through her hands, into the person seated in front of her. I have felt the heat and vibration flowing through her hands, and at times I have seen the gold-white light filling my body. These are reminiscent of the heat and biophoton emissions measured from the *qigong* practitioners.

When Kathy engages in distant healing, her procedure mirrors quantum entanglement in much the same way. Through intention, she first enters a state of attunement with what she calls the Divine Source of healing (perhaps the same source the *qigong* practitioners call universal *qi*). The next step entails visualizing the healing subject and/or saying the person's name, and asking for attunement with the Divine Source of healing for that person. In the first step, she brings herself into coherent alignment with the healing source. In the second step, she initiates attunement (entanglement) with the subject. Just as with the *qigong* subjects, the entanglement creates the non-local effect of healing in the subject. Remember the two photons? The willed entanglement between healing facilitator and subject is similar to what happened when the two photons went through the crystal together. In the healing example, the healer's capacity to link with universal healing or *qi* is transferred to the subject through quantum entanglement, just as changing the spin of one photon changed the spin of the other. Further, the subject receives the healing energy or *qi* in the Liquid Crystal Body Matrix, which is also where the attunement with the healing source takes place in the healer.

If this theory is correct, people are no doubt entangled with one another for all sorts of reasons, not all of them beneficial. The bad kinds of voodoo and sorcery probably make use of entanglement in similar ways, but for negative purposes. Knowing this, however, allows us to work with the quantum universe in ways that are for the good of the whole. One of the fail-safes of the system may be that in order to wield the energies, one must be in a state of coherence, an increased degree of liquid crystallinity. This means being in a state of harmony, a state of attunement with a universal flow that seems always to move for greater intelligence and love. We can also say that one cannot send harm without experiencing harm, any more than one can send love without experiencing love. Kathy tells me that every time she sends healing, she receives healing. In a hyperconnected reflexive universe, we do reap what we sow.

Sidirov describes certain implications of Pitkanen's "magnetic sensory canvas hypothesis," suggesting that our "selves" are composed of the physical body and a magnetic "body" that consists of magnetic structures emanated by the Earth's magnetic field, self-organized within us. In this hypothesis, the magnetic "flux tube" structures in us extend in a field comparable to the whole Earth's circumference. In other words, our magnetic "body" extends around, and perhaps through, the entire Earth! We would be able to experience this body through practicing its capacities, just as we know our physical body through practicing its senses. In this case, the capacities of the magnetic body would be things such as distant healing, remote viewing and psychokinesis—the things we call psi capacities or ESP. The extension of self into fields like those suggested in this hypothesis also indicates how *qigong* practitioners might be able draw upon universal *qi* (or the *qi* of the Earth), suggesting what it might mean to "feed on light." All such capacities would involve greater than average coherence of the body consciousness—enhanced liquid crystallinity. As we have seen, the evidence suggests that meditative practices (*qigong,* Heartmath, yoga and perhaps attunement to crystals) create repetitive patterns of coherence in the Liquid Crystal Body Matrix. These repeated patterns become stronger with use, facilitating the discovery of and successful engagement with new or uncommon capacities of sensing and action.

Our bodies and our capacities for consciousness extend far beyond what we are used to imagining. Our entanglements weave into a tapestry of being that is dizzying in its connectedness and possibilities of experience. Even what we have believed to be our physical selves turn out to be more like eddies in the cosmic whirlpool. I want to repeat here my earlier quote from Mae Wan Ho:

> The visible body just happens to be where the wave form of the organism is most dense. Invisible quantum waves are spreading out from each of us and permeating into all other organisms. At the same time, each of us has the waves of every other organism entangled within our own make-up. . . . we are participants in the creation drama that is constantly unfolding. We are constantly co-creating and re-creating ourselves and other organisms in the universe, shaping our common futures, making our dreams come true, and realizing our potentials and ideals.

Realizing these potentials, however, entails more than simply meditating. Discovery of unknown senses might be a difficult matter, since we have little frame of reference or social acceptance for them. At first, one is likely not to know what is happening, and the concept of ESP is often inappropriately ridiculed. When they are ridiculed or ignored, our exceptional capacities fall into disuse or simply remain unknown. Sidirov tells us that the psi investigator Ingo Swann believes that "a vast field of information sources has become virtually inaccessible to us simply because we have historically failed to reinforce their required processing pathways." Like the capacities for language or mathematics, if we have no teachers or models for development of psi functions, and no social environment in which to utilize them, the capacities are never developed. In one of the concluding passages in his paper, Sidirov touches on these problems, along with the problem of our agreed-upon sensory "fishbowl":

> The quest to understand our healing potential leads to inquiries into the nature and organization of living systems; the desire to understand spontaneously occurring psi phenomena leads to deep questions about the phase space of reality and our ability to navigate it more intelligently. Indeed, as Pitkanen suggests throughout his monumental "Topological Geometrodynamics," the ***illusion*** [my emphasis] of our locality is perpetuated by the data fed to us by our senses—that is, those perceptions we are habituated to pay attention to. Sight, hearing, touch, smell, taste: these are borders of our Self, and the only senses we are willing to assign meaning to. Everything else that crosses the horizon of our consciousness is neatly classified into fact, emotion, or fantasy—with the latter two carrying practically no weight in our top information-processing center. Yet the examples listed above are only a modest sample of the vast informational resources that lie hidden in the unexplored manifolds of the mind-body continuum. In fact, with perception and visualization occupying part of the same neural processing pathways, can we tell with absolute certainty that what we take for "meaningless" imagination is not, indeed, actual perception of entangled realities? In the end, the study of nature and of our potentials become entwined—and at this point we have to pause and ponder the direction of our future scientific exploration.

Although Sidirov makes no mention of meditation with stones or crystals, my own sense is that this activity provides a most accessible avenue for the development of new capacities and, in all likelihood, an increase of the coherence of our body consciousness through enhancement of our liquid crystallinity. Not everyone will take up *qigong*, and most people cannot initiate an ESP experience at will. However, a relatively large percentage of the population is capable of feeling the currents of crystals, which, in my view, resonate directly with our Liquid Crystal Body Matrix. We can become "entangled" with stones in ways that help us heal and awaken to capacities we didn't know existed. For many of us, the first new capacity we discover is our ability to feel that mysterious tingling when a stone "says hello."

I want to mention here the way I have learned to meditate with stones. To begin, I hold the stone and simply look at it and feel it. Sometimes I notice that "hello"—the stone's current of vibration in my body. I then offer it my greeting—I blow my breath across it and say, inwardly or outwardly, "I extend to you my love and blessings, and I invite you into my heart." (This is my way of entering "entanglement" with the stone.) Next I close my eyes and hold the stone, sometimes touching it to my heart or third eye. From there, many things can happen, as I report in the stone sections of this book. One of the effects, I am convinced, is the increased coherence of one's liquid crystallinity, and the consequent expansion of one's perceptual horizons. The stones, I believe, are beings whose living qualities are outside the fishbowl of our usual perceptions, and they beckon us to join them.

When we enter into relationship (into entanglement) with the stones, we also bring ourselves into holographic attunement with the Earth. Each type of solid crystal is a particular expression of (or filter for) the Earth's *qi*—its energy or life force. By engaging with the stone in quantum entanglement, we make ourselves available for resonance with its qualities (or those qualities of Sophia/Wisdom). Each stone carries the characteristic properties of its type, which I have attempted to describe in the stone sections. Thus crystals provide a variety of bridges to resonance with *the life force of the whole Earth*. (It could also be described as coming into relationship with the Soul of the World.) This resonance will enhance our liquid crystallinity and can thereby, as Sidirov implies, allow us the many benefits of crystalline coherence—including health, longevity, expanded awareness and development of psi capacities and unknown sensory abilities.

Something within us wants out of the fishbowl. Something senses that there is infinitely more life available than what we know or have settled for. When a *qigong* practitioner taps into the universal *qi*, he or she is, in a sense, being "breathed" by the world—filled with the exhalation of its life. If my dream of "breathing with Sophia" (from Chapter Two) means what I believe it does, we are invited to breathe back. That "breathing back" is our loving engagement with the world, with Sophia. It is our part of the activity of blessing and co-creation that is the essence of the New Consciousness.

THE MOTHER & THE MIND OF THE CELLS

More than twenty years ago, I stumbled upon an odd little book called *The Mind of the Cells* by a man named Satprem. In it he chronicled the amazing work of spiritual transformation of the physical body and its consciousness undertaken by Mira Alfassa, spiritual partner of Sri Aurobindo, also known as the Mother. (I introduced these pioneers in Chapter Three and will continue to refer to them in later chapters.) As I look at it now, considering the Mother's work in light of Ho and Sidirov's hypotheses about the liquid crystal body, I am struck by how closely the Mother's descriptions of her experiences parallel these ideas.

The Mother had many psychic and spiritual experiences, beginning in early childhood and continuing throughout her life. Her spiritual partner, Sri Aurobindo, envisioned an evolutionary development of humanity in which human beings would become a new species, incarnating the Divine in the body and in the entire world of matter. Aurobindo believed that the spiritual solution for humanity was not to ascend out of the world into the spiritual realms, but to draw down the Divine consciousness (the Supramental Force, as he called it) into the body, and to thereby transform our species and the Earth itself. The Mother shared his vision, and after Aurobindo's death she set about the work of transforming her own body to receive and incarnate the Divine consciousness.

The interesting thing about the Mother's work of transformation, in regard to our focus on crystals, is that she focused on the transformation of the body. She recognized the truth of what Mae Wan Ho wrote years later—the body has its own consciousness, working separately though in relationship with the mental awareness mediated through the nervous system. No one had yet discovered the liquid crystallinity that provides the medium for the body-consciousness, but the Mother's practice was directed toward bringing order and attunement to the *cellular mind,* which I maintain is identical with the consciousness arising from the Liquid Crystal Body Matrix.

Not unlike the *qigong* practitioners who focus on bringing the universal *qi* into the body through repeated practices of attunement, the Mother sought to infuse her cells with the Supramental Force through changing and unifying their vibratory patterns. Her method was to "teach" the cells to repeat a mantra, *Om Namo Bhagavate.* Her intent was to bring the *vibration* of the mantra—not only the sound or meaning of it—into the cells, such that all of them would ultimately surrender to resonant unity with the Divine consciousness. This was, she believed, the path to the realization of Aurobindo's vision.

The tale of her transformation, with its difficulties and triumphs, would take us beyond the scope of this book. However, her reports of the phenomena she experienced offer vivid validation of Sidirov's premise that the coherence of the body's liquid crystallinity can be increased through certain spiritual practices. All accounts agree—from *qigong,* yoga and Heartmath, from crystal meditation to the Mother's installation of the mantra—that it takes time and repetition to shift the body's habits and move to the desired states of coherent attunement. I will quote below some of the Mother's descriptions of the bodily phenomena she experienced. (The numbers refer to the ordering of statements in the *Mother's Agenda* books. The first two digits indicate the year.)

We begin with her report of an infusion of the Supramental Force into the body. At this time, we may imagine that the tissues making up the liquid crystalline level of the body were beginning to wake up to the new coherence.

58.169 The other day . . . it came, taking over the entire body. It went up like this: all the cells were trembling. With such power! So I let the thing develop, and the vibration kept amplifying, growing and growing, and all the cells of the body were seized with an intense aspiration . . . as if the body itself were growing bigger—it was becoming colossal. I had the feeling that everything was going to explode. And it has such a transforming power!

At other points, the Mother's description seems to depict the felt sense of full coherence. It sounds almost as though her body had *become* a crystal.

58.115 It's strange, it has a cohesive effect: the whole cellular life becomes one solid and compact mass of incredible concentration—with a single vibration. Instead of the body's many usual vibrations, there is one single vibration, there is only one single vibration. It becomes as solid as a rock, one single concentration, as if all the cells of the body were a single mass.

61.241 The entire body became a single extremely rapid and intense vibration, but motionless. I don't know how to explain it because it wasn't moving in space, and yet it was a vibration (meaning it wasn't immobile), but it was motionless in space. It was in the body, as if each cell had a vibration and there was one single block of vibrations.

As the coherence increases, new sensibilities arise. Sidirov's article mentions the magnetic body, extending to the size of the Earth. In the next quote, the Mother describes a widening of awareness into what may be that world-size body, even as she intuitively senses her inner crystallization.

60.1211 One must learn to widen, widen, not only the inner consciousness, but even this aggregate of cells. To widen this sort of crystallization in order to be capable of holding that force.

As the events initiated by the Mother's unbending intention for transformation of the cellular consciousness continue, the experiences deepen. Sometimes the Mother felt as if her body had become the entire Earth. Remember Mae Wan Ho's description quoted above: "The visible body just happens to be where the wave form of the organism is most dense. . . ." The Mother apparently began to become conscious of her body at the quantum level.

> 61.252 This body is no longer as usual: it is scarcely more than a center of concentration, a kind of aggregate of something; it is not a skin-bound body—not at all. It's a sort of aggregate, a concentration of vibrations.

As the liquid crystal coherence of the body increased under the influence of the Mother's practices (and, in all probability, with spiritual assistance from the Supramental realm), the body consciousness described by Wan Ho seems to become more vivid, to awaken more fully.

> 71.1812 You can't imagine how radical it is, my child! I could really say I have become another person. Only this, the external appearance of the body, remains what it was. To what extent will it be able to change? Sri Aurobindo said that once the physical mind [body consciousness] is transformed, the transformation of the body will follow naturally. It's the consciousness that must change, the consciousness of the cells, you understand? That's a radical change. And there are no words to describe it, because it doesn't exist on Earth—it was latent but never manifested.

Why should we want to become fully coherent, liquid crystalline spiritual human beings, with a body consciousness awakened to its full potential? The Mother and Aurobindo, and their disciple Satprem, believed that the transformation of the body consciousness—its infusion and incarnated partnership with the Divine—was evolution's purpose, supplanting survival of the fittest with the Life Divine. It was, to them, the liberation of humanity and the fulfillment of heaven's promise on Earth. Compared with this, even the powers of the most advanced practitioners and healers we have known are bare beginnings. How interesting that it is the body consciousness—not the mental—that achieves this!

> 67.3012 What the body is learning is this: to replace the mental rule of intelligence by the spiritual rule of consciousness. And that makes a tremendous difference . . . to the point that increases the body's capabilities a hundred-fold. When the body follows certain rules, however broad they may be, it is a slave to those rules, and its possibilities are limited accordingly. But when it is governed by Spirit and Consciousness, its possibilities and flexibility become exceptional! And that's how it will acquire the capacity to extend its life at will. The "necessities" lose some of their authority. . . . All the laws—the laws that were the laws of Nature—lose some of their tyrannical power, you could say. It's a progressive victory over all the "musts." All the laws of Nature, all human laws, all habits, all rules are gradually relaxed and eventually come to an end. In particular, that whole sense of rigidity, absoluteness and near-invincibility brought about by the mind will disappear.

In the Mother's story, we have a case study in willed bodily coherence and its effects on consciousness. Her scrupulous observations of her inner states provide eye-witness support for the concept of the Liquid Crystal Body Matrix. They also lend credence to the hypothesis that one can initiate practices that increase the coherence of the liquid crystallinity of the tissues, with resultant awakening of dormant or latent paranormal and spiritual capacities. In the legacy of her work, we have clues to how we can do this ourselves.

Yet the Mother's path was an arduous one. Must we also work nonstop as she did throughout her pioneering journey? Perhaps, but we may have help that was not available to her. Satprem maintained that Sri Aurobindo and the Mother blazed a trail for us to follow with greater ease than those first explorers. It may be that they created vibrational resonances bridging the Supramental and physical realms, so that our gesture of invitation, coupled with reasonable persistence and surrender, will get us there. It may take a hundred or a thousand more years, but it could also happen to you or me in this lifetime. My sense is that we can go a long way toward incarnating the Divine Light with the aid of our allies, the stones. They are alive with pure, undeviating vibration that we can welcome into our bodies. In doing so, we help ourselves find harmony, inner awakening and Light, and we help the angels of the stones fulfill their purpose in the world.

What might such a future look like? How would we experience the world and ourselves? What I have glimpsed encourages me to think that increasing our inner coherence, the liquid crystallinity of our bodies, will help us awaken to the body's consciousness as well as the heart's awareness, and to thereby become truly whole. In this condition, I can imagine us discovering within ourselves capacities for sensing and activity beyond anything we know. It may be that we can learn to incarnate higher and higher frequencies, and to "live on Light" as the *qigong* masters have learned to do. As we go further down this path, we may discover more and more Light within ourselves. This can bring us into a way of being long referred to in esoteric texts, but which has rarely been achieved. Yet these texts and numerous visions experienced by mystics throughout history have pointed to it. It may be that increasing our liquid crystallinity is an intermediate step, allowing us to effect our eventual transformation into living beings with Bodies of Light.

CHAPTER FIVE

The Body of Light & the Great Central Sun

I saw them cross the twilight of an age
The sun-eyed children of a marvelous dawn . . .
The massive barrier-breakers of the world.
The architects of immortality . . .
Bodies made beautiful by the Spirit's light,
Carrying the magic word, the mystic fire,
Carrying the Dionysian cup of joy.

—SRI AUROBINDO, *Savitri*

"'God made Man in his own image,' the idea of Cosmic Anthropos, Celestial Man of Light, or ideal arch-type of humanity, is found in a wide variety of Hermetic and gnostic teachings whether Pagan, Jewish, Christian or Islamic. Nor is the idea limited to the West. The Cosmic Man represents both the source and ultimate goal of humanity, serving as exemplar, guide, telos, the ultimate goal or fruition, and is some-times portrayed as the 'First Man,' the inventor of all arts and sciences, or Gnostic Revealer—the Logos personified. In Orphic thought the figure is represented by Phanes (Illuminator), hatched from the Cosmic Egg, who 'shines out in the darkness,' and is the seed of gods and men. . . . Light is invariably associated with the figure of Cosmic Man, for Anthropos is a manifestation of Mind, and 'Light' or illumination is the hallmark of consciousness. . . . According to the Hermetic writings, Eternity (Aeon) is an image of God; the Sun is an image of Cosmos; and Man is an image of the Sun."

—DAVID FIDELER, *Jesus Christ, Sun of God*

A heavy, wet snow had just blanketed New Haven, Connecticut, one Sunday night in early April of 1970, during my freshman year at Yale. It was after midnight, and I had been talking for hours with my roommate in one of those soul-searching conversations that tend to arise when you are young and searching, and it is your first year away from home. Telling him about my family and my childhood dreams, I had gone into the depths of difficult memories. In particular, I had recounted my most recurrent childhood dream, in which I found myself compelled to descend a dark staircase into a foreboding black basement festooned with cobwebs. In the dream, which occurred dozens of times between the ages of six and fourteen, I found myself in terror of the descent into the dark cellar.

Then, each time I had the dream, at the threshold of that awful darkness, a white horse would magically appear under me and carry me up into the sky. As it flew, the white horse grew larger and larger—to the size of a car, a house, a city block, a mile long—extending ultimately like a huge, smooth white cloud, lifting me higher and higher. I was still small, and eventually I always lost my hold on the horse's back, sliding off and falling, down and down. And as I fell, I would suddenly wake up, disoriented and frightened.

After telling the dream to my roommate, I was nervous and agitated. I stood up and walked into the living room, pacing back and forth in front of the window, gazing at the carpet of snow and the full moon that hung in the sky above a huge cloud.

Suddenly I stopped pacing and jerked my head back to the window. I *recognized* the huge cloud! It was the exact image of the horse from my childhood dream.

As I stood gaping, my thoughts raced. How could the horse from my dream be there in the sky, at that precise moment? What was real? What was a dream? I was only eighteen, and my mind had nowhere to go. It stopped. I was terrified. My idea of the real world was gone. I felt myself shatter into a thousand pieces. I called out, "Oh God, help me!"

At that moment, there was a sharp pop at the back of my head, and suddenly, smoothly, a wave of pure White Light washed through my skull. With it came a flood of ecstatic joy, peace, comfort and certainty. My terror had vanished, and I basked in rapture, watching the radiance fill my body. I was sure that I had been touched by God.

For the next few hours, I was in a state of *samadhi*, full of light, knowledge and joy. I spoke in an overflowing fountain of words, describing what I saw and understood. Anything I wanted to know I had only to think about for the answer to be there. My roommate had seen the whole thing happen, and he witnessed my state of inner radiance. The state faded by morning, though I fell asleep in the pre-dawn hours feeling as though I lay on the beach of an ocean of Light.

That experience, triggered by the synchronicity of my dream, changed my life, leading me along many spiritual paths and ultimately bringing me into contact with Moldavite and the realm of stones. The reason I tell of it here is that it was my first experience of the Light Body. I have written in Chapter Three of my second major Light Body awakening, the Moldavite journey to the Great Central Sun. In both cases, at the climactic moment, my body was filled with spiritual Light, accompanied by ecstatic joy and a sudden expansion of consciousness. Both times the radiance was visible to others. In the second instance, my wife had exclaimed, "Bob, there's light all around you!"

Among the things I learned from my two experiences was that the Light Body is real, and that the infusion of the Light Body into the physical is something of immense value. If I could be in that state at all times, I would choose it in an instant. Indeed, I have spent much of my life on the trail of those moments, trying to understand them and enter them again. The attainment of these states by as many people as possible is a major goal of my work, because I feel it is the spiritual destiny of humanity. Other things most certainly go with that—love for the Divine, for other people and the Earth is essential. One cannot live only on the peaks of Spirit, and the valleys of daily life are lovely in their own way. However, embodying the Divine Light is the goal of our transformation.

Over the past twenty years, many of my experiences with the stones have triggered infusions of the inner Light. Generally, they were less overwhelming than the two stories I have told so far, but the territories I have entered through Azeztulite, Phenacite, Herderite, Selenite and many of the other stones in this book are very much the realms of Light, and these Light-currents frequently display themselves *within* the body. Moreover, the stones are steady and consistent in their emanations. One does not have to fall into a thicket of mind-bending synchronicities to be jarred into *samadhi*. One can sit with the stones any day, and their currents will be there. Like the angels to which they have been likened, they are faithful messengers of the Divine "Word"—the vibratory patterns of spiritual Light. They can act as teachers and allies, facilitating the awakening of our Bodies of Light. Their faithfulness can help us practice and integrate the new patterns, so that we have the chance to ultimately live in an expanded consciousness, such as that which I experienced on those two extraordinary occasions.

When I prepared to write this book, I carefully chose the sixty-two stones I felt to be the most advantageous companions for our journey of embodying the Light. The essays give indications of their qualities and potentials, but it is each person's job to find his or her own path with them. The stones are like keys, and we are the doors. Each person is likely to need different keys, or a different sequence of them. I do believe that the stones in this book are the most active and helpful for awakening, stabilizing and integrating the Body of Light with our physical selves. The bringing of Divine Light into incarnation here on Earth is the true blossoming of the New Consciousness.

WHAT IS THE LIGHT BODY?

The Light Body is, in the simplest sense, a refined living mirror-image of the human body, composed of spiritual Light and radiant from within. Those who have seen a Light Body almost universally describe it as being of unearthly beauty, emanating qualities of bliss, peace, love and divinity. Most spiritual traditions that address the Light Body maintain that all human beings have a Body of Light, at least potentially. The majority of these suggest that attaining the Light Body during one's lifetime involves mastering certain inner practices.

One of the most important questions about the Light Body is its degree of materiality. Can it simultaneously be both Light and matter, or is it an immaterial projection of a spiritual image? Herein lies the mystery of our destiny. Can we become beings of Light while remaining in the physical world? And if we can, what will the Earth do? Will it also transfigure into its Body of Light?

The Light Body has a long multicultural history. It is known as "the resurrection body" and "the glorified body" in Christianity. In Sufism it is called "the most sacred body" (*wujud al-aqdas*) and "supracelestial body" (*jism asli haqiqi*). In Taoism it is named "the diamond body." In Kriya Yoga it is "the body of bliss." In Hermeticism it is known as "the immortal body" (*soma athanaton*). Tibetan Buddhism has several names for it: *Vajrayana*, "the light body" or "rainbow body." In the alchemical tradition, the Emerald Tablet calls it "the Glory of the Whole Universe" and "the golden body." All of these spiritual streams hold that the achievement of union with this luminous form of the self is among the highest potentials of the spiritual aspirant.

Traditions appear to differ in regard to what attainment of the Light Body entails, and whether the Light Body is meant to be experienced in an out-of-body or in-body state (in regard to our physical form). Gnostic groups have been portrayed as believing that our descent to Earth from the spiritual realms entailed a fall from grace that included loss of the Light Body, or the "robe of glory." Much of the attention in these groups was on recovery of the Light Body, either through *gnosis* in this life or after death. The idea that we assume a Body of Light after death is implicit in much Christian mythology, and it has been corroborated by the reports of numerous people who have undergone near-death experiences. Dream experiences or visitations featuring appearances of those who have died frequently reveal them in radiant bodies.

Some traditions have sought to "build" the Light Body as a vehicle for travel in the astral or etheric realms. In his essay, "The Body of Light in the Western Esoteric Tradition" (see bibliography), Mark Stavish first mentions an Eastern conception of the Light Body: "Under the general heading of *chi kung* [*qigong*], or Chinese internal alchemy, these practices are designed to create and mature a body of subtle astral and etheric energy that is capable of existence independent of material consciousness. This body is also thought to be capable of infusing the material body with sufficient energy to allow it to become more subtle and 'ethereal.'" I am reminded of the *qigong* practitioners discussed in the previous chapter who were able to fill their physical bodies with sufficient *qi* to live almost without food for long periods, and to heal themselves and others. We also touched on the quantum scientific view of the "magnetic body," which was not limited to the confines of the material form and was capable of extending perception and even certain kinds of action at a distance, through quantum entanglement. From this we could infer that the Light Body is the means for these kinds of actions and perceptions.

It may be that there are levels of Light Body activation or awakening, giving rise to the different descriptions of the Light Body. Later in his article, Stavish discusses Western doctrines of the Light Body:

> The three basic ideas around the subtle body are that it progresses through the levels of the spheres, increases in power and purity, and is made of light and/or fire. It is described as the spirit-body, the radiant body, and the resurrection body, depending on its degree of purity. . . . The Spirit-Body is closely aligned to the physical body, similar to the *nephesh* or vegetative-animal soul in Jewish Qabala. . . . The Radiant Body allows us to experience the vision of Beauty Triumphant as referred to in modern qabalistic schools. . . . What makes the Resurrection Body different is that while it can and does exist in the material world, it is free from material constraints.

The phrase "Resurrection Body" refers to the physical form in complete unity with the Body of Light. This is the form Jesus Christ was said to have assumed after his crucifixion and entombment, leading to his Ascension.

There are other spiritual traditions in which something akin to the Resurrection Body exists. One is the Tibetan Buddhist doctrine of the Rainbow Body. This term refers to a phenomenon—circular rainbows in a cloudless sky—seen by witnesses after the death of masters who make the transition to the Light Body.

Practitioners of Dzogchen Buddhism who have achieved a certain degree of mastery display seemingly miraculous phenomena. Upon death, the body of such an individual is said not to decompose but to gradually disappear into light, leaving behind only the hair and fingernails. Those who achieve even greater realization are said to enter the Body of Light without going through physical death. They are believed to raise their vibratory state, or Light infusion, until they become invisible to those with "normal karmic vision," although they can still be seen by those with clairvoyant vision. These beings are believed to remain invisible unless they choose to manifest a physical body in order to be of benefit to people still in the physical realm. The conscious movement into the Light Body while one is still living is called the Great Transfer. In *The Crystal and the Way of Light,* Namkhai Norbu writes:

> Both the Great Transfer and the Body of Light are in essence the same. . . . A totally realized being is free from the cycle of conditioned cause and effect . . . such a being may manifest a body for the purpose of helping others. The Light Body of a being who has made the great transfer . . . can be actively maintained for the purpose of communicating with those who have sufficient visionary clarity to be able to perceive such a body. But to help those who lack such capacity, a totally realized being may manifest in an actual physical body."

The practice of Dzogchen entails the mastery of many visualizations. To visualize is to create coherent patterns of interior light. Such practices, as we saw in the previous chapter, are more than mental exercises. They also bring the Liquid Crystal Body Matrix into greater coherence. It may be that it is when this body reaches a critical level of coherence, in union with the resonant field of the heart and a sufficiently focused mind, that the Light Body can manifest in full integration with the physical.

Sri Aurobindo's integral yoga aimed at just such an outcome. According to his teaching, not only the mind and other higher faculties of life have to be spiritualized and transformed, but the spiritual Light and force have to be brought down to the lowest level to transform the body so that it can hold the Divine Light. A weblog about Sri Aurobindo's yogic work offered the following: "Sri Aurobindo had firmly established in himself, in his very physical [body], a transformative superconscient power which he called the Mind of Light. Later the Mother defined it as the physical [body's] mind . . . opening to the Supramental." Here again we see the image of the Light's descent into the physical form, into the body-consciousness of the Liquid Crystal Body Matrix. This was the goal of the work of Aurobindo and the Mother. Their vision and intention was to ground the Supramental Light into matter through human beings, bringing into existence a literally en-Light-ened new species, free from all past limitations, including death.

The urge toward immortality was not only theirs—it is common to most of the spiritual traditions that involve movement into the Light Body. Even Christianity promises that after Judgment Day the resurrected bodies of the faithful will no longer suffer pain or death. The Dzogchen masters who made the Great Transfer are said to be beyond birth and death. Some of the Taoist alchemists of old were purported to live for hundreds of years, and Western alchemy has also involved the transmutation of the self into an immortal Light-filled condition. Who knows what is possible?

MEMORIES OF THE LIGHT BODY

Speaking of the limits of the possible, I am reminded of a past-life regression I underwent some years ago. My wife Kathy and I had been offering our wares at a gem and mineral show in Denver, Colorado. At the end of the event, we agreed to meet with a man who told us that his spirit guides wanted him to lead us into a past-life regression, which would reveal to us some important aspects of our work. After we had packed and prepared to go home, we sat with the man in our hotel room for the meditative regression induction. I placed a Phenacite on my third eye and held a piece of Moldavite in one hand and an Azeztulite in the other.

In only a few minutes, I began to view an interior "movie" of a past life. When I realized its location, I protested inwardly—it was Atlantis. One might think that a crystal-lover like myself would welcome such a vision, but I did not. I was not at that time among those who took seriously the idea that a place called Atlantis ever existed. How embarrassing to recall a past life there!

The vision unfolded, heedless of my resistance. I saw myself as an Atlantean "priest" who lived at a temple on an outlying island of the archipelago. I can still see quite vividly the white tunic I wore, the green grass outside the temple and the sparkling azure sea. My work consisted mainly of sitting in a certain spot on a white stone bench, orienting myself toward another island and allowing my heart to act as a transmission-relay point for energy currents, which were generated via a combination of human beings and crystals. It seemed that the crystals were the "batteries," and the humans directed the flow of the currents. The vertex points, such as the one where I sat, were parts of an energy grid that supported a geometric Light-structure involving and encompassing all of the islands.

As I witnessed this vision, I was amazed to see that the central island of Atlantis was the focal point for a nested group of Platonic solid energy forms. The smallest of these was a tetrahedron, perhaps only fifty feet high. Then there was a cube encompassing that, and a much larger octahedron around the cube. Even larger was an icosahedron that extended for several miles. The largest form was a dodecahedron that appeared to enclose at its base most of the Atlantean islands, as well as all the other forms.

If that were not enough to astonish me, I next became aware that there were *beings* ascending and descending through the Platonic Light-forms. They slid up or downward along the angular lines of the forms, almost like riding in an elevator. However, the beings were also undergoing a process of materialization and dematerialization as they moved. Physical people were entering the energy lines at ground level, growing gradually less dense as they moved upward. When they reached the top of the forms, they were entirely made of light, in an echo of their human form. The same process occurred in reverse for those descending—they began as Light Bodies and became physical by the time they reached the ground.

The end of my vision depicted the destruction of Atlantis by a huge tidal wave, just as numerous stories have suggested.

For years I carried that story in memory, not knowing what to think of it yet fascinated with the image of the Platonic forms and the beings moving easily between the Light Body and physical incarnation. In 2008, I received an unexpected corroboration when a woman with no knowledge of my earlier vision did a past-life reading for me in which she saw the whole Atlantean life just as I had, including the scene of the beings moving in and out of the energy forms. I still don't know whether to view Atlantis as an episode of the history of the Earth, as having been a previous version of the Earth, or as something in another realm entirely. However, the pattern of the physical body and the Light Body as dual aspects of human beings was clearly present, and in this case there were crystals involved in generating the energetic structures that facilitated the transformations.

LIGHT FROM DNA

Clairvoyants can see auras around people, and some say this is the nascent Body of Light. Is it possible that we are already walking in the world with our Light Bodies engaged with our physical forms, but in a relatively dormant state? Could it be that the Body of Light is something we can "grow" or kindle until it can manifest with much greater radiance and power? The stories we hear from the spiritual traditions suggest that this is so, although its accomplishment appears to require persons of great inner discipline and spiritual gifts.

We know that DNA emits light, and that practitioners of spiritual disciplines such as *qigong* can increase the rate of biophoton light emission from their hands. The *qigong* masters say that the *qi* with which they can heal [and the biophotonic light] come through them from the universal *qi*. Could the vehicle for this transmission be our DNA? Lian Sidirov reports that DNA has been shown to tune into the nodal points of an electromagnetic field, rather like a light antenna. DNA has been shown to emit more light during cell division and seed germination. We have here a bit of a link with the metaphysical principle that light is life.

I speculate that as we reach the level of DNA, we are near a point of overlap between the human and divine realms. As for the light emitted by DNA, I sense that its electromagnetic component is, as Steiner suggested, the "deterioration" or after-image of the spiritual Light infusing light into each cell. This may indicate why we recognize spiritual people emanating a radiance, or why, in my moment of Light Body awakening, Kathy exclaimed, "You're full of Light!" When conditions of spiritual attunement and liquid crystalline coherence are right, the flood of light enters, possibly through the portal of our liquid crystalline DNA, and the visible light we manage to see or measure is more or less the overflow.

There is an intriguing and mounting body of evidence supporting the idea of a relationship between our DNA and the mineral crystalline world. Remember that both the Australian Aborigines and the South American Desani tribe have ancient myths maintaining that the Cosmic Serpent (the spiraling, serpentine DNA molecule?), progenitor of all life, was *led* into the world by a Quartz crystal. "Led" can mean "preceded by" and/or "shown the path." In the case of DNA, it could be both, since the organizing patterns of these crystals preceded DNA's physical existence, and since the hexagonal structure of DNA is present in Quartz. Both Quartz and DNA are piezoelectric—able to transform physical pressure into light. Although DNA is known to emit light, the source of that light is unknown. Perhaps it is the same Divine source that seemed to illumine my body from within, back in college all those years ago. Certainly my heart tells me now that it is.

LIGHT FROM THE HEART

Speaking of the heart, it is good to recall that our urges toward the Divine spring most sincerely from that place. Practically all spiritual traditions identify the heart as the place that carries the Divine spark in us, and more than a few indicate that the heart is the point of origination of the Light Body. We can corroborate this idea with the fact that the heart generates the body's predominant electromagnetic field. Even if this field is not our true spiritual Light or Light Body essence (and I feel it is not), the electromagnetic field could be viewed as the overflow or after-image of the heart's spiritual Light. Both Aurobindo and the Mother taught that the body is spiritualized through the heart and feeling.

How does it feel when the heart catches fire and the Body of Light begins to form? Here is a passage written by Satprem in which he describes the incarnation of the Light Body:

> At first it is just a little flame in the mind, something groping about in search of a vaster inspiration, a greater truth, a purer knowledge, which soars, soars, and would as soon cut away all the weight of the world, the hindrances, the bonds and tangles of the earth. It soars and sometimes emerges, pure, sharp, upon summits of White Light where everything is forever known and true—but the Earth, meanwhile, remains false; life and body remain in the dark conflict, and die and decay. So this white little flame begins to take in the heart. It yearns to love, to heal, to save. It gropes about in the dark, helps a fellowman, gives assistance, offers itself and sings a song that would like to embrace all, take all life into its heart. It is already a warmer and denser flame, but its minutes of illumination are like a pale and fragile firefly on an ocean of obscure life. It is constantly quenched, engulfed, swept under the wave and under our own waves of obscurity—nothing is changed and life continues in its rut. So the seeker decides to drive this fire, this ardent truth, into his every moment and gesture, into his sleep and into his days, into his good and into his evil, into his whole life—so that everything may be purified, consumed by that fire—so that something *else* may be born at last, truer life, a truer being. . . . And the fire continues to grow. It goes down the degrees of the being, plunges into the subconscious caves . . . dislodges the misery within,

and burns more and more continuously, powerfully, as if stoked by the obscure pressure. It is already a body almost in our likeness, vermillion-red in color, already verging on gold. But it is still fluctuating and precarious; it lacks a fundamental base, a permanent foundation. So the seeker decides to drive this fire into his substance and body. He wants his own matter to reflect the Truth, to incarnate the Truth; he wants the outside to radiate as the inside. He enters upon the path of the supramental being. For in truth this growing self of fire, this ardent body which bears more and more resemblance to our divine archetype, our brother of light up above, and which seems to exceed us on all sides and even to radiate all around with an already orange vibration, is the very body which will form the supramental being. It is the next earthly substance, "harder than diamond yet more fluid than gas," said Sri Aurobindo. It is the spiritual condensation of the great Energy before it becomes matter.

But how to induce this fire into our matter, how to effect the passage, or transfusion, of this dark and mortal body to that ardent and immortal one? The work is in progress; it is difficult to talk about. We will not really know how it is done until it is done. No one knows the country or the way to it since no one has ever gone there, No one has ever made a supramental body! But it will be made, as inevitably as man and the ape and the millipede were already made in the great golden Seed of the world. This is the last adventure of the earth. Or maybe the first of a more marvelous series on a new earth of truth. We do not know the secret; we only know in what dir ection to walk—though knowing the direction is perhaps already knowing the secret, since it unfolds under our steps and is formed by walking it.

So we can at least indicate the direction, the simple direction, for as usual all the secrets are simple. *The fire is built by the particle of consciousness we put into an unconscious act.* Viewed from above, it is unconsciousness resisting and heating up from the friction of the new consciousness seeking entry—it is that futile and automatic gesture which has trouble untwisting its habitual groove and turning differently, under another impulsion; and we have to untwist the old turn a thousand times, insist and persist until a little flame of consciousness replaces the dark routine. Viewed from below, it is that unconsciousness which suffocates and calls out and knocks and seeks. And both are true. It is the memory within which summons the golden ray. It is the great eternal Sun which makes that call for sunlight well up. The process, the great Process, is simple: we must light that little fire by degrees, put the ray into each gesture, each movement, each breath, each body function. Instead of doing things automatically, mechanically, we must remember Truth there too, infuse Truth there too. And we meet with resistance, forgetfulness, breakdowns; the machine goes on strike, falls ill, refuses to take the path of light. We must begin again, thousands and thousands of times, point by point, gesture by gesture, function by function. We must remember again and again. Then, all of a sudden, in one little point of the body, in that passing little breath, something no longer vibrates in the old way, no longer works as usual; our breathing suddenly follows another rhythm, becomes wide and sunny, like a comfortable lungful of air, a breath of air never known before, never tasted before, which refreshes everything, cures everything, even nourishes us as if we were inhaling the nectar of the immortals. Then everything falls back into the old habit. We must start all over again, on one point, on another point, at each instant—life becomes filled with an extreme preoccupation, an intense absorption. A second's miniscule victory strengthens us for another discovery, another victory. And we begin to work in every nook and cranny, every movement; we would like everything to be filled with truth and with that sun which changes everything, gives another flavor to everything, another rhythm, another plenitude. The body itself then begins to awaken, to yearn for truth, for sunshine. It begins to light its own fire of aspiration here and there, begins to want not to forget anymore; and wherever it forgets that new little vibration, it suddenly feels suffocated, as if it were sliding back into death. The process is simple, infinite, perpetual: each gesture or operation accomplished with a particle of consciousness binds that consciousness, that little fire of being, to the gesture or operation, and gradually transforms it. It is an infusion of consciousness, a microscopic and methodical and innumerable infusion of fire, until matter itself, under that conscious pressure, awakens to the need of consciousness as the seed awakens to the need for sunlight. Everything then starts growing together, inevitably, irresistibly, under that golden attraction. By degrees, the fire is lit, the vibration radiates, the note spreads, the cells respond to the Influx. The body inaugurates a new type of functioning, a functioning of conscious truth.

In Satprem's description, we see how the process begins with one's everyday mental consciousness making a decision, no doubted prompted by a longing from a much deeper part of one's being but still one's own free choice. One sees the compelling attraction of the inner Light, or fire, and starts to feel an indescribable, astonishing sense of satisfaction as the Body of Light begins to incarnate. Satprem describes the difficulties of encountering the web of habit that blocks the way, accompanied by the intensity of the desire of the Divine truth of one's nature to penetrate that web.

His statement, "*The fire is built by the particle of consciousness we put into an unconscious act,*" is a key. Although it is directed toward changing habits of every sort in order to consciously open to the Light, it is also akin to what I might call "consciously engaging the Liquid Crystal Body Matrix." Here I am referring to the same gesture—bringing consciousness into an area of our being that we do not normally experience in a conscious way. We can do this, as Satprem suggests, by turning our *attention* to the body—to its tiny particles, the cells. With some practice we can feel the cells responding to us in a sort of coordinated wave of feeling, and we can feel awareness arising in the body.

It is noteworthy that Satprem describes the incarnating Light Body as resembling our divine archetype, that he describes its color (beginning in red but reaching toward gold), and that he notices its radiance beyond the perimeter of the corporeal body. He also returns repeatedly to images of the spiritual Sun, which I liken to the Great Central Sun, the source of the golden radiance of the Divine which is holographically present everywhere—in the atom, the cell, the heart, the Earth, the Sun and in the center of the galaxy. It is the source of the true Light, of which the light our eyes can see is the afterglow.

In our adventure we have allies that Satprem, the Mother and Sri Aurobindo did not have—the stones. They are mediators or messengers between the Divine and us. They can help us to become aware of the Light centers of our chakras and the resonant flows of the Liquid Crystal Body Matrix. They faithfully transmit an array of perfected patterns of vibrations—the true gestures of spiritual qualities to which we can open ourselves. Through these openings we discover ourselves, the beings of the stones, and the Soul of the World who breathes to us through them. In our mutual breathing, our activity of blessing, we can find the resonance of healing and we can embody wholeness. More than that, we can give the Divine a path into incarnation. We can co-create ourselves and the world anew. The healing upon which we have the opportunity to embark is much greater and deeper than we might imagine.

THE GREAT CENTRAL SUN

"The Central Sun emits Creative Light."

—HELENA BLAVATSKY, *The Secret Doctrine*

"The sun is the soul of all things; all has proceeded out of it, and will return to it, which shows that the sun is meant allegorically here, and refers to the central, invisible sun, GOD."

—HELENA BLAVATSKY, *Isis Unveiled*

"Perfect is what I have said of the work of the Sun."

—HERMES TRISMEGISTOS, *The Emerald Tablet*

What is the source of the Light that illuminates the Light Body? All reports seem to tell us that the source is Divine. Many cultures have used the image of the Sun to denote both the symbol and substance of the Divine. In my own meditative journey with Moldavite, I found myself orbiting in a grand and worshipful procession around a luminous golden Sun, just before discovering its mirror-image in my own heart. Years later, when the imminent arrival of Azeztulite was announced, the angelic group soul entity Azez told Naisha that the source of the Nameless Light they served (which was to flow through the Azeztulite) was the Great Central Sun. In the ancient *Rig Vedas* of India, the Divine Light was called *saura agni,* the solar fire, and it was said to be everywhere in matter—in the stone, the living wood, even in water. In Satprem's description of the awakening Light Body, he writes, "It is the great eternal Sun which makes that call for sunlight well up." As I have written elsewhere, I envision the Great Central Sun as a holographic source of spiritual Light, present in everything, as the Vedas said. If we look for its pattern, we can see that every body in the universe—from the greatest galaxy to our own sun, from the body of the Earth to the human heart, from the DNA to the core of the atom—emanates its radiance and its electromagnetic afterglow. If one sends *the particle of consciousness* to find it, the Great Central Sun with its Divine radiance of the Nameless Light is everywhere.

In the book *Jesus Christ, Sun of God: Ancient Cosmology and Early Christian Symbolism,* author David Fideler shows how deeply the idea of the Great Central Sun is embedded in our foundational myths and collective psyche. In the Pythagorean schools of ancient Greece, Fideler explains, the sun was viewed as the link between the material and spiritual aspects of existence. "Helios was seen as the heart of the celestial pattern and his physical aspect was considered as the lower manifestation of a higher principle which we may characterize as the Idea of the Solar Logos." The physical sun was not confused with the spiritual Sun, the source of life and light. It was seen rather as the Son of the Sun, or the Son of God. Numerous religions including early Christianity featured central beings who were viewed as the Son of God. In the case of Christianity, whether life imitated myth or myth imitated life is a matter of interpretation, insight and faith. This is also the case in our own spiritual explorations. Do we imagine the Divine as a radiant Light because of having seen the sun, or do we have the sun in our sky because its pattern is an echo of the Divine?

THE LIGHT BODY OF THE EARTH

Mainstream science considers the Earth to be an inanimate object—a ball of iron with a skin of water and land, inhabited by the oddity called life. The astronomical view emphasizes the Earth's insignificance within the vastness of the cosmos. Sri Aurobindo's partner, the Mother, with her spiritual vision saw the Earth as a site of supreme importance, as the following quotes illustrate:

> The formation of the earth as we know it, this infinitesimal point in the immense universe, was made precisely in order to concentrate the effort of transformation upon one point; it is . . . to make it possible, while working directly upon one point, to radiate it over the entire universe . . . the creation and the history of the earth . . . is a good symbol of universal history.
>
> —THE MOTHER, *Collected Works,* Vol. 4, p. 242, Sri Aurobindo Ashram Trust, 1972

And again, on another occasion:

> (Although it) is nothing from the astronomical standpoint . . . a thing absolutely without interest and without importance . . . from the occult and spiritual point of view, Earth is the concentrated symbol of the universe. For it is much more easy to work on one point than in a diluted vastness . . . (F)or the convenience and necessity of work, the whole universe has been concentrated and condensed symbolically in a grain of sand which is called the Earth. And therefore it is the symbol of all; all that is to be changed, all that is to be transformed, all that is to be converted is there. . . .
>
> —*Collected Works,* Vol. 5, pp. 275-276

As I read those words, my heart tells me that they are true, and they fill me with great awe. If the Earth is indeed that important, we are responsible for more than we have ever dreamed. The Divine itself may be working out the great issues of Creation right here. I am reminded of the intuitions of Christian mystics, but even more vividly I recall a personal experience from more than twenty years ago.

In an early part of our journey with the stones, in 1987 my wife Kathy Helen Warner and I journeyed to Sedona, Arizona. We visited the fabled vortices, and we climbed up onto a big one called Bell Rock. There we built a little grid of stones, and we each went into meditation while the other one stood watch. When it was Kathy's turn, she entered a very deep state, almost trancelike, and she moved into four different manifestations of her Light Body. I could not see them, but she described everything as I held a tape recorder. She first became a simple image of herself, then a great guardian spirit of the land, and next a blue Light Being reunited with other beings of her kind on a Ship of Light. There was an experience of initiation when she encountered a radiant Master; and when he placed a ball of Light into her heart, she united with the Light. From that place of unity with Light, still speaking what she experienced, she asked the question, "Why is the Earth so important that so many are trying so hard to save it?" The answer she received is printed below, along with an image of the Earth in its Light Body, illumined as a Planet of Light. You might call her words our Mission Statement:

From the Light

As I look at the universe, or this section of the universe, I see the Earth is on the outer circle of how far the Light has spread, and we need the Earth to be of the Light to continue the expansion. It is like a pivotal point, where if it turned to the darkness it would be like a black hole. But if it turned toward the Light, it would have such a brilliant radiance that it would bring the Light to much more of the universe. Once we begin to know that we are one in the Light, we will no longer be able to harm another, or the being that is this planet Earth. She is like someone that needs to rest and be nurtured and healed. She is purging, but to purge so much is weakening her. She needs all those on Earth who are Lightworkers to create a web of Light that will hold her steady—a grid through which even more Light can be poured in from off the Earth. Without these grids and these places that are as magnets for the Light, it is not possible to send enough healing Light to the Earth. It is important for those who understand to consciously draw the Light down and around our planet.

Our only purpose in all of eternity is to be one with and in the Light. We must ever expand the Light in our individual Being, and become fully conscious of that Being, so that our every everything is of and for the Light. Each breath we take, if we are conscious, draws Light into our Being. Every word we speak sends forth Light, if each word is spoken in consciousness. Every time we focus attention on another being we are opening that channel of Light and a beam of Light goes out. And if that being responds in kind, there is a great brilliance. As the master Jesus spoke, "When two or more of ye are gathered in my name, there I am." The two truly being conscious, for even a moment, connects and creates more of that network of Light.

Every connection made with every person is connecting those people with a filament of Light. Every person that has been truly met and communicated with becomes part of the network, if we acknowledge that we are of the Light and working for and serving the Light, and that they too have a responsibility to be of the Light. It does not have to be wordy and flowery. A few words, a few sentences acknowledging the Light are all that is needed. And at times all that is required is a touch or a look or even just seeing someone clearly for an instant.

There is great responsibility and there is great joy in spreading the Light.

LIGHT BODY MEDITATION

This meditation is intended to bring enhanced coherence and an infusion of Light into the Liquid Crystal Body Matrix. It can be done with a single stone over the heart, although I recommend using the full-body layout if possible. For the heart chakra, I suggest three stones—Moldavite, Azeztulite and Rosophia. I also recommend placing or holding a Phenacite at the third eye. If one can lie down for the meditation, I encourage adding a Selenite at the crown (a wand pointing toward the top of the head). To enhance the link of the heart and brain, I suggest placing a Cryolite on the chest, between the heart and throat chakras. One can make a complete full-body meditation layout of this array by putting a Strontianite and/or Libyan Gold Tektite on the solar plexus, a Cinnabar Quartz on the second chakra, a Crimson Cuprite at the root chakra and two Aegirines at the feet. Black Tourmaline at the Earth Star eight to ten inches below the feet will aid in anchoring the vibrations. Placing a Danburite and/or Petalite stone at the Soul Star eight to ten inches above the crown chakra completes the circuit. (NOTE: The above is the suggested full array for Light Body infusion, but this meditation can work with a single stone placed at the heart, or even with no stones. However, it is clear to me that the stones do offer a strong enhancement of our energetic template.)

When you have placed the stones you are using, gradually imagine each of them moving inside the body to their corresponding chakras. Pay special attention at the beginning to visualizing the heart chakra stone moving into the heart space. The space can be imagined as an egg-shaped area in the center of the chest, about the size of one's physical heart. See the image of the stone in the center of the heart. Then allow yourself to see volumes of Light pouring out of the stone, at first contained within the heart's egg. When you feel as though the heart space is filled to capacity, dissolve the boundary and allow the Light to pour through the body until it is filled with Light. Now notice or visualize a column of light running through your core, from below the feet to above the head, circulating through you. When this is fully experienced, one can be filled with intense pleasure and bliss. This is the natural state of the awakened Light Body.

If you can continue, the next part is very important: From your Light-saturated body, allow the boundary to dissolve until you can imagine the room or space in which you are meditating filled with the same Light. Then expand beyond that boundary, pouring forth the Light until the Earth is filled and surrounded by a corona of pure Light. Ultimately, this Light can link and merge with the Light emanating from the Great Central Sun, and the cosmic circuit will then be complete. Because this Light emanates from a central point in the heart, it is the same as love.

Filling the heart, the body and the world with love is the essence of healing, the key to whatever is truly meant by "immortality" and the alchemical transmutation of ego-lead into spirit-gold.

As an outer-world practice to accompany the inner meditation, one is encouraged to remember that place of Light in the center of the heart, and to relate to all others from that place in clear, loving, judgment-free truth. Wearing the heart-stones—Rosophia, Moldavite and Azeztulite—can help one stay in resonance with the Light Body currents at all times.

From this meditation we move into the next chapter, which offers a wide array of meditations to be utilized for healing, awakening to higher awareness and crystalline coherence, and for kindling the Body of Light.

CHAPTER SIX

Crystal Meditations

"The term 'meditation' implies any means that help to dispel the illusion that God and the essence of each person, as well as the essence of the whole material world, are different."

—SATHYA SAI BABA

The highest purpose of our work with stones is, in my view, the same purpose we might describe as the destiny of humanity. It involves a purposeful, willed evolutionary impulse, a chosen venture into the unknown, a leap of faith that envisions no predetermined outcome. It is guided by the heart's yearnings, and by the wisdom at the heart's core. It entails giving oneself over to the activity of blessing, meeting the world with love, trusting that the world meets us always with love and wisdom. This does not mean we will encounter no pain or difficulty. Our trust is not in expectation of getting what we think we want, but in giving ourselves to life wholeheartedly. This frees us from fear, and from the enslavement to trying to calculate and control what will happen. It is only through full surrender to the unknown that anything truly new can come to us. It is only through release of what we have been that we can be reborn. Only by bringing our shadows in from exile can we open ourselves to Light. All of these gestures express the outpouring of our heart's love into the world; and as we have been told by Novalis, "Every beloved object is the center of a Paradise." Our destiny is to remake the world and our selves through the creating activity of love, in partnership with the spirit/soul of World Wisdom, the being we name as Sophia.

So what does that mean in terms of our work with the stones? I have described the spiritual beings embodied in the stones as faithful angelic messengers, carrying the currents of the Divine patterns into the material realm. We work with them inwardly in meditation to meet and give ourselves into relationships with the stone beings and the patterns they offer. We can imagine this meeting as the overlap of two circles, forming a *vesica pisces*. On one side there is oneself, a human being in one's present state of soul development. On the other side is the stone with its soul qualities. The place where we overlap is the resonance between our selves and the stone. When we center ourselves in a state of clear attentiveness and make the inward gesture of offering, we open the door to relationship. The stones, as the angels they are, are always open to us, serving their purpose as messengers. Thus, when we turn toward the stone being with openness, attention and the generating gesture of blessing, the *vesica* of relationship is formed. The *vesica* is a sort of spiritual portal through which the Divine qualities, inherent in stone as potentials, are manifested in the world. We participate in the manifestation of these qualities by incorporating them (making them corporeal) in our own being, on all levels. These levels include thinking, feeling, healing (embodying), expressing (communicating and creating), and knowing (receiving direct understanding).

Ultimately all of these meditations serve the process of bringing greater coherence into the Liquid Crystal Body Matrix, moving toward the ultimate goal of full partnership with the Divine, incarnating it through our transfiguration into the Body of Light.

(NOTE: If you decide to work with these meditations, one way of keeping track of the process is to make a tape for yourself in your own words of the various steps, perhaps with gaps of silence between them to give time for things to unfold. After a few sessions, you will probably not need the tape any more.)

CLEARING & CENTERING THROUGH THE HEART ALIGNMENT

How do we center ourselves in a state of clear attentiveness? An excellent practice for this is a meditation I learned from Robert and Cheryl Sardello, which they developed out of the work of Rudolf Steiner. It is called the Heart Alignment, and it is something I do every day. It draws together the various currents or "bodies" of the human being and brings one into a state of harmonious, focused attention. It seems also to have other important effects, such as strengthening the chakras and helping us develop the capacity of attention itself.

I describe below the process of the Heart Alignment, which includes the felt, inward expression of several phrases. Steiner saw intuitively what the phrases for each point of focus ought to be, and, although I will not attempt to explain his reasons for choosing them, I recommend them, because they resonate inwardly in ways that work amazingly well.

Heart Alignment Initial Practice

1. Sit comfortably with eyes closed. (The practice can also be done while standing or lying down.) Take one or two deep, relaxing breaths, with a long exhale. Focus attention in the center of the forehead and inwardly, in that location, slowly pronounce the phrase, "I am." You can do this once, or more times if you feel that it increases the strength of your relaxed, full inner focus.
2. Allow attention to drop to the throat area, as if the attention in the forehead were flowing downward like a thick liquid. When the attention reaches the throat, spreading down from the forehead without leaving it, slowly pronounce inwardly the phrase, "I think."
3. Continue to allow the attention to flow downward, without leaving the higher centers, until it fills the heart level, in the center of the chest. Inwardly and slowly pronounce the phrase, "She feels."
4. Holding attention in the entire column from forehead to heart, allow attention to flow downward to the solar plexus. When it has entered there, inwardly and slowly say the phrase, "He wills."
5. Repeat or simply dwell with the process for two or three minutes. You will feel cleared and centered, and often quite refreshed. Until I began to practice the Heart Alignment regularly, I didn't realize how much I tended to be scattered and unfocused, and how much of my vitality leaked away because of that.

I like to repeat the process several times, or multiple times. Sometimes I inwardly speed up the steps, or I go through them with the feeling qualities of each phrase, rather than inwardly saying them as words. After some weeks of practice, I could also bring the feeling of alignment into all four chakras simultaneously. This process can eventually be done effectively in a few seconds, or it can go on for as long as one likes. It is a good way to calm the body for sleep as well as being an excellent preparation for working with crystals, or for any meditative work.

The Full Heart Alignment

There are, of course, three more chakras that are coordinated with three other body areas. The Sardellos explained that they found it preferable to teach students to become proficient with the four-chakra alignment before going to all seven. This is because the two lowest chakras are so powerfully linked to our physical body that they can overwhelm the others until they have been strengthened through practice. In a different way, the crown can be so open to the transpersonal currents from the higher realms that they can also override the delicate circuitry one is developing.

However, after one has practiced the first level of Heart Alignment for enough weeks or months to become strong in it, one can bring in the other three chakras. In this Full Heart Alignment, one begins at the crown with the phrase, "I am that I am," which evokes the transpersonal. Then one works as before, drawing the currents downward through the four centers one has already worked with. At the second chakra area, just below the navel, the phrase we pronounce is, "We share." Then at the base of the spine, when we have allowed the entire column to be filled, we focus attention there and inwardly say, "I belong." This affirms our appropriate link with the Earth and the realm of matter.

As with the initial practice, one should, over time, be able to go through the steps of the Full Heart Alignment within a few minutes, or even a matter of seconds. The effect of incorporating this practice into the pattern of one's way of being teaches our many levels how to line up with one another, and that they are *supposed* to be in such harmonious accord. It helps us learn how to enter a state of calm, centered attentiveness whenever we wish, and the reenactment of the practice as a personal sort of ritual (without any religious overtones) evokes the desired state with ever-increasing immediacy and effectiveness.

MEETING & GREETING THE STONE BEINGS: AN INITIAL MEDITATION

Before I sit to meditate with any stone, I do a quick Heart Alignment. This brings me into focus and reminds all my parts that I am inviting their participation. The "She feels" portion of the practice always nudges my mental awareness, reminding it to drop down into the heart and work from there.

The word *generosity* has the same root as *generate*. Starting a relationship with a stone, a person or an angel is a little bit like starting a car. You have to give some energy to get things going. When we turn the car key, the battery sends out current to spark the engine, which then runs on its own. Until we do that, it doesn't matter how much potential energy is stored in the gasoline. In our lives the heart is our source, the energy *generator* from which we can act with enough *generosity* to spark the fire of relationship. This works with all sorts of relationships, and in the case of stones, our action frees the potential energy of the stone's currents into expression in the world. This is good for the stone being and good for us, because this way we both get somewhere we couldn't have gone alone.

The way we "turn the key" is to direct attention to the heart and begin our encounter with the stone with the activity of blessing. Here is how I begin working with a stone, and how I opened each of the meditative experiences written about in the stone sections of this book.

1. From my heart, I offer a gesture of appreciation, love and gratitude. I say inwardly or with words that I greet the being of the stone, and I invite it into a love-centered relationship with me.

2. If I am working with a stone for the first time, or intending to write about its properties, I inwardly ask it to tell me its story, show me its nature, and help me to understand how we can beneficially work together. (You can ask all sorts of other questions. It is important to remain mindful to make requests respectfully, offering oneself as a receptive participant in whatever may come next. This is always good spiritual etiquette.) After my request or question and offer, I blow a breath across the stone with an inward gesture of blessing.

3. I sit looking at the stone for a few moments, taking in all I can about its physical feel and appearance. Then I close my eyes and attend to what happens in my body and consciousness while holding the stone. I may move the stone to different chakra points, almost always beginning with the heart. I am sensitive also in my third-eye area, and in my hands. Holding a pair of stones, one in each hand, can be very good. This is one of the immediate ways of allowing the currents of a stone to permeate your Liquid Crystal Body Matrix. Wherever the stone is placed, the shift in my interior state is what occurs within the *vesica* of relationship with the stone.

4. Exploration of this experience, or any number of subsequent ones, can go on for some time. One may travel interdimensionally to the realm of the stone, or to other spaces where the stone can take you. One may travel within one's own body to various points of focus, as the currents interact with one's physical being and energy fields. Sometimes the currents focus on clearing blocks or congested areas. Sometimes one sees interior "movies" that carry

symbolic messages. Sometime the tactile sensations of the currents are the substance of the interaction. In rare instances one's outer environment, or one's perception of it, can be affected. I have, upon several occasions of meditation with Azeztulite, opened my eyes to discover my meditation room filled with golden light.

5. One will usually know intuitively when the experience has completed itself. I try to remember to go to my heart before opening my eyes, and I there offer a gesture of gratitude to the stone being. These gestures of spiritual etiquette, whether the stone beings benefit from them or not, are helpful to oneself because they reinforce one's practice of the activity of blessing, which is the essence of the New Consciousness.

One can create endless variations of this practice of meeting and exploration—as endless as the variety of interactions one can have with another person, or maybe more. As with the Heart Alignment practice, repetition of this ritual of meeting the stone beings makes it more powerful. One's capacities of attention to the subtle activities of physical and non-physical body aspects will improve, and one will begin to notice consistent subtle characteristics of different stones as they interact with one's fields. Even individual stones of a single type vary widely in terms of our experience of them. It may be that some "like" us better than others, or that, like people, different ones have different things to say.

I recommend keeping a journal or even some tape recordings of one's interactions with the stones. Like a dream journal, a stone meditation journal will often reveal deeper meanings later than one sees initially. When working with self-healing or exploratory practices, one's recorded experiences may also turn out to be helpful to others in ways we can't anticipate.

MERGING THE CRYSTAL CURRENTS WITH THE BODY

This suggestion is in itself a meditation, and it is something I suggest integrating into other meditations. It involves actively inviting the currents of a stone or stones to enter and influence one's Liquid Crystal Body Matrix.

We all know how it feels when we are holding someone outside our "shell." We may be in their presence, but we do whatever we can to keep their energies, and whatever they are expressing, from getting under our skin, so to speak. There are also situations in which we are neutral to others, not really holding them out but doing nothing out of our way to open ourselves. Then there is active, glad welcoming. We open our hearts and our energy fields, welcoming the other and feeling him or her with our full attention. In order to truly meet the stone beings, it is best to find and perform our most profound gesture of opening and welcoming. This involves attending to the places in our body or chakras where we tend to first feel the stones, while also remaining centered in the heart.

1. Do a Heart Alignment and then hold the stone, greeting it with the inner gesture of blessing and appreciation.
2. Feel where the currents of the stone naturally resonate within you. Place your attention there while remaining heart-centered. Observe the activity of the currents and notice whether your attention increases their intensity.
3. When you have a clear feeling of the intensified currents, inwardly will yourself to open up throughout your body to the stone and its currents. Imagine the resonating areas within you as cups that suddenly overflow, with the abundant waters" washing through you totally. You should be able to feel this tangibly, at least after a little practice. At the same time you visualize the overflowing cups, pour out a joyful, grateful welcome from your heart, as if it is another overflowing cup, its waters blending with those of the stone's currents.

These and similar images are tools for using imagination to cross the threshold into felt experience. You may immediately be able to feel the wave of resonant attunement flowing through you as the Liquid Crystal Body Matrix takes on and integrates the emanations of the stone. Whether this felt sense comes soon or later, it happens very genuinely. One's liquid crystal nature is always working out its harmonies with the influences in the surrounding environment. However, you can learn to tune yourself at will, and the stones, with their strong, pure currents, are most helpful in regard to learning the feeling of doing this, as well as discovering the inner gestures that can be used to engage the currents of the stones, other people and the world at large. As we do this while remaining heart-centered, we develop new capacities and deeper levels of awareness, while always serving our central purpose—our loving, creating partnership with the Soul of the World.

ENTERING THE WORLD OF THE STONE

Robert Sardello discovered and developed this practice, and I encourage people to use it as a way of seeing more deeply into the nature of the stone beings. Sardello has said that it is important to discover what *they* want, because our relationship with the stones is for the sake of the world rather than our own, and the stone beings are intimately linked with the World Soul. I do agree that service to Sophia is what my heart most deeply desires to perform, and that to glimpse Her is to be moved toward a path of loving service. In any case, this practice is powerful and deep and is something not to be missed. Although it is not part of Robert's specific practice, I suggest beginning every stone meditation with the inner generating gesture of greeting the stone with loving appreciation.

1. After doing the Heart Alignment, spend some time, perhaps four or five minutes, taking in every possible sensory impression of the stone you have chosen to work with. Gaze at it in detail, on all of its sides. Smell it. Touch it with your tongue (if it isn't toxic); bring it to your ear and listen to its silent voice.

2. Gaze at it again for about a minute with your eyes simultaneously focused and diffused. I find that it can be helpful to partially close my eyes so that the focus shifts in that way. Hold the stone completely still as you look.

3. Close your eyes and watch your awareness for any sign of an after-image of the stone, or an after-effect of any type—emotional, auditory, anything. Often an after-image will look nothing like the stone. It could be a blur of light, or even a dreamlike image that is totally vivid. In feeling, it could be a longing or an exuberant rush, an inner laugh or weeping . . . anything.

4. As soon as you notice an after-effect, pour all of your attention into it. Keep doing this with as much intensity as you can muster.

5. Often, if one is patient, observant and fortunate, another image or inner experience will appear. This is the entry into the world of the stone being. It can unfold as an interior movie or in any other way. Often one will meet or see the stone being as it is in its own world.

6. Robert Sardello reports that it is possible, within the world of the crystal being, to engage in all sorts of interactions and explorations. One may communicate directly if one is able to maintain focus and a relaxed openness to whatever is present.

I once did this meditation with a Celestite crystal, and the after-image I saw was of a piece of Celestite lying in the sand at the water's edge on a beach beside a pond as little waves washed over it. In the next phase, I met the Celestite as a female being with a little silver crown and a body of long, narrow Celestite crystal. She "lived" in a cave with walls made of thousands of other Celestites. I was frankly astonished to see these visions and to get a feel for the personality of this Celestite, which was sweet, light-hearted and very merry.

Other instances of this meditation have taken me into realms of light where the beings were much more geometric and less human-looking. The after-images tend to appear for me as undulating light patterns, and the entry into the world of the stone being can span a range between the vividly visual to completely auditory, from emotional to intensely vibrational. Much of what is sensed is hard to describe because it falls within the realm of newly developing capacities, and it is perplexing to even grasp what goes on, let alone put it into words. Yet this is one of the intriguing avenues along which the New Consciousness is beginning to develop.

THE STONE ENTERS THE HEART

This meditation is simple, yet it can be very powerful. It involves entering a state of Heart Awareness and then bringing the stone into the heart. Within the realm of Heart Awareness, one can feel the stone's qualities in a way that does not require much mental processing. This can be one of the best ways to truly meet the qualities of a stone and to allow them to weave into the currents of one's body activity. (Again, I credit Robert Sardello for the original form of this meditation.)

1. Do a Heart Alignment and then hold the stone, greeting it with the inner gesture of blessing and appreciation.

2. As you hold the stone in your lap, bring attention to the center of your chest, several inches inside, at the level of your heart. Imagine an egg-shaped area about four or five inches tall. That is the space of your spiritual heart.

3. Imagine that there are fine, gentle, caressing currents surrounding the egg of your heart space, softly pressing inward on the outer boundary. Feel the currents as they soothe and stroke your heart space. Take about one minute to do this.

4. Now imagine that the soft currents are inside the egg-shaped heart space, gently pressing outward. Give this another minute.

5. Now alternate the sensing of the currents, first outside the heart space, then inside, outside and then inside. After a minute or two, you will have developed a tangible felt sense of the heart space.

6. Now bring the stone up to your chest, holding it to your heart, while still staying with the felt heart space. Then imagine the stone—its vivid image—moving into your chest and entering the egg-shaped space of your heart. While the stone is in your heart space, feel its currents within the heart. Notice what they are like. Feel how its currents entwine with the currents you felt at the boundaries of the heart space.

7. When you have reached the most tangible sense of this that you can, go back to the boundary of your heart space. Feel the currents both outside and inside, while the stone is in the very center.

8. Now dissolve the boundary and allow the currents of the stone and your heart to flow together throughout your body. This can bring forth a very powerful set of sensations, especially with practice. In this part of the process the stone currents and your own heart currents are mingled, and they are felt throughout the Liquid Crystal Body Matrix.

This practice can be very helpful in developing an inner felt sense of both the spiritual heart and the Liquid Crystal Body Matrix. In learning to sense the spiritual heart, one develops a gradually strengthening capacity to live there, to act with that as one's center of choice and activity. This is an essential aspect of the New Consciousness. At the beginning one tends to try to do all of this mentally, which produces mostly a conceptual replica, a sort of counterfeit of the real thing. But with practice, and often a helpful dose of failure, one learns the difference. Learning this is often helped along by noticing the sense of the heart's satisfaction, or lack thereof.

Equally important is the process of developing the sense of what the Liquid Crystal Body Matrix feels like. I believe that one can do this most effectively by using a number of different stones, one at a time, in this type of meditative practice. As the inner body-sense is felt shifting in response to the currents of various stones, one's awareness of the body-sense (on all levels) increases. It is like a child's way of learning to use her arms and legs. She gets the hang of it through trial and error (and success).

It is also important to "exercise" the liquid crystal body, and its self-awareness, through such practices. As Mae Wan Ho has said of the liquid crystal body, it is highly tunable and flexible. This flexibility increases with use, and one learns to work in cooperative cahoots with the body/mind, or what Satprem and the Mother called the Mind of the Cells. Their work centered on teaching the cellular mind to give up the habit pattern of disintegration and death, replacing it with attunement to the undying pattern of the Divine Light, the Holy Fire of life. Perhaps as we work more and more with the Liquid Crystal Body Matrix, or the cellular mind, inviting this long unconscious and neglected dimension of ourselves into loving relationship with our conscious self-sense and with the angelic crystal beings, we will find that it is awakening. We will meet the "other" within us and join in a partnership that is akin to our partnership with Sophia. Certainly we can encourage the body consciousness to be more awake, to feel loved by us and safe with us. And as we allow it to meet the crystal beings, the cells may realize their strength, and they may form a new mind which in its discovery of itself will reveal to us a world we have never truly known before.

GRAIL MEDITATION

This practice utilizes imagery from the Grail legend, placing it in the body, in resonant conjunction with a stone that is somehow attuned with the pattern of the Grail. I recommend Moldavite as the stone most resonant with the Grail legend. In the *Parsifal* tales of Wolfram von Eschenbach, the Grail was said to be a stone, an Emerald that fell from the heavens, out of the crown of Lucifer. Moldavite is the only gemstone ever to have fallen from the sky, and it happens to be Emerald-colored. It also exhibits qualities akin to those of the legendary Grail stone.

1. Do a Heart Alignment and then hold the stone, greeting it with the inner gesture of blessing and appreciation.

2. As in the previous exercise, while holding the stone in your lap, bring attention to the center of your chest, several inches inside, at the level of your heart. Imagine a golden goblet or a crystal one, in whatever shape and color your heart creates for you, filling the space of your spiritual heart. Observe the light that radiates from the interior of this chalice. Imagine that your point of attention is within the cup itself.

3. Now bring the stone up to your chest, holding it to your heart, while still staying with the image of the goblet. Then imagine the stone—its vivid image—moving into your chest and entering the chalice of your heart. See the cup holding the stone. Notice the increased radiance now that the stone has entered the heart/cup. Notice how that radiance feels within your chest.

4. When you have reached the most tangible sense of this that you can, watch as a liquid rises from within the chalice, filling it and then overflowing, pouring out in an increasing flow. Feel the liquid from the Holy Grail spreading through your body in a warm rush. Notice the pleasure and joy the body feels while this liquid life is spreading throughout your torso, arms, legs and head. Feel it rise up to your crown.

5. Now allow the Grail to vibrate within your heart space with increasing intensity. See a larger image of the same chalice form within your body, this time with the base at your heart and the cup encompassing your skull.

6. See the image of the stone within both cups, vibrating and emitting even greater radiance. Notice that the larger Grail now fills with a golden liquid that pours over the rim and flows downward through your body, down through the neck, the spine, the chest, abdomen and limbs. Feel all of this as tangibly as you can within the body. Give whatever sensations you are feeling a few minutes to fully permeate your body and energy fields.

7. Let the image of the larger Grail dissolve into the smaller image in the heart space. Allow this Grail to dissolve and merge with your physical heart. Allow the image of the stone to remain for another moment in your heart space, and then bring it back to rest within the stone in your hand.

8. Offer thanks, and make notes of the experience.

I like the use of vivid images in this meditation, especially since they are charged with deep spiritual resonances. This is more than fantasy. You are inviting the Grail, all that it has symbolized and the felt experiences it has generated in people over many centuries, into the temple of your heart. If you are working with Moldavite, you are also inviting the resonances of the countless people who have used Moldavite as a spiritual talisman for more than twenty-five thousand years. The image of the life-giving Grail cup is something your body consciousness can feel without having to have it as a mental concept, and without words. There is the additional and highly important aspect of the currents of the stone itself. Moldavite in particular has been felt by thousands of people as bringing warmth into the body, and the upwelling of a mysterious overflowing feeling of blessedness within the heart. I have seen this occur dozens of time, in the matter of a minute or two when someone first holds a Moldavite stone. It's easy for me to imagine that we are actually working with the very real pattern and presence of the Holy Grail.

FORGIVING MEDITATION

This is one of the most emotionally moving meditations I have experienced. I devised this practice for one of my workshops, and it worked so powerfully that I have incorporated it into most of my presentations since then. It is a fairly simple one, and I usually use two stones, Celestite and Ajoite, to facilitate it. You can use either stone separately, or combine one with a heart stone such as Morganite or Rosophia. I once combined this meditation with walking a labyrinth, and this engendered a most amazing and worthwhile experience in me, which I will recount at the end of this section.

1. Do a Heart Alignment and then hold the stones, greeting them with the inner gesture of blessing and appreciation. Ask them to help with your purpose of healing through forgiving. Blow a breath of prayer and thanks across them and bring your hands back to your lap.

2. Hold or place the stone or stones over your heart chakra. Inwardly invite the stone beings to meet you in the space between the center of your heart and the front of your chest. This is the *vesica* portal where your energy field overlaps the field of the stone. It is also in this practice the Doorway to your heart.

3. Feel the currents of the stones blending with those of your heart. Feel the resonance of the supportive energies of the stones.

4. From your heart center, call out into the realms of soul and spirit to any person or being who would like to approach you and enter your heart for forgiveness. Let your imagination see the person, persons or beings before you. Sometimes there is only one being. In other cases, there is a long line waiting. Most often you will recognize the souls who come. Sometimes, however, you may not. You are encouraged to trust the process and welcome all the beings who come for forgiveness. Some people even see an image of themselves in the waiting line.

5. Keep the stones near your heart (or in your hands on your lap if that works better for you) and feel their support. Then invite the beings to come forward and enter the Doorway of your heart, through the *vesica* in front of your heart center. Allow them in, holding an image of each one in the center of your heart, within a field of love and forgiving. Allow them to move through you and out via the back side of your heart chakra, if they are ready. If not, hold them in your heart as long as feels necessary, even after the process is finished. You are encouraged to continue this process as long as beings continue to come forward. Remember, this heals oneself as much or more than it heals the one we are holding in forgiveness.

6. When all those who come forward have entered your heart and the process feels complete, open your eyes and blow a breath of thanks across the stones, while also thanking those who came to you.

The gesture of forgiving is an essential aspect of the New Consciousness. It is a natural activity of the heart, and practicing forgiveness strengthens the heart as the center of our consciousness. Forgiving is a gesture of trust as well as generosity, both of which are implicit within the Activity of Blessing. It is also helpful to consider forgiving as forward-giving, offering oneself into the coming moment without knowing or trying to know what its nature will be. This is akin to what we usually call forgiving, although it is an expansion of the idea as well. It attunes one to harmonizing with the world coming-to-be, and to live in a state of ongoing trust.

A variation of this type of forgiving meditative activity—which produced very powerful results in me—involved a walking meditation in a labyrinth. I was a member of a group involved in spiritual practice, and we were working with bringing light into our own shadow areas through the activity of forgiving. We were instructed to enter the labyrinth, which we had gridded with Celestite crystals, while holding a Celestite crystal in our hands. As we walked, we were to hold in our heart one of our own worst shadow qualities (e.g. jealousy, dishonesty, anger, fear or other "unacceptable" trait or past action) while holding the stone near our heart for support. Inwardly we were to envision this quality in our heart while repeating, "I am so grateful for the presence of _____ in my life."

I doubt that any of us had ever expressed inner gratitude for these shadow qualities. We were more likely to be ashamed of them, and to keep them in a state of psychological exile. I remember that holding my trait in my heart, in the state of gratitude, produced powerful rumblings of dissonance in my consciousness. It was hard to do, and the feeling was rather upsetting. Yet I held to my resolve to continue as instructed throughout the labyrinth walk.

Afterwards I experienced a strange elation, a weird sort of joy. It continued for several hours, and I realized that through this process I had made myself more whole by welcoming an exiled part of myself back into my heart. Whenever we exile something, it fragments our wholeness. Even though it may be a deplorable incident or a negative pattern we have repeated, the exile keeps the wound from healing. Only forgiving can change and heal our psyche. To bring an exiled part into the heart, into the generous gesture of gratitude, is to let one's so-called "bad" side back into its home, where it can heal. I learned from this practice that the "justice" of the whole thing is not what matters. Only the healing through forgiving can change the future. It is sometimes easier to see this in regard to others than to oneself, but it is essential to make this gesture everywhere.

Walking the labyrinth helped the process, because we had used the Celestite grid and our intention to create a field of forgiving. Moving through the labyrinth pattern while concentrating on our process helped bring it into the body, where it tends toward deeper integration. However, I have led groups through a process much like this, without a labyrinth, and it is still very powerful. In addition to Celestite, I recommend materials such as Morganite, Ajoite, Rosophia and whatever other stones from one's collection "volunteer" to help.

JOURNEY TO THE GREAT CENTRAL SUN

Earlier in this book, I recounted the tale of my awakening to the currents and spiritual qualities of stones through a spontaneous meditative journey to the Great Central Sun. Although this event occurred more than twenty years ago, it is still vivid in my memory and is one of the key spiritual moments of my life. This meditation is designed to engender an inner experience of a similar journey. One cannot simply "place an order" for a spiritual experience and expect it to arrive. If something does come to us, it is often (if not always) different from what we planned or intended. However, just about everything that occurs in the inner realms, when we set a strong positive intention, is helpful to us. So in that spirit, I offer this.

1. Choose the stone or stones that most strongly appeal to you for this journey. I recommend any form of Azeztulite, especially Golden Azeztulite Crystals, Himalaya Gold Azeztulite or the original white Azeztulite from Vermont and North Carolina. Moldavite was the talisman of my own journey to the Central Sun, so I must also recommend taking it along. Additional possible allies might include Nirvana Quartz, Natrolite, Herderite, Phenacite or Brookite, all of which are aids to interdimensional travel. Agni Gold Danburite is specifically attuned to the currents of the Great Central Sun, and its cousin, white or transparent Danburite, is a wonderful stone of uplifting. Primarily, I still believe your own intuition should lead you.

2. Do a Heart Alignment and then hold the stone or stones, greeting it or them with the inner gesture of blessing and appreciation. Ask for their aid in your intended journey to the Central Sun. Blow a blessing, a prayerful breath across the stones, close your eyes and begin. (NOTE: I sometimes use background music for inward travel meditations. If this is appealing, I suggest a solo flute or other instrument, and a recording that flows like a musical journey.)

3. Create in inner image of yourself, siting just as you are in your meditation space. See yourself rise out of your body. Your spirit image may or may not look just like your everyday self. Notice any differences that you can see from your point of view within the second image-self, and allow your second image-self to float upward, looking down at your meditating form.

4. Allow your point of view to float further upward. Look down upon your home, your neighborhood, your area. Notice that you are flying more and more rapidly. See the shape of the countryside, the continent, the Earth, receding behind you.

5. Now you are flying through space, still away from the Earth, which continues to shrink behind you. Eventually it is lost among the fields of stars. Remind yourself of your intention to travel to the Great Central Sun and then let go, allowing your point of view to be drawn toward your goal rather than steering yourself through the will.

6. Hold to your intention while releasing control of the journey. Do this moment by moment. Be aware of any direction in which your journey draws you, but wait and allow it to unfold on its own.

7. When you feel yourself becoming aware of a certain star, check to notice whether your heart is attracted to it. If so, allow your will to send you more quickly and directly toward it. If you are able to approach this star, notice its color, feel its radiance and take in its beauty. If these sensibilities are engaged and you feel a longing to venture nearer the star, let yourself do so, falling into orbit around it.

8. At this point, allow your heart to guide you. You may simply experience a wordless rapture at the beauty before you, or there may be some more personal, intimate communion. If your heart generates a question or gesture, put your intention behind it. Notice any unexpected perceptions, images or thoughts.

9. When you feel the experience is fulfilled, allow yourself to imagine your return journey. Offer gratitude for the gifts of the journey and retrace your flight back to Earth, the room and your body. (In my own original experience of this journey, the interior movie reached a crescendo when I noticed a replica of the Great Sun within my own heart, followed immediately by the sizzle of the Moldavite in my hand and the full-blown opening of all my chakras. I like the idea of bringing journey meditations to a graceful return as a way of concluding them, but in my first such experience, more powerful events took over.) One never knows what surprises such journeys will evoke, and these gifts should definitely be taken in, rather than adhering to any predetermined scenario. Most of the steps in this meditation are there to help one get into the flow where the journey generates itself. When that happens, you can abandon the plans.

10. Write in a journal all the details you can recall, especially anything unexpected. It is generally a good practice to keep a meditation journal, but this is especially true when one is journeying. The richness of images takes time to assimilate, and you may learn more in reading your narrative later than you were able to grasp in the moment.

TRAVELING INTERDIMENSIONALLY

This sort of meditative practice is different from an imaginal journey such as the trip to the Great Central Sun or a Shamanic journey. Both of those practices are incubated through initiating some intentional images. In what I am calling interdimensional travel, one selects a stone ally with the quality of stimulating the third eye's capacity for visionary experience and holds the intention to simply travel through the spiritual worlds. The practice involves following the lights, patterns or images that arise. Often one finds one's point of view moving through "corridors of light" which open in a sort of succession of geometric forms. Sometimes there are openings or portals that look into other planes of consciousness. This is one of the most uncharted areas of inner research with the stones, so I can only offer some sketchy instructions.

1. Select a stone to aid you in opening the third eye and traveling interdimensionally. I suggest Phenacite as my first choice, and secondly a Herkimer Quartz "Diamond." Of course, one may work successfully with any stone that strongly stimulates one's third eye chakra.

2. Do a Heart Alignment and then hold the stone or stones, greeting it or them with the inner gesture of blessing and appreciation. Ask for their aid in your intended interdimensional journey, and request that you be guided to the destinations that serve the highest good. Then release expectations. Blow a blessing, a prayerful breath across the stone, close your eyes and place or hold the stone at the third eye chakra. (If simply holding the stone is equally stimulating to your third-eye area, you need not hold it at the third eye.)

3. Watch the inner lights or images that appear before your closed eyes. If you see a light pattern, try "jumping in" by pouring your attention into it. Allow the pulsations or currents of the stone's energies to bring the third eye into a higher state of activity. You can also follow the pulsations with your attention until they begin to generate light patterns. Send your point of awareness into the pattern or patterns. Notice when you begin to journey, as the patterns become corridors of light. Allow your attention to continue through these corridors. They may divide, shift or undulate up and down. You may see potential "stopping places" where there are window-like portals that allow you to view or enter a number of different realms.

4. Continue this journey as long as you like. Holding a relaxed attention while using one's "soft will" to move about is the best way I have found for these explorations. To the best of my knowledge, one need not be concerned with finding one's way back. The intention to return is enough. Also, one can return rather more abruptly by simply opening one's eyes. (Ah, the benefits of having a body!)

5. Note interesting experiences, messages or insights. Write down your most detailed possible description of the topographies of the inner landscapes, the way it felt to travel and the sorts of beings one observes or encounters. This area is very exciting to me, and I hope that others engage in helping to see if it is possible in any way to map this inner landscape.

SHAMANIC JOURNEYING

Shamanic journeying has been practiced for thousands of years, in cultures all over the world. A shamanic journey is an intentional inward venture into a parallel dimension, a dimension of the soul realm. The beings and situations encountered there are often represented as animals or spirit guides and protectors. Their appearances, as well as the other images one sees in these journeys, are symbolic of the conditions and dynamics of one's soul being and its relationships within that realm. It is possible within the framework of a shamanic journey to glean information about the condition of other souls as well. Individuals with the capacity to act as shamanic healers can take actions in the shamanic realm that have beneficial effects on the health and soul life of others. One can also enlist the aid of inner guides and animal allies in the shamanic realms for one's own physical and soul healing.

A particularly helpful type of shamanic healing involves an activity called soul retrieval. Practitioners of this modality assert that most or all of us have experienced a fragmentation of our soul, our natural wholeness, which involves fixations—often around traumas—that have caused pieces of one's soul to split off and be left behind, attached to the pattern of the fragmenting cause or event. Much of this fragmentation happens in childhood, and when one works to retrieve the lost soul fragments, one may find that certain unconscious habits or patterns, over which we seemed to have no control, resolve themselves. One often has to work very consciously to welcome and integrate the returning fragments into one's psyche and present life situation. I remember that in my own period of working with soul retrieval, I spent a few weeks imaginally bringing the child versions of myself everywhere I went, showing them the life they had helped to create and inviting them out of the dark where they had been lost and into the light of my present life.

Not all shamanic work involves soul retrieval, and one may be best advised to consult an experienced shamanic soul retrieval practitioner for assistance in this sort of work. At the same time, many shamanic journeys involve going inward with a purpose in mind—to ask for help in healing physically, psychologically or spiritually—and one often receives some sort of gift. The gift can come in the form of a spirit animal ally, a talisman from a guide or even as directions to carry or wear a certain stone for a number of days or weeks. In all cases, one is advised to take to heart the messages received and to work consciously to integrate them into one's life.

From my experience, a shamanic journey typically involves inducing an altered state of consciousness by means of sound, usually drumming. On can recline with eyes closed, on the floor or a massage table, preferably in a darkened room, while listening to a friend's drumming or a recording of shamanic drumming. One uses intentional imaginative visualization to initiate the journey, usually involving crossing an inner symbolic bridge (such as a tunnel for the Underworld or a tree for the Upper World) between the everyday world and the shamanic realm. One then continues, following the "interior movie" that proceeds to unfold. When the process feels complete, one returns to this world by coming back across the inner bridge symbol. This sort of process is mirrored somewhat in the Journey to the Great Central Sun meditation.

In the language of shamanic practitioners, the crystals and minerals are known as the "stone people." Shamanic workers are perhaps the humans most readily prepared to view and understand the stones as *beings* rather than objects. This also means that a shamanic approach holds great potential for developing real relationships with the beings we meet as the stones.

There are others with much more experience than I have in working with stones and crystals shamanically. I recommend in particular that interested readers find books and trained practitioners to assist with soul retrieval work, if a draw is felt to that. The meditation below suggests a way of going into the shamanic Underworld or the Upper World to meet and form a relationship with a Stone Guide. After this initial meeting, I recommend working with the stone or stones that come to you on a repeated basis. If the shamanic approach is fruitful for you, it is likely that ongoing repetition and expansion of these types of practices will make for clearer communications and more fulfilling results.

How shall we engage in shamanic work with stones? There are a number of possibilities. One can "take a stone along" on a shamanic journey simply by selecting the specimen one is most drawn to work with in the journey. Look at your collection and ask for volunteers. Then see which stone "chooses you." If you pay attention, you can feel this when it happens. For the best results, hold in mind the purpose of your journey, as you understand it (e.g. meeting an animal ally or spirit guide, healing a specific physical or emotional issue, looking for insight regarding a difficulty in one's life, etc.). As you prepare to enter the journey, let intuition guide you regarding whether to wear the stone in your pouch, hold it in your hand or place it on your body. If you are working with more than one stone, check this for each one. In this sort of journey, your chosen stone allies have been called upon before you begin.

It is also possible to utilize the inner journey to find an appropriate stone ally. Often this ally will come to you in the journey and identify itself. There are at least two ways to do this. First, one can undertake the journey with no stone in mind or on one's person, and wait to see what sort of stone being approaches during the journey. Then, if a stone being comes to you, wear or carry that type of stone with conscious intention to work in partnership with it for the intuitively felt appropriate number of days or weeks.

A second approach involves placing an array of possible stone candidates around one's body. I like to make a sort of ring of various stones around my head, placed on the floor or massage table. One then goes into the journey state with the request that the most appropriate of these stone beings come to help in this journey. A journey of this sort can incorporate a more complex intention than simply meeting the guide. One can ask that the most appropriate stone helper or helpers come forward for whatever the intended purpose may be, and then follow the inner course that presents itself.

Here is a sequence of steps for a journey involving the array of stones, with the intention of meeting and working with the one that is willing to aid you in your purpose.

1. Look at your collection of stones. Allow yourself to relax your vision and bring your inner state into a condition of receptivity. Ask aloud or inwardly which stones will be the appropriate candidates to work with you. Then feel which stones draw your attention. Place these stones in a semicircular array around the place on the floor or table where your head will be when you go on your journey.

2. Do a Heart Alignment, and then gaze at the array of stones, greeting them with the inner gesture of blessing and appreciation. Ask for the aid of the appropriate stone being or beings in your intended shamanic journey, and request that you be guided to the experience that will fulfill its purpose. Then release expectations. Blow a blessing, prayerful breath across the stones.

3. Start the drumming recording or ask your friend to begin drumming. Lie down with your head in the center of the semicircular ring of stones and close your eyes. Allow the drumming to fill your consciousness for a few moments, relaxing your body and emotions.

4. You can choose whether to journey to the Underworld or the Upper World. Both are helpful places, although the beings one meets tend to appear as animals or medicine people in the Underworld and as more angelic forms in the Upper World. If you are going to the Underworld, begin by visualizing a place in nature, such as under a tree or in bushes or near a cave entrance. Go there inwardly and look for a tunnel or cave, or a downward-leading stairway. Enter it. If you are going to the Upper World, begin in a meadow or forest, and look for a tall tree or a cliff. Climb it, and when you reach the top, jump off. You will fly or be carried upward.

5. Look for a doorway or gate, some sort of threshold. Go through it and you will have entered the other realm.

6. As you explore this realm, notice what is around you. Look for the beings that approach. If one comes near you, ask if it is a true teacher or ally for you. If it says yes, greet it with gratitude and ask its name. If it is not a true ally, it must withdraw. If it says it is not your true teacher or ally but does not withdraw, ask it to withdraw.

7. If you have met an ally, ask it if there are any others coming to help you. If not, ask it for help with your intended purpose. If there are any other allies to come, you can ask whether to wait for them or go forward. Proceed with your ally or allies, exploring the countryside. Hold to your intention, while releasing any expectations about the form the experience should take.

8. There may come a moment when you can ask a question, if you are looking for guidance. When you feel this moment, ask the question of your ally, or perhaps a higher teacher if one presents itself. Stay with the unfolding experience until you feel it is beginning to resolve itself.

9. If you are with one or more stone beings, be sure to pay attention to everything about their appearance and gestures to you. Before you return to this world, you may want to ask whether you are to work with the stone or stones in your outer life. Ask how this should be done.

10. Find your way back to the dimensional bridge. Before crossing it, thank your ally or allies, and ask whether there is any service you can do for them. Make a gesture of respectful departure (a bow, an offering of the heart, or a blessing breath, etc.) and turn toward the dimensional bridge by which you entered. Return as you came, and see yourself back in the original safe place—on the threshold of the tunnel, beneath the great tree, etc.

11. Wiggle your toes to ground yourself in your body. Take a deep, cleansing breath and open your eyes when you are ready. Turn off the drumming if it is still playing. Write down or record as much as you can recall from your journey.

12. Integrate what you learned into your everyday activities and thoughts. Work with or wear any stones that were requested or advised by the beings. Develop a deeper relationship with the beings by making more journeys, or by sleeping with the stones with which you feel the most kinship.

While I feel it is important to be open to all possible alliances with any of the stone beings, I recommend a few in particular for the facilitation of the shamanic journey itself. For the Underworld journeys, both Nuummite and Master Shamanite are powerful allies and protectors. For the Upper World, there are many choices, perhaps because the stones represent angelic entities. It is especially true in this book, where our focus is on the awakening of the Light Body. My own favorites include Danburite, Phenacite, Cryolite, Nirvana Quartz, Herkimer Quartz "Diamonds" and all forms of Azeztulite.

ASCENSION OF THE HEART

There are many tales of spiritual ascension in the poetry, myths and religious stories of cultures worldwide. In Western culture, the best known (and the most laden with dogmatic baggage) is the resurrection and ascension of Jesus. Although I do not mean to espouse any religious belief system in this book, I want to use an artistic image of Jesus' ascension as a diagram for this meditation.

If we look for a moment at the fundamental "blueprint" or gesture of the Jesus story, it fits several of the patterns we are considering in regard to our own spiritual evolution. Jesus, considered mythically, is a personification of the spiritual Sun (the Great Central Sun) or the Solar Logos. He is a Man of Light and perhaps most notably a personification of the Heart. Countless artistic renderings of Jesus depict his heart as visible *outside his chest,* emanating radiant Light, displaying visually the unbounded love and compassion from which he is said to have lived and taught. One might say that his crucifixion is more or less what has happened to the heart itself in human history. Love, which moves through the world in a gesture of generosity and trust, has been subjugated to the tyranny of the mental, calculating consciousness that responds to its fear of the unknown future by trying to master and control the world. This pattern is everywhere—throughout our political and economic structures, within our education systems, and deep down in the habits of our personalities. The magnificence of the Jesus story (as history as well as myth, whichever is the actual case) is that it asserts the ultimate victory of the Heart, which neither avoids its enemies nor fights them, but which triumphs over death through its absolute love and trust. This pattern is offered to us as our way of transcendence.

To go a few more steps, let us remember that in the tale of Jesus, this Great Being of the Heart was crucified at a place called Golgotha, which means the Hill of the Skull. The symbolism could not be more clear. The Heart, which holds our own spark of the Divine, our Love, has been crucified on the Skull, the seat of our mental, calculating consciousness. As in our own body, the Heart is the true Sovereign, the King or Queen of the realm of our being. Our fear has taken us into a fragmented state in which the true Sovereign is not recognized, is denied and nailed to the Cross of matter. (Our physical hearts are placed at the center point, the "crossroads" of our physical body.) Yet the spiritual Heart, because it holds the Divine spark, cannot be contained, even by death. It can rise up, in our own psyches and bodies, and in so doing it illuminates the darkened mental consciousness. At that moment, if we open ourselves to it (because love offers but does not compel), the transformational "resurrected" Heart rises into its seat of Sovereignty at the center of our consciousness. Metaphorically, energetically and perhaps even physically through neuronal channels, our Heart awareness rises into our skull, which is illuminated with golden radiance, the Light of the spiritual Sun, transforming our interior darkness into the dome of heaven. Seeing fear dissolve into the joy of Love's victory, all the mental forces in us that sought to control the future, thereby putting the heart in bondage, recognize their true place as servants of the Heart's life-generating activity of blessing.

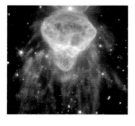

The small image to the left is a photograph of a part of a nebula formed from an exploding star, taken by the Hubble telescope. I was struck by the similarity of this image to the painting on the opposite page. Notice the apparitions of "angels" below the illumined "skull," and the brilliant "capstone" at the crown!)

All of this can be seen in the reproduction of a portion of the painting by Antonio Campi, *Mysteries of the Passion of Christ.* The whole painting depicts an array of scenes from the story of Christ's crucifixion and resurrection, with the portion relevant to this discussion occupying the top right corner area. We see in this image the pattern of the ascension in which Christ, the Being of the Heart, rises triumphant into the cranium-shaped vault of heaven. His entire body radiates Light, and in my view, it is the Light Body that we also seek to incarnate. The fact that this cranium is in the clouds yet is a portal into another realm signifies the Air element we link with mental energies, and the complete transformation of the mental self through the ascension of the Heart being. The golden-domed vault is held up by innumerable beings, symbolic of the willing service of all aspects of ourselves, when the Heart is seen as the true Sovereign. Below the Christ figure, the lower, earthly figures are being drawn up behind him, perhaps to be seen as the transfiguration of the lower, bodily self by the Heart's ascension. Around him are four rejoicing angels, perhaps meant to signify the four elements or the four directions. The great sphere in the center of the dome is the transfigured World, the World in its Body of Light. Its image contains a smaller sphere, the physical Earth, with Sun and Moon above it within the larger World sphere. The fact that the World Body has ascended as well as the Christ figure reveals that our own transfiguration and ascension are intimately linked to that of the Earth. We don't ascend to leave the world. We ascend together *with* the world. In fact, the painting suggests this, as it appears that the World sphere is being lifted into the heavenly dome by the ascending Christ. At the top of the dome is a golden capstone depicting the newly illumined crown chakra, the Gateway to the Great Central Sun, the Light of the Divine Source.

All this is a lot to think about, but I wanted to set the stage here for the important meditation I have named the Ascension of the Heart. I feel that this Ascension, which takes place simultaneously within our bodies, our consciousness and the world, is a key to the New Consciousness. It essentially *is* the New Consciousness, and it is inseparable from the Activity of Blessing, which is what the Ascension of the Heart does by its very nature.

So now, if you have come this far, I invite you to follow along a bit more. I encourage you to try on the idea and image that this Ascension of the Heart into the kingdom of heaven (the transfigured self, the New Consciousness) is available within each of us now. When we open our everyday selves to the astonishing reality that the Divine itself is present in our own heart—that the will of our heart, which acts always toward the good, is our spark of the Divine will—our consciousness can be awakened and our mental habits transformed and brought into the illumined state of joyfully serving the Heart. In the meditation that follows, we will work with the image from the Campi painting, which is a symbolic diagram of this transformation in the moment of its successful accomplishment. We will combine our image work with the helpful presence of four stones—Danburite, Azeztulite, Moldavite and Rosophia. (You can also work with stones like Agni Gold Danburite, Himalaya Gold Azeztulite, Golden Azeztulite Crystals or others that seem most resonant with the purpose of this practice.)

Here are the steps of the meditation as I envision it:

1. Spend a few minutes looking at the Campi painting meditatively. Give it your full attention, both visual and imaginal. Let yourself sense it in every way—visually, symbolically, emotionally and in every way you can. Stay with this until you can see the image of the painting with your eyes closed.

2. Do a Heart Alignment and then hold the four stones, greeting them with the inner gesture of blessing and appreciation. If you are working with the four stones I mentioned, I suggest putting the Moldavite and Rosophia over the heart, perhaps in a pouch or on a chain or string. You can hold the Azeztulite and Danburite, one in each hand, at least for the beginning. You may want to place the Azeztulite at the third eye chakra and the Danburite on the crown as you move deeper into the process.

3. As you are holding/wearing the stones, close your eyes and place your attention in the center of your spiritual heart center, about four inches in from the center of your chest. While you are doing this, picture in the heart center an egg-shaped form of golden light, radiant with brilliance and edged with gold/pink rays.

4. Feel the currents of the stones on your chest (Moldavite and Rosophia) as they resonate with your heart center. Imagine the stones in the form of light (however your imagination depicts that) moving inside your chest and entering your heart. Feel the radiance increase in your heart as they enter.

5. Feel the Azeztulite and Danburite currents awakening the third eye and crown chakra centers. If necessary, place the Azeztulite at the third eye and the Danburite on the crown. Notice that the currents in your heart and head are mutually attracted to one another. Stay with that feeling for a minute or two.

6. Now, using your imagination, overlay the image of the Campi painting on your own body. I suggest imagining that the golden skull/cloud shape be larger than your physical head, so that the base reaches to your heart. However, try to sense what feels right to you. As you imagine that overlay, allow it to move into your body so that its image touches the feelings of the stone currents in your head and heart.

7. Hold this combination of the image and the feeling of the stone currents, keeping focus on the entire heart-to-crown area. Now remember the symbolism and feeling of the painting. Remember the joyfully upraised arms of the resurrected Christ. Remember the lower beings that are drawn up along with him. Remember the rejoicing angels around him, and the resurrected Light Body of the World that he lifts above him. Recall that he is the Being of the Heart, of your own heart as much as any other.

8. Bring attention to your heart center, allowing it to move upward toward your head. Remember all that is shown in the painting, while feeling the helpful currents of the four stones (your own four rejoicing angels), holding the heart's powerfully vibrating radiant field as it moves upward. Remember the gesture of the Heart as you allow it to rise—the generative gesture that loves and blesses all. As you are feeling all this, say to yourself, "All of this is happening in me." Go over all the meaning and feeling of the pattern you have created with the image and the stone currents, and repeat, "This is happening within me now."

9. Let go, let it become real within you.

I suggest that you continue until your heart tells you it is ready to come back to calm, if that is possible or necessary. I can't really tell you how to end this meditation because, in a sense, it never ends. It is one of the ways of seeing and entering the New Consciousness. There are other ways, other diagrams or ritual enactments one can create. The fact that we use an image of Christ for this is not an endorsement of any religion. It is an attempt to see *through* the religious iconography to the essential spiritual gesture behind it, and to make that gesture our own. If you find it preferable to use another image, by all means do so. It is the opening to the Heart's ascension that we care about.

One of the crucial corollaries to this meditative work is that for it to really happen within us, we have to take it outside our houses and into our worldly lives. I suggest making a practice of remembering the meditative image and the feeling of the currents of the four stones, and the possibility that the Ascension of the Heart is our destined condition. I encourage those who are moved to embody this reality to work with the image/feeling from this meditation as you move through your life. When you are driving, working, taking a walk, etc., bring the image/feeling back to your heart/head corridor and say again, "This is happening within me now." Try to realize that it truly *is* happening. Let your gestures and actions within the world grow out of the New Consciousness of the Ascended Heart. Let your mind practice serving the wise counsel of the Heart as your Sovereign self. Engage, as constantly as you can, in the Activity of Blessing.

Another important opportunity: We don't want to see ourselves as alone in this process. If our hearts are ascending, so potentially are all others. (One of Jesus' famous purported sayings is, "If I am lifted up, I lift all men with me.") One way of recognizing and honoring this is to make a practice of seeing others as also within this process of the Heart's ascension. It is both impractical and potentially rude to start telling this to other people, but we can wordlessly "see" it when we look at them. I like to imaginally project the image of the Campi painting overlaid on the other person and say to myself, "This is also happening in her (or him)." This plants an invisible seed—in ourselves, perhaps in those we encounter and certainly within the soul body of the world. Whether we or others are aware of it or not, the great spiritual process of the Heart's Ascension is unfolding, within us and around us. Another famous saying of Jesus is found in the Gospel of Thomas, when he was asked when the kingdom of heaven would come: "The kingdom of heaven is spread out on the Earth, only men do not see it." We are called to see this reality, and so to help give birth to it.

SLEEPING AND DREAMING WITH STONES

Although sleeping and dreaming with stones may fall outside the bounds of meditation, it is one of the most profound ways to enter into relationship with them. When we sleep our personalities, with all of their desires and fears, subside. We let go of everything, even consciousness itself. If we take a stone into our sleeping time, its currents are able to interact with us in different ways, most of which are rather mysterious to me even now. Nonetheless, I trust this activity, and I have done it numerous times. In fact, for the past six months or so, I sleep almost every night with a Rosophia stone. As I have written in the section on Rosophia, it offers the sweetest heart currents I have ever experienced from a stone. It is deeply soothing and, I feel, healing on many levels. When I sleep with Rosophia, any residual stress or too-active mental processing dissolves and fades away within minutes of lying down. I sometimes awaken in the night and am able to feel a mysterious, delicious exchange of a sort of life-nectar flowing between my heart and the Rosophia stone. My conscious self can observe it but apparently has little to do with it. The effect I can attest to is that I wake up each day deeply refreshed by my night's sleep.

Other stones offer other currents, and they affect us differently in sleep. The most potent stone I have worked with for inducing vivid and plentiful dreams is Moldavite. If one tapes a small Moldavite to the forehead before sleep, one is guaranteed a night of multiple dreams that can run the gamut from the weirdly ridiculous to the profoundly spiritual. When I sleep with Moldavite, I usually have to remove it by 3 AM or so, in order to get a little sleep *without* those incessant dreams.

Dreaming with Phenacite is likely to precipitate a profound opening of the third eye and crown chakras. This can sometimes feel too intense, but it is a way of reaching for visionary experience in one's dream life. Cryolite can invoke the pleasurable opening and enlivening of the Corridor of Light between the heart and the brain.

I highly recommend sleeping with all forms of Azeztulite. Azeztulite is the most important of all stones for the Light Body awakening. Sleeping with Azeztulite, one will often enter a state in which innumerable tiny "fingers of silence" caress one's entire body-outline. This is a most pleasant sensation, and an initial stage of Light Body awakening. Each of the Azeztulites brings in a different frequency spectrum of the Nameless Light, thus resonating with various aspects of our nascent Light Body. Although I am very much working to develop this within myself, I am still too much at the beginning to report more than the fact that I feel it holds tremendous promise for those willing to engage Azezulite's help in the evolutionary leap it portends.

There are only a few steps I follow when I work with stones in sleep. Here they are:

1. Before lying down to sleep, I invite the stone or stones to enter the dream realm with me, and to teach or show me what I most need to know. I blow a breath of blessing and gratitude across the stone and then place it under my pillow, near my heart or (with tape) on my third eye.

2. Before falling asleep I affirm my intention to enter the dream realm for learning and healing, and I inwardly assert that I will remember my dreams.

3. *(Optional)* Sometimes I will inwardly ask a question over and over as I am falling asleep. Upon waking, I will try to recall and record the first thought I have, or the dream that was going on as I awoke. The dream or the first thought is my answer. It often comes in symbolic form. (This is described elsewhere in the book as Robert Sardello's Last Thought/First Thought exercise.)

4. In all cases, I try immediately upon awakening to recall my dreams and write them in a dream journal. I also note any physical sensations or impressions of the stone energies which I experienced during the night or when I wake up in the morning.

My intention is to work my way through all the stones in this book, inviting them to join me in the realm of sleep and dreams. I hope others will be drawn to this path and will record the stories of what they discover.

ABOVE: Outdoor labyrinth with Azeztulite stones at the School of Spiritual Psychology.

RIGHT: Indoor labyrinth inset in the floor of Chartres cathedral.

WALKING THE LABYRINTH

When my wife Kathy and I were taking one of the courses at Robert and Cheryl Sardello's School of Spiritual Psychology, we had the privilege of each morning going out with our group to walk the large labyrinth that had been laid out and constructed by earlier classes of students there. Its pattern is a replica of the labyrinth in Chartres Cathedral in France, which is a very magical architectural creation, resonating powerfully with the presence of Sophia. The labyrinth we walked at the school was large enough to easily accommodate our class of fifteen people, and we did our walks together as group meditations.

The labyrinth is a sacred pattern, and walking that pattern in a reverent way brings forth amazing inner experiences. It helped us develop and deepen our sensitivities to subtle currents, and there were often synchronous events—gestures from nature—that occurred during our walks.

On one occasion I brought six large Azeztulite stones to class, and we laid them out in a hexagonal grid around the labyrinth. Everyone immediately felt that the potency of the labyrinth as an energy field increased dramatically. (Someone who later measured the field reported that it had increased manyfold, stretching well beyond the boundaries of the property.) We later added 128 additional Azeztulite stones at the "lunation points" around the labyrinth's perimeter, and the power of the field was multiplied again. One phenomenon we noticed in our first walk after the Azeztulite's arrival was that the many river stones that had been used to define the labyrinth pattern seemed to have "woken up" under the Azeztulite's influence. They glinted at us as we walked among them, and the whole field felt charged with life force.

In the description of the Forgiving Meditation above, I mentioned the power and efficacy of carrying a Celestite through the labyrinth gridded with other Celestites, while engaging in the meditative process. I very much recommend the active meditation of the labyrinth walk, for a number of reasons. First, the walking itself helps the body integrate the intention of the meditation. One experiences it kinesthetically as well as mentally and emotionally. This helps retain the benefits of the activity. In addition, the labyrinth pattern and the intentionally created sacred space of the labyrinth both work to deepen one's experience. There is a sweetness and a feeling of beauty to ritually performing the labyrinth walk. We always did this in silence, which helped us stay focused on our meditative intention.

And, of course, the stones add a great deal, as they do in all our work with them. There seemed to be a mutually empowering resonance between the stones, the labyrinth and the people when all three were present together. The labyrinth deepened our resonance with the stones, and vice versa.

To work meditatively with a stone during a labyrinth walk, I recommend holding the stone over one's heart and keeping one's attention primarily in the heart. I think it is helpful to carry a question into the labyrinth, holding it in one's heart, where one also invites the presence of the stone. Upon reaching the center, one can stop for a few moments of prayer and receptivity, and during the walk out of the labyrinth, one can remain receptive for the development of the "answer" to one's inner question. This answer may well up in the heart as a feeling, an image or simply a recognition of oneness with the stone, the sacred labyrinth space and the surrounding world. If this occurs within the field of pure heart awareness, one may feel as if brushed by an angel's wings.

The possibilities of meditative activity with stones are endless. I offer these practices as suggestions of the sorts of directions one might wish to explore. These are invitations into the unknown rather then recipes to achieve certain results. Readers are encouraged to modify the practices or come up with their own, and to remember that we are all on a voyage of discovery together. Any limits we encounter are likely to be those we brought along with us.

CHAPTER SEVEN

Healing with the Stones

"There is only one kind of problem in the human body, one way to diagnose that problem, and one way of treating it. The common denominator is energy."

— JAMES OSCHMAN, PhD, *Energy Medicine: The Scientific Basis*

Books on crystal healing abound, and I highly value their contributions to the field of experimentation that we are involved in with the stones. It has been a big step to simply recognize that the currents we feel from the stones, and even those we do not experience in a tactile way, can be beneficial to our health and well-being. Even as mainstream medicine has been on a path that increasingly acknowledges the body/mind connection in healing, the metaphysical pioneers of crystal healing (as well as some other modalities) have championed the body/mind/ *spirit* triad of factors, each of which can provide wholesome influences that are beneficial to one's natural state of optimum health.

Everything I say below about healing with the aid of stones is to be considered in a spiritual light. It presupposes that the spiritual dimension of life, which some may not even believe exists, can be a vital factor in healing. Yet it is important for me to assert that what I say below and throughout this book in regard to healing is speculative, experimental and not grounded in scientific research. I am not a medical doctor, nor do I intend to give any medical advice. I do not recommend that anyone use stones or anyone's ideas about them as a substitute for conventional medical or psychological care. For myself, I believe in a sort of "chicken soup" approach. If I wear a crystal or meditate with stones as a practice with the intention of improving my health, well, it can't hurt and it might help. When I feel ill I consult my doctor, I take my vitamins, and I wear my stones. Personally, I wouldn't leave any of them out. I strongly recommend that each person take responsibility for his or her choices in regard to all aspects of self-care. We are not at a place in our spiritual research with stones to be able to say with any certainty or precision what, if any, benefits these stones provide for our physical health.

Having said this, I'll go on with the ideas and practices that I use. Those who want to experiment with spiritual healing with stones might use them as a jumping-off place for their own self-care activities.

ALTERNATIVE PARADIGMS FOR HEALING

Who are we? Are we animals with consciousness that arose as an accident, as a sort of ornament to the survival imperative? Is life no more than a big, savage game of musical chairs on the food chain, and when the music stops the unlucky ones get eaten? Is love a romantic embroidery on the drive to reproduce? Are our spiritual aspirations no more than a vain effort to cope with the fearful knowledge that we all die?

You can guess that I wouldn't answer "yes" to any of these questions, but from the purely materialist perspective "yes" is the only right answer. So we are going to jump the fence of materialism. (It is actually "material conceptualism," since the world view to which I am referring dwells not so much in real matter as in *concepts* of matter.) We have already made this jump in positing that both we and the stones are beings with a spiritual core, that we humans have had past lives, that there is a Soul of the World, and that love is the truest quality of the essence of the All. Most people reading this book are likely to be on this side of the fence already, so I won't make all the arguments here for regarding life as this sort of multi-dimensional experience. For those who aren't sure, I invite you to suspend denial and take an "as if" approach. Let yourself imagine "as if" this were our situation, and see where it takes you. That's how I got here.

In the new paradigm we are imagining together, we are all beings whose existence in the spiritual realm does not terminate with physical death. Our spiritual aspect has a history of lives, like beads on a string, and future lives as well. From the spiritual perspective, our multiple lives may not even have a meaningful temporal sequence. Our soul aspect is much more concerned with this particular life, its relationships, joys, sorrows and lessons. We might say that spirit flies high and stays dry, while soul goes low and gets wet. Our corporeal body involves a joining of our soul and spirit with the World—this vivid realm of matter, density, limitation and those amazing qualities, the senses. Some visionaries such as Rudolf Steiner describe levels of body-composing activities, such as the astral body and etheric body, plus the self-sense he names the "I." When we say "I," we are usually referring to all of this, though generally in a rather casual way. In fact, the "I" we actually talk about and from is primarily the personality, a set of habits that add up to a pattern or a way of being in the world. Our soul and spirit give a certain flavor to this pattern, as do our pasts, our wounds, our family history and our educational programming. All of these affect us throughout our being, however little we might be aware of it.

When we speak of our health, we usually mean the state of the corporeal body, as if it were disconnected from the rest of us. Our materialistic culture tends to more or less ignore the body until something goes wrong with it. (Granted, there are diet, exercise and psychological regimens intended to keep us healthy, and they work more or less well.) When we feel ill, we are conditioned to take in some physical substance (a medicine) that will help the body machine fix itself so we can go back to what we would rather be doing. I am making a little fun of this, although within its self-imposed boundaries it works. The material route is definitely one of the roads to healing. It just may not be the only path. And in this book, we are looking for some off-road avenues.

Psychology has shown us that wounds to the psyche and soul can make us ill in the body as well as in the mind. Clearing up old issues by bringing them to light and trying to form new, conscious belief patterns in place of the old, unconscious, unhealthy ones has been shown to bring good results, at least in some cases. We can say that conscious delving into the unconscious, unhealthy patterns we carry and efforts to create new habit patterns constitute a sort of mental or mental/emotional mode of healing. It is another road that can work, although one must often expend a great deal of will to make and hold on to the new patterns. Also, the labyrinth of inner entanglements that holds us tends to show itself only a bit at a time, like the tip of an iceberg, and we can work therapeutically only on what we can see.

Shamanism offers an interesting alternative path. Here, as in traditional medicine, we enlist the help of an expert, although the shaman is a "doctor of the soul." Leaving aside for a moment the herbal medicines and tonics they dispense, shamans often work to help their clients by journeying into the "Other World," the soul realm where they can see the destructive patterns that have spread from that realm to this one, causing the health of the corporeal body to deteriorate. Soul and body are intimately joined in the eyes of the shaman, and healing the soul will lead the body to heal. The shaman works to overcome the soul sickness, often with the help of spirit animals and allies in the Other World. Some of these maladies are recognizable as complexes the psychologist might also see and endeavor to treat. Others are viewed by the shaman as being caused by malevolent spirits or the ill will of other people. Some appear to be patterns from previous lives. We can see that the shaman works on certain levels not entered by either the medical doctor or the psychologist. Again, we are viewing the many roads into the whole of the human being, and we are not intending to judge which roads are best or even the most "real."

Deeper even than soul are spiritual patterns—so say practitioners of crystal healing and other modalities that work to invoke the potential of our wholeness. Distinct from looking into various levels of the person for where "problem areas" may be, a spiritual healing tends to focus on striking the chord of one's essential pattern of well-being, the so-called Divine blueprint. This pattern then reverberates through all levels of one's being, bringing them into resonant alignment with the essential perfected pattern of oneself. Imagine that one's wholeness is a musical note or chord, and that the vibrations from some source of "energy," like a crystal, can move within one's being similar to the way sound enters a room and strike the instrument of oneself where the originating spiritual pattern lies. Through sympathetic resonance, the chord or note then resounds through one's being, "tuning" all the levels—spirit, soul, emotional, mental and physical. The dissolution of the dis-ease or destructive pattern comes about because it has been "overwritten" by the resonant pattern of one's wholeness.

This sort of healing through the invocation of wholeness is to some extent what other modalities do as well, though perhaps less directly. From this description it might seem that crystal healing, hands-on energy treatments or even prayer directed toward embodying one's Divine blueprint might be expected to achieve better results than other methods. So why doesn't everyone who receives such a treatment reorganize on a higher level and simply get well?

My sense is that in order for the Divine blueprint to be installed in all levels of one's being strongly enough to repair whatever damage has been done and to regenerate the physical body, one must overcome the awesome force of that great nemesis, habit. Biologist Rupert Sheldrake's work, including his seminal book *The Presence of the Past,* shows that one of the deep operating principles of nature is habit. When something happens in a certain way, it tends to continue happening that way until a more powerful pattern overcomes it. My favorite example of this is how a path forms through a forest. Imagine that you are the first person ever to walk through a great dark forest. You choose your way, and you leave behind the marks of your passage, both physically and in the form of memory. The next time you enter, you might see your previous trail or simply remember various landmarks you passed before. There is a tendency to go the same way again, because it is easier to follow the familiar than to ignore memory and form another original path. A few more trips make the remembered route into a physical trail, as well as a mental habit. You may even forget that there is another choice, or that you made this trail in the first place. It simply becomes "the way through the woods." Now other people walking into the woods notice your trail and follow it, or they just take the easiest way and follow your path without noticing it. Eventually the path becomes popular, and even more inevitable. People drive their cows along the path and it gets wider. Eventually the highway department chooses it as the site for a new road. After it is paved, the path becomes permanent, and almost no one goes any other way.

Sheldrake suggests that all sorts of processes and behaviors have been formed in this way, and that even the "laws of nature" as scientists have described them are more like persistent habits than inviolable laws. Quantum physics supports such an idea, in that it describes the fundamental activities of matter and energy in terms of probabilities. This means that there is no ultimate determinism about how *anything* will happen, although the odds are that things will tend to go as they have in the past.

So how does that apply to us and our health? It is easy to see how difficult it is for one to break a habit like smoking or drinking. Our eating habits are hard to change, even when we know that a better diet will help us live a longer, healthier life. Unhealthy psychological habits such as low self-esteem are just as difficult. Shaming or fearful events that happened in childhood can be hard-wired into the brain. (Especially problematic in regard to making conscious change is the amygdala, a part of the primitive "reptile brain" in us, where the emotional "shape" of threatening early childhood events is stored in order to trigger survival programs. Any moment that reminds the amygdala of a past trauma or shame tends to trigger fear, shame and/or anxiety, along with defensiveness. The dysfunctional habit of equating even mildly distressing personal interactions with threats to survival is created before we are three years old, unless our early environment is unusually supportive. (See Joseph Chilton Pearce's book *The Biology of Transcendence.*) Examining even deeper levels of the psyche, studies of past-life memories indicate that people tend to repeat the same unfortunate patterns, in one form or another, life after life.

What starts these unhealthy soul patterns, which become the habits that hold back our highest potential and limit our lives? In cases where the pattern is self-destructive, the fixing force is often fear, or the low-level fear we call anxiety. Imagine this rather dramatic past-life pattern: Four hundred years ago, a certain self was hanged as a religious heretic. In the next life, he was strangled by a robber. In the next, he dies by drowning. In this life, he suffers from asthma, is fearful of authorities, avoids turtleneck sweaters and tends to get rashes around his throat. Examples very much like this are recounted in past-life research literature. They indicate that not only do individuals repeat habits within a lifetime, their souls tend to echo resonant patterns of experience until they are brought to consciousness and cleared. When the subject in past-life therapy remembers and releases the fear held from the past-life traumas, the symptoms in this life often disappear. I have experienced this myself.

We all know how a strong fear can throw us into irrevocable decisions that can have severe consequences. Fear produces fixations. Patterns formed in moments of fear produce a potent imprint in the psyche, like burning that first trail through the woods with a flamethrower. Because fear often produces unhealthy choices, which we tend to repeat through force of habit even when no danger is present, we can end up unconsciously choosing all sorts of things that result in bad health on any and every level.

Although one can invoke the pattern of spiritual perfection that I and many other practitioners envision as the essence of each person, the pattern may not "stick" because of the persistence of habit. If you walk through the woods once in a new way, even if it is the most beautiful way imaginable, that big road is still there from the past, and it takes attention and willpower not to fall back onto it. A further difficulty is that our habitual dysfunctions may affect our capacities for attention and will, weakening the very tools we need to free ourselves. And even if our mental capacities of will and attention are relatively strong, there are levels of us such as the "cellular mind" (the consciousness of the Liquid Crystal Body Matrix) that are not directly accessible to the mental self. The emotional body feels closer, more in the neighborhood of our mental awareness, but even that requires a good deal of digging before we can uncover the destructive habits and effectively remind that dimension of ourselves that it is not necessarily under siege right *now*. This also ultimately entails convincing the emotional body that it is always loved.

Elsewhere in this book I have mentioned Sri Aurobindo, the Mother and her confidant Satprem. I admire these three because they dared to challenge humanity's greatest habit and limitation, death itself. They each explored the possibility that evolution is more than a Darwinian game of adaptation and survival—that it is the playing-out of the intention of the Divine will, working its way into conscious manifestation; that evolution desires a spiritual *revolution* within matter. The Mother viewed death as a deep, long-standing habit of the cellular mind, but not as an inviolable law. She spent decades working inwardly to reach the levels of the cellular consciousness, where she believed that not only the habit of death but also the key to the new human species dwells. She attempted to take the light of consciousness down into the depths of the matter of her own body. There she found death, linked in a million places to fear. The presence of fear in the cells triggers the habit of death, as she taught Satprem. It is such an old, deep link—the fear of death and death itself—that it seems the cells tend to take the arousal of fear as a suggestion to die, and obediently follow it.

How was she to overcome this? With great simplicity, she introduced into the cellular consciousness an affirmation of the deathless. It was a simple Sanskrit mantra, *Om Namo Bhagavate*, which has been translated as "I surrender/salute/offer myself to the Supreme Divine." She worked it into the cells as a new habit, a habit to replace the bondage to fear and its mortal suggestion. Instead the cells were taught to sing a hymn of trust to that which does not die—the Supreme Divine. By resonating with that pattern, she believed the cells would have no death, because the Divine is eternally self-renewing.

Her work was astonishing, to herself as much as anyone else. Satprem's book, *The Mind of the Cells,* provides a summary of it. Even though she began the work "late in life," she carried herself through into her nineties, and she mapped inner terrain that no one else had ever entered, at least in recorded history. She marveled at both the persistence and myriad means of the death habit, and at the absolute unfamiliarity and life-power of the "other consciousness." She spent many years at the interface of these two worlds, trying to find the way.

Did she die? The answer is controversial. She warned her confidant Satprem that in order to make the crossing into the new way, she would have to go through a state in which her body might seem to have died. She instructed him not to allow anyone to disturb her body, which she intended to reanimate. But Satprem was overruled by ashram authorities, was kept away and could not carry out her wishes. He believed that she was buried alive.

I am not necessarily trying to suggest that we attempt to follow in the Mother's footsteps—I simply don't know whether what she tried was possible—but I hope to illustrate an approach to healing that attempts to overcome the habits of dysfunction and disease by resonance with the Divine pattern of wholeness. (My analogy of the "blueprint" is only partially apt, because the incarnation of the Divine is not static—it is an ongoing, moment-to-moment creation and regeneration of the body as a living activity.) Our bodies do regenerate themselves quite effectively, at least in our younger years. Cells die and are replaced with new cells, and we are "as good as new." Over time the regeneration process starts working less effectively. We age, and the body is eventually overwhelmed as its diminishing capacity to repair itself is overcome by more and more going wrong. (One might say that some cells give way to death, generating the suggestion of more death, until the pattern spirals into the complete failure of the organism.) Some scientists have written that there is no reason in principle that the body can't keep regenerating indefinitely, even though it doesn't. Some say the breakdown begins in the DNA, which starts to make mistakes in self-replication. (We will return to DNA as we later try to imagine another possibility for life.)

If this is true, then the Mother intuitively knew where the problem lay—in the core of the cells—decades before our science found it. Her vision of the solution involved inviting the Supreme Divine into expression in her own body, her own cells—linking the persistent goodwill of the cellular consciousness with a trusting surrender to whatever the nature of the Divine Light might be, or wish to be within us. This is not so different from what I have called "breathing with Sophia." (Recall that in the dream experience I described in Chapter Two, the Sophia figure breathed life into my body, and I into Hers, in a rhythm of mutual trust.) In fact, Satprem has described his experience of engaging the Divine power—which Sri Aurobindo called the Supramental Force—as "a new way of breathing . . . a kind of double breathing."

I have brought these examples into our discussion of healing to show how the spiritual way of healing endeavors to go to the core of our being, our spiritual blueprint, or perhaps our untapped potential for co-creating with the Divine—our resonance with the Divine itself—and to bring that into expression fully, wholly and holy. What stands in the way are millennia of habits of fear, disease and self-destruction, so ingrained that we view the world through the lens of our belief in their inevitability. Yet if Sheldrake, Satprem, the Mother and Aurobindo are right, the "inevitability" is simply composed of all the billions of repetitions of the dis-eases we hope to overcome.

It is important to remember that healing through attunement with the Divine pattern can work. Unconventional modalities such as prayer, *reiki* and crystal healing have their success stories. Many miracles are dismissed because they don't fit the paradigm of belief to which we may subscribe without even realizing it. And even if we mentally glimpse the glimmer of a different way, there are still all those invisible layers of ourselves to be untangled and regenerated.

It looks hopeless, and it certainly would be if we had to do it alone. If we had to consciously unwind every knot of our twisted and fallen nature, the lives of even the most dedicated would most likely end before the task was half done. However, I will assert here that wholeness is our natural state, and healing is our coming into alignment with truth, overcoming or dissolving the layers of fear and life-negation that assail and enmesh us. The Divine offers us the living pattern of grace, our ever-flowing perfection. We do not have to construct the answer. We have only to find our resonance with the truth.

WORKING WITH STONES FOR HEALING

So why work with crystals and stones? What do their properties have to do with helping us overcome the patterns that make us vulnerable to illness? Let us recall the Sanskrit chant *Om Mani Padme Hum* and the Dalai Lama's teachings about these sacred syllables:

> The first, *Om,* symbolizes the practitioner's impure body, speech and mind; they also symbolize the pure exalted body, speech and mind of a Buddha. The path is indicated by the next four syllables. *Mani,* meaning jewel, symbolizes the factors of method—the altruistic intention to become enlightened compassion and love. The two syllables *padme,* meaning lotus, symbolize wisdom. Purity must be achieved by an indivisible unity of method and wisdom, symbolized by the final syllable *hum,* which indicates indivisibility.

As I mentioned earlier, we could construct a new, literal translation for *Om Mani Padme Hum* using the Dalai Lama's meanings: *The Body, the Gemstone, and Wisdom are Inseparable.* "Wisdom" is the most direct translation for the Greek word *Sophia,* Soul of the World. Our bodies (in both their perfect nature and their current imperfect expression), the gems and crystals (the solid embodiments of perfected Divine patterns), and Sophia (the vast, intimate intelligence of World Wisdom) are *inseparable.* This is the ideal that we will carry into our healing work with stones.

It might be fruitful to think of the stones as our spiritual "doctors" in our quest for wholeness and healing. Remember that Rudolf Steiner described crystals and minerals as "the gods," and elsewhere as "the sense organs of angels." Plato, Pythagoras and other ancient Greek philosophers used what we now call Sacred Geometry to depict the emergence of the basic ideal forms found at the underlying levels of all matter and the patterns of nature. In the material world, crystals are the form of matter that most perfectly adheres to these sorts of fundamental geometries. In fact, the regularity of crystals, which I like to call their "faithfulness," is what makes them so helpful to us in multiple technological applications. The silica in silicon chips "remembers" whatever we tell it to hold for us with a perfection and faithfulness that would do justice to the most ardent angel.

It was discovered relatively recently that our living bodies exhibit, on the microscopic level of the cells, a visible adherence to the same sorts of ideal forms that govern the patterns of crystals. This suggests not only that there is a true "Divine blueprint" for our bodies, it also provides another point of resonant likeness between ourselves and the stones, encouraging us to see how natural it is to turn to them in our quest of actualizing wholeness. Biologists M. J. Denton, C. J. Marshall and M. Leggae of the University of Otago in New Zealand have written:

> Before the Darwinian revolution many biologists considered organic forms to be determined by natural law like atoms or crystals and therefore necessary, intrinsic and immutable features of the world order, which will occur throughout the cosmos wherever there is life. The search for the natural determinants of organic form—the celebrated "Laws of Form"—was seen as one of the major tasks of biology. After Darwin, this Platonic conception of form was abandoned and natural selection, not natural law, was increasingly seen to be the main, if not the exclusive, determinant of organic form. However, in the case of one class of very important organic forms—the basic protein fold—advances in protein chemistry since the early 1970s have revealed that they represent a finite set of natural forms, determined by a number of generative constructional rules, like those which govern the formation of atoms or crystals, in which functional adaptations are clearly secondary modifications of primary "givens of physics." The folds are evidently determined by natural law, not natural selection, and are "lawful forms" in the Platonic and pre-Darwinian sense of the word, which are bound to occur everywhere in the universe where the same twenty amino acids are used for their construction. We argue that this is a major discovery which has many important implications regarding the origin of proteins, the origin of life and the fundamental nature of organic form. We speculate that it is unlikely that the folds will prove

to be the only case in nature where a set of complex organic forms is determined by natural law, and suggest that natural law may have played a far greater role in the origin and evolution of life than is currently assumed.

Recall from our discussion in Chapter One that Jeremy Narby uncovered myths on opposite sides of the globe in which the Cosmic Serpent, the progenitor of life, was "led" into manifestation in the world by a Quartz crystal. This is not too different from what the New Zealand scientists affirm—that life on the level of the cells emerges in ideal forms that echo those of crystals!

There is a growing body of scientific information linking mineral crystals to the origins of life. In the article "Diamonds May Be Life's Birthstone," Michael Schirber reports the following:

One of the hurdles in origin of life theories is that the pieces that make up complex biomolecules do not readily come together by themselves. A group of scientists proposes that diamonds provided a kind of "work bench" for biomolecule manufacturing on early Earth.

He recounts the work of Andrei Sommer, who has proposed that certain kinds of Diamond crystals, called hydrogenated diamonds, have the unique property of causing water molecules to line up on their surfaces in highly ordered formations. Schirber continues, "Sommer's team proposes that small organic molecules in the primordial soup landed on hydrogenated diamond and were helped by its robust crystal water layers into linking together to form proteins and DNA." This is potentially an amazing confirmation of the Cosmic Serpent myths of the Desani and the Australian Aborigines. That the crystal in question is Diamond rather than Quartz is less important for our purposes here than the recognition that life may have originated because of having been *guided by a crystal*. The water and the proteins got the Message, and the crystal was the Messenger!

Speaking of Divine messengers, let us recall Rudolf Steiner's suggestion that crystals and gems are the embodiments of angels, the Divine messengers that offer us truth from the spiritual realms. I want to suggest here that we should view crystals almost literally as angels. Their patterns of structure and behavior are much more orderly, closer to the Divine originating forms, and far less variable than ours. This means that they are, like angels, faithful "messengers" of the Divine Word (or what I might call the vibrational pattern of the Divine blueprint). They carry the Message, although it is frozen in them as a potential. In order to bring it any further into the world, they need us. We are the ones with free will.

In religious mythology, angels were created as servants to humanity, though we should not make them our slaves. Service should be mutual, and all will benefit. Certainly the crystals are generous with us, offering their currents and responding with astonishing willingness to work with us in whatever ways we ask or attempt. Yet, if we only take from them, we miss the opportunity to set free their qualities, expressing them in the world through our own being. This "service" from us would mean that we allow ourselves to take in the qualities offered by the stones, and we let those qualities change us. It means "listening" to the stones through intending and allowing their currents to interface with our own Liquid Crystal Body Matrix. It means that we trust completely, opening ourselves to the Divine pattern of wholeness, which is something we have never experienced. It will feel alien to us, and possibly quite disconcerting at first to the old tangled layers of ourselves. Yet it will be perfect. When this healing fully occurs— who knows?—we may find out that Sri Aurobindo was right. We may live what he called the Life Divine.

Om Mani Padme Hum = The Body, the Gemstone and Wisdom are Inseparable

What is the nature of the body in its state of perfected wholeness? Honestly, I cannot say, because we have yet to reach the fulfillment of that potential. Any fixed image we make of it will be limited to our current level of consciousness, which is not yet the consciousness of the New Body. If we say anything, it has to be viewed as a thread of potential coming in through the faculty of imagination. Yet we can weave our threads together by intuition and see what emerges.

HEALING THROUGH THE BODY OF LIGHT

All the great spiritual traditions, when describing experiences of encountering the Divine, speak of Light. Many refer to the source of the Light as a great Sun, center of the Universe and yet present everywhere. When we are attuned to the Source, our body fills with Light, or it becomes Light. In my own work with the stones, my most profound and ecstatic experiences involve an infusion of spiritual Light into my body, or the body itself becoming a source of Light. I want to suggest that the Divine blueprint of our wholeness and perfection is that of a Body of Light. It is not another body in some heavenly realm, but this very breathing body typing these words on the page. However, it will have become a body filled with Light.

Where does this Light come from, and how do we initiate its flow into and through us? My intuition is that we can do this by making ourselves aware of the "body consciousness" of our Liquid Crystal Body Matrix, by feeling it and befriending it, by paying continual *attention* to it and offering our cooperative *intention* to it. We can find it through listening and trusting. That is what the Mother did with her meditations and her mantra.

The stones, with their currents streaming in from the spiritual realms, can aid us—stimulating, awakening and shifting the alignments of our Liquid Crystal Body Matrix. They offer us pure patterns of the qualities we have perceived within them (loving heart currents through Rosophia; soft, uplifting joy through Danburite, and so on), untainted by the convolutions we have knotted into ourselves through our confused and fear-driven choices. Yet there is a saving grace—it is through this same free will that we can bring these vibrations into ourselves and into manifestation in the world.

At the core of our cellular makeup lies DNA, the spiral molecule that displays a striking likeness to the many Cosmic Serpents found in myth, from the Rainbow Serpent of the Australian Aborigines to the twin Serpents of the Greek caduceus, universal symbol of healing. We know that our DNA emits light, and we guess that if we were in a state of alignment with the Divine, our DNA could emit more light, giving us the radiance artists have long portrayed around the bodies of spiritually illuminated people.

We don't really know whether DNA is what emits this spiritual Light, although its emanation of physical light has been measured. We may be speaking of two kinds of light, or it may be that the visible, "physical" light is a sort of afterglow of the original spiritual Light. My own intuition is that DNA, as the essential molecule of life, acts as a portal via which the spiritual and material worlds interface. I think that our DNA transmutes spiritual Light into life, with the visible light it emits appearing as a sort of by-product. Therefore, if we were to fully open ourselves to the Divine, *on the cellular level*, as the Mother attempted, not only would we be filled to overflowing with life, we would appear as Bodies of Light to both physical and spiritual vision.

Consciousness can no doubt exist without a physical form, but if that were preferable to the Divine, why would there be a material world? I believe that the Divine desires incarnation here in the physical world, through us, and through all that we behold. The amazing stability of matter would add a fantastic dimension of clarity and strength to consciousness. If this is true, then our evolution into our perfected potential as Light Beings in physical incarnation is truly a co-evolution with the Divine. We breathe life into Sophia, just as She breathes it into us. In this, the stones are our allies. The healing upon which we have the opportunity to embark is much greater and deeper than we might have imagined. We have the chance to heal not only our particular pains and illnesses, but perhaps the very source of these.

CRYSTAL HEALING PRACTICES

Wearing Stones

This is the simplest self-healing stone practice you can do, yet it is among the most effective. Wearing or carrying stones whose vibrations correspond with the qualities you wish to embody brings their currents into engagement with the Liquid Crystal Body Matrix. To facilitate bringing the body into resonance with the stones' qualities, I recommend sitting in meditation with them at the beginning of the period in which you will be wearing or carrying them. Hold the stones or the piece of jewelry over your heart and center your awareness there. Imagine the stones moving into the heart area. Invite the currents of the stones to enter the heart, and then imagine them spreading throughout your body. During the day, whenever you remember, repeat the invitation and try to feel the currents in your whole body. To get the most out of wearing or carrying stones, try beginning each day with the meditation for one to three weeks, or as long as your intuition suggests.

You may notice over time the phenomenon of energetic integration. You may initially feel the currents of the stones very tangibly, and over time the sensations may diminish. I believe this is due to the fact that one's body and vibrational field have internalized the stones' currents and adjusted to them, making them a part of one's own vibrational makeup. At this point one is free to take a break from wearing stones, or to choose other stones. In some cases it is best to continue long-term with certain stones that support one's overall well-being, or with those that are in alignment with one's evolutionary goals. My analogy here is that some stones are like a course of medicine that one takes to overcome a problem, whereas others are like vitamins that one will keep using indefinitely.

Regarding which stones one should choose for this sort of application, I hope that the individual essays on each stone in this book, and in *The Book of Stones,* will help seed your intuition. There is no better "stone doctor" than your own knowing. When I make these types of choices, I like to use a technique that my wife Kathy taught me. Hold the stone or stones in your hand and visualize it or them on a table. Then imagine yourself approaching them or walking away. Look into your heart for the image. Whatever you see will usually indicate your best choice in that moment.

Meditation with Stones

The classic practice for aligning oneself with any and all stones involves meditation. When we center and quiet ourselves, gathering our attention and intention for the purpose of self-healing and connection with Spirit, we have already taken the first necessary step toward creating the inner harmony out of which good health can arise. If you have chosen one or more stone allies to assist in attuning to the Divine blueprint of your optimal state, holding the stone(s) during meditation is an ideal way to engage their energies.

I find that the most helpful way to begin a meditation session is with the Heart Alignment practice, which is described in Chapter Six, "Crystal Meditations." This takes only a couple of minutes, and it works wonderfully for calling in all the aspects of one's being—the astral, etheric and causal bodies, the emotional and mental layers, and the Liquid Crystal Body Matrix. After this initial centering, one can pick up the chosen stones and work with visualization and intention/invitation to engage fully with the stone currents.

One helpful visualization for healing and overall well-being involves establishing strong connections with the Above and the Below—with Heaven and Earth. After the Heart Alignment, and either before or while holding the chosen stone(s), visualize a strong dark root extending from your base chakra to the center of the Earth. Feel it going deeper and deeper, branching out and providing a strong and deep Earth connection. Allow any stress, negative energies or confusion to drain out into the Earth. When this feels as real and tangible as you can make it, direct your attention to the space a foot or two above your head. Visualize a golden Sun, perhaps about the size of a basketball, above your head. Feel the warm golden radiance penetrating your crown chakra and gradually working its way through your whole body. Imagine the Sun's warm currents and Light blending with the currents of the stone(s), filling your body with Light, warmth, harmony and health. Notice how these currents dissolve and disperse any tension, stress, fear or dysfunction in the body. Visualize any inner "debris" or negative remnants flowing down the root to be grounded and transmuted in the Earth. As you continue allowing your body to be saturated with the healing and transformative golden Light, allow any surplus of the beneficial currents to also flow through the root into the Earth.

This simple meditation can be altered for individual needs. For instance, if working to heal or rejuvenate a particular organ or area, you can put special attention there, inviting the stone currents and the spiritual Light to permeate that area. A vivid visualization of the organ, or of a Light-filled space in that part of the body, can be especially helpful.

Other meditations are suggested in Chapter Six. All of them can be modified to fit one's particular focus. It can also be very interesting and helpful to sit and inwardly ask the stone beings to assist in designing the most appropriate meditative practice. The results can be amazing. In the Crystal Meditations chapter, and throughout this entire book, it is probably apparent that my focus is less on healing different conditions as such, and more on moving into a new state of being that is, in a sense, beyond healing as we have known it. That state is what one might call alignment with the Divine blueprint, living in the Light Body, becoming the New Human Being, or simply becoming Whole and Holy. It may seem to be a lofty goal, but it is where I believe our destiny is beckoning. None of us can see the form, because there is no fixed form for this. It is an adventure into the unknown.

Shamanic Journeys with Stones

Speaking of adventures into the unknown, we turn now to shamanic healing with stones. Shamanic practitioners utilized stones in their journeys and healing practices for many centuries. I asked my friend Herb Stevenson, who is a Native American shaman and crystal healer, to tell me something about the function of stones in shamanic healing. This is what he wrote:

> Each stone can raise the vibration of the individual or space that has been created. It's a matter of the interaction of the vibrations of the stone with those of the person. This kind of shift can explain how, individually, the crystal can clear auras and remove dis-ease from the body. Spatially, the stones' vibrations create a liminal space so that a person can cross over, in order to return to one's original, natural, high-vibrational state of being; then one can come back to the everyday world. Using stones in combination with shamanic journeys makes the person's entry into the visionary state happen more quickly, and the journey usually goes deeper. Stones support the entrainment of the brain in ways that lead to expanded perception and inner visions.

Shamanic journeys often include drumming, which facilitates entry into liminal space in a way analogous to that of crystals. The drums are used to generate vibratory energies—in this case they are the physical vibrations of rhythmic percussive sound. Shamanic drumming, which is usually fairly loud and repetitive, serves to break up the energetic habit patterns within one's vibratory field. When the habits of everyday consciousness are dissolved by the power of the drums, it is possible for unconscious material to emerge because it is no longer held at bay by habitual consciousness.

The stones also have a way of dissolving the habits that hold one apart from the realms of soul and spirit. They work via their own kinds of energies, which we sense as their vibrational currents. These currents, as Herb said, interact with our patterns in a way similar to the wave interference one can see in a pan of water or a pond. When one drops a pebble into the water, waves flow out in a circular pattern. If one drops a second pebble, the two wave patterns interact in ways that alter both of them, creating new wave patterns that would not have existed without the interaction. This is a helpful way of visualizing something I have described elsewhere in the book: It is important to see what is going on between ourselves and the stones not so much as our "getting something from stones" as our freeing something new into the world through our interaction with them. Shamans understand that this sort of thing occurs all the time, and that our shamanic journeys affect not only ourselves and our lives, but also the Other World that we visit. That world and our physical domain are utterly woven into one another, and shamanic journeying is a powerful way to experience this.

Although it is possible to induce a shamanic state in oneself via the use of a drumming tape and one or more stones, I believe it is preferable to work with an experienced shamanic practitioner, especially in the beginning. Shamanic journeying can free all kinds of repressed and difficult unconscious material, and it is possible to encounter negative forces, especially if one does not do appropriate cleansing rituals. I do enthusiastically recommend shamanic journeying with stones—I have taken a number of journeys, and the results have been excellent. However, rather than write a how-to for the do-it-yourselfer, I recommend trying one's first journeys with a vigilant guide who knows the territory.

It's possible to venture into the shamanic realm to meet the stone beings themselves, and to partake of their wisdom. I have learned a great deal and seen some beautiful visions in this way. I have recounted two such journeys in this book, in the stone sections on Nuummite and Master Shamanite. In the liminal realm of the Other World, the beings behind the stones can compose themselves into symbolic personifications—they may look like people, animals or who-knows-what. I recommend viewing such visions in a way that seeks their essence but does not concretize their image. The images are, from this point of view, costumes the beings put on to display themselves. We can, however, learn to experience these beings in their vibrational essence, in or out of the shamanic state, without necessarily "seeing" them. It is helpful to hold both the image and the vibration, as this provides a fuller view of the being of the stone.

Stones with Massage

Combining stone energies with massage is a practice that has been developing in recent years. Hot stone massage does not overtly employ the vibrational qualities of stones, but there is doubtless a sort of "passive" effect beyond the heat itself that enhances the relaxation qualities of the bodywork. In the realm of metaphysical stones, suppliers have been making and selling massage wands of various crystals and mineral materials for at least a decade. Utilizing tools such as these in massage sessions can bring in a definite vibrational component.

I have worked with massage wands made of Selenite, Rosophia, White Azeztulite, Himalaya Gold Azeztulite, Lemurian Aquatine Calcite, Mystic Merlinite, Sanda Rosa Azeztulite, Satyaloka

MASSAGE WANDS (left to right): Rosophia, Master Shamanite, Sanda Rosa Azeztulite, Satyaloka Azeztulite, Lemurian Aquatine Calcite, White Azeztulite, Mystic Merlinite

Azeztulite, Satya Mani Quartz and Lepidolite. The Selenite wands did an excellent job of stimulating the chakras and meridians. Rosophia is a wonderful stone for relaxing the body and infusing one's field with love. It is of great help to those who can benefit from a deeper connection with the Divine Feminine. Lemurian Aquatine Calcite is deeply relaxing, and it aids in experiencing visions during the massage process. Mystic Merlinite is an ideal adjunct to polarity therapy. Lepidolite is pure relaxation, sometimes leading to euphoria. All three Azeztulites work to awaken the Body of Light, and stimulation of the physical body with massage tools made from Azeztulite encourages the cells and the Liquid Crystal Body Matrix to open to the spiritual Light that emanates from Azeztulites of all types. Massage tools of this type make versatile tools. The rounded ends can be pressed into the muscles in bodywork, while the pointed ends focus the stone currents for stimulation of the chakras and meridians. The wands can also be placed on the body in stone layouts, and other stones can be affixed to them to make more complex energy tools.

Body Layouts

One of the most popular, powerful and interesting ways of working with stones for healing is the body layout. In this practice, one lies on a massage table, bed or yoga mat. A crystal practitioner or friend (or with somewhat less ease, oneself) places appropriately chosen stones over the chakras, meridian points and/or organs that one wishes to bring into vibrational resonance with the stones' qualities. This process can be enhanced with music and/or meditation. When one is working for purposes of healing, it can be helpful to work with the Heart Alignment, followed by a version of the root below/sun above meditation described earlier in this chapter. Consciously opening to the currents of the stones—inviting them into engagement with one's Liquid Crystal Body Matrix—is an essential element of this process. After placing the stones it is best to relax for thirty minutes to an hour, holding the intention for beneficial engagement. If one is working with a practitioner or helper, some of the stones can be removed or changed during the session. Usually body layouts are done with the recipient lying on the back, but certain layouts, such as those concentrating on opening and clearing the chakra column, may be more efficacious if one lies on the stomach and has the stones placed directly along the spine.

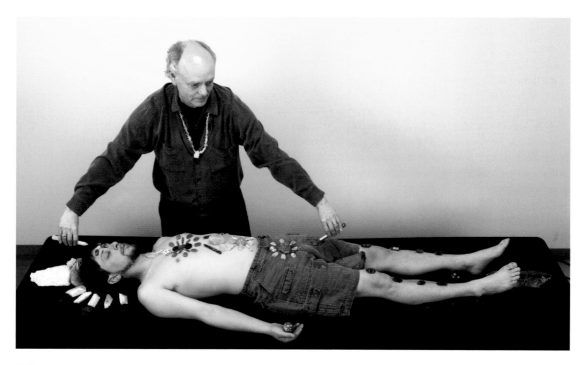

Body layouts can be very powerful experiences, and it is a good idea to allow oneself some grounding and recovery time before leaving the healing space and re-entering the flow of normal life activities.

Stone Combinations for Body Layouts

Below are several lists of stones suggested for different sorts of layouts designed to facilitate self-healing and/or consciousness expansion. I concentrate here primarily on the stones discussed in this book. Since these stones are mostly on the high-vibrational end of the scale, the layouts tend toward expansiveness. For a wider spectrum of stones one may wish to work with in different kinds of body layouts, see *The Book of Stones*.

STONE POSITIONS FOR BODY LAYOUTS. Earth Star (on table, about ten inches below the feet); Ground Interface (on table, touching bottoms of the feet); Root (1st chakra, base of spine or perineum); Sexual/Creative (2nd chakra, midway between sexual organs and navel); Solar Plexus (3rd chakra, about one inch below bottom of rib cage); Heart (4th chakra, on chest, over the heart); Throat (5th chakra, on throat, just below larynx); Third Eye (6th chakra, on the forehead, about one half to one inch above the eyebrows); Crown (7th chakra, on the table, touching the top of the head); Soul Star (8th chakra, on table, about six to ten inches above the head).

GENERAL HEALING LAYOUT. Earth Star: Aegirine; Ground Interface: Black Tourmaline; Root: Healer's Gold, Tibetan Black Quartz; Sexual/Creative: Crimson Cuprite; Solar Plexus: Agni Gold Danburite, Lemurian Golden Opal; Heart: Seraphinite, Seriphos Green Quartz; Throat: Ajoite, Celestite; Third Eye: Cryolite, Magnesite; Crown: Danburite, White Azeztulite; Soul Star: Selenite, Scolecite.

DIVINE BLUEPRINT. Earth Star: Aegirine; Ground Interface: Prophecy Stone; Root: Crimson Cuprite; Sexual/Creative: Cinnabar Quartz; Solar Plexus: Himalaya Gold Azeztulite, Libyan Gold Tektite; Heart: Moldavite, Morganite, Staurolite; Throat: Lemurian Aquatine Calcite, Satya Mani Quartz; Third Eye: Phenacite, Moldau Quartz; Crown: Satyaloka Azeztulite; Soul Star: Clear Apophyllite.

SHAMANIC HEALING JOURNEY. Earth Star: Master Shamanite; Ground Interface: Black Tourmaline; Root: Nuummite, Mystic Merlinite; Sexual/Creative: Healer's Gold; Solar Plexus: Sanda Rosa Azeztulite, Sunset Gold Selenite; Heart: Master Shamanite, Diamond; Throat: Fulgurite, Prophecy Stone; Third Eye: Herkimer Quartz "Diamond," Strontianite; Crown: Mystic Merlinite, Glendonite; Soul Star: Petalite.

EMOTIONAL HEALING. Earth Star: Healer's Gold, Tibetan Black Quartz; Ground Interface: Black Tourmaline; Root: Pink Azeztulite; Sexual/Creative: Rosophia, Seraphinite; Solar Plexus: Sanda Rosa Azeztulite; Heart: Morganite, Kunzite, Hiddenite, Green Apophyllite, Seriphos Green Quartz; Throat: Ajoite, Celestite; Third Eye: Lepidolite, Lithium Quartz; Crown: Danburite, Nirvana Quartz (pink); Soul Star: Scolecite.

PAST-LIFE REMEMBRANCE JOURNEY. Earth Star: Master Shamanite; Ground Interface: Prophecy Stone; Root: Nuummite; Sexual/Creative: Cinnabar Quartz; Solar Plexus: Lemurian Golden Opal, Sunset Gold Selenite; Heart: Mystic Merlinite, Moldavite; Throat: Lemurian Aquatine Calcite; Third Eye: Phenacite; Crown: Alexandrite; Soul Star: Selenite.

POWER OF MANIFESTATION. Earth Star: Master Shamanite; Ground Interface: Tibetan Black Quartz, Sanda Rosa Azeztulite; Root: Nuummite, Mystic Merlinite, Cerussite; Sexual/Creative: Strontianite, Cinnabar Quartz; Solar Plexus: Himalaya Gold Azeztulite, Agni Gold Danburite, Golden Azeztulite Crystals, Libyan Gold Tektite; Heart: Moldavite, Rosophia, Circle Stone; Throat: Satya Mani Quartz, Diamond; Third Eye: Datolite, Phenacite; Crown: Cerussite, Mystic Merlinite; Soul Star: White Azeztulite, Fulgurite.

MARRIAGE OF HEAVEN & EARTH. Earth Star: Master Shamanite; Ground Interface: Prophecy Stone; Root: Tibetan Tektite; Sexual/Creative: Circle Stone; Solar Plexus: Libyan Gold Tektite; Heart: Moldavite, Rosophia; Throat: Creedite; Third Eye: Moldavite, Phenacite; Crown: Tibetan Tektite, White Azeztulite; Soul Star: Golden Azeztulite Crystals.

DIVINE LOVE. Earth Star: Tibetan Black Quartz; Ground Interface: Rosophia; Root: Crimson Cuprite; Sexual/Creative: Pink Azeztulite; Solar Plexus: Moldavite, Libyan Gold Tektite; Heart: Rosophia, Morganite, Kunzite, Hiddenite; Throat: Celestite, Ajoite; Third Eye: Danburite; Crown: Lepidolite; Soul Star: Petalite, Scolecite.

SYNERGY OF SELF (SYNERGY TWELVE). Earth Star: Sanda Rosa Azeztulite; Ground Interface: Satyaloka Azeztulite; Root: Tibetan Tektite; Sexual/Creative: Pink Azeztulite; Solar Plexus: Himalaya Gold Azeztulite; Heart: Moldavite, Petalite; Throat: Tanzanite; Third Eye: Phenacite, Brookite, Herderite; Crown: Danburite, Scolecite, Tibetan Tektite; Soul Star: White Azeztulite, Natrolite.

MERKABAH INTERDIMENSIONAL TRAVEL. Earth Star: Merkabite Calcite, Master Shamanite; Ground Interface: Himalaya Gold Azeztulite; Root: Nuummite; Sexual/Creative: Cinnabar Quartz; Solar Plexus: Agni Gold Danburite; Heart: Merkabite Calcite, Green Apophyllite; Throat: Herderite; Third Eye: Phenacite, Magnesite; Crown: Clear Apophyllite, Natrolite, Brookite; Soul Star: Merkabite Calcite, Spanish Aragonite.

LIGHT BODY AWAKENING. Earth Star: Mystic Merlinite, Glendonite; Ground Interface: Cryolite, Moldau Quartz; Root: Spanish Aragonite; Sexual/Creative: Natrolite, Sunset Gold Selenite; Solar Plexus: Himalaya Gold Azeztulite, Agni Gold Danburite; Heart: Pink Azeztulite, Rosophia, Moldavite; Throat: Satya Mani Quartz, Satyaloka Azeztulite; Third Eye: Circle Stone, Phenacite; Crown: Magnesite, Spanish Aragonite; Soul Star: White Azeztulite, Golden Azeztulite Crystals.

ANGELIC ATTUNEMENT. Earth Star: Staurolite; Ground Interface: Seriphos Green Quartz; Root: Sanda Rosa Azeztulite; Sexual/Creative: Seraphinite; Solar Plexus: Agni Gold Danburite; Heart: White Azeztulite, Rosophia, Nirvana Quartz (pink); Throat: Celestite; Third Eye: Nirvana Quartz (white); Crown: Danburite; Soul Star: Petalite, Selenite, Scolecite.

ASCENSION. Earth Star: White Azeztulite; Ground Interface: Sanda Rosa Azeztulite; Root: Glendonite; Sexual/Creative: Pink Azeztulite, Scolecite; Solar Plexus: Agni Gold Danburite, Himalaya Gold Azeztulite, Golden Azeztulite Crystal; Heart: Nirvana Quartz (pink), Rosophia, Moldavite; Throat: Herderite, Brookite, Satya Mani Quartz; Third Eye: Nirvana Quartz (white), Phenacite, Satyaloka Azeztulite; Crown: Spanish Aragonite, Danburite, Natrolite; Soul Star: Scolecite, Magnesite, Merkabite Calcite.

Healing Grids

Healing grids are a logical extension of the body layout practice, and they can be used in conjunction with one another if it feels appropriate to do so. A grid is made by placing a pattern of stones around a flat area within which the body will lie down for a session of meditation and current-infusion.

For basic healing grids, I usually prefer to place the stones in a six-sided or twelve-sided pattern. (Special grids follow other patterns, and three of these are pictured below.) The regular arrangement of stones encourages a smooth overlapping of the currents emanating from the stones around the perimeter, creating a harmonious sacred space. As with body layouts, I like to select a synergistic medley of stones, keyed to a chosen purpose. In general, Selenite provides good amplification of whatever other stones are chosen, as well as produces an infusion of high vibrations into the body. Because of the importance I place upon activation of the Light Body and evolutionary change in our selves and the Earth, most of my grids include several types of Azeztulite. For a maximum infusion of the stones' currents, I have sometimes combined a healing grid (or another sort of stone energy grid) with a body layout of a similar vibrational spectrum. It can also work well—when one receives guidance to do so—to interface a grid for one level or segment of the vibrational spectrum with a body layout keyed to another. This can be tricky, because one does not want one's client or oneself thrown into confusion or disharmony. However, if the two spectrum segments are compatible—such as those of Divine Love and Ascension—bringing two complementary vibrational patterns into engagement with one another and with one's energy field can be very powerful and beneficial.

FULL ASCENSION GRID

STONES: White Azeztulite, Golden Azeztulite Crystals, Pink Azeztulite, Himalaya Gold Azeztulite, Sanda Rosa Azeztulite, Satyaloka Azeztulite, Selenite Wands, Nirvana Quartz, Petalite, Creedite, Cinnabar Quartz, Crimson Cuprite, White Danburite, Agni Gold Danburite, Mystic Merlinite, Tibetan Black Quartz, Circle Stone, Phenacite, Moldavite, Moldau Quartz, Prophecy Stone, Fulgurite, Spanish Aragonite, Satya Mani Quartz.

MERKABA GRID

STONES: Merkabite Calcite, Selenite Wands, Mystic Merlinite, White Azeztulite, Cryolite, Petalite, Phenacite, Spanish Aragonite, Datolite, Tibetan Tektite, Darwinite, Moldavite, Libyan Gold Tektite, Sanda Rosa Azeztulite, Natrolite, Circle Stone.

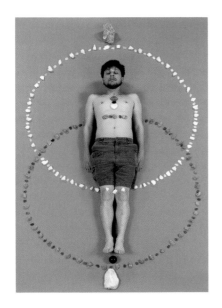

HEAVEN & EARTH (VESICA PISCES) GRID

STONES: Rosophia, White Azeztulite, Master Shamanite, Phenacite.

The possible good stone combinations for healing grids and energy grids are infinite, and they should be created intuitively. However, if one is looking for ideas, one is advised to consider combinations similar to those listed in the preceding "Body Layouts" section. One main difference between a body layout and a grid is the use of multiple stones for the grid, laid out in a balanced geometric pattern. I suggest using some powerful stones around the perimeter of the grid to create a sort of "temporary energy vortex." Azeztulite and Selenite are two of my most highly recommended choices for this. Rosophia is another, especially when the goal is an infusion of love and/or engagement with Sophia. One can add Black Tourmaline, Nuummite and/or Master Shamanite to ensure sufficient grounding and spiritual protection. Smaller stones can be interspersed to make the grid into a sort of vibrationally woven "net" of stone currents.

Crystal Acupuncture

Acupuncture is a healing modality that works on the subtle levels of the body, at their interfaces with the physical body—the meridians. This ancient practice has been proven to work for a wide variety of applications, from anesthesia and muscle spasms to cancer treatment. One of the frontiers of self-healing with stones is the development of crystal-enhanced acupuncture.

I have worked with two different practitioners in this area. In one case, we continued to use acupuncture needles, and we augmented them by applying them through holes drilled in selected stones. It looked a bit like little buttons strung onto the needles. With this method, one retains the strong stimulation of the needles while adding the vibrational enhancement of the stones at the appropriate points.

The second way of doing crystal acupuncture is completely on the subtle level. A trained acupuncturist uses small polished wands of various stones, directing the energy flow through the points of the wands into the chosen meridian points.

This emerging modality has not yet been explored deeply enough for me to say anything about its efficacy, or to offer any sort of instructions. I mention it here to encourage interested persons to experiment with it and to share their research. Of course, one should only work with a trained practitioner, especially where needles are involved.

The words *whole* and *healing* have the same root. Much of the discussion in this chapter has been about uncovering our fragmentation and discovering and integrating the Divine pattern of our wholeness. All beneficial healing modalities work to dissolve dysfunctional patterns in the body, soul and/or psyche and to replace them with one's optimal state of well-being. The stones, by their unwavering fidelity to the Divine patterns they carry, provide us with offers of harmony and attunement to the perfection of their many qualities. Our work is very much a labor of undoing the "knots" in ourselves and reconnecting with the truth. The stones offer their radiance of truth to us at all times, perhaps as they have done since time's very beginning. The Diamond may have "taught" water molecules how to line up so that organic life could begin. In the next chapter, we explore how crystals and water may once again combine to help us live more fully and with greater joy.

CHAPTER EIGHT

Waters of Life: Crystal Water & Elixirs

"Water is a primordial element which underlies creation myths and stories around the world. The Egyptian Heliopolitan creation story recounts that the sun-god Atum (Re) reposed in the primordial ocean (Nun). In Assyro-Babylonian mythology, first the gods and subsequently all beings arose from the fusion of salt water (Tiamat) and sweet water (Apsu). The holy books of the Hindus explain that all the inhabitants of the Earth emerged from the primordial sea. At the beginning of the Judeo-Christian story of creation, the spirit of God is described as stirring above the waters, and a few lines later, God creates a firmament in the midst of the waters to divide the waters (Genesis 1:1-6). In the Koran are the words 'We have created every living thing from water.'"

—PROFESSOR CHRISTOPHER L.C.E. WITCOMBE, "Water and the Sacred"

For the past twenty-five years I have worked with crystals, gemstones and minerals, investigating their usefulness in areas such as self-healing, meditation, spiritual evolution and consciousness expansion. Over that time I became interested in learning whether water can be "charged" or "programmed" to carry the beneficial properties of stones. As I began to understand the similarities between living (organic) organisms and crystals, it seemed increasingly logical that one very tangible medium via which the currents of the stones could be brought into our bodies is water. If water could be attuned to the vibrations of the stones, and if it could hold those vibrational patterns, we would have a means of directly infusing the beneficial qualities of stones into our body, at the cellular level. There is considerable scientific evidence to suggest that water may be able to do just that.

Human beings are about seventy percent water, and water is something we must constantly take into our bodies in order to live. Though one can live a month or more without food, one will die in as little as a few days without water. Water moves through us, builds our tissues, cleanses our organs and makes up much of our blood, which carries nourishment to all the cells. Without the proper amounts of water, our digestion, nerve impulses, thinking, sensing and even breathing cannot function. Water is everywhere in us and in fact *is* us more than any other substance.

Water is an essential component of the Liquid Crystal Body Matrix. The relationship between water and the connective tissues that make up the majority of this structure is key. Biologist Mae Wan Ho has written that the liquid crystallinity of organisms is what makes them so dynamically coherent and adaptable. She has asserted that communication through the liquid crystal structure (Liquid Crystal Body Matrix) occurs much faster throughout the body than it can occur through the neurons of the nervous system. The body tissues transmit electrical impulses as semiconductors, which are a great deal faster than conventional conductivity. Mae Wan Ho concludes that the liquid crystalline continuum of the body acts as "the basis of sentience," a "body consciousness" working in tandem with the nervous system and representing the primary control center for instantaneous coordination of body functions. She sees the body consciousness as existing prior to the brain consciousness, maintaining that "Brain consciousness associated with the nervous system is embedded in body consciousness and is coupled to it." In my own words, I would say that the Liquid Crystal Body Matrix is the foundation of consciousness, and that the nervous system works with it cooperatively. Learning to feel and engage the body consciousness is part of what our work with crystals can facilitate. Elixirs are one way to bring the stone currents into deep interactive resonance with the body.

What about water in all this? It is the vehicle for information. There are ten thousand water molecules in the human body for every molecule of protein. When molecules trigger a biological effect, they are not directly transmitting the signal. The final job is done by perimolecular water, which relays and possibly amplifies the signal. Proteins are complex molecules forming the major support structures for animal and plant cells, and they also regulate biochemical reactions. The shape and movements of protein molecules determine their function, and scientists have long known that proteins can't function unless they are immersed in water. Water forms a very thin layer—only three molecules thick—around the protein, and this layer is essential in maintaining the protein's structure and flexibility, lubricating its movements.

Homeopathic medicine works on the principle that water, which is used in preparing the remedies, has a "memory" of the presence of the substance introduced into it. Dilution does not degrade the memory. (In fact, it increases its potency, according to homeopathic principles.) It has been established that water molecules fall into discrete and specific patterns of alignment in the presence of a foreign substance. When the substance is removed, the water retains those patterns, and it transfers them to water which is later added to the original batch.

Water is an ideal medium for the introduction of the vibrational patterns emanated by stones. It crystallizes in a hexagonal pattern similar to that seen in Quartz and numerous other minerals. It is tremendously sensitive, as has been shown through a gamut of research, ranging from the rigorous experiments of molecular biologists to the more spiritually based research of Japan's famous Dr. Emoto.

In his book *The Messages of Water,* Dr. Emoto displayed photographs of water crystals, formed from water that had been "programmed" by writing words on paper taped to bottles containing the water. His results seemed to show that water programmed with positive or loving words formed much more symmetrical and beautiful crystals than water programmed with angry or negative words. It even appears that water distressed by the application of chemicals or other detrimental events can be "healed" by programming it positively.

Since we are water, such results play into the entire realm of self-healing that is based upon producing states of well-being through meditation, positive affirmations, laughter and loving attention. Even the "placebo effect" comes into play. Could it be that the success of all these practices and even the placebo effect come out of the "programming" of the water in our bodies? All of them seem to offer a positive "imprint" for the body to somehow take in. Perhaps it is the malleable, sensitive, impressionable water within us that receives and carries forward the positive (or negative) influences we encounter. Perhaps our capacity for self-programming comes directly out of communication between the brain/mind and the Liquid Crystal Body Matrix.

In regard to our liquid crystallinity, I will again quote Mae Wan Ho:

> Organisms are so dynamically coherent at the molecular level that they appear to be crystalline. There is a dynamic, liquid crystalline continuum of connective tissues and extracellular matrix linking directly into the equally liquid crystalline cytoplasm in the interior of every single cell in the body. Liquid crystallinity gives organisms their characteristic flexibility, exquisite sensitivity and responsiveness, thus optimizing the rapid, noiseless intercommunication that enables the organism to function as a coherent, coordinated whole. The organism is coherent beyond our wildest dreams. Every part is in communication with every other part through a dynamic, tunable, responsive liquid crystalline medium that pervades the whole body, from organs and tissues to the interior of every cell.

One of the key words in Mae Wan Ho's quote is the word "tunable." The liquid crystal medium of an organism can be "tuned" to different patterns, frequencies or states of being. Such attunement may explain why and how we "resonate" so sympathetically with our environment. If we are with depressed people it depresses us, just as happy people can cheer us up. This is very similar and may be the very same effect evident in the experiments Dr. Emoto did with water.

From this it is clear that we will most likely benefit from taking in water that has been intentionally imbued with positive qualities. Even something as simple as Dr. Emoto's practice of writing words on bottles of drinking water is promising—write the words "good health," "happiness" and/or "prosperity" on your jug of drinking water and watch the results. But is there an even better way? My interest in crystals and their beneficial properties led me to try methods of using them in combination with water. The initial results are so interesting that I am planning a much wider series of experiments.

Crystals and precious stones have been valued throughout world cultures over many centuries for their healing virtues, as well as their capacities to imbue courage, strength, invulnerability, clairvoyance, love and numerous other qualities. (At least as far back as the Middle Ages, people have created gem elixirs for healing purposes. One of the best-known and most prolific practitioners was Hildegard of Bingen.) If crystals can help us attune to helpful patterns and bring them into our own being, how does that work? The theory of crystal resonance suggests that the characteristic energy patterns emanated by any stone can be transferred into the liquid crystal medium of our bodies through resonance. Our bodies, being composed of tunable liquid crystal, can mirror and mimic any consistent pattern with which we come into contact. Just as we fall into cheerful resonance with happy people, we can resonate with the healthful qualities of Seraphinite, or the evolutionary quickening of Moldavite. If we add to this the information-carrying capacities of water molecules, the permeation of the entire body by water and the instantaneous communication of body consciousness through the Liquid Crystal Body Matrix, we can understand how both homeopathic remedies and stone elixirs might work very well indeed.

If we want to expose our bodies to the benefits of the vibrational patterns of stones, the fuller and more penetrating the contact, the better. This is where the idea of drinking water enhanced by crystal energies comes from. If water takes the imprints of what is projected into it, as Emoto suggests, it stands to reason that water can carry stone energy patterns. If we drink that water, those patterns travel throughout our bodies into the tissues and all the cells. By this theory we can, for example, "teach" the cells of the body the pattern of good health transmitted by Seraphinite by bringing Seraphinite-charged water that we drink right into the cells. (NOTE: Use the double-bottle method described below in making a water or elixir using Seraphinite.)

Using crystal water elixirs to program the body for overall health is just "the tip of the iceberg," so to speak. We can also utilize elixirs for quickening our spiritual evolution and/or awakening the Light Body. In bringing the vibrational patterns of the stone currents into physical contact with our cells and body consciousness we can, to an extent, bypass the brain/mind with its multiplicity of inner conflicts, doubts and patterns of self-sabotage. And if Mae Wan Ho is correct, the consciousness of the Liquid Crystal Body Matrix is actually much "faster" than the brain/mind, at least in terms of its internal communication. Satprem and the Mother would say that the Mind of the Cells is definitely more stubborn and consistent than the brain/mind. Once it grasps a new pattern, it sticks with it and will repeat it indefinitely. That is its nature, and the reason our bodies retain their functional patterns so well. The Mother understood that the work to be done was to find the way into the cellular consciousness and to teach it the new pattern—the pattern of truth, attunement to the Divine and immortality. Whether our goals are that ambitious or not, the means are the same—making the new suggestion to the body consciousness with sufficient purity, consistency and power for it to catch hold. The stones can be of great help in this work because they faithfully and undeviatingly emanate their qualities. This is their constant offer and love gesture. One of the means for these gestures to reach our bodily core is through the stone elixirs.

I have worked on my own with stone-charged waters over the decades, and the results have been promising. In recent years I wondered if the nature of the water used made a difference. I wanted to avoid chlorinated or fluoridated water, since chlorine and fluoride both carry their own energy patterns, which can deplete or harm the body. Spring water is good, and I thought it would be my choice until I found crystal water from Arkansas. I began working to create elixirs using water from one of the most prolific and high-quality Quartz crystal mines in Arkansas, the Ron Coleman Mine. The ground in this area is full of crystals, and the water is filtered right through the crystal layers. This water comes out of the ground already patterned with the beneficial properties of the Quartz that has permeated it for millions of years. My sense of this water is that it carries a strong pattern of Quartz, which is the most "programmable" of stones. Quartz is said to be capable of amplifying and strengthening any intention placed within it. The Quartz-enhanced water from this location is ideal for making drinking water and elixirs enhanced with other stones, in addition to its native Quartz. My feeling is that this water holds the patterns of stone currents more effectively and longer, and it magnifies the desired effects. If this type of water is available, it is probably the best choice for stone elixirs. Otherwise, a good, pure spring water should work well.

SOME NOTES ON MAKING CRYSTAL WATERS & STONE ELIXIRS

I present below a couple of simple methods for making crystal drinking water and stone elixirs. These recipes are only a beginning. You can make them much more elaborate, selecting all sorts of stone combinations to accentuate chosen spiritual qualities. (If you look back to the previous chapter, the stone combinations for the various body layouts can just as easily be utilized for making more complex elixirs. One special elixir I prefer for Light Body activation uses all the forms of Azeztulite. Another one, which I call the Tree of Life, combines Master Shamanite, Azeztulite and Rosophia.)

I also recommend experimenting with making your water-charging area more potent by laying out a grid of crystals around the vessel. For example, I like to use a hexagonal pattern of six raw Azeztulites around most of my elixir containers, especially those having to do with Light Body activation. Regular Quartz crystals can also be used for basic amplification of the charging of the water. The six stones create overlapping spherical fields in the Flower of Life pattern. The hexagon is also the natural crystallization pattern for water (i.e., snowflakes), so this sort of grid provides macroscopic resonance with the microscopic forms.

Use Caution in Making Crystal Waters & Stone Elixirs

However beneficial the energies of different varieties of stones may be, some of them can leech out toxic compounds into water or alcohol. Even stones such as Quartz, which should be safe, may have been treated with chemicals when they were mined or cleaned. Others, such as Cinnabar, contain toxic compounds in their own structures. If you don't know for certain whether a stone is "dirty" or if it might be toxic, you are better off treating it as if it is. In such cases you can still make elixirs, but you will need to place the stones in a glass jar or bottle that can be closed tightly. Place the stone or stones in the sealable jar or bottle and tighten the lid before starting the elixir-making process. Be sure that the container does not leak. Then you can submerge the sealed jar of stones into the water you will be charging. It is okay to fill the stones jar with water so that it will submerge more easily, but be sure to discard that water afterwards. Never use: Realgar, Orpiment, Stibnite, Galena, Azurite, Malachite, Cinnabar or other compounds of mercury, arsenic or lead.

RECIPE FOR HEALING WATER Use two liters of spring water in a glass container. Write the words "Pattern of Perfect Health for My Body" on a piece of paper and tape it to the bottle. (You can add other words like Love, Well-being, Strength, etc.) Take a clear, clean Amethyst point and a clear Quartz point and hold them while you meditate, imagining the intention for your optimal health going into the crystals and filling them. (You can add Sanda Rosa Azeztulite to intensify the process, or other healing stones of your choice.) Then place the crystals in the water. If you are not sure whether they are clean, non-soluble and non-toxic, seal them in a glass container, wash the outside of the container, and then immerse the container in the water. Put the glass container(s) in the sun for four to twelve hours to charge it. Then refrigerate the water and drink it as you normally would over a few days. Repeat as you wish.

RECIPE FOR MEDITATION ELIXIR Take a one-pint or one-quart glass jar of spring water. Write the words "Deepest and Most Beneficial Meditation" or the phrase of your choice on paper and tape it to the container. Other helpful words can be added. For this elixir I recommend that Moldavite, Phenacite, Danburite, Azeztulite and Petalite be placed in the container. If you are not sure whether they are clean, non-soluble and non-toxic, seal them in a glass container, wash the outside of the container, and then immerse the container in the elixir water. It is all right if the container floats in the water you will be charging. Prepare the stones beforehand by holding them and placing your intention within them, as described immediately above. Tighten the lid on the elixir jar (outer jar) and place it in sunlight for an entire day. Moonlight, especially of the full moon, is also recommended. After at least twenty-four hours of this charging, add fifty percent vodka or other 80-proof alcohol for preservative purposes (you can substitute vinegar if you prefer). Dispense the liquid into clean dropper bottles. Before meditation, place a few drops under the tongue. Note your inner experiences.

Both of these recipes are the simplest possible. Much more can be done to make the preparation process more powerful, and many more stones can be brought together to create the perfect blends for one's desired purposes. Since this water is for consumption, I want to repeat: take special care that the stones you use are completely clean, and do not use stones that could be poisonous if they leech any of their constituents into the water. Don't use porous stones. Crystals are best. When in doubt, check in a good mineral reference book for potential toxicity before trying a specific stone and/or use the sealed inner container method. Don't use any stone or material soluble in water or alcohol. These are experiments. No results are promised or implied, but I hope to hear about yours! I am collecting stories about people's experiences with stones, elixirs, body layouts, grids and other modalities of crystal resonance. Write to me at heavenandearth@earthlink.net.

CHAPTER NINE

Crystal Tools & Jewelry

"Very early, and very naturally, the religious nature of man led to the use of precious stones in connection with worship—the most valuable and elegant objects being chosen for sacred purposes. Of this mode of thought we have a striking instance in the accounts given, in the book of Exodus, of the breastplate of the High-priest, and the gems contributed for the tabernacle by the Israelites in the wilderness. Another religious association of such objects is their use to symbolize ideas of the Divine glory, as illustrated in the visions of the prophet Ezekiel and in the description of the New Jerusalem in the book of Revelation."

—GEORGE FREDERICK KUNZ, *The Curious Lore of Precious Stones*

We know from the resonances we feel in the body that crystals emanate tangible, if immeasurable, currents. Books like this one try to describe and categorize the currents or energies of stones, and we know from experience that there is quite a bit of commonality in what different people feel. There are many differences as well. Those of us who study the stones try to pay attention to all of that, and to our inner experiences, in order to learn how to derive the greatest benefit from our work. This benefit is not just for us but ideally for the spiritual beings of the stones as well, with whom we endeavor to work cooperatively.

People love stones, and apparently stones love people. Like the angels they may be, they seem endlessly willing to serve the well-being of humans and to help us achieve our desires for health, protection and spiritual awakening. As the inventive creatures we are, humans have long attempted to utilize stones and their powers in tools and jewelry for our betterment and beautification. In the technology industries, crystals are constantly incorporated into tools. Computers are filled with silicon chips, expensive watches have jeweled movements, lasers are focused through gems. Kings and queens, as well as lesser mortals, enhanced their images and perhaps their powers with crowns and scepters. In the Old Testament, the High Priest was said to have worn a breastplate of gems through which the Divine Will was revealed to him.

Unlike peoples of the ancient past, we now have access to virtually the entire mineral kingdom. We have the opportunity to work like modern alchemists, combining and arranging the stones and their currents, looking for combinations and patterns that can help us enhance our inner and outer lives. I am one of the most enthusiastic of these "alchemists," and I have tried many combinations of stones for different purposes or just to see what responses they generate in me.

Although the stones do seem quite willing to help us, I will inject this note of caution: We should always approach the stones with an awareness of them as beings. When we want something from them, it makes sense to ask, holding the stone or stones and listening with reverence and respect. (We wouldn't think of just grabbing an angel's wing and plucking a feather for a pen!) When we ask in this way, the answer comes into one's heart, so it is essential to center one's attention there. This sort of asking and listening helps us practice placing attention in the heart, so it is good for us in any case. My experience is that the answer does come, often in the form of an urge or feeling. It is important to pay attention to the feeling. Most often the answer is "yes," but when it is not, one should look for another design idea, another combination of stones or wait for another time. Meditation with the stone or stones can help clarify the issue and may lead to a new and better idea. The beings behind the stones do wish us well, and their counsel, when we can hear it, is for our benefit. When I practice this sort of listening, I feel that it unerringly leads me to bring together stones which will work in the most harmonious way

Crimson Cuprite

Pink & Clear Azeztulites

Merkaba Pendant with
Rosophia, Azeztulite &
Moldavite

possible. Feeling for harmony in the potential toward which one is leaning is a way of developing deeper sensitivity to the stones themselves, and it is a joy to find later that the harmony is tangibly present in the tool or jewelry piece one has designed.

Shaping a stone is one way of creating an energy tool. When a stone is faceted in a symmetrical form, this can focus and direct its currents. Likewise, spherical forms make for an even diffusion of the stones' currents in all directions. Other geometric forms such as the Platonic solids and the Merkaba Star can activate resonant patterns within our subtle energy bodies.

JEWELRY

The most obvious and yet overlooked type of stone energy tool is jewelry. The placement of gems on the body, especially in ways that allow them to be worn continuously, is an ideal means of incorporating the currents of the stones into one's vibrational field. Pendants are among the best items, because they align the stone over or between the heart and throat chakras. Wearing a combination pendant and earrings can be especially effective, since the placement of the pieces puts them in a triangular pattern, which tends to amplify the effects of all three.

Stone Combinations in Jewelry

Like the ancient alchemists, who were always seeking new combinations of metals and other substances in their search for the Philosopher's Stone, we can put together jewelry pieces in an effort to create new and powerful synergies of the vibrational currents of the stones. With practice one can learn to feel whether the juxtaposed gems are singing in harmony or are out of tune with each other. Pictured here are four of the most significant beneficial combinations we have found in our twenty-three years of experimentation.

CHAKRA PENDANT. This eight-stone piece is designed to offer a wearable template of gems, providing the auric field and chakras with the appropriate pattern for general health and well-being. We use eight gems in this piece—one for each of the physical chakras and the top stone for the etheric chakras above the head. Some people prefer the traditional seven-stone alignment, and we make those as well. From top to bottom the gems and chakras are as follows: Etheric—Danburite; Crown—Amethyst; Third eye—Iolite; Throat—Aquamarine; Heart—Moldavite; Solar Plexus—Citrine; Sexual/Creative—Padparadscha Sapphire; Root—Garnet. I like to wear this pendant when I am working with the public at shows and conferences. It helps me stay centered and adds to my overall energy level, enhancing stamina and the ability to be present for other people.

SYNERGY SEVEN. This piece works differently from the Chakra Pendant—it helps one attune one's personality and outer expression to the wisdom and higher purpose of one's soul and spirit. When I wear this piece I feel that my higher awareness is present, yet I am fully grounded and able to articulate new insights and ideas gracefully. I think of this piece as attuning one to the morphogenic fields of knowledge-at-large, so that one may suddenly "know" about something just by turning one's attention to it. It certainly seems to enhance intuition, and it gives a feeling that something more than one's everyday self is present. The gems, from top to bottom, are: Azeztulite, Tanzanite, Danburite, Moldavite, Phenacite, Tibetan Tektite and Petalite.

ASCENSION SEVEN. We have long sought the ideal combination of gems to enhance the process of Vibrational Ascension. This process is, from my perspective, about bringing the Body of Light into incarnation here on Earth, rather than any sort of ascension that causes one to leave the world. Wearing this I experience a very definite heightening of my vibrations, together with the feeling that I am sensing everything on the etheric level. This pendant provides a very exhilarating sensation, and it is best to allow time to integrate its currents into one's own field before wearing it while driving, etc. On the other hand, it is excellent for attuning to spiritual guidance or channeling and is an excellent aid in meditations of all types. I can personally testify that it is especially helpful for attuning to the many high-vibration stones described in this book! The stones, from top to bottom, are: Azeztulite, Petalite, Satyaloka Azeztulite, Danburite, Satya Mani Quartz, Golden Azeztulite and Nirvana Quartz.

Multi-Stone Combinations: Chakra Pendant, Synergy Seven, Ascension Seven, Azeztulite Power Pendant

AZEZTULITE POWER. This pendant incorporates all seven of the known varieties of Azeztulite, the Stone of the Nameless Light. Azeztulite is perhaps the most advanced of all Stones of the New Consciousness, having been purposely attuned and activated by interdimensional beings since the early 1990s. It is completely aligned with the awakening of the Body of Light and is said by the Azez to aid in reprogramming our cellular structure (or Liquid Crystal Body Matrix) to receive infusions of spiritual Light. This Light infusion helps dissolve the habit patterns of contraction, fear and limitation on the cellular level, opening one to harmonious attunement with the Light of the Great Central Sun. This is one of my personal favorites, because when I wear it I feel conscious on multiple levels yet able to focus and be present here on Earth.

MASSAGE WANDS

One of the most popular designs for a stone tool is the massage wand. A form of this kind usually echoes the shape of a natural Quartz crystal, with six sides and an elongated body. The pointed end directs a focused flow of the stone's currents, which can be used to stimulate chakras and meridians. The rounded end acts somewhat like a sphere, sending a diffuse flow of currents, usually experienced in a "softer" way by the subject. The rounded end is the part used in actual massage because it can be used to apply pressure to tight muscles or other places where blockages exist. See a picture of several massage wands in Chapter Seven, and look at the Stones section of this book for descriptions of their qualities.

SELENITE SYNERGY WANDS

Selenite is in itself a very powerful stone, and it is known for its special capacity to amplify and harmoniously blend the vibratory qualities of other stones. I have been designing and constructing what I call Selenite Synergy Wands for more than twenty years, and it is always exciting to try new combinations. The Selenite's fibrous structure has a way of channeling the currents of whatever stones are attached to it along its axis, sending a stream of synergized vibrations out through both ends of the wand. The stones on the wands pictured here are as follows: 1. AZEZTULITE POWER: White Vermont Azeztulite, Himalaya Gold Azeztulite, Original North Carolina Azeztulite, Pink Azeztulite, Satyaloka Azeztulite, Sanda Rosa Azeztulite, Golden Azeztulite Crystal. 2. RADHA'S WAND: Tibetan Tektite, Lithium Quartz, Herderite, Celestite,

White Azeztulite, Phenacite, Brookite, Danburite, Moldavite. 3. ASCENSION SEVEN WAND: White Azeztulite, Petalite, Satyaloka Azeztulite, Danburite, Golden Azeztulite, Satya Mani Quartz, Nirvana Quartz. 4. SYNERGY TWELVE: Moldavite, Phenacite, Tanzanite, Danburite, Azeztulite, Herderite, Satyaloka Azeztulite, Brookite, Petalite, Tibetan Tektite, Scolecite, Natrolite.

GEMSTONE TEMPLATES

To utilize a group of stones at a particular spot on the body, or to hold a group of stones in meditation, a Gemstone Template can provide the ideal means. Since my work focuses primarily on the high-vibration stones, I like to create templates that bring together groups of the stones in this book since they are, in my estimation, the most powerful and beneficial materials available. These templates (or others you create yourself) are excellent when held in meditation or when placed on the appropriate chakra or meridian in a healing session. The templates shown are as follows: 1. ASCENSION SEVEN: White Azeztulite base with Petalite, Satyaloka Azeztulite, Danburite, Golden Azeztulite, Satya Mani Quartz, Nirvana Quartz. 2. EARTH MAGIC: Mystic Merlinite base with Fulgurite, Black Tourmaline, Master Shamanite and Nuummite. 3. PHILOSOPHER'S STONE: Rosophia base with Moldavite, White Azeztulite,

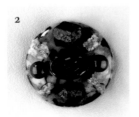

Himalaya Gold Azeztulite, Master Shamanite. 4. HEALING: Sanda Rosa Azeztulite base with Morganite, Seraphinite, Healer's Gold. 5. GREAT CENTRAL SUN: Himalaya Gold Azeztulite base with Libyan Gold Tektite, White Azeztulite, Moldavite, Agni Gold Danburite, Clear Azeztulite. 6. POWER OF THE AZEZ: White Azeztulite base with North Carolina Clear Azeztulite, Pink Azeztulite, Himalaya Gold Azeztlite, Satyaloka Azeztulite, Sanda Rosa Azeztulite, Golden Azeztulite.

CRYSTAL VIAL PENDANTS

Knowing how much I enjoyed combining stones in wands and jewelry, a friend some years ago showed me his invention—a transparent Quartz or glass tube, sealed at each end, filled with harmonious combinations of stones and wrapped in a spiral of gold or silver wire. These Crystal Vials facilitate creation of a wearable combination of almost any stones one could imagine. The spiral wire and the crystalline tube both serve to amplify the currents of the enclosed stones, and the vertical way that the vial hangs around the neck puts the entire array in alignment with one's chakra column. Many of the combinations I use in the Selenite Synergy Wands and Gemstone Templates, as well as the Power Strands described below, are also utilized in Crystal Vial 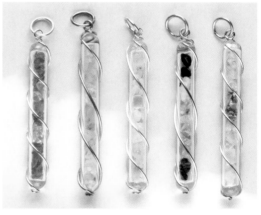 form. The vials shown are, from left to right: TRANSFORMATION, with Moldavite and Herkimer Quartz "Diamonds": ASCENSION, with Petalite, Satyaloka Azeztulite, Danburite; LIGHT BODY, with Satyaloka Azeztulite, Rainbow Moonstone, White Azeztulite; SYNERGY TEN, with Moldavite, Phenacite, Tanzanite, Danburite, White Azeztulite, Petalite, Brookite, Herderite, Tibetan Tektite, Satyaloka Azeztulite; CROWN CHAKRA, with Cryolite, Seraphinite, Petalite, Natrolite, Danburite, Satyaloka Azeztulite.

POWER STRANDS

These necklaces are aptly named because they undoubtedly provide the most powerful dose of high-vibration stones one can wear or carry on one's person. They evolved out of our first such creation, which was a simple strand of raw Moldavite nuggets. (Those in themselves sent many people into some amazing states of consciousness!) Over time we experimented with combinations, just as we did with our wands, templates and jewelry.

Power Strands are exceptional for multiple reasons. First, they are relatively large, giving one a high dose of whatever stones are in them. Second, they are worn around the neck, and we usually make them long enough to encircle the heart chakra. Because the heart is the central point of generation for the multiple levels of one's vibrational fields, bringing synergistic groups of high-powered stones into conjunction with the heart allows them to permeate one's entire field and to thereby generate effects on all levels simultaneously. I consider these necklaces to be initiatory pieces, and wearing them means that one is taking a conscious step on the path

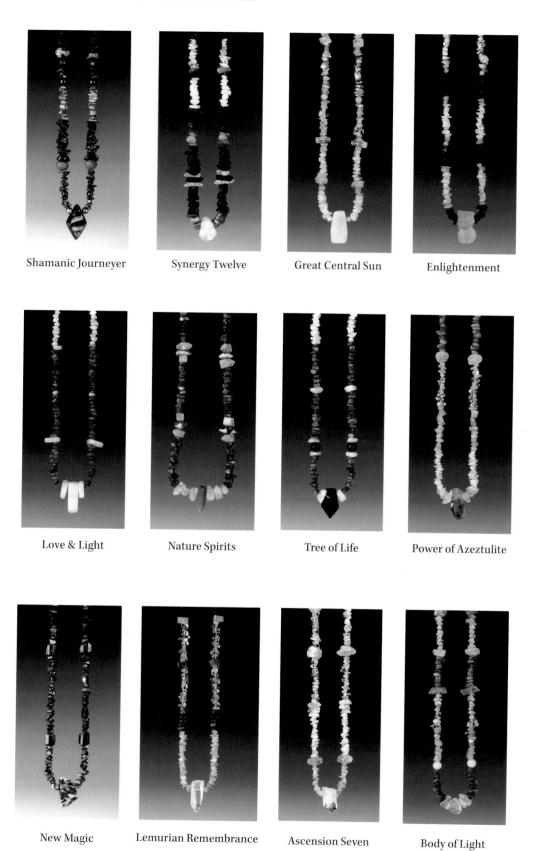

Shamanic Journeyer

Synergy Twelve

Great Central Sun

Enlightenment

Love & Light

Nature Spirits

Tree of Life

Power of Azeztulite

New Magic

Lemurian Remembrance

Ascension Seven

Body of Light

of awakening, healing and vibrational ascension. Like the stones themselves, these strands provide different sets of qualities, and they are designed for different purposes. For information on the stones in each strand, check the Web site www.heavenandearthjewelry.com.

PLATONIC SOLIDS

The Platonic Solids are the only three-dimensional geometric forms that can be made by combining equilateral flat geometric shapes. They were considered by the Pythagoreans of ancient Greece to be the essential building blocks of nature. Three are made from triangles, one from squares and one from pentagons. The Platonic Solids are fundamental to Sacred Geometry, and meditation with them or upon them is said to provide a pathway to understanding the Universal Design. Making Platonic Solids from gemstones is difficult because of the unusual angles for cutting them. However, we have long made a point of being able to make and provide high-quality Platonic Solid gemstone sets—first in Moldavite and later in a variety of gem materials. The pieces pictured here have been cut from clear Azeztulite. They are, from left to right, Octahedron, Icosahedron, Dodecahedron, Cube, Tetrahedron. The sixth form is the Merkaba Star, which is not a Platonic Solid.

STAR TETRAHEDRON (MERKABA)

Another form of importance to those interested in Sacred Geometry is the Star Tetrahedron. Also called the Merkaba, this form combines two interpenetrating tetrahedrons, forming a three-dimensional Star of David pattern. The name "Merkaba" is derived from three words in the Hebrew language: *Mer* = Light, *Ka* = Spirit, *Ba* = Body. Thus the Merkaba is viewed as a geometric representation of the human Light Body, and working with it meditatively is said to be of great help in incarnating the Light. The Merkaba is also used for interdimensional travel. Imagining two counter-rotating tetrahedrons of Light encompassing one's physical form is believed to activate the Merkaba Vehicle of Light for such travel.

Working with a crystalline Merkaba form can be helpful for those wishing to attune to the Merkaba Body of Light, especially if the stone is itself one that vibrates at the highest frequencies. We have made Star Tetrahedrons from Moldavite, Phenacite and Azeztulite, all of which proved to be of exceptional power. The Merkaba in the picture was cut from clear Azeztulite.

MEDITATION PYRAMIDS

One of the classic forms of Sacred Geometry is the pyramid. It was clearly believed by the ancient Egyptians to act as an antenna or amplifier of great power, and in modern times a great deal of research has been done into the potentials of "pyramid power." For the past fifteen years I have worked with pyramids made from copper tubing and filled with stones. As with many of the other tools discussed in this chapter, one can create an infinite number of stone combinations in this sort of device. I have built pyramids filled with combinations of Quartz, Moldavite, Azeztulite, Phenacite, Tanzanite and numerous other stones. Two of my favorite groupings are

the Synergy Twelve and Ascension Seven stones. In the picture above, I am sitting within a pyramid filled with a combination of Rosophia and Azeztulite. This is one of my all-time beloved pairings! The Azeztulite offers the heavenly Light from above, while the Rosophia reaches up with Earthly Love from below. When one sits in this space, the two currents join in one's heart, and they then flow throughout one's whole body, on all levels.

Having a pyramid filled with one's choice of high-vibration stones is like living next to an energy vortex. One can enter at any time, and one's whole body will be infused with powerful and beneficial stone currents. Depending on the choice of stones, a meditation pyramid of this type can be used for clearing and cleansing, opening the heart, traveling interdimensionally, awakening the Light Body or any number of other applications. The pyramid itself can be enhanced by laying out grids around the base, hanging stones above the apex, placing a small "crown" pyramid on top (the one in the picture is Azeztulite) and/or wearing a Power Strand or other talisman.

This chapter has shown a sampling of the tools we have devised and experimented with over the years. The possibilities for this sort of work are endless, and I hope others will be inspired by the pieces presented here to do their own work in this area. The stones seem to enjoy getting together (most of the time), and if you pay attention, you'll know when they don't!

CHAPTER TEN

The Tale of the Azez

"The [Philosopher's] Stone of victory can penetrate and conquer all solid things and every precious stone. . . . In addition, the Stone of victory receives a new name pronounced by the mouth of the Lord."

—JEFFREY RAFF, PhD, *The Wedding of Sophia*

In the entire array of amazing Stones of the New Consciousness (with the possible exception of Rosophia) there is nothing with such a strange and amazing story to tell as Azeztulite. This stone (and now its several varieties) carries some of the highest currents of any stone, and it is alive in a way that is unique in the mineral realm. Its awakening to its current vibrational activity occurred only recently, and that activity is increasing. I was lucky because I had a front-row seat to watch it all unfold.

There is no way to explain Azeztulite without telling a personal story. Azeztulite emerged and came into the world of crystal lovers through a series of inner communications and synchronicities that began in 1991. They concern myself, my wife Kathy Warner and my friend and co-author of *The Book of Stones,* Naisha Ahsian.

Late in 1991, Kathy and I received a telephone call from three women who were working together in channeling. The person doing the primary work was Naisha Ahsian, who later came to work for us at Heaven and Earth and created the *Crystal Ally Cards.* At that time we did not know her well, but when she called she told us that she and the other women had been in communication with a group-soul angelic being. Through this apparent telepathic contact, they had been directed to have a special piece of jewelry made for one of the women. It was to contain five powerful stones—Moldavite, Tanzanite, Danburite, Phenacite and Azeztulite. We were excited about making the piece, but we had to tell Naisha we had never heard of Azeztulite. She answered that the beings communicating with her said that if our company did not yet have the stone, we would soon. Apparently Azeztulite was a stone that already existed on Earth, but it had not yet been "activated" or awakened to its full potential and spiritual purpose. She went on to say that the term "Azeztulite" is a spiritual name, and that the beings themselves were called *Azez.* They told Naisha that this stone would become a very important tool for Lightworkers. Naisha described the new stone we were asked to seek—she had been told that it would be colorless or white and irregularly shaped, not like the prismatic crystals of Quartz and other minerals with which we were familiar.

The tale of Azeztulite is full of synchronicities, and I want to recount some of them so readers will get a feeling for the mystery and numinosity that pervades our eighteen-year saga with these stones.

After speaking with Naisha, we agreed to look for stones that might turn out to be the prophesied Azeztulite. Over the next few weeks I called stone suppliers and browsed rockhound magazines, looking for rocks that might match Naisha's description. My searching seemed to be going nowhere. Every week or so, Naisha called to check in, but I had nothing to report.

During the same week Naisha first contacted us, we were hosting some friends visiting from Arizona. One of them fell in love with a large Phenacite crystal I kept on my desk, but she decided it was too expensive for her to buy. After she returned home at the end of the week, she called us to say that she just couldn't live without the stone and asked if we would sell it to her. I agreed, and after hanging up I went to my office desk to get the stone. However, the Phenacite was missing.

We looked for the stone for days, literally taking our offices apart trying to find it. After a few weeks I gave up searching, though I kept hoping to recover it. At that point I received one of Naisha's calls. I told her that I hadn't found the Azeztulite, but I had lost a big Phenacite. I asked her to try to tune in psychically to help me find the lost Phenacite.

Two days later Naisha called again. She said, "I have interesting news. The Azez have told me that they 'borrowed' your Phenacite, and that they are using it to complete the activation of the new stone, Azeztulite." She went on to say that although the Azeztulite already existed on Earth and had begun its activation, the Azez were still working to maximize the stones' potential. The Azez, she explained, in serving the Nameless Light emanated by the Great Central Sun, travel the universe seeking planets nearing the threshold of spiritual awakening, and they facilitate the awakenings by "energetically engineering" a native stone from each planet to carry the frequencies of the Nameless Light. If inhabitants of the planet utilize the stone with the intention of opening to this inner Light, they will receive its currents and become carriers of the Light, grounding it in their planet and seeding its awakening. Because Azeztulite was to be attuned to frequencies that overlap with the vibrations carried by Phenacite, the Azez had "borrowed" my stone. Naisha told us that at the moment my Phenacite was not in the physical world, but the Azez had promised to return it when they were finished with it. "Look for it in a box, in an odd place," she added.

Even though I was a crystal-loving New Age entrepreneur, that story was pretty wild for me. However, we did look in every box we had, to no avail. Over the next two months we moved our office to a new building, but even all our packing and unpacking did not reveal the missing Phenacite. Nor did the predicted Azeztulite appear.

Then, in the month of May, we received a package from a North Carolina rockhound. It contained about two pounds of odd-looking crystal shards. The note inside explained that the man had seen an ad I placed looking for sources of Phenacite. He had dug up these crystal fragments twenty-five years earlier, believing them to be Phenacite, but he had kept them in his garage for all those years. Suddenly, when he saw my ad, he got the impulse to sell his cache of stones.

I was strongly attracted to the stones, which carried a very high vibration and powerfully stimulated my third eye chakra. I did a specific gravity test, which indicated that the stones were not Phenacite. They did, however, match the specific gravity of Quartz. I considered returning them because the rockhound was asking a high price, far more than the usual cost of Quartz. However, the stones' powerful energies intrigued me, and I decided to call Naisha. When she arrived at our office, she took a moment to touch the stones. She turned to me and said, "This is the Azeztulite. You have to buy it."

From that point, things evolved quickly. We purchased the stones in that first box and made the jewelry piece for Naisha's group. Azeztulite was also immediately popular with our other customers. Over the next ten years, we bought all the Azeztulite the rockhound had discovered back in 1966. I theorized that the stones may not have always had the powerful currents they now carry; they had only recently been activated by the Azez . . . if the Azez were real.

As if in answer to my skeptical musings, another event happened the same week that the first Azeztulite arrived. One morning I reached down below my desk, putting my hand into a wooden message box as I do every day when I check my phone messages (taken for me by an assistant). On this day there was more than paper in the box. My fingers touched something hard. When I pulled out the object, it was a stone—the Phenacite that had disappeared three months earlier!

It was quite an astonishing moment. I use that message box every day, and I was certain the stone had not been there before. It seemed the Azez had kept their word, returning my Phenacite right after the newly awakened Azeztulite arrived. And, of course, the stone was found in a box, in an odd place! My wife pointed out the humorous implication of the particular place where the Phenacite was found: "It was in your *message* box. It's as if they're saying, 'Do you get the message?'"

But the tale is not over yet. Several days later, as I left the office to go home, I noticed a bright, transparent stone on the steps. I picked it up and examined it. It appeared to be an Azeztulite, and it carried the same energies, but it was larger than anything that had been inside our box from the rockhound. I showed the stone to Naisha and asked her what she thought about it. Once again, she consulted the Azez. The next day she called with their answer: "They say to tell you that the stone on the steps was something they left—it's 'interest' for the loan of your Phenacite." This incident opened my mind to another paradigm-shifting implication. At face value, what happened suggests that the Azez are capable of taking a physical stone—my Phenacite—into their realm and returning it. Not only that, the stone found on our steps seemed to indicate that they can also precipitate an Azeztulite *into* this world.

Even after that very tangible confirmation, it took years for me to fully accept what happened. Over the course of that time, hundreds of additional small and large confirmations occurred. But before I go on with the story, I want to backtrack to some of Naisha's original messages from the Azez, which I quote below:

The beings with whom I am communicating are part of a society of interdimensional, extraterrestrial beings, and they have said we may call them the *Azez*. From what I understand, their reason for being centers on anchoring the "Nameless Light" onto planets and into societies coming under the influence of that energy. The word "Azez" seems to mean both "Nameless Light" and the embodiment of that Light in the universe, which is the Great Central Sun. The stone Azeztulite is not only for communication with the Azez, it also holds and channels the energy of the "Nameless Light" and its manifestation from the Great Central Sun. These beings have bases all over the world at energy centers known and unknown to us, including the Andes, the Himalayas, the Adirondacks and other mountain ranges.

I'm not sure if channeling is the correct term for how I communicate with them. It is much more of a direct telepathic link.

Next came a transcript of the words she received from the Azez:

Interdimensional travel involves "pulses" of energy in the universe. These pulses act as bridges. When we travel through many dimensions, the energy pulses cause disruptions—making it difficult for us to communicate with other bases in other dimensions and on other planets. Here enters the stone Azeztulite. It is used by us in creating channels for our communications with other bases. On each base or planet we inhabit we have chosen a stone to be the anchor for these channels.

After some manipulation and alteration, we engineered the stone Azeztulite. It has the capacity to handle the intense energies being carried by it. Until recently, we did not have the technology to engineer a vessel to contain this energy frequency. Azeztulite is that vessel. In our culture, "Azez" is the term for that which is the "Nameless Light," the embodiment of which is the Great Central Sun. Please understand the implications of what we are explaining. This stone is the embodiment of the Azez and carries with it the manifest energy of the Great Central Sun. This is a powerful stone. This stone heralds many changes!

This stone will enable those of you who are telepathic "windows" and dimensional engineers to begin to reclaim the knowledge of these practices from your genetic memory banks. We will now begin to make ourselves known more fully to those beings to aid in this awakening and transformation.

Disease on your planet is the result of certain frequencies of light. You block cellularly these light waves through thought-form shields and contracting emotional patterns. Your cellular consciousnesses are therefore unable to properly learn and expand, resulting in disease. Azeztulite carries energies and frequencies of Light that help release the shields and blocks, healing disease and aiding in cellular rejuvenation and expansion. Likewise, its activation at certain points on your planet will aid in healing the total organism of Gaia.

Since our initial encounter with Azeztulite I have seen thousands of people connect with this stone. At trade shows I have told the story of its discovery many times, yet almost every telling brings me goose bumps of excitement. I have seen people experience such profound contact and recognition that they were in tears. Azeztulite remains the stone that seems to carry the highest spiritual vibrations. It fascinates me to observe that some people feel it as extremely powerful while others notice nothing when they hold it. A number of people have purchased entire necklaces of Azeztulite beads or nuggets, and I have felt each time that the necklaces were talismans of initiation that the owners were meant to use to awaken others as well as themselves.

Since its discovery I have found that, chemically speaking, Azeztulite is a Quartz. This deepens the mystery of these stones, for energetically sensitive people agree almost universally that the vibrations of Azeztulite are nothing like those of ordinary Quartz. Personally, when I handle Azeztulite, I instantly feel an unmistakable tingling sensation in the hands, which can quickly spread over and through the whole body. Regular Quartz doesn't do this!

Some months after her initial contact with us, Naisha offered the following insights:

> Azeztulite speaks to us of alternate realities. As humans, we inhabit a very narrow range of reality. It is as though we walk this Earth with blinders on, never seeing the incredible depth and beauty of all the levels of reality that surround us. Azeztulite was sent as an ally to aid us in connecting with the other realms around us, enabling us to open to the true scope of perception of which we are capable.

> The coming Age of Light is about opening ourselves to these other, more expanded levels of reality. It is about reconnecting with the Source of energy that exists beyond us all and is embodied in the Great Central Sun. Azeztulite carries this energy, and when we resonate with it, it shares this broadened perspective with us. From this connection we will gain a greater wisdom and understanding of the beings that we truly are—beings of Light.

After seeing how accurately Naisha predicted the arrival and the qualities of Azeztulite, I paid close attention over the next eighteen years to the things she had said, comparing them with the experiences I had with Azeztulite as well as the experiences of other people. I also considered Azeztulite in light of references I found in spiritual and alchemical literature to the Philosopher's Stone and the Great Central Sun. In early chapters I mentioned some of these parallels, and there are more in the Azeztulite portions of the Stones section of this book. However, I will also continue here with excerpts from an essay I have written about Azeztulite's similarities to the fabled Philosopher's Stone, the goal of alchemy.

THE PHILOSOPHER'S STONE—
a common substance, found everywhere but unrecognized and unappreciated

Legend tells us that alchemists were continually searching for the Philosopher's Stone, often depicted as a white rock which was outwardly unimpressive but which had the power to convert lead into gold and to convey longevity, enlightenment and even immortality. Mythologists and lore keepers have in more recent times viewed the Philosopher's Stone as a metaphor rather than a real object—symbolic of the wholeness of self, achieved with completion of the Great Work. Some of us who work with stones have looked at this and other legends, such as that of the Stone of the Holy Grail, as possibly resonant with actual stones that are able to mysteriously bridge the apparent chasm between the spiritual and physical realms. It may be true as well that the "chasm" is only a micron wide, and the step across is a shift in perception. Whatever the truth of such speculations, the story of Azeztulite's rise from the utter unknown to its prominence in the world of spiritual seekers is, to me at least, highly provocative and worthy of consideration by those open to some rather astonishing possibilities.

When we consider the Philosopher's Stone—whether one imagines it as a metaphoric object or a real rock—it is worthwhile to think about its function. The Philosopher's Stone provides a bridge between matter and Spirit. No object rooted exclusively in the material world could convey gifts such as enlightenment, longevity or immortality, let alone the transmutation of lead to gold. Such transformations would require supernatural intervention in the natural world. Thus the Philosopher's Stone, like Azeztulite, must be a talisman that links one with the powers and blessing capacities of the Divine realms.

One recurrent phenomenon around Azeztulite is head-to-toe, full-body goose bumps. I have learned to associate these with the invisible presence of the Azez. That is because the sensation inevitably comes when I am behind the showroom counter, speaking to someone about the story of Azeztulite. Somewhere during the story either I, the customer or both of us (in some cases as many as four people at once) get a sudden rushing current of vibration in the body, which brings out the all-over goose bumps. It is as though the Azez are called when we speak of them, or they come because they want to facilitate the connection that is occurring. It has been happening now for eighteen years, almost every time I tell the story, even though I have recounted it hundreds of times. Aside from validating the reality of the Azez, these phenomena indicate that Azeztulite is the sort of talisman one could compare to the legendary Philosopher's Stone. People's experience with it is one of consciously connecting with the spiritual realms—the goose bumps are a very tangible piece of evidence for that.

Let us continue considering Naisha's comments and the parallels of Azeztulite to the fabled Philosopher's Stone. The latter was said to be the catalyst for the transmutation of lead to gold. In alchemical writings, this was often viewed as a metaphor for the transmutation of the self from the crude ego-bound person to the awakened spiritual human. This is precisely the transmutation that Azeztulite is meant and said to facilitate. So, where is the knowledge that allows us to reclaim our capacities of clairvoyance, healing and rejuvenation? According to the Azez, it is in our cells, our *"genetic memory banks."* This resonates with the old alchemical assertions that the "gold" is inherent within the "lead," and that the processes of transmutation will "free" the gold within the lead.

Another correspondence to the alchemical transmutation of lead into gold concerns the human aura. People who are able to see auras will often say that a sick, frightened or depressed person's aura is gray. By contrast, an enlightened, joyful, love-filled person's aura is golden white. By its infusion of the currents of the Nameless Light, Azeztulite can effect just such a color shift in one's auric field—changing the "leaden" gray habit-enslaved person into the "golden" radiant spiritual human being. Spiritual treasure has always been viewed as a kind of "inner gold," and spiritual alchemy's goal has always been the transmutation of the self.

The word "enlightenment," another of the promised gifts of the Philosopher's Stone, means "to be filled with Light," and this is the primary purpose and function of Azeztulite—to bring the Nameless Light—the *saura agni*, the Sun in darkness of the Hindu *rishis*—into full expression in the world through us. This was the ultimate goal of the Mother, and to me it seems the same goal as that prophesied by the Azez.

This brings us to the issue of the world. As Robert Sardello points out, we tend to think of stones too often as the means for ourselves to "get something," when their highest use is undoubtedly to move into partnership with the spiritual realms for the sake of the world. If I myself am healed, enlightened or even made immortal, what good is that if the world remains ill and its people enslaved to fear and death? There is no doubt that our planet needs healing, and I believe our participation in that is crucial. Here again Azeztulite enters the picture. The Azez tell us, *"Its activation at certain points on your planet will aid in healing the total organism of Gaia."*

Even as I write all of this, I am rather awed by the implications. My past experiences with Azeztulite are numerous and convincing enough to prove to my skeptical side that something very real, and of a truly spiritual nature, is going on with Azeztulite. Its parallels with the Philosopher's Stone are striking. And I love the fact that, like the Philosopher's Stone, Azeztulite appears common and unimpressive. It looks like any other chunk of Quartz, but the currents it emanates are extraordinary. As with the virtues of the Philosopher's Stone, not everyone on the planet is yet capable of perceiving Azeztulite's currents; however, feeling them is not a matter of fooling oneself with a fantasy. If that were so, how to explain the incidents in which people who actively disbelieved in the possibility of the spiritual properties of stones were brought to tears at the touch of Azeztulite?

How should we all work with Azeztulite? I think the answer is multifaceted. Simply bringing these stones into our vibrational fields is probably the most important. Then the transmutation of our personal "lead" into spiritual "gold" can begin. The process of cellular reattunement—the repatterning of the liquid crystal structure of our own organism—can proceed, in part, on a subconscious level, simply by our exposing ourselves to the Nameless Light and being open to its influence. Our emerging cellular mind may be able to feel and assimilate Azeztulite's currents more effectively than our usual mental consciousness.

Meditation with Azeztulite can introduce a more active element of choice into the process of growth and evolution. Giving our attentiveness to the currents of Azeztulite speeds and enhances its influence dramatically. Saying an inner "yes," surrendering to the gift being offered, is a way to align our consciousness with the new pattern. As the Azez said, "Disease on your planet is the result of certain frequencies of light. You block cellularly these light waves through thought-form shields and contracting emotional patterns [fear]. Your cellular consciousnesses are therefore unable to properly learn and expand, resulting in disease. Azeztulite carries energies and frequencies of Light that help release the shields and blocks [habits], healing disease and aiding in cellular rejuvenation and expansion."

We can participate in overcoming the old patterns of dis-ease by witnessing and actively releasing our "contracting emotional patterns" (e.g., fear and judgment). We can learn to release fear and its ilk by going to our heart, dwelling there, finding the truth within and living from that truth. The deepest truth of the heart that I know of is that our genuine identity is love. This is, from my perspective, essentially the same love that the Azez call the Nameless Light. Perhaps one might say that the Nameless Light is Divine Love, and human love is our particular resonance with that. Denial of love, succumbing to fear, is the same *"contracting"* the Azez describe. *Cellular rejuvenation* entails overcoming the *habits* of degeneration we have carried for millennia. Habits are usually not conscious—they can exist deep within the unconscious, as deep as the mind of the cells. Azeztulite works directly on this level by bringing its Light into the darkness of our corporeal fear and the habitual destruction of the body that goes with it.

A third means of working with Azeztulite involves "seeding" its energies wherever we go. We can do this by literally giving away pieces of Azeztulite and/or by embodying the loving currents of the Nameless Light and choosing to meet each individual and each moment of life with blessing. Just as fear leads to degeneration, trust can instill the capacity of regeneration. Implicit within trust is the activity of *generosity*. To be generous is to generate something new, out of the generative gesture of trust. This action is the antithesis of fear. We can and must center ourselves in our heart (the body's literal *generator*) and follow the heart's natural impulses to make such gestures. Light is, in a sense, the most generous phenomenon of the universe. Stars radiate their light freely, in resonant likeness with the inner Light of Spirit that has generated all of being. (What more generous and generative act could there be than the Big Bang, in which the Divine Unity gives itself into the void?) To make the Light the center out of which our actions come is to seed the world with Azeztulite's pattern and purpose. I like to give Azeztulite stones away, and to plant them in the Earth, as one of the many possible tangible gestures of generosity, but seeding the intention of the Light is at least as important.

Of one thing I feel certain. We human beings are needed in order for the Nameless Light to manifest here on Earth. I liken the connection to an electrical circuit. The potential blessing energy of the Nameless Light dwells in a realm that is vibrationally "above" the level of most of us, and above where the Earth is vibrating. The Azez carry the current as close to us as possible, offering themselves and the stone Azeztulite as conduits. Now it is up to us humans to make the gesture of opening ourselves in trust to receive and ground that Light. We are like the "wires" through which the current can pass, but as living beings we are also blessed, healed and illumined by it. As more of us do this, more Light can pour in, healing (making whole) and regenerating all of us and the world. As this increases, both we and the stones will carry even higher intensities of this current, and more people, as well as more stones, will catch and carry this pattern of vibration until ultimately the entire world is filled with it. At least, this is what I believe is possible.

The unconsidered point of view that most people who work with crystals have regarding stones and their spiritual properties is that the stones, with whatever properties they may have, are more or less sitting there in or on the ground, broadcasting their qualities, and when we find them and start working with them, we feel their energies, receive their benefits and evolve as a result.

This may be part of how it is, though I suspect that our participation plays a much greater role than we suspect. Certainly the Azeztulite story has always been different. From the fact that it was prophesied before we had it to the goose bumps at the mention of the Azez, it has been clear that we are called to participate in the evolutionary leap of consciousness for which Azeztulite was activated. These stones, as the Azez said through Naisha, carry currents of Light that can help us to awaken, to heal, and to dissolve all our old habits of fear, illness, destruction and death. They carry the spiritual pattern of regeneration, and they hold the longing of the Divine Light to incarnate in us here upon the Earth.

That's pretty big stuff, and it has taken years for me to see it as clearly as I feel I do now. It is rather daring to say all of this so plainly. And all of this is not fate, but destiny. Fate one cannot avoid, but destiny must be chosen in order to be fulfilled. What Azeztulite offers can change us, and change the world, but only if we claim the destiny that is available to us, only if we choose to accept Azeztulite's gift. And, as we have been told, we must offer our gift as well—the gift of ourselves, of our conscious attention and evolutionary intention. If enough of us work with Azeztulite, we make it possible for more Light to be grounded in the Earth, and for more Azeztulite to be awakened.

Naisha's original messages stated that the Azez were stationed etherically in power spots around the Earth, and that over time, more Azeztulite would be activated and then discovered. Think of that! It is different from the old assumption that stones are just sitting around broadcasting the same energies forever. Azeztulite seems unique, an intentional gift from high angelic beings, perhaps from the Light itself. Chemically, it is Quartz, but clearly not all Quartz is Azeztulite. Will that always be so?

Perhaps not! As the Azez predicted so many years ago, more Azeztulite has been found. (We always identify a new form of Azeztulite by testing its energy currents. Their presence is what reveals it as Azeztulite.) After the original Azeztulite from North Carolina surfaced, Vermont Azeztulite was discovered, and then Satyaloka Azeztulite from South India. In the spring of 2008 we came upon a new variety of Azeztulite from North Carolina, which we named Sanda Rosa Azeztulite. This material, in addition to Quartz, contains Spessartite Garnet and Green Mica. I found it to be an excellent stone for my own physical healing.

In the fall of 2008, Pink Azeztulite (Rhodazez) was found in the Rocky Mountains. This was another mixture, containing Quartz and pink Dolomite. It unmistakably carries the Azeztulite currents, but the pink Dolomite attunes it perfectly for the soothing and regenerating of the emotional body.

The winter of 2008 brought forth the first true Azeztulite prismatic crystals, once again from the North Carolina mountains. Because they were mostly citrine colored, and because they evoked the gold-white spiritual Light, we named them Golden Azeztulite.

The energetic wealth of Azeztulite has come to amaze me, as has the rapidity of Azeztulite's recent expansion into new varieties. In the early months of 2009, a friend from India brought yet another new stone, a bright yellow quartz from the lands bordering the Himalaya mountain range. It revealed itself, when we tested it in meditation, to be a newly activated Azeztulite, keyed to the development of creative manifestation and will. We have named it Himalaya Gold Azeztulite.

Why is all of this happening? I believe we are seeing the development of the original agenda of the Azez and the Light they serve. These beings said that they serve the Nameless Light, and that they come as helpers to planets ready to make the next great leap of their spiritual evolution. The most recent communication Naisha shared with me was that the ultimate agenda of the Azez is for *all the Quartz on Earth* to eventually carry the energies of Azeztulite! I have written of this before, but I must repeat it, because the implications are so important. Those who have felt the currents of Azeztulite, and who have felt the response to Azeztulite in their soul and body, can readily imagine what this could mean. If all the Earth's Quartz, which makes up *seventy-three percent of the Earth's crust,* begins to vibrate at the frequencies of Azeztulite, at the intensity of Azeztulite, we will be living on a different kind of planet—a Planet of Light. And we, ourselves, will change simultaneously with the Earth into our true nature—Beings of Light. As I think of this, and as I see the gradual (though actually quite rapid) unfolding of this agenda through the new Azeztulite discoveries, I am awed. It is so big, it is hard to take it in, hard to feel the enormity of it. Yet I am moved, as others have been, to try my best to help it all come true.

So, naturally, I invite everyone who is stirred by this vision to join in and help. How? By working with Azeztulite, opening ourselves to the inner Light of the Central Sun, the seed of which is in our hearts. Let all our fearful habits dissolve, and trust the Light, trust the heart and trust the unknown. I think it is good to meditate and sleep with Azeztulites of all sorts, and to wear it. I like and encourage giving Azeztulite to others and planting pieces of it in the Earth, in the ocean, in rivers and cities and vacant lots and houses—everywhere that the heart suggests. I planted pieces of Azeztulite at Stonehenge in 2007, inviting the giant megaliths to wake up and become like Azeztulite. I like to do this—leaving bits of Azeztulite and the invitation to the "beneficial contagion"—in different places where inspiration dictates. Even if you are not planting stones, I encourage you to invite the Quartz embedded in all the fields, woods and yards you walk upon, in the sidewalks, in the buildings you pass, in the highways, the beaches, the tombstones, the gravel, the layers of Quartz deep under the soil—invite them all to wake up and carry the currents of Azeztulite. This invitation from us is a way of inviting the Nameless Light of the Divine to fully enter the Earth, and to weave its way into our whole being. Because it is based in Love, this Light will never force itself upon us. It, like love, will only enter where it is welcomed.

In 2008 I learned that Azeztulite has a partner—the stone called Rosophia. (See the Rosophia entry in the Stones section of this book.) I like to imagine Azeztulite as the Divine Light from the spiritual realms, reaching down from above. And Rosophia is like the spirit of the Divine Feminine—the Soul of the World, already deep within matter—reaching for union with the heavenly Light. The Light of heaven can meet and marry with the Love of Earth, and our hearts are the place we can offer for them to incarnate. We are their living vessels, if we choose, and when they have joined in our hearts, their joy becomes our own. And if we invite it, this Joy/Love/Light will pour from our hearts and flow to every cell, and our bodies will become bodies of Love and Light.

This is the vision I hold. I invite all who feel a resonance with these stones, or these words, or the energies behind the words, to try some of these activities and meditations. (You may want to start with the Azeztulite meditation at the end of this chapter.) If it is true for you, your heart will know. We create as much as we discover, and we discover as much as we create. We have the opportunity, and the help of the Azez, in bringing about what I have called the Azeztulite Awakening. I hope those who feel the intention behind my words will be moved to join in imagining and creating this awakening.

FOOTPRINTS OF THE AZEZ?

I have long been intrigued by the connection of Azeztulite to the Great Central Sun. As I wrote earlier in this book, the stone Moldavite once took me on an initiatory journey to that spiritual Sun, and that was the day when I first awoke to the currents of the stones.

Early in 2009 I was seeking information online regarding Azeztulite. I wanted to see what other people were saying about it, and whether anyone else was communicating with the Azez, as Naisha had. Late one night I happened upon an obscure website that mentioned the enigmatic word *azozeo.* The text said the word came from the ancient Coptic gnostic gospel, the *Books of Ieou,* and that *azozeo* meant "light passing through a crystal." I was, of course, quite excited to find such a reference from a source not involved with the metaphysical uses of stones, and who had never heard of Azeztulite.

That was all I could find until I came upon the source of the quote, a book by David Fideler entitled *Jesus Christ, Sun of God.* The spelling of the word Sun was of key significance. I ordered the book and discovered in it dozens of mind-bending references to the Great Central Sun and its meaning in various ancient spiritual traditions. As the title of the book implies, Jesus Christ was shown here as a personification of the Logos, as the Son of the Great Central Sun.

Fideler's book contained only one page from the *Books of Ieou*. (Ieou is in this case an alternate spelling of the name Jesus.) The *Books of Ieou* is one of the most unusual and least studied manuscripts of early Christianity. It contains not only text but diagrams relating to Ieou as "the true god." The diagram reproduced in Fideler's text shows concentric squares, text, and a circle divided into six pie-slices around a small central circle. This pattern is remarkably similar to a top view of a Quartz crystal. The text on this diagram page mentions the name Izema Ieou, His Character, and the names of the Three Watchers and the Twelve Emanations.

Fideler tells us that elsewhere in this text, "Jesus reveals to his disciples the magical names, numbers, and seals they will need in the afterlife ascent to the realm of light." He then gives the following example of Jesus' instructions:

> When you reach the fourth aeon, *Samaelo* and *Chochochoucha* will come before you. Seal yourself with this seal:
>> This is its name: *Azozeo*.
>
> Say it once only. Hold this cipher: 4555 in your hands. When you have finished sealing yourself with this seal and you have said its name once only, say these defences also: "Withdraw yourselves *Samaelo* and *Chochochoucha,* you archons of the fourth aeon, because I call upon *Zozeza, Chozozazza, Zazezo.*" When you have finished saying these defenses the archons of the fourth aeon will withdraw to the left. But you [will] proceed upward.

These instructions appear arcane to say the least, but I am struck by the similarity of the names of the angelic protectors to the name Azez. The last one, Zazezo, even contains the word Azez. (If one were to coin a group name for these three—*Zozeza, Chozozazza, Zazezo*—it is plausible that *Azez* would be a reasonable choice.) It is interesting that their role is to assist human souls in the process of spiritual ascension. This is much like what the Azez are attempting to do with us now. It is also important to recall that the instructions are purportedly coming from Ieou, or Jesus, whose mythic role is that of the Son of the Sun, the personification of the Great Central Sun or the Logos.

In Naisha's communications, the beings described themselves as a *group soul angelic being,* whom we could call Azez. It is a small (though rather astonishing) leap to imagine that the Azez, a group of angels who serve the Light of the Great Central Sun, could be identical with the entities whom Jesus, as the personification of the Light of the Great Central Sun, instructs his followers to call upon.

All of the above is speculative, yet I must report that my heart leapt when I came upon this surprising set of parallels. If it should be valid, we can say that the Azez may have long served the Light, and they may have been stewards of human evolution for millennia.

The facts we do know are just as astonishing as these speculations. Here are the Azeztulite stones, which were predicted to arrive, which were activated by spiritual entities whose avowed purpose is to serve the Light, and we can feel in our own bodies the powerful currents entering us through the stones. As promised, more varieties of Azeztulite have been found. We are told that the goal is for all the Quartz on Earth to awaken to these currents. What that would do to change the vibrational reality of this world is beyond our imaginations, but many of us have glimpsed the vision of the Earth as a Planet of Light. If our hearts direct us toward that vision, we can help to make it so.

I first heard the phrase Great Central Sun in the mid 1980s, when my wife Kathy had the intuition that Moldavite emanated from that Sun. She herself had never read or said that before. The second time was when Naisha came to me in 1991 with her story of the Azez. She wrote, "The word 'Azez' seems to mean both Nameless Light and the embodiment of that Light in the universe, which is the Great Central Sun." It was 2009 when I learned that one of the mythological names for the invisible Central Sun, or the "Black Sun," was *Isis*. I was struck immediately by the similarity of the sound of the word *Isis* to *Azez*. Doing a little more research, I discovered Isis' alternate name, *Aset*. This too sounds strikingly like *Azez*! Isis was a black goddess, the original goddess from whom the Black Madonna artworks and spiritual streams have descended. The Black Madonnas, in turn, are images of Sophia. The Azeztulite was said, from the beginning of our encounters with it, to carry the currents of the Great Central Sun, for the purpose of infusing the cells of our bodies with Light—in other words, the realignment of the Liquid Crystal Body Matrix and the awakening of the Light Body. Thus, we could say that the group soul Azez, as servants of the Nameless Light of the Great Central Sun, might also be considered servants of Isis/Sophia. (They had said from the beginning that their name was taken from the Light they served.) Thus the currents of Azeztulite may be intimately related to Sophia/Isis/Aset. Perhaps she has chosen to embody in Azeztulite her Life/Light for the purpose of awakening our Light Bodies, and, by bringing the currents of the Nameless Light into all the Quartz on the planet, awakening the Light Body of the Earth.

AZEZTULITE MEDITATION

A suggested meditation along the lines of this chapter's discussion is to sit quietly with attention placed in the heart space. The space can be imagined as an egg-shaped area about the size of our physical heart, in the center of the chest. One can then place or hold an Azeztulite stone over that area on the chest and gradually imagine that the stone has moved into that heart space. See the image of the stone in the center of the heart. Then allow yourself to envision volumes of Light pouring out of the white stone, at first contained within the heart's egg. When you feel as though the heart space is filled to capacity, dissolve the boundary and allow the Light to pour through the body until it is filled with Light. When you can see this clearly, there may be an accompanying feeling of bliss throughout your awareness.

If you can continue, the next part is very important: From your Light-saturated body, allow the boundary to dissolve until you can imagine the room or space in which you sit filled with the same Light. Then expand beyond that boundary, pouring forth the Light until the Earth is filled and surrounded by a corona of pure Light. (The image in the center of the cover of this book is an attempt to depict this, and it can be used as a meditation aid.) Ultimately, this Light can link and merge with the Light emanating from the Great Central Sun, and the circuit will then be complete. Because this Light emanates from the heart, it is the same as love. Filling the heart, the body and the world with love is the essence of healing, the key to whatever is truly meant by "immortality" and the transmutation of ego-lead into spirit-gold.

As an outer-world practice to adjoin the inner meditation, one is encouraged to center oneself in that place in the center of the heart, and to relate to all others from that place in clear, loving, judgment-free truth. Because Azeztulite has the effect of softening our rigidities and melting our fear-bound structures, it is helpful to wear or carry Azeztulite during one's daily routine.

Having said all this, I want to state clearly that no one necessarily needs Azeztulite. Everything that matters in the meditative exercises and life practices mentioned here can be done on one's own, without any stone. Yet I am astonished by the story of Azeztulite and the aid that is offered through it. To think that one holds in one's hand the very embodiment of the angelic consciousness called Azez, that the stones are the means through which they perceive us, as well as our link to them—these are awesome possibilities. To think that such humble, common-looking stones carry the most profound spiritual gifts makes me smile and agree.

After all, it is like that in us. The heart is a common organ, and rather humble, too. It works unceasingly throughout our lives, never speaking in words or equations, yet carrying the spark of the Divine within. The brain thinks, but the heart knows. The brain analyzes, disassembles and reassembles the patterns found in the past, while the heart feels into the future. The heart trusts, carrying us forward into what can be. This is the essence of Azeztulite, which I view as one of the most profound stones of the heart—carrying the spiritual pattern of human destiny, our highest future.

CHAPTER ELEVEN

Co-Creation & Transfiguration

"Everyone practices magic, whether they realize it or not, for magic is the art of attracting particular influences, events and situations within human life. Magic is a natural phenomenon because the universe is reflexive, responding to human thoughts, aspirations and desires...."

—DAVID FIDELER, *Jesus Christ, Sun of God*

"There may be no such thing as the 'glittering central mechanism of the universe.' Not machinery but magic may be the better description of the treasure that is waiting."

—JOHN A. WHEELER, quantum physicist, Princeton University

In these opening chapters, before entering the world of the sixty-two stones I have chosen as the harbingers of the New Consciousness, we have looked at the stones and our work with them from multiple perspectives. We have seen that crystals and gems have been prized for their spiritual gifts in the history, folklore and myths of many cultures. We've discussed the crystalline nature of our own bodies and our capacity for entering into resonant union with the currents of the stones. We have examined the proposition that the stones are spiritual and/or angelic beings, and that through relating with them from our hearts we can free their highest potentials, and ours, into expression in the world. We've looked at how the vibrational qualities of the stones can help us heal ourselves, and we have seen how we can enter the inner world of the stones in meditation. We have touched upon the notion that our evolution into beings of Light is the destiny to which we are ultimately called, through our work with the stones and in other ways. We have even seen the vision that as we attune ourselves fully to the Light, the Light Body of the Earth can also awaken. Most profoundly, we have glimpsed the intimate, subtle, yet undeniable gestures of the Soul of the World, coming to us through the currents of the stones, as well as through the synchronicities, beauty and wisdom of the world.

Where are we going now? If we take seriously all that has been written here about the magic of the stones, and all that we have experienced in our lives, what shall we do with it, and how can we be of service in the world?

If I have convinced you of anything, O Reader, I hope it is that the stones and the world are spiritually alive, and that we live in constant relationship with the Soul of the World, whom we can call by the ancient name Sophia. My encounters with her—in the realm of dreams, in the waking world of synchronous moments and with the healing, loving, consciousness-expanding currents of the stones—have shown me that her intelligence is vast, that her presence is all-pervasive and that her heart is all-loving. Think of it. What we call synchronicities—those astonishing moments of meaning that seem to arise *just for us*, with connections that only we could notice or appreciate—imply a mind that is aware of *each person and event individually*. Not only that, for a synchronicity to work the intelligence out of which it arises must extend through time, as if that intelligence were a choreographer of perfection, so that the perfect meaningful "coincidence" occurs at the precise moment when it fits with the flow of events in a person's life. And then, we must recognize that this is going on constantly, circulating through the lives of billions of people, and that there are doubtless many more synchronicities than we ever notice. It is no wonder that the name Sophia is synonymous with Wisdom.

If you are looking for a synchronicity with the stones, try holding a thought (preferably in image form) about some aspect of your spiritual aspiration, or some wound you want to heal, or anything else your heart genuinely desires. Then thumb through the Stones portion of this book (or *The Book of Stones*), opening a page a random. Quite a number of people have told me that in doing this, they always find something that responds to the very core of their question. Certainly when we work with oracles like the I Ching or Tarot, we see that the randomness of our card shuffling or coin tossing is not random at all. Our release of control allows "chance," which is actually Sophia's wisdom, to enter and bring unforeseen meaning into the moment for us. All oracles based on any sort of "randomness" work in this way. If the universe were not permeated with the invisible living Wisdom of the Soul of the World, there would be no working oracles and no synchronicities. Because Sophia does not walk up and *talk* to us, we have to learn to notice and interpret her gestures, and it is in this coming-to-meet her that our own creative imagination has its role.

From her gestures, we can surmise that Sophia's essential gesture is always love. The harmony of the world seems designed to instruct us, to offer us opportunities to glimpse the loving hand that life extends to us in each moment. The minerals and gemstones always seem to do this. Virtually every stone I have encountered in twenty-five years of work emanates vibrations that feel beneficial to the body, supportive to the emotions, expansive to consciousness and/or grounding and protective to my whole being. Although I am careful around radioactive or toxic minerals, I feel strongly that the currents of the stones provide powerful evidence that we live in a loving world that wishes us well.

All of this makes me wonder: does the world need anything from us? At our current level of awareness, we humans tend to look at the world in terms of *our* needs and desires. We feel separate from the world rather than united with it, and out of that consciousness of separation we tend to act from fear and greed.

Imagine a couple living together. The woman in this imaginary scenario knows that she is living with her beloved but, in our tale, she cannot speak. The man in our story is blind and has amnesia. He does not understand where he is or who he is living with, or even that someone else is there, and he tends to be suspicious, and his handicaps make him fearful and greedy. She provides food, flowers, a comfortable environment, and she performs many little acts of love. He finds the food and other things but does not realize where they have come from or who has provided them. He cannot see her, and he only occasionally suspects that *someone* may be behind the good things that happen to him. Still, in his fear, he does not trust the situation, so he grabs and hoards food and whatever else he thinks he needs. All she can do is keep making her gestures in hopes that he will eventually notice her and realize her love.

This is a little like the way I imagine our situation in regard to Sophia. We need to learn to see with new eyes in order to recognize how much love surrounds us. We need to trust first, because it is trust that opens our eyes. We need to open our hearts toward her before we *can* know that she is present, and has always had her heart open to us.

All of this makes me want to offer a little story of something that happened one morning in the fall of 2006. Some months after reading Robert Sardello's book, *Love and the Soul,* my wife Kathy and I enrolled in one of the courses offered by the School of Spiritual Psychology, which Sardello and his wife Cheryl operate together. Following the introductory weekend, the morning after we returned home to Vermont I took a walk along a nearby country road. I felt inwardly softened, expanded by the first session, and I was also holding a notion I had felt since childhood, which had resurfaced on the trip home. I had always felt a concern that the world was in peril, and a longing to somehow "save" it. Though experience and cultural indoctrination had forced me to table such a grandiose idea, deep down I had never forgotten it. As I walked, I decided I would try out some of this heart attentiveness and interiorizing of the world. And I held the question: if I could save something of the world, what would I choose? What I did next was simple enough. As I walked, my attention was caught by various creatures and things— chickens in a yard, geese honking overhead, an apple tree, a collapsed barn. As I noticed each one, I said to myself, "I'd save these chickens. . . ." Or those geese, or this tree, or that barn. I placed each of them imaginally within the area of my heart. All of those little gestures of imagination felt good, good in my heart, as if a bit of the world was now inside me. Near the end of my walk I thought, "I can put anything I want in here; why not the whole world?" So I did that. There was plenty of room, and I felt my love for the world as a warmth in my chest, very intimate.

In the next moment I was astonished by what happened. Inexplicably, but without a shred of doubt, I felt the world loving me back! It was as if She was acknowledging with gratitude my own little turning toward her. In that moment I knew within myself what Sardello had been saying—the Soul of the World is a feminine being, she is both inside and outside us, and her way is the way of wisdom transformed in love. Her soul cannot be separated from ours. She is wisdom and love, and she is always in danger, and she will not defend herself.

I have been learning that when I take the world into my heart, the heart expands to fill the whole world. It isn't exactly *my* heart—it is *heart itself* that encompasses everything when I initiate the process by taking each thing I notice into my heart. It becomes as though the sweetness of the heart fills all of the space around me. I believe that when this comes about, it means that my heart is overlapping with the heart of Sophia. The little gesture of my loving intention encounters the vast love that was always there, and their meeting does something that seems to transform the world. It is the same world, full of all the same things to see, taste, hear, smell and touch, but the feeling within which I do all of this is one of blessedness. In this state the flow of synchronicity is almost constant, and every encounter reinforces the atmosphere of love. It is not that the world changes. It is that meeting the world in this way allows us to truly experience it for the first time. The world loves us and responds to whatever we ask, but our asking must be done in feeling and gesture rather than words. We are met not with words but with inner and outer event—with gestures that match up with those we make. This is a taste of what co-creating is.

The above is my effort to describe more fully what I mean by the New Consciousness and the Activity of Blessing. The love gesture of appreciation and praise, taking the world into our hearts—all at once or piece by piece—is our blessing gesture. The joy we experience—the wonder of feeling ourselves and the world together within heart-space—is our spontaneous response upon recognizing the world's loving attention to us. Think of the amazement: the world is *really* alive, it is conscious of us and loves us! And we can feel it.

In this last chapter before the Stones section, I want to mention again how I now engage each stone before working with it. I begin by sitting quietly in a comfortable chair and doing the Heart Alignment meditation for a minute or two (see Chapter Six). Then I pick up the stone and blow my breath across it, offering myself into relationship. I say, inwardly or outwardly, "I offer you my love and I welcome you into my heart." Other words can be used—it is the welcoming intention that matters. Then I hold the stone against my chest, allowing myself to sense it, imagining the stone's image entering my heart and surrounding the image of the stone with love. It is important to really *feel* all of this. Doing this sets the blessing activity in motion from my side, and it allows me to meet the currents of blessing that are always coming from Sophia through the stones. It is fascinating to consider their identity—each stone species is a being, and at the same time they are all the gestures of Sophia, the "words" of a Sophianic language of love and wisdom.

Remember that at the beginning of this book I quoted Rudolf Steiner, who called the stones the "sense organs of angels" and the embodiments of the gods. I suggested that, through their crystalline structure, stones are able to be the faithful messengers of the Divine "words" (the patterns of vibration that we feel and intuit as the qualities of the stones). This gives us another lens through which we can view the stones. As angels they have different characteristics from one another, yet none of them are separate from the Divine. As messengers they carry the pure expressions of the Divine Word. This is another way of understanding their qualities as the words of a Sophianic language.

This is why I now attune to the stones through the inner gesture of love and invitation. I am attempting through this to meet their emanations by "emanating" something that is in harmony *with them*. Here is something I think is of great importance. We have a tendency to think of stones and their energies in terms of *what they will do for us*. This greatly limits what is possible, because like the man in our fantasy example above, we are seeing things through the lens of what we think we want or need, rather than through the intention of *what we can create*. Even if the stones could and would give us what we want (which it seems they do at times, though not in the ways we expect), this is much less significant than the possibility of co-creation with them. (Would one rather win a lottery or learn how to co-create abundance on a level much deeper than money?)

Let's try an example of what this co-creating might be like. In the old consciousness, if one decides to work with a stone that carries the qualities of physical healing, one might wear the stone and wait for it to heal one's illness. In the New Consciousness, one would wear or carry the stone while continually *holding the intention of healing*, bringing the intention of healing into every encounter and every perception. Instead of focusing only on oneself, one takes the healing intention *into the world,* with the help of the stone. One becomes a sort of walking intention for the presence of healing. When we align with this inner gesture, we harmonize with the qualities of the stone, and our world becomes an environment of healing.

As another example, if we work with a stone that vibrates with frequencies of expanded consciousness, we can bring the intention for greater awareness into all our encounters—offering it, looking for signs of it, encouraging it everywhere. In all such cases, we do not *receive* the benefit from the stone; we allow the stone's patterns to align with us in *creating* the benefit. And, of course, we experience what we create, so the benefit is ours, though it comes to us through our *offering it into the world*. When we do this, we are truly aligning ourselves with the stones and with Sophia, because their way of being is one of continually offering themselves and their qualities into the world. This sort of activity is the very essence of generosity, and we may recall that to *generate* anything we must be generous.

This is closely akin to the story I have related above about the Activity of Blessing, in which one lives out of the intention of bringing each perceived object or activity into one's heart, into love. This has the astonishing effect of turning the world inside-out and outside-in, so that one experiences the entire world as *within heart awareness,* within loving relationship with the World Soul. If we hearken back to the tale of the blind man and the mute woman, we can imagine that, if he were to begin trusting his world and acting from love, he would soon be permanently in the arms of his beloved, and in a different world than the one he had created out of fear.

The idea of reversing one's attitude in the ways I am suggesting sounds difficult, and it can be. We run immediately into the wall of our habits, which may turn out to be the only wall there is. There are thousands of habits that make up our ways of seeing the world and acting in it, and we rarely think about them. That is the problem. Habits just happen, while living in a mode of continual conscious co-creating requires awareness and intention *in every moment*. We can figuratively live in an "asleep" state when habits run the show, while co-creation requires us to be awake all the time. We all know that we can't create anything new without paying attention to what we are doing. We are not going to bring the qualities of Divine Love into the world by wearing a Morganite and forgetting about it.

The New Consciousness is exactly this: being awake, centered in the heart, acting in every moment from a place of love and generosity that blesses the world, and that encourages in the world everything one might wish for oneself. This is in alignment with Sophia and the angelic nature of the stones. It might be an impossible task, except for one electrifying truth. *Each moment we spend in the New Consciousness is filled with joy!* No thing we might acquire can bring us joy, but co-creating in a state of love is joy itself. Once we experience this, we have a new compass by which to guide our choices.

Our new compass is, of course, located in our hearts. The heart knows only truth, and its impulses to action are always for the well-being of the whole. When we experience joy, we are in our hearts. The heart's mode is generosity, which is how it generates our life. Rudolf Steiner even said that the entire world is generated by the heart. That is a hard concept to imagine, except when I recall how heart awareness can permeate the world, given a little encouragement from us.

So in place of habits, in the New Consciousness we have the commitment of our conscious intention. When we are acting out of that, our choices are weighed on the heart's scale, and we always know what to do. We will always act from love and generosity, unless we go to sleep or fall into fear (the same thing, really). Things do not move in a straight line, of course. It takes time and practice to replace old habits with a new, conscious way of being. But it is all right. The world doesn't collapse when we fall asleep—we just lose our joy. When we wake up and again offer ourselves into our new way of being, we find that our joy is there waiting for us.

Here is where the stones can help. They offer an abundance of positive, helpful qualities, and they never forget or fall asleep. Indeed, the more we work with them, the more powerful they seem to become. (It may be that *we* are becoming more powerful, though I suspect it is mutual.) Every meditation we do with them brings us more into alignment with their beneficial vibrations. Wearing a stone while holding the intention to encourage its qualities in the world fills us with those qualities. Giving someone a stone mirrors its very gesture of generosity, and this too implants within us its way of being. When we commit ourselves to *embody the qualities of the stone* with which we are working, we become much more powerful (in the most wholesome way) than we would if we were seeking to "get" those qualities from outside ourselves. We embody the stone's properties by *acting from them,* in both inner perception and outer gesture. It is a self-reinforcing activity. We begin it with our intention, which the stone supports, which makes the intention more full and powerful, and so on, in an ever increasing co-creating activity that brings the qualities we have chosen into the world as well as ourselves.

My aim in describing what I believe to be the properties of the stones in the coming pages is to offer a kind of map of the qualities we have to work with, and to allow the reader to get a feel for the stones that most powerfully attract each person to his or her highest destiny. There are hundreds of types of minerals in the world, and all of them offer different gifts. The ones in this book were chosen because I felt them to be the ones most resonant with the unfolding of the New Consciousness in ourselves and in the world. We are called to give up the illusory security our fears try to build for us, and to enter a world in which our foundation is built from our trust in the unknown. I don't know what events will occur in that world, but I do know one thing that will happen—joy.

If you have seen someone's face when they are in fear, and if at another time you have beheld the same face in a state of joy, you have seen transfiguration. It is the transfiguration for which every heart lives in longing, and it can change much more than our faces. Nothing will do it for us, but there are many beings ready to do it *with* us. The stones are unique among these beings because they are embodied, right here in the world with us. They are most amazing angels because they have sacrificed everything (even the ability to move) in order to make themselves and their qualities available for partnership with us. They are lying around—on the ground, in caves, in shops—waiting for us to turn toward them with our eyes and hearts open. Behind those beings, permeating our world, is Sophia. She is the Beloved whom we do not see, yet she is everywhere. Every gesture we make to her is met, although we need to trust in that *before* we see it, even if we never see it in the way we expected. That is how our mutual blessing and creating with her can begin.

You may remember that I began this book with a quote from the poet Novalis: "Every beloved object is the center of a Paradise." By now I hope that idea is alive within you, and that you are beginning to try it out. It is great fun, and very much a generator of joy, to begin extending one's love to the objects of the world—indiscriminately, to as many as possible, with no evaluation of "worth" or judgment involved. It is easy to do this with the stones, because many of them are beautiful and all of them offer themselves to us. The world is the same way, and so are we, when we choose. When every object is beloved, all the world is Paradise.

If I don't fall asleep, I'll meet you there.

SIXTY-TWO STONES OF THE NEW CONSCIOUSNESS

INTRODUCTORY NOTE

For this book I selected the sixty-two stones that seemed to me most aligned with the emerging New Consciousness. Because the premise of this book is that the stones are the physical aspects of spiritual beings, and because the New Consciousness is one of relationship and co-creation, I felt the need to revisit the stones in a way that went deeper and attempted to give them a fresh look. I wanted readers to be able to join me in meeting the beings behind the stones, and I hoped to inspire them to re-imagine what is going on between us and our rock collections.

I worked meditatively with each of the sixty-two stones, attempting to find my way into *their* interior worlds and to establish relationship with them. This provided me with many fascinating journeys and a number of surprising and powerful moments of illumination. The sections of the individual stone essays marked "New Attunement" were dictated into a tape recorder during these meditations, and they display a variety of perspectives. Sometimes the information came in discursive form, almost like a newspaper report. At other times my awareness was filled with images that I reported and attempted to interpret. Some meditations flooded me with so much inner Light and feeling that it was difficult to speak. On several occasions the stones took me on amazing shamanic journeys, which I simply described. At the end of each meditation I attempted to allow the stone its own voice. These "quotations" are at the end of each section.

Looking at these meditative essays, I was happy with having been able to take the role of investigative reporter, and deeply moved by the experiences engendered by opening to the stones in new ways. I also felt that readers deserved to see information about the stones that was more in the tone of my previous writings and the writings of others. My solution was to add the "Background" section of each stone entry, which combines excerpts from my *Book of Stones* essays and other articles. I think it is useful to read and compare the Backgrounds and the New Attunements, in order to get as complete a picture as possible and to notice the differences between the two approaches. In some cases, these are subtle, but in others they are not subtle at all!

Reading this can be interesting and fun. Writing it certainly was. However, *doing* it is far more important than either. I reiterate to the reader what I have told myself many times: This stuff is *real,* and it can matter immensely in one's own life. The stones extend to us their offers of relationship and co-evolution from the spiritual worlds. If we offer ourselves in kind, amazing things can happen, which have the potential to change us and our world more profoundly than we can know. Spirit and matter have long been split in the consciousness of humanity. The stones offer themselves as bridges between the worlds. Reading about the country on the other side of a bridge can be interesting, but there is no substitute for walking across and experiencing it for yourself. Let's go.

AEGIRINE

KEY WORDS Clearing, protection, cleansing, confidence, dispelling negative attachments

ELEMENTS Earth, Fire

CHAKRAS All

Aegirine (also known as Acmite) is a sodium iron silicate mineral with a hardness of 6. Its crystal system is monoclinic and it forms in columnar, prismatic crystals, which are sometimes striated with pointed terminations. It is dark in color, often black, greenish black or brownish black. It occurs most commonly in alkali-rich volcanic rocks. It is found in Greenland, Russia, Canada, South Africa and the United States.

BACKGROUND Aegirine is excellent for removing negative or stuck energies from all levels of the subtle bodies. It provides a high degree of spiritual protection from negative energies or entities. There are few stones as effective as Aegirine for breaking the attachment of negative entities to one's etheric body. Such attachments are not normal for energetically healthy and balanced individuals, but anyone can become vulnerable in moments of strong fear or anger. Working with Aegirine in body layouts or in conjunction with other subtle energy healing modalities can, in time, regenerate the damaged protective auric shield.

NEW ATTUNEMENT When I first sat to meditate with Aegirine, holding a black crystal over my heart, it was only moments until I felt, in the space between the stone and my heart, a kind of sparking discomfort. It was not a pain but more of a sense of something within my heart brought out into the space between the stone and my heart, and there, in some way, being burned, consumed. This signifies Aegirine's purpose of cleansing and healing all sorts of knots of disharmony throughout the physical, etheric and astral levels of the human being.

Aegirine presents itself as a stone deeply dedicated to service in healing and purification. It has offered itself in a sacrificial act of willingness to go deep and cleanse all of the worst and most difficult places within us. While many stones resonate best in the heart and upper chakras, Aegirine is willing to enter into the lowest chakras. When I held the Aegirine near my base chakra, I felt a steady pull toward the crystal of every sort of impurity in the places within my energy bodies that corresponded to physical disharmonies in the corporeal body. This stone carries a vibrational charge that is so deeply opposite the negative charges of our disharmonies that they are drawn to Aegirine as inexorably as to a magnet. One can imagine this by visualiz-

ing the way something charged with static electricity can pick up bits of paper that will cling to it. In a similar gesture, Aegirine attracts everything in us that is impure. This is indeed a great service to the evolutionary potential of the human being, for in our daily lives in the world there are innumerable possibilities for attaching or being attached to by negative complexes. We are not consciously aware, in most cases, of these attachments, Aegirine, in relationship with us, if we invite it to enter our field and share its pattern of identity, will cleanse us energetically, perhaps more deeply than we have ever been cleansed. Aegirine is unafraid of what we may find repugnant and what we therefore may not wish to regard in ourselves. Aegirine is like the diligent worker who does what is needed whether it is agreeable or disagreeable. In the short minutes between beginning to meditate with Aegirine and reaching this point in my narrative, I found that a digestive upset I was experiencing dissipated under its influence.

When placed at the third eye, Aegirine again seemed to magnetically draw something out. My intuitive sense is that it once again pulled the patterns of

discord, or what might be called psychic pollution, out of the head. This also occurred when the stone was placed against the throat, and again I felt the sense of little sparks, with heat pulled out of the spot where the stone was placed.

Aegirine has a resonance with the being sometimes known as the Black Madonna, and with a being known as Kali. It is a stone of the Dark Mother energy and a resonant ally of the stone Master Shamanite. Both of these stones work from and within the Underworld or the un-conscious realms for the evolutionary benefit and healing of the human being.

Aegirine is a strong ally and willing helper, offering service by taking upon itself the impurities and disharmonies we carry. Because of its affinity for the darkness coupled with its dedication to healing, this stone, as deeply as any other, serves the Light—for the well-being of us all.

AEGIRINE SPEAKS "I am a stone of the nourishing darkness. I am a being that dwells in the dark places where many things are exiled. I do not seek light, although I am a friend of light. In the dark place, the realm of silence, I redeem and heal the negative entanglements that I draw out of you."

AGNI GOLD DANBURITE™

KEY WORDS   Clarity, truth, joy, clairvoyance, attunement to higher spiritual realms, alignment with the Great Central Sun

ELEMENT   Storm

CHAKRAS   Solar Plexus (3rd), Heart (4th), Third Eye (6th) Crown (7th)

In 2006, a new Danburite deposit was discovered in southern Africa. This material differs from the clear or white Danburite found in Mexico, the dove-gray crystals from Peru and the champagne-colored Russian Danburites. This African variety is unusual both in its irregular massive form and in its color, which is a brilliant golden yellow. Danburite is a calcium borosilicate crystal with a hardness of 7 to 7.5. Its crystal system is orthorhombic. The name Agni Gold Danburite is derived from its color and the intensity of the fiery *(agni)* currents it is said to emanate.

BACKGROUND   Agni is the Sanskrit word for "fire," and this stone carries the stream of the inner holy fire of the Great Central Sun. Working with this stone can aid one in discovering one's link to Source and can facilitate the process of clarifying and purifying consciousness so that one speaks and acts from the place of truth. The currents of Agni Gold Danburite resonate with the third chakra, seat of the will, and the third eye, window of inner vision. There is a stream of joy carried by Agni Gold Danburite. Simply gazing at the stones or holding them can initiate a sense of enthusiastic well-being.

Agni Gold Danburites are resonant with the angelic beings who attend the Great Central Sun in an unending procession of joyful celebration. What is being celebrated there is the presence of the Divine within the Universe. In us, this may mean that the stones stimulate our senses of joy and gratitude in relation to life itself.

Agni Gold Danburite can ignite the inner fire of purpose, and the joyful participation in the fulfillment of one's destiny. Moldavite and Nirvana Quartz can magnify these effects. The

angelic connection of Agni Gold Danburite can be enhanced by combining it with Petalite, Azeztulite or White Danburite. Its stimulation of the mind centers is deepened when it is used along with Herderite. For healing, especially of the third chakra and heart, Seraphinite is its best ally.

NEW ATTUNEMENT   In meditating with Agni Gold Danburite I sat first with the stone in a pouch over my heart and one stone in each hand. I found, moments after sitting down with the stones, that the currents from them went to the third-eye area in the center of my forehead just above the eyes. The currents seemed not to pulse, as other stones often do, but rather to be selectively stimulating small areas of my third eye chakra and perhaps the brain as well, in the area between the eyebrows about one-half inch above my eyes.

My intuition as this occurred was that the Agni Gold Danburite's currents were stimulating points involved in the capacity to generate images in the mind that display the invisible currents and beings of the Other World. By "Other World" I simply mean the vibrational realms that are imperceptible to us in everyday consciousness. The Agni Gold Danburite continued the stimulation of the third-eye area for some time, and it was interesting to notice that the currents moved in very small and symmetrically precise ways on both sides of the center of the third-eye area, and these movements were felt as a progression of activation (in the initial stages only).

My felt sense is that Agni Gold Danburite has the capacity, when we open to it, to awaken clairvoyance, in which one's intuition is made more acute and is displayed visually to the inner observer. This allows the spiritual domains and beings to present their communication with us as images. The spiritual worlds do speak often in images rather than words because images have multiple associations and do not train themselves to a linear progression the way our language does. Thus we may see images which are at first hard for us to understand but which actually convey more accurate representations of what is being communicated than could be carried by words. This type of seeing has long been an aspect of my intuitive work with the stones, and stone properties often present themselves as images.

I then held a piece of Agni Gold Danburite up in front of my eyes and opened them, gazing upon it with diffused vision in order to allow the formation of an after-image, or subtle image, displaying the stones' message and purpose. I was surprised when the image of the stone was overlaid with an image of a face. As I gazed upon the face, it appeared to move as if speaking. Although I could hear nothing inwardly, it seemed clear that the stone was presenting me with an image representing its nature, and the moving lips indicated that it was offering communication. Then the face on the stone changed, and I was able to see and recognize, to my astonishment, the face that is also impressed upon the ancient relic known as the Shroud of Turin (reputed to be the burial cloth of Jesus and said to have been supernaturally impressed with his image). My knowledge of this relic was limited, so I simply recognized the face and saw its striking resemblance to the Shroud image. All of this was portrayed upon the surface of Agni Gold Danburite.

The felt sense was that the Christ image is related to Agni Gold Danburite's resonance with the currents of the Great Central Sun. The Great Central Sun is the spiritual sun, or center of the universe, which is holographically present in the center of every planet, every star, every heart and even every atom. It is what the Vedic *rishis* of ancient India called the *saura agni* or the Solar Flame—the Solar Fire. In Christian mysticism, Christ was referred to as the Sun behind the Sun. Therefore, Christ is the same entity as the Great Central Sun or the *saura agni* of the *rishis,* for *saura agni* also was not a physical fire but the spiritual fire underlying all matter.

Agni Gold Danburite invites us into awareness and even embodiment of the underlying fire of pure golden-white light that some mystics view as the spiritual core of all being. Other stones such as Azeztulite, Moldavite and Rosophia also have relationships, linkages or currents resonant with the Great Central Sun. Agni Gold Danburite is a very pure stone expression of the Central Sun energies.

In meditation I found that I was able to attune through the heart to Agni Gold Danburite, and to travel inwardly on a visionary journey to the Great Central Sun. I had gone to this place many years ago with Moldavite and I recognized it as the same. The Central Sun to which I was taken in my heart meditation with Agni Gold Danburite appeared as a golden sphere of light and warmth out of which, in a single flat plane at its equator, emanated a myriad of golden threads of light, which flowed away from it in a spiral pattern. Each thread connected with the heart of one of the innumerable beings that circled the Central Sun, in a kind of joyful, praising procession that goes on eternally.

If I correctly understood the face of Christ as I was given it in my visual meditation, I would conclude that it expresses this stone's connection to the spiritual heart of All-That-Is, and its offer of reaching into our heart and bringing us there. Over a period of some minutes meditating with the Agni Gold Danburite upon the heart chakra, the resonance in my heart became stronger and stronger and could be felt as a kind of ache. There was even a longing tension of the heart toward the spiritual Sun. Or this aching tension may have been the spiritual Sun's thread of longing toward my own soul, as it longs for conscious union with all beings.

My entire etheric body began to vibrate at a greater and greater rate and intensity as the meditation continued. The crown chakra became stimulated and thousands of tiny needle-like (although not uncomfortable) tingles covered the entire top of my head. The third eye continued its pulsations and the heart its intense longing toward the Light.

Agni Gold Danburite's message is that we are on a path into the Light, into an evolutionary leap, from all that we have known and believed ourselves to be now becoming beings of Light—seeing at all times in our own heart the Great Central Sun, and recognizing that each of us also is a Sun and that the Earth is a Sun in potential. When we unite with the Earth, the light of our heart joins with the light of the Earth's spiritual core in conscious, joyful, loving surrender. Through this, we can facilitate the process of the awakening of the Earth as a spiritual sun.

Agni Gold Danburite is clearly a stone of Light Body activation. It belongs in the same category of such high-frequency crystals as white or clear Danburite, which is an angelic-realm stone. Agni Gold Danburite resonates with the entire family of Azeztulites, the visionary stone Phenacite, and the other Light Body stones such as Natrolite, Herderite, Scolocite, Nirvana Quartz and others. Moldavite is highly capable of intensifying the heart connection of the currents that pour through Agni Gold Danburite.

AGNI GOLD DANBURITE SPEAKS   "I am a Light Seed being. I reach my golden hand into you and plant a grain of Light. If you nourish my seed with your attention, it will grow and fill your being with the Light of the New World that is coming to be. Those who reach toward me with an open heart will find within me an ally for all you may wish to create. The current of creating is the current of love and liberated intention. Allow yourself to follow your heart's desire with all your will and with a surrender in every moment. Thus you reach the threshold of the consciousness wherein all creating lies."

AJOITE (AJO BLUE QUARTZ)

KEY WORDS   Love, healing, emotional support, moving
through sorrow and grief, goddess and angelic connections
ELEMENT   Storm
CHAKRAS   Heart (4th), Throat (5th), Third Eye (6th), Crown (7th),
Etheric (above the head)

Ajoite is a blue or blue-green copper silicate mineral. It is named after Ajo, Arizona, where it was first identified. It is a rare mineral, most frequently seen as an inclusion in Quartz. The most beautiful and plentiful Ajoite specimens in Quartz crystal points came from the Messina Copper Mine in South Africa. In addition to Ajoite, some of these crystals contain Hematite, Limonite and/or Papagoite. Another small discovery of Ajoite in agatized Quartz was made in Zimbabwe. This is sometimes called Ajo Blue Quartz. As of this writing, both of these finds are exhausted, and the only Ajoite in the marketplace comes from old stocks from the two African discoveries.

BACKGROUND   Ajoite in Quartz is a pure bearer of the vibrations of the Earth Mother, the aspect of Sophia or the Divine Fem-inine expressed through the living world. Ajoite can cleanse the heart of sorrow, wash negativity out of one's thoughts, and open the floodgates for the ocean of love to lift one to the higher planes. It clears and activates the throat chakra, assisting in communicating one's deepest inner truth. It helps one connect with the Goddess energies, both within oneself and throughout the natural world. Ajoites can clear the auric field and align the Light Body with the physical. They can harmonize the energies of any chakra, disperse contracted thought forms that are creating pain, dispel any amount of negativity and call forth the truth from oneself and others.

Ajoite is a strengthener, healer and harmonizer of the emotional body. Meditation with Ajoite can bring both tears and laughter, as feelings arise in what is often a deep yet gentle release of inner tensions. Ajoites not only help us to release our old grief and pain; they facilitate strength and confidence, a clear-minded sense of our own goodness and our ability to move forward on the spiritual path. Ajoite inspires us to bring more beauty into the world. It can help awaken the emotions of compassion and forgiveness. These emotions are key in the healing of the many conflicts that exist on all levels of human life.

NEW ATTUNEMENT   As I began working with Ajoite in meditation, I first experienced the greeting of the stone. By greeting, I mean a physical encounter with its particular vibrational pattern. I felt this in my heart, in my third eye and in the crown chakra, as well as the chakra point in the back of the head known as the "Mouth of God." I expected to feel Ajoite strongly in the throat chakra, yet in this initial session it was apparently important for the currents of the stone to stimulate other centers. As I began speaking about the Ajoite into the tape recorder, I became aware that my throat chakra had become vibrationally active. My sense is that before speaking about Ajoite, it was necessary for me to see and feel Ajoite within me. Therefore the heart chakra and the mind centers needed to be activated first.

I held the Ajoite crystal to which I was attuning in front of my eyes and looked at it with diffuse vision for some minutes in order to make an inner connection with the crystal. I then closed my eyes and looked for the after-image of the stone, which is a kind of psychic impression of the stone in its overlap of physical and spiritual qualities. Throughout the attunement to Ajoite, my Liquid Crystal Body Matrix was feeling pleasurable currents and had become very relaxed. Ajoite's gesture entails a relaxation of one's astral and etheric bodies and a kind of soothing caress to one's body conciousness. Ajoite seems to have a strong influence and capability of calming and comforting the emotional body. As I worked with the stone, I felt the longing to simply rest in the arms of this loving angelic presence.

Next there was a visionary experience of the being of Ajoite. An image arose of a very lovely female figure, clothed in a gown of blue, and the blue was the same shade as the Ajoite inclusions in the crystal. This dress or gown in its coloration and form resembled an Ajoite crystal. There were shades of gray and white, within which the clouds of blue appeared. The being was tall and slender, and her demeanor was wistful and contemplative. She walked through a misty landscape, touching trees, stones, mosses and other plants. She leaned down to take a cupped hand of water from a small pool. There was a deep impression of longing and sadness about this being. I sensed that the sadness was related to the dream of the World, which this being held in her heart, and the longing was her longing to see the world in bloom.

A number of thoughts arose in me about how spiritual beings, and perhaps the Divine itself, might feel about the condition of the Earth. By this I mean more than the depletion and pollution of the Earth, although these obvious symptoms are part of the sorrow. I also was thinking of what spiritual beings might feel about a world that failed in its promise, or in their hope for what it could be.

Even though my own point of view is one of great hope for human beings and the world, I can imagine that what was attempted thus far by the great creative effort, which made the world we know, may be less fruitful than was envisioned. Whether or not this set of ideas is true, it is consistent with the being of Ajoite as I saw her. The sense of deep longing and of some unknown sadness was tangibly present. I cannot know for sure if this sadness and longing was some aspect of my own feelings, brought to consciousness through the influence of Ajoite on

my emotional body. Nonetheless the image of the beautiful, sad, feminine being is very clear. In exploring this, I also felt that in order for me or other people to reach the ecstatic experiences for which we long, it is necessary to open to all of the loss and grief present in us and in the world. We often attempt to push aside this sorrow, or to hold it below the threshold of consciousness. However, it is clear—so I hear from the Ajoite—that the heart not open to grief is also closed to ecstasy. Ajoite seems to say that our path to joy must be through the misty forests of sorrows, which have grown very large over long stretches of time. She is present in that domain because, in her faithfulness and service to us, she knows we must also go there.

Ajoite is also very much a stone of joy. It longs for joy and wishes, as we all do, that the path into joy will be short and easy. Whether this can be so or not, if we place ourselves in our heart and ask if we are prepared for the journey through grief, the heart is always ready.

As I am speaking now I see the woman of Ajoite extending her hand in a gesture that says, "I am present for you and will walk with you." Ajoite's gift is one of emotional, soul and spiritual healing through opening the heart, and through speaking, thinking and knowing the truth. She has more strength than the beauty and delicacy of her inner image or her crystal embodiment might

suggest. In our inner work, Ajoite can be a steadfast ally as we turn to face difficult emotions and past wounds. Ajoite will lend our heart greater intensity of purpose and will help us persist in going all the way through the journey of grief. It will unerringly lead us to the full resolution of whatever hurts and losses we carry, bringing us fully into the truth. Ajoite allows us to appreciate the present moment and to find our way into the future. The image I see is of myself, or any of us, facing the unknown future in a gesture of open-armed embrace. Ajoite reminds us that as long as we are trying to avoid the next moment of pain, we are closed. Through the full and conscious opening to whatever is within us, we free ourselves and truly begin to live.

AJOITE SPEAKS "I am a healer of the wounded heart. I can be what I am because my own heart has been wounded. I am one who loves, through all conditions, and if you turn toward me, I will soothe your heart and show you your tears, and mine. Let the cleansing rain of tears come, let the heart's power arise, let us align as partners, and let us continue."

ALEXANDRITE

KEY WORDS   Joy and wisdom, release of sorrow
ELEMENTS   Wind, Water
CHAKRAS   Heart (4th), Third Eye (6th), Crown (7th)

Alexandrite is a variety of Chrysoberyl, a beryllium aluminum oxide with a hardness of 8.5. It is one of the hardest gemstones, second only to Diamond and Corundum. Its crystal pattern is orthorhombic, and it sometimes forms in hexagonal-looking twinned crystals. It was discovered in the Ural Mountains of Russia in 1830, on the birthday of Czar Alexander II, and was named after him. The magic of Alexandrite is in its property of color change—it is light red or red-purple in incan-descent artificial light, and green or blue-green in daylight. (Appropriate to its name, the red and green colors of Alexandrite were the same as those of the Russian Imperial Guard.) In addition to the Russian discovery, Alexandrites have been found in Sri Lanka, South Africa, Burma, Brazil, Madagascar and the United States. The largest cut gem, weighing sixty-six carats, is in the Smithsonian Institution in Washington, DC. Alexandrite is one of the world's rarest gemstones, and the finest specimens are more costly than Diamonds.

Since its discovery, Alexandrite was believed in Russia to be a stone of good fortune. As belief in the magical properties of stones faded with the rise of science and rationalism, Alexandrite was the only gemstone Russians still widely believed to be a beneficial talisman as late as the nineteenth century.

BACKGROUND   Alexandrite carries a very joyful vibration. It is a powerful agent of inner transformation and spiritual evolution. It embodies both the heart energy (green) and the higher mind energy (purple). Its property of changing color in different lights symbolizes the ideal of inner adaptability in which one is able to respond from the mind, the heart or both together, in whatever way is most appropriate. It can stimulate a harmonic opening of the heart chakra, third eye and crown chakras, in which the three operate as an integrated whole.

Alexandrites are truly stones of joy, teaching us that the joy of the celestial realms is also simultaneously here at every moment, and that we are free to choose how much of it we receive. It encourages us to take in all energies that come to us, to transmute them into such harmony and beauty as is possible, and to do this with the inner resilience of a commitment to joy.

NEW ATTUNEMENT   When I sat down to meditate with Alexandrite, I first held the stone in front of me with my eyes open, and I gazed carefully and intently upon it. Then, closing my eyes, I immediately saw its outline in blue-white light. This indicated to me that Alexandrite is a highly energetic stone that leaves an instant impression upon one's vibrational field, which is experienced as the presence of light. Upon my watching this inner radiance for several minutes, it shifted into other colors—including golden, green and purple. Even orange and red lights came forward. One way of understanding the multiplicity of radiant colors stimulated in the mind's eye by Alexandrite is to say that this is a stone of flexibility, adaptability and transmutation, as many meditative experiences with it have suggested.

Alexandrite in the physical world appears green in sunlight and red-purple in incandescent light. This is reflective of Alexandrite's inner resonance with the heart, as well as the third eye and the crown chakras. Green is the color of the heart; purple is associated with the crown and sometimes the third eye. The fact that Alexandrite appears green in sunlight and green is the color of the heart is especially fascinating in light of the fact that the heart in us is our point of resonance with the Great Central Sun. Thus outer sunlight changes Alexandrite to the color of the heart, which is itself a Sun.

On the other hand, Alexandrite is purple in incandescent light, something created by human beings that is not otherwise existent in nature. This has a resonance with the fact that the center of our individualized consciousness is the mind, where our thoughts (and inventions, like incandescent light) arise. Alexandrite's stimulation of the brain/mind centers displays a fitting resonance with the purple color it assumes in (human-created) incandescent light. Fittingly, purple is the color associated with the third eye and crown chakras—the centers of the conscious mind.

In meditating with Alexandrite, I found—as I held one crystal at the heart and another at the third eye—that the stones strongly stimulated the energy centers of the heart, third eye and crown. Initially, each of these chakras was pulsing at a different rate, but within a few moments, in the presence of the Alexandrites, they moved into a unified vibration. This is resonant with Alexandrite's higher purpose—unification of mind and heart. Some esoteric teachers maintain that the heart chakra, as we evolve more fully into the human Light Body, will ascend to the location now known as the crown. This suggests the pattern of a fully integrated union of heart and mind and is signified by this new expansion of the heart chakra. My intuition suggests that the evolutionary shift we are experiencing may bring about a unification of the neural dimensions of the heart and brain, awakening a spiritual heart/mind consciousness.

Alexandrite engenders a powerful awakening of one's entire being through its harmonization of the heart and mind centers. When the heart and mind become one, we enter a consciousness in which feeling and thinking are in unity, and in which the heart's wisdom is expressed with the full eloquence of our best mental capacities. The throat chakra, residing between the mind centers and the heart, then becomes the expressive tool of the unified heart/mind. Alexandrite encourages all of this. Alexandrite's emotional tone is one of exuberant joy. It calls forth the heart's natural state of delighted engagement with all that occurs in each moment.

Alexandrite, in its own color change, embodies an inner pattern of flexibility, adaptability and willingness to shift its expression in the presence of varying conditions. In us, a similar flexibility and adaptability are encouraged by Alexandrite. It engenders in one's heart and mind a feeling of comfort and relaxed engagement with each moment. It allows us to feel the shape of each experience and adapt ourselves most advantageously for all concerned. Thus Alexandrite extends the heart's predisposition to act always for the well-being of the whole. In this, it is a true stone of the heart. Yet the violet resonance of Alexandrite encourages the infusion of the personal heart with the great column of Light descending from the Heart of the All. Alexandrite is therefore a stone of the Higher Self, and it initiates the integration of one's earthly, everyday identity with one's true expression as the Higher Self. Thus, just as Alexandrite encourages the unity of mind and heart, it brings forth a new unity of one's known self in earthly life with one's Higher Self—one's Perfect Nature emanating from the spiritual realms.

ALEXANDRITE SPEAKS   "I am a blossom of the Earth's joy. I offer the experience of Her Heart through me. She wishes the flower of your heart to bloom, and to reach ever upward toward the Light. Her gesture through me is a sweet beckoning, and you, as beloved partners—beloved children—are invited into the garden of Her joy."

APOPHYLLITE

Apophyllite is a hydrated potassium calcium silicate mineral with a tetragonal crystal system and a hardness of 5. It is most commonly colorless, white or gray. Rare specimens can be seen in varying shades of green. Apophyllite often appears in cubic or pyramidal shapes. Most specimens on the market are from India, especially the Poona and Nasik districts. Apophyllites are also found in Italy, Germany, Canada, Iceland, Greenland and Brazil.

CLEAR APOPHYLLITE

KEY WORDS   Interdimensional awareness, bringing spiritual Light through the DNA

ELEMENTS   Wind, Earth

CHAKRAS   Crown (7th), Third Eye (6th)

BACKGROUND   Clear Apophyllites excel at attuning one to the higher-frequency energies of the angelic and interdimensional domains. These crystals can serve as windows into many other worlds, and those wishing to experience interdimensional travel will enjoy working with them. In meditation, if one can imagine one's point of awareness moving into the interior of a Clear Apophyllite crystal, one will find, once "inside," that geometric corridors of Light lead off in all directions, and that one's consciousness can travel along these corridors to myriad realms of inner experience. Angels are attracted to the Light and high vibrations emanated by Clear Apophyllites. One may use these stones to contact guardian angels and spirit guides, or to visit the higher angelic realms.

Clear Apophyllite works synergistically with Azeztulite, Scolecite, Natrolite, Phenacite, Herderite and Brookite, all of which are "Ascension Stones." Using Selenite with Clear Apophyllite can open the pathway to conscious communion with the Higher Self.

NEW ATTUNEMENT   Resonating with Clear Apophyllite is a most pleasurable experience. When I began to work meditatively with three small clusters of Clear Apophyllite, I was immediately buoyed up in my mood and made aware of an interior presence of joy. There is something that delights one's heart in Clear Apophyllite, something that feels like the stones' own attitude of delight. The effect that Clear Apophyllite had on my chakras was immediate. The energy was quick-moving and it vibrated each chakra very noticeably, and in a way that felt precisely like the appropriate amount of stimulation. As I sat with closed eyes, I became aware of shimmering patterns of silvery-white light, apparently generated by the Clear Apophyllite. This light beckoned me to the angelic realm. There was a wave of revitalized feeling that went through the liquid crystal matrix of my physical body. And it seemed that it was awash in a replenishing Light.

The felt sense was that Clear Apophyllite draws Light—spiritual Light—through the mol-ecular corridor of one's DNA. We know that DNA emits light although we do not know why. Several stones touched upon in this book seem to stimulate or attract more light through the DNA. Apophyllite intuitively feels to me that it is among the stones with this beneficial effect. It is certainly capable of making the body feel happy inside without any other stimulus.

I worked in visualization with the Clear Apophyllite, imagining my point of attention entering a pyramidal crystal at the top of one of the clusters. It was surprisingly easy to do this, and the imagery came vividly. I opened a kind of doorway at the base of the pyramidal crystal and saw myself moving into it. Once inside there was a sense of spaciousness and light within the pyramid, and I looked up to see what—to my physical eyes a moment before—had been a tiny rainbow in the Apophyllite crystal. In my inner vision, this rainbow was now almost as large as my own body, shimmering in the space above me. Again my felt sense of enjoyment and delight was palpable. Continuing this meditative exercise, I turned toward one of the triangular walls of the interior of the Clear Apophyllite pyramid and dived through it.

This took me into a series of triangular geometric openings that formed a sort of Light corridor, and my point of attention pulsed along this corridor at a very rapid speed. It seemed to be endless, but it did eventually open into a scene in another realm. In this place there were trees and other features such as water, a bridge, a beach. All of these were tinged with the silvery light I had first perceived in my body as the effect of the Clear Apophyllite. All the images in this realm emanated the silvery light, as a kind of gauzy gloss over their natural shades or base colors. This was a beautiful place. I looked about for beings, and I was able to see a female form emerging from the rock of a silvery mountain. She identified herself as the being of White Apophyllite. She is a goddess of expanding consciousness and attunement to the Divine mind. She, as Apophyllite, gestured, and an array of images appeared. I was shown white caves—glowing caverns of crystals that were light-filled, with no outer source. She said, "This is my home." She looked to the water and I saw some dolphin-like creatures swimming toward her. She gestured upward, and white geese seemed to fly to her hand. By the time they reached her, her hand had become much larger, as her own stature had grown to perhaps ten times the size of a human being. Her face exhibited a serene calm, and I was given to understand that this face is the countenance of Clear Mind.

More gestures from her produced more symbolic phenomena in her world. At her prompting, I gazed across a bridge over the water. I saw a hole in the crystal mountain and felt that this was the opening to the Light corridor for my return. I entered this and was whisked quickly back to the interior of the Apophyllite pyramidal space. I saw other corridors leading from different faces of the crystal, and I was aware of many realms that one may visit through those

dimensional doorways. My felt sense was that Apophyllite is a tremendously helpful stone for those who wish to explore the inner universes and to meet the beings within them. It is like a universal attuning crystal that can aid in finding the resonances by which one can come into coherence with these other worlds.

Clear Apophyllite is, in my view, the most versatile and easy stone to access for interdimensional travel and communication. This traveling is for spiritual growth, as well as for adventure and enjoyment. One will be drawn to the corridors that most immediately serve the purpose of one's spiritual evolutionary progress. Thus the stone offers opportunities to enter realms that fit one's current state and take one to the next level. Other doorways open when one is in the inner state that resonates with them. Clear Apophyllite can help one attune to the various frequencies required for interdimensional travel. The state of vital, joyful, clear-thinking awareness is Clear Apophyllite's signature of inner balance. One's buoyancy is helpful in attuning to the spiritual realms of Light. We are cautioned not to become so serious in our exploratory research that we forget the joy, for without joy we can go nowhere.

CLEAR APOPHYLLITE SPEAKS   "I am a face of the Feminine in her aspect of Clear Consciousness. I am a mirror that can reflect as perfectly as the calmest water, and I can open the portals to myriad worlds."

GREEN APOPHYLLITE

KEY WORDS   Connection with nature spirits
ELEMENTS   Wind, Earth
CHAKRAS   Heart (4th), Third Eye (6th), Crown (7th)

BACKGROUND   Green Apophyllite resonates with the abundant life force of the world of nature. It can open one's perception to seeing and interacting with nature spirits and devas, and even to telepathic communication with animals and plants. Carrying or wearing this stone will increase the flow of life force throughout one's whole being. These are ideal stones for people recovering from illness—invoking the energies of rebirth, healing and growth.

Green Apophyllite can assist with animal communication, opening the psychic channel whereby one can interact with both individual animals and the collective minds of entire species. It can work similarly with plants and even other minerals.

Green Apophyllite resonates strongly with Seriphos Green Quartz, Seraphinite, Hiddenite, Staurolite and Ajoite.

NEW ATTUNEMENT   In beginning meditation with Green Apophyllite, I was quickly drawn to place all three of the stones with which I was working upon my heart. The heart was immediately filled with a deeply comforting sensation and I felt a wish to keep the stones there—a wish that seemed to emanate from my heart itself.

The felt sense was that Green Apophyllite was providing a kind of nourishment which was refreshing to my heart, and which replenished my heart's supply of energy. Not only energy, but also happiness and pleasure flowed through my heart and upward into my brain, beginning to fill my skull with pleasant, curling currents.

The next area in which I felt the currents of Green Apophyllite was my crown chakra. Rising up from the heart there was an impulse of White Light like a thin wire or thread, maybe one eighth of an inch thick. When it reached the crown, it spread fluidly along the inside of the skull, throughout the top "layer." Like white liquid, this light circulated within the skull, filling it with pleasing sensations and tingling currents. The Green Apophyllite seemed, in a sense, to be "playing" with my body, encouraging my body to become playful.

Next, the currents that coursed between my heart and crown entered the third eye, beginning to open it and bring the pleasant tingling sensation there as well. After a few minutes, the third eye and crown chakras were united by a kind of L-shaped energy flow between them, all of which was fed by the steady current of Light that rose from the heart.

Green Apophyllite is much more resonant with the heart than is its cousin, Clear Apophyllite. It soothes and enlivens the emotional body. I was able to sense this throughout the time I was holding it in meditation. It brings a light, positive atmosphere into the body and one's consciousness. It brings imagery of the natural world to one's inner eye. Sitting with Green Apophyllite I saw visionary landscapes of forest, grasses, rich green plants waving in the breeze, and the many shades of green one might see in a summer field. Green Apophyllite delights us with the panorama of the living Earth's beauty. If one works meditatively in this landscape, Green Apophyllite will bring forth beings and inhabitants of this beautiful reflection of the physical Earth, in its less dense, more joyfully alive dimensions. Green Apophyllite helps one see the forms of nature spirits and to initiate loving communication with them.

In my own experience, the "conversation" was not linguistic but gestural, and it was enacted by the nature beings as a dignified ritual, carried out with radiant smiles. The beings of nature revealed by Green Apophyllite were most gracious to me and honored me with their well-wishing. Leaving this realm behind and attuning again to the stones' qualities (as they are usually discussed), I sensed that Green Apophyllite is so alive with life force that it is almost animated. This is an ideal stone for anyone who is convalescing from illness, or who is recovering from depression or grief. Its positive influence is unflagging, and very difficult to resist. It is not easy to feel unhappy near Green Apophyllite. Green Apophyllite offers healing currents that most beneficially affect the heart area. It aids one in developing compassion and motivating oneself to altruistic activity.

GREEN APOPHYLLITE SPEAKS   "I am a joyful being who delights in life, and I offer this delight as a happy contagion for your whole being."

ARAGONITE (SPANISH)

KEY WORDS Awareness of the living world, awakening higher awareness, attunement to the future stream, grounding heavenly energies on Earth

ELEMENTS Wind, Fire, Storm

CHAKRAS Third Eye (6th), Crown (7th), Etheric (8th to 14th)

Aragonite is a calcium carbonate mineral with a hardness of 3.5 to 4. It occurs in various colors, including white, gray, reddish, yellow-green and blue. Aragonite's crystal system is orthorhombic, and it can be found in prismatic crystals, concretions, and stalactitic masses. Aragonite forms the skeleton of a number of marine organisms, either living or recently fossilized.

Beautiful bi-color (reddish purple and gray-green) Aragonites come from Molina de Aragon, Spain. The most plentiful forms of Aragonite in the metaphysical marketplace are the reddish Aragonite Star Clusters found in Morocco. Other Aragonites include white clusters from Greece and Mexico, and sky-blue material from Peru and China. For the purposes of this book, because it is by far the most energetically active form, we have chosen the columnar Spanish Aragonite bi-color crystals.

BACKGROUND Spanish Aragonite is the most highly energetic form of Aragonite. It stimulates the third eye and crown chakra very powerfully, and it allows one to attune with the frequencies of the etheric chakras above the head. Spanish Aragonite has the unique capacity to step-down the vibrations of those centers so that one can link with them. This facilitates connection with the higher-frequency domains such as the angelic realms.

One of the strengths of Spanish Aragonite is its ability to help us connect empathically with animals. It is highly recommended for those working with animal communication. On a deeper level, Spanish Aragonite encourages one's capacity to link with the living world. Working with this stone in meditation or carrying it through the day can sensitize one's energy field to the subtle currents operating beneath the visible surface of things and events. Perceptions are experienced as participations. One recognizes one's own creating activity, and the creating activity of the world. Such experiences bring recognition of an intimate involvement with all that one perceives, and engenders the felt sense of life in everything.

Spanish Aragonite carries powerful life-force currents. With most stones, these currents enter from below, through the root chakra. In the case of Spanish Aragonite, the energies come in through the crown chakra. The life force entering us through this portal is involved with the infusion of the Light Body into the physical form, as well as the regeneration of the organism.

NEW ATTUNEMENT In attuning to Spanish Aragonite, I began by carefully looking at my chosen crystal and then closing my eyes and waiting to see the after-image of the stone in my inner vision. In this case I saw a column reflecting the shape of the crystal itself, except that this column was flared open at the bottom like the end of a trumpet. It seemed to indicate a downward fountain of a spiritual force traveling through the crystal. It moved into my physical body and the etheric body, widening as it entered at the crown. The spray of this energy fountain filled the body with a tangible spiritual force. This column was a blue color, although the stone itself was a mixture of green and reddish purple.

Every time I hold the Spanish Aragonite, I feel drawn to bring it to the top of my head—to the crown chakra—and to open the crown chakra through intention, allowing the energies to enter there. Each time I work with the Spanish Aragonite, I experience first a kind of pulsing, even a pounding (though not unpleasant) entry of spiritual current through the top of my head. It is as though there is a kind of percussion of energy working its way down through my head and then the spinal column in a kind of energetic "hammering" that is very discrete and rhythmic. As this energy or current moves steadily down, pulse by pulse, it reaches all the way to the base chakra, and the spray (or the widening of the current flow) increases as the energy moves completely through my body.

I feel that Aragonite of this type has (in regard to working with human beings) the purpose of opening and clearing and raising the vibrational activity of the entire column ranging from the crown down to the base chakra. This stone's intention is to work in unity with us to bring a New Consciousness into the incarnated world. The consciousness that this insistent, pulsing current represents is of a kind rarely experienced up to now. The feeling in the body of the downward-pulsing current can be likened to a flow of heavenly nectar entering the body from spiritual worlds. Although this pulsation can feel initially quite intense, it is highly pleasurable if one opens to allow it to penetrate all the way into and through the body. I have the intuitive sense that other beings—spirits of human pioneers, in unity-of-purpose with benevolent spiritual beings—are pouring their intention through the willing conduit of Spanish Aragonite. I feel they are operating from a realm somewhere between our dense-matter plane and the high frequencies of pure Spirit. They are working to bridge the Divine realms with this world, and this is not only for our benefit—the high-vibration beings are fed and fulfilled through our recognition of them and our engaging in relationship with the Divine through their (and our) efforts. I sense that they experience considerable joy in the fact that this living being—the Aragonite crystal—has been recognized and will be utilized and cherished for the purpose of bringing these beneficial frequencies into the material world.

After the initial opening and the current flow down, I touched the Aragonite to my forehead and then back to the crown. This initiated or coincided with the beginning of a different sort of pulsation. Actually, before doing this I held the stone to my heart, and I felt intensely "busy" electrical sparkings. These occurred in the area between the stone on the surface of my chest and the location of my physical heart. It felt as if the stone being and my own essence were meeting in that "overlapping" space between the stone and my heart. During this, I continued to feel the pleasurable currents of the Aragonite. Yet the feeling of pounding or pulsing diminished, and the overall sense became more of a humming vibration throughout my body— still a very good feeling.

Then I moved to my forehead and my crown with the crystal, and this initiated another phenomenon. When the stone was on my forehead I experienced a vibrational current permeating the front part of my brain. Sometimes a stone will enter through the third eye and go to the center of the head and then up to the crown in a kind of L-shaped current. This stone, however, seemed to concentrate its forces in the very front part of my brain, near the forehead. And, amazingly, more pulsations began in the front part of my brain, alternating from right to left and from left to right in a rhythmic manner. I felt certain, as these pulsations surged back and forth across the center line, that their purpose was to integrate, align and increase instant communication between the right and left hemispheres of my brain. The feeling came that this integration was essential in order for there to be a completely balanced set of capacities and activities. One's consciousness could then draw as needed upon the specialized areas of both sides of the brain without any dominance of one side or the other.

This stone can join with other stones for the activation, awakening and alignment of the Light Body. It is helpful to intend for the energy stream that enters us with Spanish Aragonite to be grounded into the Earth. Our destiny is a joint destiny with that of the Earth. The Earth needs the currents and love of the heavenly domain as much or more than we do. Although Spanish Aragonite can be a conduit, it can only fully benefit the Earth when we work together with it and attune ourselves also as conduits, as transmitters—as receiver/transmitters. We can be like the "hollow bone" of the shaman, through which Spirit flows both up and down, and the worlds meet.

Spanish Aragonite brings a great feeling of peace into the cellular consciousness of the body. It first fills the cells with pulsing living currents of energy and then encourages all levels of the body, including the etheric, to release into the Universal Wholeness all coalesced negative identifications. That is to say, when we have identified with some experience or feeling of difficulty, this coalesces a negative pattern. Aragonite, as it spreads its higher-realm vibration through the body, dissolves these, as long as we are prepared to agree to this.

There are many other Aragonites, and some—such as the White Aragonites of Seriphos, Greece—are capable of carrying some of the high-vibrational currents that Spanish Aragonite carries. Other varieties of this stone are awake to a lesser degree, although they may eventually be more fully activated. Meanwhile, the Spanish Aragonites resonate and ally themselves with other stones that carry the same mission—that of bringing down the Light. Many of the stones chosen for this book are aligned with this purpose. I invite people to work with all of the Ascension Stones (Azeztulite, Phenacite, Petalite, Danburite, Nirvana Quartz, Herderite, Satyaloka Azeztulite, Himalaya Gold Azeztulite and Golden Azeztulite from North Carolina) in conjunction with these Aragonites. I feel a strong quality of a potent, unknown future potential as I hold and attune to this stone. It is resonant with the idea of carrying the memory of the future, and it is strongly linked to the manifestation of that unknown potential in the world.

As deeply as I wish to delve, there remains a great deal that is hidden about the purpose and possibilities to which these stones are attuned. As we open in trust, if we work with these Aragonites, we will begin to see more readily the shape of the world to come. Until then, the first task of the Spanish Aragonite is to trigger and aid in the transfiguration of the human body into the Body of Light. However, its ray is the transparent or invisible ray, so its radiance is one that is felt rather than seen, even inwardly. It links us to what is known as the Midnight Sun in the heart, and it is in resonance as well with the being sometimes known as the Black Madonna. This attunement is accentuated if one uses a stone such as Master Shamanite, which is a stone of the deep realms. The stone and the being of the stone are devoted to nourishing and protecting the Feminine hidden in exile in the darkness of matter. It wishes us to be as dedicated, so that the work we do with the Aragonite is unified with the purpose of the stone being.

We as humans have great influence with the stones. Their intention of service is one that means they will try—they will attune or adjust their capacities to fit our wishes and needs. At the same time, if we are willing to ask what *their* purpose is, and agree to support it and bring it into the world, they rejoice.

SPANISH ARAGONITE SPEAKS   "I bring the memory of the future. I am carrying the Love/Light waves of the superconscious realm into incarnated matter. My talent is my capacity to perfectly conduct, with no resistance, the heavenly energies for their transmission to the Earth. I was awakened recently. I have always been potentially what I now am, yet now the request has been made and I am willing. I am very fast. In my speed, I am like unto the being once called Hermes. My devotion is total, and I reach through the membrane of worlds that I may serve Her, the Life within life."

AZEZTULITE™

Azeztulite has one of the most unusual stories of any stone in this book. Chemically it is a variety of Quartz with a hexagonal (trigonal) crystal system and a hardness of 7. The original and most powerful Azeztulite came from a single find in North Carolina around 1970, and more than thirty years later a second deposit was uncovered in Vermont. Since then, Azeztulites have been discovered in South India (Satyaloka Azeztulite), the Rocky Mountains (Pink Azeztulite) and the regions near the Himalaya range (Himalaya Gold Azeztulite). There have also been two new Azeztulite discoveries in North Carolina (Sanda Rosa Azeztulite and Golden Azeztulite Crystals). All of these new forms carry Azeztulite frequencies, yet each has its own special qualities as well.

If one were to make a scale of the intensity of the currents emanated from Azeztulites, one might place Satyaloka Azeztulite at the highest intensity, followed next by Golden Azeztulite Crystal Points from North Carolina and followed closely by the original white Azeztulite from North Carolina and Vermont. Next in intensity and again almost exactly tied with original Azeztulite is Himalaya Gold Azeztulite, the newest discovery. Next, and in a decidedly softer and gentler spectrum, is Sanda Rosa Azeztulite. The gentlest, softest, most heart-based and feeling-centered Azeztulite is Pink Azeztulite (Rhodazez). This spectrum may be of some use, although it is a gross measure. The qualities of all kinds of Azeztulite have much overall similarity, yet they differ distinctly from one type to another, as mentioned above, and also from one specimen to another. The way they interact with different individuals constitutes another variable, but I believe these general principles can be helpful.

Because I have devoted a whole chapter to Azeztulite (Chapter Ten, "The Tale of the Azez") I will not include a background section here on the original Azeztulite.

WHITE AZEZTULITE (Original Azeztulite)

KEY WORDS   Receiving the Nameless Light, link with the Great Central Sun, reattunement of the Liquid Crystal Body Matrix for healing and regeneration

ELEMENT   Storm

CHAKRAS   All (including the etheric chakras above the body)

NEW ATTUNEMENT   I have written more about Azeztulite than perhaps any other stone, with the possible exception of Moldavite. Yet each time I sit to meditate with Azeztulite, I am impressed anew. In this meditation, I placed a pouch with Azeztulites over my heart and I held two pieces of Azeztulite, one in each hand. All these are the original types of Azeztulite, the white or clear materials found in North Carolina or Vermont. In my experience, the Azeztulites from these two locations are energetically matched to one another, and one is not better than the other in any overall sense. The initial impulse of Azeztulite's currents in me caused very powerful pulsations in my third eye and crown chakras, with more subdued resonating pulsations in my heart. The throat chakra played the role of a current-carrying connecting link between the two areas.

Holding Azeztulite over the third eye, the currents of the stones are experienced as high-frequency energy that, intuition suggests, must originate in the spiritual realms of Light. Indeed, seeing light in the interior of the skull is one of the hallmarks of Azeztulite, and as I meditated, I experienced vivid inner imagery and sensations of undulating liquid currents of White Light in my skull. These currents were accompanied by pleasurable sensations that were hard to compare to any others. The feeling is somewhat as if consciousness is being sweetly caressed by angelic hands, and these hands work with a purpose, for they are not only there to soothe the consciousness; they are much more there to work Light and expansion into one's consciousness. The feeling that accompanies

Azeztulites is one of reverence. Being in the presence of something holy is felt when one opens up to Azeztulite.

I tried placing two Azeztulites at different points of my skull, one at the third eye at the forehead, and one behind my head at the base of the skull where it joins the top of the spine. This point is one at which I had experienced powerful currents and openings in the past. When I placed the Azeztulites in these two spots, I was awed by the immediate and powerful current connecting the two areas, flowing right through the skull. It seemed for a moment that I might slip into a full-blown mystical experience, and echoes of one such experience from the past flooded my memory. Apparently, for purposes of this attunement, I was to stay just outside, at the boundary edge of complete mystical immersion. However, I must report that resonance with Azeztulite can take one far down that road.

Since applying Azeztulite to the front and back skull points, my entire skull remained, at least for this meditation time, resonant with currents moving through it. The sense of holiness and Light was so potent that it was difficult to continue composing consciousness into words. Azeztulite is said to represent the Great Central Sun. In other words, it is said to conduct the currents or light of the Central Sun, the spiritual core of the universe, and to direct those currents into us for our ultimate spiritual awakening and our service as the people of Light.

There is a history of traditions asserting that the Divine Light from the Central Sun longs for incarnation in the world of matter. This is resonant with traditions such as those related in Gnostic writings and other early Christian myths. The statement "I am the Way, the Truth and the Light" is highly resonant with the qualities of Azeztulite. Azeztulite brings forward the inner experience of spiritual Light, and through its presence suggests to us a path of truth to Light. This path must be, and naturally is, followed with an ardent intensity. One might say "a zest." It has been pointed out to me by a friend that the name Azeztulite could be rewritten as "a zest to Light," or an ardent approach to the inner Light. I do feel that Azeztulite stimulates this potential in us.

The Liquid Crystal Body Matrix probably resonates more strongly with Azeztulite than any other stone I know. Certainly, comparisons do not matter, though I would say that Azeztulite can be felt as bringing Light into every cell in the body.

I'll try another way of saying this: Each cell has a nucleus, each nucleus contains DNA, and each molecule of DNA is known to emit light naturally. The source of this light is unknown; the reason for it is unknown. It is interesting also to note that Quartz crystal, which is the substance carrying the currents of Azeztulite, emits light when put under pressure. Thus Azeztulite as

Quartz and the nuclei of each cell of our bodies both emit light. What is this light?

Robert Sardello has suggested that what we know as electromagnetic energy is not in itself true energy but is the kind of echo or after-effect of true energy, spiritual energy. The currents of the Great Central Sun may thus also be seen as the underlying Light, expressed in the world of matter as the light we experience from the sun in our sky. It is also known that our heart is a generator of an electromagnetic field, and I would agree with Sardello that this field is again the echo, the after-effect, the epiphenomenon of the true radiance of the heart, the spiritual radiance of the heart. We know that each atom of matter generates a tiny field that is again, from this perspective, the after-effect or shadow image of the true energy within it. I would describe this true Light as emanating the holographic presence of the Great Central Sun in the core of each atom.

Our DNA is the molecule of life and it emits visible light. This means, in the context of our explanation here, that spiritual Light pours into the world through DNA and is expressed first as life and secondarily as its echo, light. I mention all this because the purpose of Azeztulite, as I understand it, is to help us incarnate the human Body of Light. This is the New Body of spiritual Light, and I believe very deeply that this Light Body is to be incarnated at the level of our cells, perhaps through our DNA.

Here is the idea/image I am seeing: Our cells are the level at which the physical and spiritual worlds interface in our bodies. DNA is the portal through which spiritual Light, which is the animating force of life, enters the world. With physical vision or instruments, we can detect only the "echo" of this spiritual Light—the physical light, electromagnetic energy. The light emitted by DNA is a by-product of the spiritual Light of life. When people are deeply attuned to the spiritual dimension, more spiritual Light pours through them, and perhaps more physical light would also be detectable around them. Everyone has seen paintings of holy people depicted with light emanating from them. This may be an actual visible phenomenon caused by an infusion of spiritual Light through the DNA.

From this viewpoint, we can say that we already have a Body of Light. It is most likely that Light Body which animates one's material body, and it is perhaps that Light Body which leaves the physical form at death. However, the words of the Azez tell us that an infusion of spiritual Light from the Great Central Sun, such as that carried by Azeztulite, can dissolve the patterns of contraction (fear), degeneration and disease on the level of the cells. This seems to suggest that working with Azeztulite has the potential to bring about an alchemical transmutation of the body. With enough infusion of spiritual Light, we might enter a higher vibrational frequency in which the very matter of our bodies becomes less dense, more radiant.

If this occurs, I do not view it as our simply "becoming Light" and leaving the material world behind. The vision I am seeing is even more amazing. I see the realm of matter marrying and fusing with the realm of Light, creating something that has never existed before. And this is not for ourselves alone. Remember that the Azez intend to awaken all the Quartz on Earth, which is most of the Earth's crust, to the currents of the Nameless Light. This means that our Light Bodies would awaken at the same time or within the same process as the Earth's Light Body. I am seeing not only our own transmutation but that of the Earth itself into a new kind of Light-filled matter. And our participation is essential. It is only through our bodies, with our voluntary co-creative cooperation, that this process can be fulfilled, because we are the portals through which the Nameless Light can be grounded on the Earth. As long they are in the Azeztulite alone, without the engagement with living beings such as ourselves, the currents are not fully active. Like all gestures of true love, the infusion of the Nameless Light is an offer, not a compulsion. For it to actually happen, we have to say "Yes."

It is fitting to consider this as a kind of marriage. The Solar Logos (another name for the Great Central Sun) is thought of mythologically as a male archetypal energy or pattern. The Earth has been viewed almost universally as female, and if we think of Sophia as the Soul of the World, then the fusion of Heavenly Light with Earthly Matter is a Divine Marriage. Since we humans are integral to the unfolding of this process, we may play the role of the Holy Child, and we would experience within ourselves the ecstasy of the Divine Union. (It could even be this ecstasy that fully "ignites" the Light Body.) All of this may seem like a far cry from where we are today, but it is nonetheless the vision that arises as I contemplate the Azeztulite, and my heart leaps to affirm it.

We naturally have the connection to the Great Central Sun; every atom of our bodies carries its holographic aspect. By this I mean that the energy field around each atom is resonant in form and function with the field around the sun, the Earth, the galaxy and even our own heart. Azeztulite works as a means of increasing the flow of spiritual Light into our bodies and through them. My felt sense is that Azeztulite, with our invitation, can fill the entire Liquid Crystal Body Matrix with its spiritual Light. The Liquid Crystal Body Matrix is found throughout the human body, even in the interior of every cell's nucleus—for every cell nucleus contains

water molecules, which, in the case of DNA, hold its pattern of molecular folding. Therefore if the pattern of the liquid within ourselves shifts in resonance to the pattern offered through a stone such as Azeztulite, the DNA itself may refold to accommodate the shift. In my impression of what happens, it will feel the shift, and does feel it, and begins to open itself to express more of the light of the Great Central Sun. Think of this molecule as a tube through which Light from the inner world pours into the outer world, the world of incarnation.

Thus Azeztulite has many beneficial effects upon us, spiritually, soulfully, physically. The habits or patterns carried in the cells that take us into states of deterioration and contraction can be reconfigured through the influence of the Nameless Light pouring into us through Azeztulite. The Azez said in the very first contact through Naisha that Azeztulite currents would dissolve and dispel patterns of contraction, degeneration and deterioration in the cells. Thus, Azeztulite was promised always to be an influence toward healing. Since death itself is only a habit in the DNA and the cell—not an inviolable law—it is within the potential of the effect of the spiritual Light to increase health and longevity beyond any parameters we know.

This is my intuitive and deeply held vision for the potential of Azeztulite, yet there is more. The human Light Being is the highest potential of the human being and is something of the Divine incarnated within us. We all know this spark of the Divine lies within us. The purpose of Azeztulite is to fan our spark into a full radiant Sun.

Azeztulite gleams with the Light of the highest realms. It is not for Light alone, however, that we exist. The complement of Light is what we might call the darkness of matter. This is not an evil darkness but a fertile one, like the womb. In the expression of this that we can experience through the stones, one could say that the Light of Azeztulite represents the masculine Logos and that the dark of Rosophia, or of the Earth as Rosophia express it, is the feminine. My heart says that the love of the Earth longs for the Light of heaven, and that the Light of heaven reaches out for the intimate love of the Earth. Azeztulite and Rosophia are a mated pair in the world of stones when they are allowed to meet one another through us. There is no pair of stones I recommend with more enthusiasm than these.

The meeting of their currents within us is an occasion of great joy, and I have seen many people come to tears simply by feeling how these stones interact when they hold them at the same time. It is a gift of great potential that we have the opportunity to work with the streams carried by these two stones now.

I spent a few moments holding an Azeztulite at my forehead and a Rosophia over my heart. The pulsations that were previously going through my skull now aimed downward through the third eye toward the heart. My heart resonated with powerful swirling upward-gesturing currents, reaching up for the Light the Azeztulite offered, and the heart currents were something I can only speak of as love. The heart pulsed up and the third eye pulsed down. The stones at each position seemed to reach toward one another through me, and a sense of sweet, resonant union developed in the space between my heart and my head. The entire corridor of their meeting was luminous with joy, and they pulsed together as one.

To fully embody the tree of life we must be rooted. Azeztulite and Rosophia resonate best with the rooted qualities of the stone Master Shamanite. Its carbon-based substance is a strong influence for both grounding and spiritual purification. Thus, it aids in the work that Azeztulite and Rosophia naturally do. In addition Master Shamanite provides a link to the world below, our waking world. And this world, too, belongs in union with the Divine, for it is a reflection of it. Heaven and Earth are resonant with Azeztulite and Rosophia. Heaven, Earth and the Underworld, the depth world—not a demonic world, but a world of what lies beneath—are resonant with Azeztulite, Rosophia and Master Shamanite. I encourage readers (and myself) to spend time working with the combined current of these three stones.

Moldavite too, as Grail stone, is highly resonant with Azeztulite and Rosophia, which are aspects of the Philosopher's Stone of alchemy. Moldavite is resonant with the Emerald Tablet of Hermes Trismegistes—another essential element of the transformations offered through spiritual alchemy.

AZEZTULITE SPEAKS   "I am the Light in darkness. I banish nothing. I bring light to all things and all beings, and I represent the true living Light of love, which pours forth infinitely from the Source of all."

SANDA ROSA AZEZTULITE

KEY WORDS   Healing, inner harmony, grounding spiritual Light in the body, purification attunement with the soul of the Earth

ELEMENTS   Storm, Earth

CHAKRAS   All (1st through 7th)

BACKGROUND   Sanda Rosa Azeztulite, which was found in North Carolina (where Azeztulite was first discovered), is different from the original Azeztulite in that it contains particles of Spessartite Garnet and Green Black Mica. Whether it is for these reasons or others, meditation with Sanda Rosa Azeztulite indicates that this stone, while still resonating at the high frequencies of Azeztulite, is a more grounded and grounding form of Azeztulite. Its primary resonance remains with the upper chakras and the heart. However, on a spectrum of Azeztulite qualities, Sanda Rosa Azeztulite is most likely the variety with which highly sensitive people will be comfortable.

NEW ATTUNEMENT   In meditation with Sanda Rosa Azeztulites I experienced a comfortable feeling of warm vibrational stimulation at the third eye and crown chakra. These chakras are certainly strongly activated by Sanda Rosa Azeztulite, but there is no sense of being overstimulated. There is not the need to ground excess energies that some people feel with the original Azeztulite or Satyaloka Azeztulite. The currents of Sanda Rosa Azeztulite descend readily to all parts of the body after entering from above, as Azeztulites most often do. They spread through the Liquid Crystal Body Matrix in a graceful flow. Sanda Rosa Azeztulite is very soothing to the etheric body. Its interface with the energetic membrane of the physical body is a smooth and nurturing one. I have experienced the most physically healing qualities from Sanda Rosa Azeztulite that I have felt from any of the forms of Azeztulite. For example, I have several times been able to instantly quell digestive discomfort and difficulty by placing Sanda Rosa Azeztulite over the affected areas. This can occur in me in a matter of only a few minutes. I have seen people who were generally attracted to Azeztulite, but who felt ungrounded by the other varieties, find a pleasing and comfortable fit with Sanda Rosa Azeztulite.

The Spessartite Garnet in these stones carries a vibration of its own, which harmonizes beautifully with the pure white Azeztulite portion of the stone. The Spessartite Garnet is a very Earth-friendly, body-friendly material. It resonates strongly with the first and second chakras, providing the grounding influence one experiences from Sanda Rosa Azeztulite. It helps spiritualize the densest aspects of one's physical self. It also provides a vibrational stepping stone so that the Liquid Crystal Body Matrix can find resonance with the Azeztulite currents by means of the Garnet's harmonizing, mediating energies.

Sanda Rosa Azeztulite's currents move at a relaxed pace as they undulate through one's body. They are warm, and they resonate well with our corporeal selves. They also encourage our bodies to vibrate at a higher spiritual frequency, without losing touch with the Earth. The Mica portion of Sanda Rosa Azeztulite seems to stimulate a certain reflective quality in the consciousness. It is a strengthener of what I might call the witness, the observer in oneself,

141

who watches without judging all that passes within one's body, mind and soul. Sanda Rosa Azeztulite stimulates the third eye and crown chakras in a way that allows one to see into very deep levels of meditative awareness. It is calming to the emotional body, and this benefits those who are working to quiet the mind.

Sanda Rosa Azeztulite is a good stone to take into the realm of dreaming. It stimulates vivid images in the psyche in both meditative and sleep experiences, and it helps one remember dreams.

This stone has a particularly good and easy resonance with Rosophia. Together they facilitate the deepest release of stress and the strongest repair of the emotional body and the etheric body of any Azeztulite, perhaps of any stones at all. Sanda Rosa Azeztulite resonates very well with Moldavite. It is also a potent and guiding ally with Circle Stones. Together they can be used to explore the mysteries of the Crop Circle formations and experience inwardly a unity with the consciousness that has been creating them. Sanda Rosa Azeztulite is a powerful talisman of healing and it seeks alliance with stones such as Seraphinite, Tanzanite, Morganite, Seriphos Green Quartz and others that attune to the Divine blueprint of the body.

Sanda Rosa Azeztulite can be used in conjunction with Master Shamanite for spiritual purification of the physical body. It provides the most directly beneficial spiritual influence for healing of all the Azeztulites, and its agenda is to make the body comfortable with the presence of the Divine Light within every self.

SANDA ROSA AZEZTULITE SPEAKS "I am of both the Light and the Earth, and I am a kindred soul with nature. I can remind your bodily self of the truth of its forever-living nature."

GOLDEN AZEZTULITE CRYSTALS

KEY WORDS Attunement to the Gold-White Light, Light Body awakening, time travel, accessing the Hall of Records, kindling the Sun of the Heart

ELEMENT Storm

CHAKRAS Heart (4th), Third Eye (6th), Crown (7th), Soul Star & Transpersonal (8th through 14th)

BACKGROUND The only actual prismatically crystallized Azeztulites, except for a few tiny clusters from Vermont, are the recently discovered crystals from North Carolina, which I have named Golden Azeztulite. Although they span the range from milky white to smoky brown, with various shades of golden citrine color in between, we call them all Golden Azeztulite, because they engender within one's awareness a ray of gold-white light—the ray of the Great Central Sun. All Azeztulite is attuned to this source, but these crystals are the most powerful catalysts for awakening a consciousness imbued with the gold-white light.

NEW ATTUNEMENT As I meditated with three of these crystals, I first experienced Azeztulite's characteristic and very powerful opening of the third eye and crown chakras simply by holding the Golden Azeztulite Crystals. Placing them at the crown and third eye areas created a highly charged conduit of vibration between the third eye and crown. I experienced those chakras being linked by an L-shaped bar of light which was so strong and intense that it felt nearly solid.

Golden Azeztulite crystals are important in their stimulation and awakening of the Light Body. I speak of this in many places in this book, because I feel that the evolution into Light is essential and is an aspect of the joint destiny of human beings and the Earth. The currents that vibrated through my body as I worked in meditation with these stones gave rise to the sense that my entire Body of Light was awake, all at once, and perhaps for the first time. There was a sensation of having another body overlaid upon the physical form that I usually call "my body." And this overlaid body was only partly integrated with the physical. It was bouncing, almost but not quite within the outline of the physical form—a bit like a tethered balloon.

The felt sense was that the awakened Light Body, unaccustomed to awareness of itself, was suddenly present and overlapping (though not completely woven into) my physical form. This was my most vivid experience of the Light Body, and yet I sensed it was only the beginning of what we will experience as we proceed down this path of our evolution and destiny. I feel we have the potential to become fully spiritual human beings, wearing the garment of Light.

The currents of the Golden Azeztulite Crystals continued to course through me very powerfully, and the L-shaped flow of energy pouring though the third eye and crown chakras became a great torrent. Because of this I opened my eyes, and I saw that the room itself was filled with golden light. This is always an astonishing occurrence. It was unmistakable that the atmosphere had become golden. I have been in this situation two or three other times in group settings after meditation, usually with some form of Azeztulite. This atmosphere of gold was spoken of by Sri Aurobindo's partner, the Mother. Her project, which I think of as encompassing (though not limited to) Light Body awakening, aimed to engender a kind of human transmutation into immortality. (Many esoteric teachings say that the Light Body is an immortal body.) In her explorations, the Mother sometimes entered a realm she described as an atmosphere of "warm gold dust." This is precisely what I saw upon opening my eyes after feeling the Golden Azeztulite current move through my skull. The Great Central Sun, from my past meditative experiences, apparently emanates this same gold-white light. A holographic likeness of this same Central Sun is present in our own hearts, and it is sometimes kindled in one's consciousness in the presence of the Golden Azeztulite, as I experienced moments later.

In holding the Golden Azeztulite crystal to my heart chakra, I was quickly immersed in a vision of a golden radiant glow within my chest, where the physical heart is. And this golden glow was filling the interior of my body with gold-white light, while rotating on its axis like a planet or a sun. This vision came moments after I pointed the Golden Azeztulite Crystal toward the heart chakra.

After some time, I tried pointing a small crystal of the Golden Azeztulite at the secondary chakra at the back of the skull, while holding another crystal at the third eye. Once again a powerful circuit was formed, accompanied by a feeling of movement and held tension, as though a curtain were closed over my third eye. I sensed that with the lifting of this curtain could come vivid visual inner experiences, and perhaps the capacity to see truth, and only truth, with clarified spiritual vision. That is my intuitive sense of what Golden Azeztulite is attempting to awaken in us. Such visionary consciousness is among the dormant capacities that this stone can stimulate and bring forward.

Golden Azeztulite, like all Azeztulite, is aligned with the purpose of our evolution into spiritual human beings. However, it specifically is attuned to the unknown latent capacities of the brain/mind and nervous system. It stimulates the prefrontal lobes of the brain very intensely and very precisely. I wish I could report the nature of the coming capacities! My felt sense is that they involve direct knowing,

simply by turning one's attention to a question or a subject, or toward the so-called Hall of Records on the inner planes. It's simply a turning toward knowing.

Another potential that Golden Azeztulite can help awaken is our capacity as time beings—capable of moving in conscious awareness through the fluidity of time. When we are fully attuned to what we are capable of being, I feel that the movement of one's indivdual consciousness through time—both past and future—is a strong potential.

Another capacity enlivened through working with Golden Azeztulite is empathy. We have empathy now, but the empathy of which I speak is the ability to move one's self-sense into union with the self-sense of another. In this, one knows precisely how the other person feels and what his or her concerns are. More significantly, one may be able to feel the patterns of the other person more deeply and clearly than she or he is consciously capable of doing.

In my meditation, I saw a vision that the interior of the skull, in concordance with Golden Azeztulite's strongest and most full-blown manifestation in us, can be inwardly illumined. In such a state the space behind our eyes would not be dark but filled with golden light, always. We do not understand—when all the light we see is actually generated within the brain/mind—why the skull itself feels inwardly like a kind of darkness. We take it for granted, but if the vision I had was true, it is not necessarily the case. I have experienced moments of this interior illumination. It is akin visually to the image in the painting of the ascending Christ by Antonio Campi that is featured in Chapter Six, "Crystal Meditations." I encourage looking at that painting and imagining that the golden dome into which Christ is ascending is one's own skull—that the human pillars and radiant spheres and all the golden imagery are truly present within one's own skull, one's own body. Golden Azeztulite makes such an identification much easier by providing us with the quality of Light, interior Light, that gives rise to such experiences.

THE GOLDEN AZEZTULITE CRYSTALS SPEAK "We are the tools of the surgeons of Light. We are the allies of the explorers of Light. We are the messengers of Light. We are the kindlers of the radiant Heart of Light."

HIMALAYA GOLD AZEZTULITE

KEY WORDS Creative manifestation through the will, co-creating with Sophia, kindling the Great Central Sun in the heart, filling the body with Gold Light

ELEMENT Storm

CHAKRAS Heart (4th), Third Eye (6th), Crown (7th), Soul Star and Transpersonal (8th through 14th)

BACKGROUND Himalaya Gold Azeztulite was discovered in 2008, in the regions near the Himalaya mountains. Like other Azeztulites, it is a form of Quartz, in this case displaying a bright yellow color. Himalaya Gold Azeztulite emanates Azeztulite's whole pattern of energies, and one of its special qualities is its resonance with the solar plexus chakra. This is the seat of power and manifestation in the human being. As with other conditions we carry from the past, within the solar plexus are patterns of limitation that severely restrict our capacity to create. We literally do not know our power, and in the past this may have kept us from abusing it. Yet with evolution into expanded awareness comes the necessity of taking up our full range of potentials. The arrival of Himalaya Gold Azeztulite coincides with the beginning of our development of new capacities for creative manifestation through the will. The stimulation of the solar plexus, in alignment with the Seat of Vision in the third eye chakra, is an important aspect of this activation.

NEW ATTUNEMENT   I began meditating with Himalaya Gold Azeztulite holding a stone in each hand and another one in a pouch over my heart. Some stones require me to place them over the third eye or other upper chakras—especially if they are high-vibration stones—in order for me to really feel their energies. The currents pouring through Himalaya Gold Azeztulite are so potent that no such placement is necessary. Simply holding the stones in my two hands, I felt their currents move to several chakra points where their flow was emphasized. The third eye and crown were stimulated very powerfully, and I felt an impulse of strengthening current move into and then back out of my solar plexus chakra.

Relatively few stones reverberate so strongly in the solar plexus as does Himalaya Gold Azeztulite, and those that do rarely emanate the high-frequency currents as powerfully as Himalaya Gold Azeztulite does. As I continued holding the stones, I felt my Liquid Crystal Body Matrix shift into resonance with their currents, flowing through the whole body. The primary focal points of the third eye and solar plexus continued to resonate, and their resonance became a strong mutual pulsing with each other. My felt sense was that Himalaya Gold Azeztulite potentiates the power of creating, which is latent in us and is an essential part of our coming destiny.

The solar plexus currents were enhanced and strengthened by putting my attention there, and my resonance with the stone became something I could influence through my will. In fact, I believe that this was possible primarily because of an enhancement of the strength of my will forces, brought about through the currents of these stones. One of the most amazing capacities we have as human beings is the will. We can choose what we do! This gives rise to both exhilarating freedom and terrible difficulty, since our free will allows a myriad of errors. Another mixed blessing is our limitation—we do not "create our own reality," at least not in a direct way. Yet when we create, the will is always deeply involved. In my view, it is the activity of the will (both the "hard" will of doing and the "soft" will of agreement or surrender) in union with our visionary capacity that comprises our gesture in the activity of creating. I refer here primarily to our individual conscious will.

There is more to geniune creating activity than our own self-aware aspir-ations. The creating we can do—in which we are truly creating a world, our bodies and our living experience—is not isolated within us; instead it is co-creating in a kind of union with the Soul of the World, whose impulses we feel in our hearts. Individually, we can utilize the third eye to envision something mentally and the solar plexus to "push" things into manifestation, yet this is a much more limited sort of creating. When we work in co-creative unity with Sophia, we are simultaneously setting our intentions and letting go of any expectations regarding what the results must be. We imagine the essence of what we want and then we "exhale" it, releasing it to Sophia. It is the heart's natural gesture of trust, not in fulfillment of what we imagine in our minds that we want, but in whatever may come to us. This rather circular gesture of intending and releasing in trust allows the spontaneous genius of the World Soul's creating to engage with us in a sort of continuous dance. The results of this are seldom what we might have expected. Rather, they are infallibly preferable, more perfect and appropriate for the harmonious well-being of the whole, of the All. We can often recognize our original intention bearing fruit that reminds us of our original hope, yet the result is far better.

Himalaya Gold Azeztulite facilitates this kind of co-creating activity in several dimensions. Its stimulation of the third chakra lends greater "power" to our intention. When we are strong-

willed (and avoid trying to be tyrants), we have more to offer on our side of the dance. We can focus our intentions better and keep our actions in alignment with the intentions we have set, even though we have released expectations. Second, having more awareness and control of the third chakra's currents allows us to learn to consciously project them (intend) and withdraw (surrender). If we can feel ourselves doing these gestures, it is very helpful in learning to practice them continuously. Our strengthened third chakra also increases our capacity to feel the will of others, giving us the opportunity to align or disengage with them. Third, we can even learn how to feel the flow of the World itself—what the Chinese call the Tao, and we might think of as the creating activity of Sophia—and we can then learn how better to swim with its currents.

As my meditation continued, I began to notice that the heart and solar plexus chakras were "burning into one another." There was pleasant but intense fiery activity in both areas, and the tingling in them grew until the two chakras seemed to merge into a single huge center. Simultaneously, I felt a powerful longing in my heart, and a great release of tension in the solar plexus. This brought tears to my eyes, accompanied by feelings of exaltation.

I feel that this merging of the heart and solar plexus—the unification of our love and will—is an essential component of the New Consciousness. When we give all our power to what our heart desires, we are also surrendering to the will of the Divine, since that is the source of the longing in our heart. To live in a state within which one's will is powerful, yet fully given over to the heart, is to live in co-creative union with the Soul of the World—for the will of the heart is inseparable from Her will. The dance we then embark upon is a life of grace. We feel ourselves as instruments that are, at last, in tune, and we play with the great intelligence of Love—intertwined so completely that we cannot tell whether our hands or Hers have touched our inner strings.

We can find our way to such a place without the help of stones, but the Himalaya Gold Azeztulites can introduce us to capacities we did not know we had, and it can aid us in maintaining our awareness and intention as we learn how to walk this invisible path of co-creating the world and ourselves through love.

As I sat with the Himalaya Gold Azeztulite on my forehead, heart and solar plexus, I was drawn to place the solar plexus stone on the crown. I saw an inner image of a golden sun or a radiant starlike form over my head, and as I sat holding the stones, I felt the radiance of this golden sun begin to penetrate my crown chakra slowly. Like liquid light with the consistency of honey, this golden light from the radiant sun above my head descended into the skull, bringing yellow-golden light into the consciousness. As I sat with it, the gold light descended slowly through the region of the third eye, and as it descended I began to inwardly see a field of golden light. The felt sense accompanying this was one of quiet bliss and a kind of soft willingness to allow the experience to unfold.

The gold light continued its descent and reached the area of my mouth, making it more of an effort to dictate, in part because my consciousness was most interested in attending to the gold light. The descent continued, reaching the throat, filling it with light, making my breathing through the throat a greatly pleasurable sensation. It descended further, through the shoulders and the upper chest—all this golden light from the radiant sun above my head—and I felt the light being pulled down through my root chakra into the Earth, although my sight showed it still just slowly, softly dripping down toward the heart.

Then I had a sudden vision of the heart as an organ of gold, wrapped in gold, radiant with gold, illuminated by an inner shining golden light; and the chest center became its own radiant source of light, and a great joy and recognition of the nature of my own heart as a radiant star came into my consciousness. "We all have this," so said my intuitive voice—we all have this golden Heart Light, and there is a star within us, kindled by the golden Sun from above. I was given the intuition that the golden Sun above my head is a holographic image of the Great Central Sun, which is present at the core of each star, each heart, each atom of matter. And by inviting this golden light I kindled, unexpectedly, the Sun of my heart.

The gold light continued its descent, stimulating the will center in the solar plexus, and I discovered (because I was seeing images arising very quickly with each step of the descending light) that my solar plexus had been wounded in my early life and in earlier lives. My will had been broken and overturned by violence in other lives, and I had been a fearful child in this life because of it and because of like happenings in my childhood years. As this golden light descended, I felt as though my third chakra became like a powerful beacon that shined out from me. It felt as though the broken ray of the will was repaired, and now in gratitude or appreciation, my will center seemed to turn up to the heart as if to ask its will. The radiant light of the heart shone.

The golden light dropped further to the second chakra area, and there I felt a kind of soft pleasurable glow, and the intuition was that this chakra will strengthen through imagination and play. Finally the golden light reached my root chakra and flowed from there down into my legs and feet and down into the Earth. It was a great moment of completion, and I was flooded with gratitude. I sat for some time, filled with the radiant gold, aware of the star above my head and its counterpart in my heart. I was aware of the ray of the will, now held within but prepared to extend out to any commitment or choice I might make. I was reminded that many years ago, a meditation with Moldavite brought forth a more abrupt and in some ways more amazing link with the golden light. Yet in both cases there was a Sun in my heart, and in both cases I was filled with gratitude and joy. In the case of my attunement with Himalaya Gold Azeztulite, there was more of a sense of walking with a kind of sure-footedness that I did not feel in the Moldavite experience. This may be from the more stable golden-light energies of this stone or my own level of experience now. Nonetheless, this descent of the Golden Light is accompanied by a great feeling of having been blessed, and it is a door this Himalaya Gold Azeztulite seems very well-suited to open.

There was and is a strong sense of clear-headed awareness which arose as I held the stones. I feel from this that there is a clarifying quality for consciousness emanated by Himalaya Gold Azeztulite. It is also a stone that makes the heart happy when the eyes behold it. I feel this is because its bright yellow color somehow reminds the heart of its own true radiant nature, which is often veiled.

HIMALAYA GOLD AZEZTULITE SPEAKS "I call out to the seat of your sovereignty, the throne of the heart, to awaken the One that dwells within. I invite all the noble citizens of your inner kingdom to awaken and serve the One."

PINK AZEZTULITE

KEY WORDS Deep heart awareness, emotional healing, serenity, compassion

ELEMENT Storm

CHAKRAS Heart (4th), Third Eye (6th), Crown (7th), Soul Star & Transpersonal (8th through 14th)

BACKGROUND Pink Azeztulite has the alternative name of Rhodazez. Although it is a mixed mineral containing both Quartz and Pink Dolomite, it is unmistakably an Azeztulite, as becomes recognizable when one meditates and opens to its frequencies. Like the other forms of Azeztulite, Pink Azeztulite resonates rapidly through the Liquid Crystal Body Matrix, and one senses tingles over the entire surface of one's skin, as though being gently touched by innumerable tiny hands. These may indeed be the hands of the Azez, the Light Beings who have awakened these stones to their potential and purpose. Yet even with its

tingles, Pink Azeztulite is a deeply soothing stone. As it awakens sensitivity, and as it sweeps through the liquid crystal body with the pattern of the Nameless Light, it also soothes the emotional body. It goes to the heart and seeds there the pattern of compassionate acceptance and love toward all aspects of oneself.

In our culture we are taught not to accept or love ourselves too much. We are taught that the demands and customs of society are more important than our own self-esteem. This leads to deep fragmentation, which may manifest as a contraction of self, as shame, fear, defensiveness or another manifestation that might be called egoistic self-esteem. These are two sides of one coin, and they have their roots in the fragmentation of self that is rampant in human societies. Wholeness begins with wholeheartedness; and Pink Azeztulite, as it centers in our heart and initiates the currents of compassionate self-acceptance, moves toward healing our fragmentation. In meditative work it often induces imagery from one's past to arise, especially moments in which the particular instances of our wounding have occurred. As one goes back and feels the breaks in the psyche that are brought forward in these visions, the compassionate heart qualities encouraged by Pink Azeztulite wrap themselves around the images of our fragmentation and bring those images into the center of our heart. Thus the lonely, forgotten child is comforted.

One is encouraged in these meditative practices to actively engage with the images and to inwardly welcome them as they are drawn into one's heart. It is good to extend the invitation to the lost fragments of self to come into the now and to view yourself in your wholeness, your healed state. It is appropriate to thank those lost parts for all they did and have tried to do to help you survive fearful situations. All of these are empowering choices that we can make under the inner circumstances to which we are led through meditative work with Pink Azeztulite. Even without doing the meditative work, wearing the stone brings into the emotional and the physical body the spiritual currents of forgiving, of loving, of gentleness, softness, calm, quiet, certitude, loyalty and heartfelt compassion.

One may not differentiate all these qualities, and one may not see the specific sorts of visions I have described, but anyone who turns attention to what occurs within themselves as one wears, carries or meditates with Pink Azeztulite will notice the sweet, calm, serene, yet highly activated state which is the signature of these stones. Ultimately, Azeztulite's purpose is to ignite the light of the Great Central Sun within our hearts and to encourage and enable us each to become a Light Being in human incarnation. To be the bridges between heaven and Earth is Azeztulite's pattern of destiny for us. It is a stone of ascension, but not of departure from the Earth. It is a stone of awakening to wholeness and enlightenment. Pink Azeztulite has been activated by the Azez for the purpose of healing our fragmentation in the realm of feeling. This is such a vast problem among humanity that a special stone, a special variety of Azeztulite, has been dedicated to it, or so my intuition states.

Upon longer exposure to Pink Azeztulite, I find its deep calm is transmuted into a state of reverence within heart awareness. It seems as though the entire interior of my body feels like the interior of my heart, and within that space my awareness assumes a posture of reverence. Pink Azeztulite can, of course, be applied to all kind of conditions for which the simultaneous gifts of Light-awakening and calm healing serenity can be of benefit for the individual. It is also important to work with Pink Azeztulite as an initiator of self-giving through the heart. As the heart is healed and one's old wounds cleared away, and even before this process is complete, one is enabled and encouraged to open the door of the heart and pour one's love into the world each moment.

Pink Azeztulite allows one to do this in a modest, unassuming way, with tenderness, graciousness and gentleness. Thus one is not only healed emotionally, one can become a healer of emotions—a healer of the wounds of others. This can be done through conversation and compassionate listening, and the heart will help one find the skillful words. Yet this capacity to facilitate emotional healing comes also, and primarily, from the state of one's being—the condition of the serene and open heart.

PINK AZEZTULITE SPEAKS "Do not hold your Treasure within your heart alone, for it is through the pouring out of the heart's Treasure that all become wealthy."

SATYALOKA AZEZTULITE

KEY WORDS   Spiritual awakening, planetary consciousness, receiving Light and knowledge from the higher planes

ELEMENT   Storm

CHAKRAS   Third Eye (6th), Crown (7th), Soul Star (8th), Transpersonal (9th through 14th)

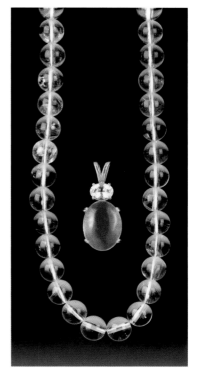

BACKGROUND   Satyaloka Azeztulite (aka Satyaloka Quartz) is a variety of Quartz from the Satya Loka moun-tains of southern India. It is a silicon dioxide mineral with a hardness of 7. Its crystal system is hexagonal (trigonal). Satyaloka Quartz forms as small, prismatic crystals and also in massive form. The massive material is primarily transparent, translucent or white, sometimes with inclusions of reddish brown or gray. The crystals are colorless, with fogginess at the base end of some pieces, and an occasional reddish coating.

This Quartz was originally gathered by monks of the Satya Loka monastery, who sent it into the world as a means of spreading the energy of spiritual enlightenment. The monks believe that this energy is a quality of the mountains where they live and that the stones are capable of carrying and dispersing this energy throughout the world. The region where Satyaloka Azeztulite is found in South India has been called by some the crown chakra of the world. The impression one experiences in meditation with Satyaloka Azeztulite makes it easy to understand how the land got this designation.

NEW ATTUNEMENT   Satyaloka Azeztulite opens the crown chakra with a tremendous flow of energy. I felt it pouring downward through the crown as soon as I held the stones in my hands, without even placing them anywhere near my head. The crown chakra opened and a pulsing energy cascade thrust down again and again through the top of my head all the way to my heart. As it extended further, it seemed to be exploring or slowly penetrating the column of my chakras below the heart, with each pulse reaching a little deeper.

Satyaloka Azeztulite placed upon the heart in a pouch produced a deep sense of reverence, an appreciation of the presence of the Holy in my heart. It became difficult to speak or form words as I allowed this vibration of the Holy to move

into my heart center. This stone carries deep currents of what I would term the Holy Silence. It has a direct resonance with the vastness of consciousness at the site of Origin. It opens a stream via which one may venture toward the Source. It is a rather magnetic feeling, as the Source draws one toward itself. As one gets closer and closer to it, words are left behind, and as one approaches nearer, one is conscious only of the swirling White Light that whirls around the center void in a spiraling cloud. One feels like a moth might feel when approaching a flame. Even if merging with the center of the flame is annihilation for the moth, it cannot do other than propel itself toward that irresistable Light.

Satyaloka Azeztulite is a stone of India, and as such it is soaked in the energy of spiritual aspiration which has prevailed on the subcontinent for so many centuries. Satyaloka Azeztulite vibrates to the frequency of enlightenment, and it is more intense in its currents than any other form of Azeztulite. If one wishes to experience the maximum Light infusion possible through Azeztulite, the maximum expansion of consciousness that Azeztulite can stimulate, and the maximum intesity of energy currents one can receive through a stone, the best stone for these purposes is indeed Satyaloka Azeztulite. All Azeztulites carry the currents of the Great Central Sun, spiritual core of the holographic universe. What distinguishes Satyaloka Azeztulite from other Azeztulite varieties is perhaps less important than what unites it with them, for all are paths to the Central Sun.

Yet if I am to make distinctions, I must say that Satyaloka Azeztulite is what one might call the most "hard-core" of all Azeztulites, perhaps of all stones. Certainly it is unswervingly attuned to the source of pure White Light radiance, and it tends to infuse one's mind, body and chakra system with pure White Light.

Azeztulite from the original sources in Vermont and North Carolina carried a somewhat more gentle frequency, perhaps a bit less potent. Satyaloka Azeztulite is tremendously powerful. Throughout the entire mineral kingdom I know no currents more intense than these. It organizes and re-centers brain activity. It brings consciousness to a deepening sense of quiet and gives a heightened sensitivity to subtle energies and streams of consciousness. It asks a great deal of the heart, for it pulls Light through the heart and into the rest of the body. It is not a difficult or painful thing at all; it is a lovely feeling. It is simply powerful.

Satyaloka Azeztulite is resonant with the energies described in India's mystical traditions as *sat-chit-ananda*. *Sat* means truth, *chit* is consciousness and *ananda* is bliss, so this *sat-chit-ananda* is the quality of truth, consciousness and bliss as one whole pattern. Satyaloka Azeztulite can infuse the Liquid Crystal Body Matrix with the intense high frequencies of *sat-chit-ananda*. There is, I can only say, a tremendous Light in these stones.

When meditating with Satyaloka Azeztulite stones, after initially just holding some of them in my hands I placed several in a pouch over my heart, several more in my hands and one on the crown chakra.

The resonance with the heart is powerful. It stills the extraneous currents that might circulate around or through the heart and puts the heart in a kind of high-frequency pulsation in attunement to its core, its center point. It feels so deeply powerful, it is difficult to speak of it. For those who wish to transfigure themselves into beacons of spiritual Light in the world, for the uplifting of humanity and the world itself, there is no better tool than Satyaloka Azeztulite.

It is a stone of powerful spiritual dedication. It can guide in purification of one's energy bodies, of one's intention, will, even of one's love activities and energies. It encourages one-pointed focus of consciousness through the will in the third chakra. This is an extremely powerful capacity, because one-pointed focus through the will is the most powerful inner "posture" for specific co-creating activity and manifestation of what one envisions.

Satyaloka Azeztulite can be used to travel through the realms of Light to many higher planes of reality. It can be ridden all the way to the archetypal first emanations from Source. It is a powerful stone for conducting one on conscious journeys into the spiritual worlds via the geometries of Light. It enables one to more readily place the Light geometries along and within the body/temple. Satyaloka Azeztulite encourages us to envision ourselves and our world as temples, as holy places.

Its adherence to the purpose of Light in the world is absolute, and it engenders absolute devotion to Spirit in the individual.

Satyaloka Azeztulite resonates with all other forms of Azeztulite, as well as Moldavite and many of the other high-frequency stones such as the Synergy Twelve and the Ascension Seven. Among the stones that will help modify and ease its intensity are Rosophia and Pink Azeztulite, as well as Morganite. Satyaloka Azeztulite is a stone of our great journey into the Light, and the great infusion of the Light into us.

SATYALOKA AZEZTULITE SPEAKS "I am the stone most capable of carrying the currents of Nirvana. I am a Master stone through which spiritual Masters may speak to those who work with me. Indeed, those who work with me may find that spiritual Masters are speaking through one's own voice, through one's own heart and mind and consciousness. I can awaken the body to its purpose as a living expression of, and vehicle for, the Light."

BLACK TOURMALINE

KEY WORDS Purification, protection, grounding, becoming the New Human Being

ELEMENT Earth

CHAKRA Base (1st)

Black Tourmaline is a complex aluminum borosilicate with a hardness of 7 to 7.5. Its crystal pattern is hexagonal (trigonal) with prismatic crystals and striations running parallel to the main axis. Though less colorful than other varieties, Black Tourmaline (also known as Schorl) is one of the most popular stones for spiritual purposes. It forms in a wide range of sizes, from the half-inch double-terminated crystals of Nepal to large Brazilian crystals of several pounds each. Some of the best specimens come from Brazil, China, Africa, Pakistan, and the U.S. state of Maine.

BACKGROUND Black Tourmaline crystals are ideal for psychic protection. Carrying or meditating with one of these stones can keep the auric field clear of imbalance, even in the presence of destructive energies. In addition, Black Tourmalines can provide high levels of purification that serve to elevate one's consciousness. These crystals are also recommended for ridding oneself of negative thoughts, anxieties, anger and ideas of unworthiness. Black Tourmaline's energies of protection can be further enhanced by combining it with Master Shamanite,

Tibetan Black Quartz, Jet, Obsidian, Smoky Quartz, Sugilite, Charoite and Amethyst. Its grounding qualities can be increased by Hematite.

NEW ATTUNEMENT   Black Tourmaline has for a number of years been considered the quintessential stone of grounding and protection. This reputation is clearly deserved, and my meditation with Black Tourmaline gave me an immediate sense of this. I sat holding a large Black Tourmaline in each hand, and a third Black Tourmaline in a pouch over my heart. I sat there for only a few seconds before noticing a kind of flushing-out of innumerable minute tensions, which seemed to exit my body through the points of contact with the Black Tourmaline. A very noticeable wave of relaxation and relief went through my body, and my energetic bodies as well. It was clear to me that the Black Tourmalines had pulled out the "wrinkles" of disharmony from my various fields and from the Liquid Crystal Body Matrix.

Purification and cleansing are among the most crucial of spiritual activities. We cannot possibly be conscious of the many patterns that hold us, or that we hold. There are innumerable patterns, large and small, that are detrimental to our wholeness and well-being. We, as sensitive living beings, readily pick up all sorts of patterns from our environment and our explorations of the inner and outer realms. Because we cannot attend consciously to all points of our being, many linkages occur between ourselves and detrimental or limiting currents and patterns. Black Tourmaline, when one invites it to do so, will very naturally draw all such patterns out of the auric field, physical body, and etheric and astral bodies. The sense of relief—the sigh of relaxation—comes from the felt recognition that all sorts of difficult frequencies are no longer present, and all that remains is one's optimal pattern of wholeness.

Those who are working to bring in or build the Light Body, and to weave together the physical body and the Light Body, are serving to give birth to the New Human Being. These people will find a ready ally in Black Tourmaline. As we take on new vibrational layers that work together to build the Body of Light, we benefit from Black Tourmaline's way of cleansing and purifying. This is akin to the alchemical term coagulation. In the process of building the Light Body, one encounters many high-frequency currents offered through stones or via other means, and one opens oneself to take on these new patterns. This is integral to the process. As one adds layers of vibration to one's core being, there is a need to hold those patterns steady within the matrix of the self. To take on multiple elements or layers and to synthesize them into a new form is coagulation.

It's a bit like acquiring a new habit. If you do something once and do not hold steady with your will to repeat the new desired behavior, it can drift away easily. Conversely, as you practice the new pattern as a chosen habit, its repetition—its entwinement with the fullness of oneself—becomes stronger, more solidified, more integrated. This is as true with new vibrational spectrums as it is with diet or any other outer behavior. One must practice the presence of the new material within the fullness of self. Because it has the quality of grounding and purifying, Black Tourmaline helps one solidify and integrate new layers much more quickly. This is essential in the Light Body process, and Black Tourmaline ought to be a part of everyone's array of stone allies for this work.

As I mentioned, coagulation is a term that describes the solidification of all that one has learned and become in the process of spiritual alchemy. Coagulation is in fact the forming of a solid out of a solution. I love this play on words, for our embodiment of Light is indeed the "solution" to our human evolutionary dilemma, and its full embodiment is indeed a coagulation, a solidification of the new patterns of selfhood. Black Tourmaline is like a coagulating agent, pulling together the new patterns into a synthesis; and a new substance—a new way of being—is created. This is our goal as spiritual alchemists of the self. I know of no other stone that so powerfully acts to ground, strengthen, purify and solidify the newly grasped patterns of our potential into the fullness of the New Human Being than Black Tourmaline.

BLACK TOURMALINE SPEAKS   "I am the great Attractor of all that you must release and all that you can become."

BROOKITE

KEY WORDS   Higher-chakra awakening and alignment, interdimensional travel
ELEMENT   Storm
CHAKRAS   Third Eye (6th), Crown (7th), Etheric (8th and beyond, above the head)

B rookite is a titanium oxide crystal with a hardness of 5.5 to 6. Its crystal system is orthorhombic. It often forms in metamorphic rocks, especially high-grade gneisses or schists. It occurs, rarely, as an inclusion in Quartz and more commonly as squarish charcoal-colored crystals under a half-inch in size. Good specimens are found in England, the French Alps and in the U.S. state of Arkansas. Its color is most frequently dark gray or black, but it can also be yellow-brown or reddish-brown. In the Alps, veins with Brookite often contain Rutile, Anatase and Albite.

BACKGROUND   Brookite is one of the primary power stones for expansion of awareness be-yond the physical body. It is a powerful activator of the sixth and seventh chakras and the etheric chakras above the head. It can align all the upper chakras with the rest of one's energy body, allowing one to explore the subtle realms with a highly sensitive and stable awareness. Brookite facilitates reaching an ex-panded state in which one can communicate and commune with beings on the higher vibrational levels. It can help one gain the "cosmic perspective" that allows one to see even unpleasant situations as beneficial to growth. It is inspirational and energizing, assisting in overcoming old patterns and moving ahead to greater inner development.

Brookite combines well with other high-vibration stones such as Phenacite, Azeztulite, Danburite, Herderite, Seraphinite, Natrolite, Scolecite, Tibetan Tektite, Satyaloka Azeztulite, Petalite, Tanzanite, Merkabite Calcite and Moldavite. If one feels the need to ground Brookite's energy more deeply in the body, Black Tourmaline and Master Shamanite are recommended.

NEW ATTUNEMENT   Brookite, for all its modest appearance, is one of the fastest and most intense stones for stimulating the third eye, the crown chakra and the etheric chakras above the head. For those who have never had the experience of sensing these nonphysical chakras, Brookite provides ready access and enables you to consciously notice and dwell in the reso-nance of the connection with the higher worlds. This connection is the function of the etheric chakras.

Brookite is primarily resonant with the highest energetic frequencies we can experience in our present form. It links to the physical body at the third eye and crown chakras exclusively. Currents from Brookite are seldom experienced below the third eye. Brookite is an excellent stone for the expansion of consciousness into higher dimensions of Light. It is a beneficial ally for those who wish to experience and understand the inner geometries of interdimensional

travel, as well as the archetypal forms underlying the manifest world. Brookite, through its intense high vibration, stimulates the areas of the brain/mind that can intuitively see and understand the Divine principles of form. Those drawn to the practice of sacred geometry or geomancy—applying the principles of higher-dimensional understanding to the living currents and patterns of the Earth—will find that Brookite enhances the capacity to see these patterns clearly.

Brookite can take the inner traveler to realms in which the living beings—or perhaps I should say the vibrational beings—exist within Light geometries and express and communicate symbolically through a geometric language. This high-vibrational domain is a place rarely visited by our species, in our current level of evolution. However, Brookite seems to ask me to say that we will find these beings to be our vibrational neighbors and evolutionary friends. These seemingly alien beings are not space travelers; they are mind travelers. They say, through their ally Brookite—which is working as a kind of energetic line of communication with these higher-frequency domains—that they know and see us and wish to learn from communing with us about the "mysteries of imperfection" and the spontaneous activity of creating within the unknown. These vibrational entities are beings of the higher Logos—the perfected and eternal patterns—expressing themselves in highly complex, intricate geometries, such as we might see when viewing fractal forms. Fractal patterns go on infinitely, unfolding perfections that continually generate deeper and deeper levels of detail and complexity. These beings, to which Brookite attunes us, seem to say that the fractal world is deeply akin to their domain of existence, and that their world is deeply entwined with ours.

The "mystery of imperfect expression," which—although fully entwined with that which is perfect—is from the perspective of the geometric realms an astonishing quality of the Earth and all the manifested universe. These intelligences from the unmanifested realms are fascinated by us, and we will understand ourselves and our universe better by finding our way into attunement with them. As I reflect upon this surprising experience of communication through this meditation with Brookite, I see that the opening of awareness to the higher-vibrational realms that Brookite promises is quite genuine. I am guided to say that Brookite offers a multiplicity of such interior vibrational gateways for our exploration and learning.

BROOKITE SPEAKS "I invite you to travel with me into lands which you do not know, to view realms which eyes have never seen, and to meet inhabitants who will expand your consciousness vastly."

CELESTITE

KEY WORDS Angelic communication, access to higher dimensions, serenity, forgiveness

ELEMENT Wind

CHAKRAS Heart (4th), Third Eye (6th), Crown (7th), Transpersonal and Etheric (8th through 14th, above the head)

Celestite (also known as Celestine) is a strontium sulfate mineral with a hardness of 3 to 3.5. Its crystal system is orthorhombic. It forms both tabular and prismatic crystals, and Celestite also occurs in massive, fibrous, granular or nodular configurations. It can be colorless, white, gray, blue, green, yellow, orange, reddish or brown. The Celestite most frequently found on the market is a gray-blue variety from Madagascar, which tends to occur in clusters and geodes. A rarer variety is Ohio Celestite, which often forms in single gray, whitish or blue-gray tabular crystals, from under an inch to over eight inches long. Some of these crystals are at least partially transparent, and a few are double-terminated. The tabular Celestite crystals from Ohio have become popular with energy workers.

BACKGROUND   Celestite offers a gentle, uplifting energy that can raise and expand one's awareness into the higher realms. It is one of the most effective stones for accessing the angelic realm and can facilitate communication between oneself and one's guardian angels or angelic guides. It stimulates the third eye and crown chakras and the etheric chakras above the head. It is a soft stone both physically and energetically. As it elevates awareness, Celestite makes one feel as if floating on a cloud rather than zooming in a rocket.

Madagascar's Blue-gray Celestite comes primarily in clusters, and it is ideal for place-ment in a bedroom, healing room or meditation space, as an environmental cleanser and source of soft positive energies. Its vibrations radiate in all directions, making it wonderful to have around any healing or meditation space. Tabular Celestite points from Ohio are ideal for body layouts and jewelry.

NEW ATTUNEMENT   In placing two Celestites over my heart and holding a large Celestite crystal in my hands, the immediate effect was a profound soothing and quieting of my energy field. Celestite, without a doubt, is one of the gentlest, softest and most intimately loving stones in the mineral kingdom. Whereas some stones such as Strontianite may reflect a very impersonal sort of love, the qualities emanated and received in the heart from Celestite are the most delicate, loving and softly nurturing energy currents. One readily senses the angelic presences behind Celestite, and the most prominent among them is one's personal guardian angel. Recognizing that Celestite seems to act as a portal for connection with one's guardian angel and other angelic beings, I notice an immediate upwelling of joy and gratitude.

Through Celestite, one feels the sense of being individually loved and cherished by higher spiritual beings. By "higher" I mean beings on a higher vibrational plane, not "of higher impor-tance." For they themselves hasten to tell us that they are not superior to us and that, in fact, they lovingly serve our highest good and are constantly available to help us.

The softening feeling that enters one's emotional body upon contact with Celestite is remarkable. Celestite soothes and soothes deeply. It is an ideal stone to aid sleep and reduce stress. In fact, Celestite is highly attuned to the realm of dreaming. While I held the Celestite crystal to attune to its properties, I fell into dreaming several times. The dreaming engendered by Celestite is of a teaching nature for the feeling self. Take, for example, the dreams I unexpect-edly experienced as I meditated with Celestite. These were quite unusual—almost waking dreams—and each dream showed me people and situations that I was called to forgive. Forgiv-ing is the most important activity that Celestite encourages within us. In order to realize our destiny of evolving into spiritual human beings, in order to achieve our capacity to awaken and live within and as the Light Body, we must be able to release attachments to entanglements in the past. Various attachments to past events hold pieces of the psyche fixed and keep us from living and acting with the fluidity that allows us to embrace each new moment wholeheartedly. When one's feelings are attached to some wound or trauma from the past, or even when attached to a pleasant memory, our conscious awareness and soul body are not fully present for the coming moment's arrival.

Of course, much suffering is experienced in relation to these sorts of attachments. In the case of positive attachments, one longs for what has already happened to still be present. With attachments having to do with wounds or painful memories, the feelings are sometimes grief or depression, and often anger and resentment. Sometimes these are mixed. All of these, including attachment to positive memories, are dispelled in the activity of forgiving.

The word "forgiving," if taken apart, becomes fore-giving, giving forward. This is the very gesture of offering oneself into the moment that is constantly coming into existence. And, as quickly as each moment flows into awareness, it passes and is followed by another moment, in a continuous flow. In order to fully embrace the coming moment, one must be present to the constant creating activity of living. The attachments we have to the past must be dispelled. Forgiving is that process: fore-giving.

Celestite offers an opportunity for healing resolution of attachments to the past. It engenders inner experiences that rekindle the memories of those attachments. In the case of memories attached to wounds and pain, around which we may still carry anger, resentment or fear, the soft, soothing qualities of Celestite help us love all those involved in these memories, unconditionally and therefore without attachment. Celestite awakens compassion within the heart, and through the heart's eye of compassion we are able to revisit the occasions of past attachments and to forgive all who were involved. Celestite allows us to invite that situation and those people into our heart, and to give each of our memories a home in the heart. We need not die to our memories, only to the attachment that keeps us stuck in the past.

Many of our entanglements are unconscious, and meditation with Celestite can bring forward unhealed patterns and memories for clearing, which occurs through loving acceptance and release. A good meditation to practice with Celestite is this very simple one: Hold or wear a Celestite near or over your heart and quiet your thoughts. Align and center in the heart, and from the place in the heart, inwardly say, "I invite all beings who wish forgiveness to come into my heart. I invite all beings who long for my forgiveness to come into my heart, including myself." Hold this intention quietly and remain centered in the heart. Watch as beings appear in order to come into your heart and be forgiven. Imagine the image of each one entering your heart and finding its proper place there. Then release that image and continue until no more beings appear, or until you feel the process is complete.

Often when I practice this meditation, I see a line of people in front of me, waiting for me to take them each into my heart for forgiving. Sometimes I, myself, am in that line. When I am, the image of me brings with him a memory of some past wound that I have brought upon myself or someone else. Forgiving oneself is a powerful act of healing.

The forgiving encouraged by Celestite is one in which we do not deal with the right and wrong or the "injustice" of any event. Rather, we see who comes for forgiving and take them into our hearts with compassion. The Celestite provides a resonance that softly and gently encourages the heart to open. This softness carries with it the current of compassion. All of these words are more complicated than the inner experience, which is simply a soft opening. Seeing

the forgiven ones within my heart engenders a kind of inner sigh of release, accompanied in me by feelings of gratitude toward those who have stepped forward.

I want to describe another powerful forgiving meditation to practice with Celestite. This again involves sitting and holding the Celestite over the heart, or even walking outdoors holding the Celestite crystal over the heart. Before beginning the meditation, think of one of your worst, darkest traits or deeds. Place an image or memory of that trait or deed within your heart, and hold it there. As you sit or walk with eyes closed, or partially closed, repeat inwardly (with heartfelt emphasis) the following words: "I am so grateful for *blank*." Fill in the blank with the trait or memory you are holding in your heart. For example, you could say, "I am so grateful for my dishonesty" or "my greediness." Keep repeating this, with as much emphasis as you can muster, for three to five minutes, while sitting or walking. I like to make this a

walking meditation, because the movement seems to bring the process more fully into the body.

Holding gratitude in the presence of one's darkness brings the exiled parts back into the heart, so that we may be whole rather than fragmented. The feeling of a meditation like this, in which one purposefully speaks of gratitude for qualities of which one is either afraid or ashamed, is powerful spiritual medicine. The only possible way we can be whole is if we heal our fragmentation, and the most potent way I know to recover our exiled fragments is to bring them into our heart. With the help of the soft compassionate currents available and offered freely to us through Celestite, we can use our will to bring forgiving into every corner of our being, into every negative fragment of our past. As we continue to develop the activity of forgiving as a constant flow, our attachments become fewer and the length of time to which we are attached to some difficult moment diminishes. Ultimately, when we can forgive each difficult moment or person (or ourselves) instantly, we will be available for full engagement in the joyful activity of co-creation in each moment.

Celestite raises one's awareness, without in any way depersonalizing consciousness. We retain the intimate feeling qualities natural to the heart, even as consciousness rises and expands to the domains above the crown chakra. It has been said that the Universe is essentially love, and Celestite helps one attune to the inner currents through which this idea becomes one's felt sense of being.

Celestite resonates synergistically with all forms of Azeztulite, as well as Morganite and other stones attuned to the heart. Rosophia and Azeztulite are particularly lovely when used together with Celestite. Rosophia most tangibly awakens the heart and invites one's individual self into relationship with the Soul of the World. Celestite's soft heart-opening influence makes it easy for us to gently allow the relationship with the World Soul, Sophia, to unfold. Celestite is very helpful in softening the intensity of certain stones that can be very strong and beneficial but sometimes rather overwhelming. It has a resonant connection with Strontianite and combines with it in such a way that the willful intensity of Strontianite is modulated by Celestite's soft attunement to the heart. Celestite is deeply attuned to the blue ray—the medium-blue ray or the silver-blue ray—and has close kinship with the stones Angelite and Larimar.

CELESTITE SPEAKS "I am a being so woven in love that there is no other thread in my loom. Love is joy, and no pain is worth departing from love or joy. Forgive, and live, and go on loving."

CERUSSITE

KEY WORDS Alchemical transformation of self, infusion of Light, embracing evolutionary change

ELEMENT Storm

CHAKRAS Root (1st), Crown (7th)

Cerussite is a lead carbonate mineral with a hardness of 3.5. Its crystal system is orthorhombic, and it typically appears in association with minerals such as Sphalerite, Galena, Pyromorphite, Anglesite and Smithsonite. It often forms crystals, which are colorless, gray or brown, and it has an adamantine luster. Good-quality Cerussite crystals have been found in the Czech Republic, Sardinia, Austria, Scotland, Namibia and the U.S.

157

BACKGROUND Cerussite is a stone of inner alchemy. For those spiritual pioneers who desire self-transformation, it can be a helpful ally. It stimulates the energies of the root chakra and links them to the crown chakra. It builds a vibrational spiral up through the spinal column, energizing each of the chakras along the way. In so doing, it creates a pattern of realignment which reverberates through all levels of one's being, offering the opportunity to choose to restructure one's life at a higher level of spiritual functioning. It can also assist those who are going through unexpected transitions—in health, relationships or self-awareness—to find the most appropriate new pattern for their life.

Cerussite harmonizes with Nuummite, Black Tourmaline and Master Shamanite, which give extra emphasis to the lower chakras. At the crown, Cerussite links synergistically with Azeztulite, Petalite, Scolecite and Natrolite, which aid in opening one's consciousness to awareness of the Divine. Celestite helps Cerussite attune's the physical self to the frequencies of the higher worlds.

NEW ATTUNEMENT As I meditated with Cerussite I placed one stone over my heart, one at my base chakra and one upon the crown. There was noticeable infusion of powerful currents, which worked their way down from the top of my head and resonated powerfully at the base chakra. Few stones with the ability to stimulate the crown are also powerful at the root chakra. Cerussite resonates with the polar axis of the human body. It was interesting to notice that the currents pulsed at both ends of this axis—linking them—but did not do anything I could feel in intervening areas of the body or the chakra system.

Placing a Cerussite on the third eye, I felt no currents there, even as the crown continued to vibrate. This is most unusual. There had been an initial resonance in the heart, but after a few minutes this became very still and only the two polar points continued to vibrate. In monitoring the two polar positions where the Cerussite was resonating, my attention seemed to open a connecting circuit between them. The felt sense was of rays of Cerussite's currents reaching down from above and up from below toward each other, as though they were mutually magnetic. The two currents began pulsing toward one another, sending thrills of energy nearly all the way to my heart. Although I still did not feel the stone currents in my heart, I did see a vision of the heart as golden, transparent, living matter. This was a striking image to me.

At this point I remembered Cerussite's reputation as an alchemical stone—a stone that could be understood through applying the ideas of alchemy to its working. Of course Cerussite

is a lead carbonate and therefore is akin to the alchemical element of lead. The "external" goal of the alchemists was to transmute the metal lead to the metal gold. If they were spiritual alchemists they also hoped to simultaneously transform (through sympathetic magic) the lead of their everyday personality into the gold of the Divine human being. This is much the same as our goal in developing or awakening to the New Consciousness. Cerussite itself appears often as gold-tinged crystals, thus displaying a kind of crystalline embodiment of the alchemical transmutative process. As I thought of this, the currents that Cerussite was generating—upward from my root chakra and down from my crown—began to display themselves to my inner vision as currents of gold-white Light. And the heart, which I could see inwardly, although it did not feel the current was a golden heart.

After a few more minutes I began to feel Cerussite's currents entering my heart area. The pulsing continued, and as the currents joined they became swirling, undulating movements, which encapsulated my heart in a bath of living energy. This was a great and holy sensation. It was accompanied by a slight itching of the skin over my heart chakra, and I assumed this to be an effect of the currents merging there from above and below.

The ancient saying, "As Above, so Below," is the essence of sympathetic magic. Cerussite draws the Above of the crown chakra and the Below of the root chakra into the alchemical vessel of the heart. Under Cerussite's influence, the heart itself becomes golden, and it can transmute all things it touches into a Golden condition. My image of the heart—the transparent, golden heart—seemed to fill with a liquid like water, pouring in from above and below. And as the heart filled with the living water from the two poles of my being, it began to radiate light like a sun.

I sense that Cerussite, in alliance with the many transmuting, transfiguring stones of spiritual metamorphosis in this book, works to carry the pattern of evolutionary transformation into the body, and in its own particular way. Its currents are the only ones I felt entering the body from both directions (above and below). This seems to suggest that Cerussite can teach us how to incorporate both our higher and lower aspects, in a way that draws nourishment from all aspects of our being. This is not a hierarchical flow that works down, from above to below.

Cerussite is indeed an alchemical stone, which resonates with both the Above and the Below, bringing that resonance into us. Cerussite seems to tell us that it is a helpful talisman for all forms of sympathetic magic. If one wishes to bring the qualities of another stone more fully into oneself—or even the qualities of some other being or teacher—placing a Cerussite near a sample of the stone, or a picture of the teacher or being, is the first step. In fact, it is best to place two Cerussites there and to do a prayer of grateful request. Then wear, carry or meditate with one of the stones while leaving the other with the talisman. Through sympathetic magic and Cerussite's aid, we may begin to feel ourselves assimilating the qualities we seek.

CERUSSITE SPEAKS: "I am the highest and the lowest. You are the in-between. Through me you can become your fullness, and through you I can fulfill my purpose."

CINNABAR QUARTZ

KEY WORDS   Alchemy, magic, transformation, insight, manifestation, wealth, mental agility

ELEMENT   Fire

CHAKRAS   Root (1st), Sexual/Creative (2nd), third eye (6th)

Cinnabar Quartz is a mixture of red Cinnabar, white Quartz and other trace minerals. It is found in Arizona. Cinnabar is a mercury sulfide mineral with a hardness of 2 to 2.5. Its crystal system is trigonal. Its color is vermillion red, or brownish when impurities are present. It forms around volcanic vents and hot springs and may also occur in sedimentary rocks associated with recent volcanic activity. Cinnabar is the principal form of mercury ore and is processed to produce refined mercury. Since mercury is a toxic material, caution should be used in handling Cinnabar.

Cinnabar sometimes forms in conjunction with Quartz, and Cinnabar Quartz is perhaps the most beneficial form of Cinnabar for metaphysical use. The Quartz serves to increase the durability of the stone, and to magnify the Cinnabar's energetic properties.

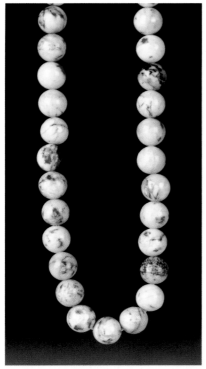

BACKGROUND Cinnabar Quartz stones are talismans of the alchemical transformation, aiding in fulfillment of the Divine pattern we carry within. Cinnabar stimulates the first and second chakras, enhancing life force and creativity. It also awakens the third eye, making for greater insight and the ability to see visions of the potential future. It helps ground visions in physical reality, making it an ideal stone for creative people as well as business owners, both of whom can use it to actualize their dreams and create prosperity. Cinnabar Quartz can align, balance and remove blockages in one's energy body. Such attunement is at the core of transformation.

As a stone of the Magician archetype, Cinnabar (or Cinnabar Quartz) can facilitate alignment of personal will with Divine will, allowing one to sometimes "tweak" the Divine currents so that one influences the form of creative manifestation. Cinnabar is aligned with the god Mercury, also known as Hermes or Thoth. These stones can help increase mental agility, speed of thought and intellectual brilliance, traits for which these gods were known.

Cinnabar and Cinnabar Quartz work in synergy with Crimson Cuprite and Creedite, as well as Phenacite, which aids in manifesting inner visions.

NEW ATTUNEMENT As I wrote in *The Book of Stones*, Cinnabar and Cinnabar Quartz are associated energetically with the domains of magic, alchemy, quick leaps of thought and inner transformation. Transformation might also be called metamorphosis, or shape-shifting. The fluid metal mercury has always been associated with magic and alchemy, and with the capacity to rapidly change states. Cinnabar is composed of mercury and sulfur. It is a mercury sulfide, and both mercury and sulfur were key elements of alchemical processes.

Cinnabar in crystal form—or in veins, as in Cinnabar Quartz—is bright red. This color is resonant with the color of one of the images of the Philosopher's Stone, the goal of alchemy. This is the Stone of the "lovers of wisdom" (*philo*= love; *sopher*= Wisdom, or Sophia), which helps the alchemists attain wisdom. This Stone has been described as white at one stage, and red in its completion stage. There is no stone more perfectly red than Cinnabar, and there many other correspondences between Cinnabar and the Stone of alchemy.

As I began to work meditatively with Cinnabar Quartz, the piece upon which I was focusing exhibited interesting phenomena. I initially felt unusual currents in the third eye, going through the skull at an angle, down toward the back of the neck at the top of the spine. The pulsations of Cinnabar were unlike those of any other stone. There were repetitions of three short pulses, without any extension of the current past the forehead point, followed by one long pulse in which the current flow went straight through the head and down the first section of the spine toward the shoulders. It felt as though the stone was building up its charge with the three short pulses and then extending its influx into the body with the long pulse. With time, this worked its way lower and the pulse became longer.

I believe that Cinnabar Quartz has the capacity, like the ancient alchemical Philosopher's Stone, to stimulate and awaken dormant areas of the mind. It seems to quicken the pulse of thought and to trigger rapid associations of ideas. It initiates leaps of understanding from one domain of knowledge to another. One makes surprising connections that shed new light on familiar ideas. This stone is resonant with the god Hermes (Mercury), who could travel so fast that he became the Messenger of the gods. The quickening of mental powers was one of the characteristics of the Wisdom the alchemists were seeking in their work with elemental forms of mercury. In fact, for their laboratory processes they frequently extracted their mercury from Cinnabar.

As I gazed upon the piece of Cinnabar Quartz used in this meditation, I was struck by the shape-shifting quality of the appearance of the stone itself. I began noticing that the swirls of red and the other markings appeared to be moving and coalescing into recognizable patterns. I initially noticed a face, seeming to emerge from the surface of the stone—a rather friendly face, with the curling hair one sees in representations of the Greek Gods. I thought, "Oh, this is the face of Hermes!" Then this shifted and seemed to disappear, and the next image I saw was a goblet, again appearing to compose itself from the stone's markings, shifting even as I watched. This is so like the malleable, changeable Mercury of alchemy that it made me smile. And the goblet form was reminiscent of the Grail, which is itself a powerful alchemical image. Above this Grail there seemed to be another face that was shouting or singing, clearly attempting to communicate. It was reminiscent of the so-called "severed head" of the Templars' meditations. (For the Templars, this image signified the mental capacities separated from their bondage to the body, nothing worse!) I took this to mean that the Cinnabar acts, like the Grail, as a catalyst for freeing the mind and liberating our thought.

Then I turned the stone and gazed upon it anew, finding this time another face. This third face had lips of red Cinnabar that seemed to move as I gazed upon it. It was a face sharply divided between a light-filled side and a dark side. The side to my left was the darkened side, and the right was the light-filled side. This was another alchemical image, for the processes of spiritual alchemy involve mixing and blending one's inner darkness and light until they become one body—the wholeness of the Self. As these thoughts arose, I continued to observe the Cinnabar Quartz stone, and the half-dark, half-light face was moving its lips, silently speaking.

I recognize that such moving imagery is not necessarily physically present. I believe it to be a phenomenon of the interaction of my consciousness with the being behind the stone. The images, and the manner in which they appeared, are resonant with the qualities of Cinnabar and Cinnabar Quartz—they were fast-moving, shape-shifting symbols that illustrated alchemical ideas—and I marveled at their vividness and the originality they displayed.

For our aspirations for spiritual growth and evolution, Cinnabar is a potent quickener. It speeds the processes by which one's transformation takes place, regardless of which other stones one may be working with. It enables leaps of insight that allow one to turn toward the most promising areas of inner development. It facilitates the process of alchemical change within the individual, from what may be called the "leaden self" of the everyday consciousness into the ultimate expression of golden illuminated awareness. That is the inner meaning of the alchemical transmutation of lead to gold, the goal of many alchemists. "Changing lead to gold" has various resonances, among them the fact that Cinnabar and Cinnabar Quartz have long been considered to be stones of prosperity. Lead-into-gold is also the change from the beginning of a business or project into its fruition as a generator of wealth. Therefore Cinnabar and Cinnabar Quartz are recommended to those wishing to work in this "outer" dimension of alchemy. Alchemy is not necessarily the repetition of old alchemical practices; it is much more a matter of recognizing the underlying gestures of alchemy, as they are akin to the movements we make in our own evolutionary growth. The change of lead to gold is a prime example.

Because of its facilitation of rapid change and growth, Cinnabar Quartz is a stone of so-called invisibility. This means that it enhances one's capacity for rapid adaptation to changing circumstances, whether inner or outer. This is an advantage on all levels, from survival to inner fulfillment. There are few stones as rapid in their entry into one's energy field, or their engagement with one's interior sensing capacities, as Cinnabar and Cinnabar Quartz. Their vibration speedily moves through one's energy field, influencing the entire Liquid Crystal Body Matrix.

Cinnabar does not suggest a new pattern; it enhances one's capacity to take on new patterns, dissolve them and take on other new patterns as the need of the moment inspires. In this sense, Cinnabar Quartz can be of great aid in the fundamental transformation called for by the times in which we live and the development of Light Body awareness. The integration of the physical body and its senses with the Light Body and the additional senses and capacities it carries is the call and challenge of our destiny in these times.

By infusing us with an enhanced readiness for rapid metamorphic change, Cinnabar and Cinnabar Quartz fulfill a vital function. As we begin to claim our capacities for continuous co-creation of our lives and world, in partnership with Sophia, Soul of the World, the need for a flexible, adaptive consciousness becomes stronger and stronger. For those on the path of stones and evolutionary transformation, I highly recommend bringing Cinnabar or Cinnabar Quartz into your toolkit (or, you might say, into your band of Allies!).

Cinnabar Quartz also serves a function for the heart. The heart's consciousness has been, for some centuries, dulled or hidden, covered by mental layers. Heart consciousness is an essential quality of the newly evolving spiritual human being. The dismantling of old mental structures is vital in this process, and Cinnabar Quartz is a great facilitator of this. As an ally for the removal of blockages between the heart and mind, Cinnabar Quartz is a catalyst for the alchemical inner "wedding," the unification of all aspects of the self.

CINNABAR QUARTZ SPEAKS "I am the most adaptable of beings. My love of swiftness makes me a helpful teacher for those who wish to make rapid and great strides in the coming years. Human beings are called to become conscious creators, and to create well—with beauty and with expression of the harmony that radiates from the realms of Spirit. As a magician, I offer to show you the means to affect the manifestation of the elemental forces entering the world. You may become true magicians, if you are guided by your heart's wisdom, if you give effort to developing powers of attention, and if you exert your strength to maintain watchful awareness of all that occurs within and without you. There is much to be discovered in the resonance of patterns that you see looking inward to your heart and mind, and looking outward to the world. When you begin to knit together the likenesses of the inner and outer realms so that both are illuminated by each other, you have entered and become an ally of the process of transmutation. This is the desire of the Divine and the destiny of humanity.

CIRCLE STONE™

KEY WORDS   **Attunement to Earth's consciousness, awakening of dormant capacities, co-creative union with the World Soul**
ELEMENT   **Storm**
CHAKRAS   **Third Eye (6th), Crown (7th)**

Circle Stone is the name given to pieces of Flint that have been gathered from within the crop circle formations in England. Flint is a sedimentary rock composed entirely of silica. It occurs as concretions, in band or nodule form, in limestones, especially chalk. Its color is usually black, brown or tan. It is marine in origin. Flint is a hard, tough stone that fractures conchoidally. Flakes of Flint were used by primitive peoples for making arrowheads, scrapers and other tools. Flint frequently contains invertebrate fossils. What appears as crypto-crystalline silica in Flint may be organic Opal that has formed in the contained sponge spicules. Some of this crypto-crystalline material appears in the Circle Stone Flint.

The areas of England where crop circles occur are rich in the chalk that creates optimal conditions for the formation of Flint. A few feet below the surface in many parts of Wiltshire—the nexus of crop circle activity—the entire area is underlain with white chalk. Raw chunks of Flint are common in the fields. Some investigators speculate that the mineral content of the land in these areas somehow facilitates the creation of the crop circle formations, by whatever intelligence brings them about.

BACKGROUND   In the summer of 2007, I traveled to England with my wife to speak at a Crystal and Sound Healing conference in Glastonbury. On our first day of sightseeing, we were surprised to discover one of the mysterious crop circles in a wheat field adjoining Avebury Stone Circle, a megalithic monument akin to such ancient sites as Stonehenge. Upon entering the crop circle, both of us felt powerful spiraling currents of energy rising out of the ground and moving up through our bodies. On the ground within the circle, Kathy found several unusual-looking stones, which we later identified as Flint. As we held the stones, we suddenly realized that they were carrying the same currents as the crop circles themselves! Even though it was nearly sunset, we hurried back to our car and went searching for more crop circles.

A series of synchronicities led us within forty minutes to a field where there was another crop circle, and also two other people. The second crop circle had formed only the night before, and the currents rising from the Earth there were far more powerful than those we had felt earlier. Once again, there were pieces of Flint on the ground, and these, too, carried the powerful currents of the strange formation. When we spoke to the people, we were surprised to find that they *recognized* me, having just bought a copy of *The Book of Stones* the week before. We formed an instant friendship, and the couple we had just met offered to show us an even larger and more complex crop circle a few miles away. When we arrived at the huge 450-foot formation, it was nearly dark, but we could see the amazingly complex patterns of "woven" wheat, laid in perfect symmetry within the complex multi-petaled "flower" of the formation. Again the ground displayed scattered pieces of the highly charged Flint.

Having been convinced that these amazingly lively Flints were a part of the crop circle mystery, and that their energies were of importance to the metaphysical community, we arranged with our new friends to gather stones in order to bring them to America and begin distributing and working with them. Like Azeztulite, it is not so much what the stones intrinsically are that matters but rather what is being expressed through them. We have found Flint that is not from crop circles to be a solid and helpful ally, and even the Circle Stones, as we call them, hold the qualities of Flint. Yet they also carry the currents of the crop circles themselves, and as such they are keys to unlocking mysteries that may lead human beings into conscious communion with spiritual worlds and beings beyond our current imaginings.

Here are some quotes from my original attunements with Circle Stones: "The stones of the Circles are awakened by the Self that is the heart of the Earth. They have waited for the ripeness of time and are brought to their present joy by the gesture of her love. Her wisdom flows through them like living water, and the chords of her rhythms resonate through their inner lattices as music goes through harp strings. She speaks to us through them, as through the patterns of the circles themselves, and her speech is more than words—it is that which reaches into us and brings forth the awe of recognition. The Earth is alive, awake and aware of us, with an intelligence we can glimpse but have not yet awakened fully enough to comprehend. We may never comprehend her, yet we can feel the astounding joy of beholding her, and the intense love engendered by our first glimpse of her. She offers us the grace of spiritual nourishment beyond measure and invites us to a higher calling than we have ever known, a kind of spiritual marriage of our hearts with hers."

The vibrations of the Circle Stones deeply stimulate the heart chakra, sometimes bringing tears of appreciation and gratitude. They stimulate the third eye and crown chakras, facilitating visionary states. The currents of the Circle Stones can penetrate deeply into the brain, stimulating dormant areas and stirring inner capacities. They stir the dark areas of mind/brain and heart where our forgotten or never-known potentials are sleeping. Carrying, wearing or meditating with these stones can help us become aware of more of what we can be. Sleeping or meditating with the Circle Stones can help bring one into conscious relationship with the spiritual intelligence that gives rise to the crop circles themselves. Longer meditations with the stones can take one very deep, much deeper than any other stone I have worked with.

"The Circle Stones resonate very strongly with Moldavite and Azeztulite, with mutual amplification of their currents and qualities. Phenacite will bring an enhancement of the third-eye stimulation that Circle Stones provide, and Herderite will strengthen its effects for waking dormant brain areas."

Speaking now from outside the meditative perspective, I believe that crop circles may be efforts to communicate with human beings, made by a highly aware and intelligent self which can be viewed as the mind/heart of the Earth or the life-intelligence of the world. It may be the intelligence of Sophia herself. Whatever is making these formations is clearly aware of human ideas and symbols. This much is indicated by many of the patterns that appear. As we have begun to give more attention to crop circles, their complexity, number and geographic range have all increased.

NEW ATTUNEMENT Beginning a meditation with several pieces of the Circle Stones, I noticed quickly that the natural entry points where the stones resonated with me were the third eye, the crown chakra and the entire interior of the skull. Although I am able to feel pulsations in the heart from Circle Stones as I hold them there and invite them inside, the brain seems to be where the being behind these stones is focusing its currents.

The mysterious formation of the crop circles is an enigma, with many people offering different ideas about their origin. Because of the way these stones so powerfully resonate in the brain, and because of images arising during this meditation, I want to say that the crop circles are expressing the Earth's consciousness. It is, according to what I am seeing, neither aliens nor hoaxers but the Earth's own growing self-awareness that creates these patterns. Crop circles are a gesture up from the interior of the Earth, one might say. If one looks historically at the evolution of the complexity of crop circles, it is easy to imagine that the Earth itself may be evolving in consciousness and discovering in herself the capability of gesturing to us through ever more complex and meaning-imbued patterns.

The feeling I sense from the stones found in the crop circles is one of an intense wide-awake longing for communication. I feel that the Soul of the Earth, whom we speak of as Sophia, is nearing the time of her opportunity for full expression, for fully awakened presence in partnership with humanity. The patterns of the crop circles are her efforts to express, in a kind of visual and tactile language, her presence to us.

The Circle Stones trigger a state of highly activated currents moving throughout the brain. These are the strongest currents I have felt in the brain in my twenty-five years of meditating with crystals and stones. The sense I have is that these stones carry within them or express through their currents an intense desire for human beings to awaken, to kindle capacities unknown to us and latent within our nervous system. I see an image of our whole being as a great vessel of water attempting to pour through a pinhole. The consciousness that is presently expressed through our minds and brains is a tiny fraction of the potential we carry.

Sophia is our Mother and yearns for our fulfillment. Our fulfillment includes a kind of consciousness that we have never experienced before. "It is a whole-world consciousness," says the stone. It is a shared consciousness with the Soul of the World. If our dormant capacities begin to function, one quality of this expanded awareness is direct knowing. The usual processes of learning we experience in our daily lives are slow and painstaking, and our gains are genuine and to be valued. However, people referred to as savants are able to know astonishing things, not through study but through resonant attunement. It is as though they need only to turn inwardly toward the question and the answer is present.

My intuitive sense as I work with the Circle Stones is that, through these stones that received their awakening "charge" when the Earth gestured by forming a crop circle, we can connect with the intelligence behind the gesture. The stones, in that moment, became imbued with the consciousness of the Soul of the World. That is to say, the Circle Stones carry her living imprint, her message. And her wish (so I am hearing) is for us to share consciousness with her. We will remain individuals and yet we will be one with the world. This is the New Consciousness.

What I feel inside my own head as I meditate with the Circle Stones is high-intensity vibration filling the entire skull, and an insistent sense of longing. The longing seems to come from the intelligence behind the stone, and the desire is for me, and all the rest of us, to wake up—wake up to our potential and experience shared consciousness with the One, the Soul of the World.

Geometry has been considered for many centuries to be a kind of language, or Logos, through which eternal principles of the Divine are expressed. The amazing formations of the crop circle phenomenon—sometimes depicting these geometries of the eternal—are ephemeral. They are of the moment. It is in the living grains, in the living fields of the Earth that these patterns appear, stay for a time and disappear. Many who enter them feel a numinous presence, a mysterious something much greater than we are used to encountering. The same is true when we hold the Circle Stones. A Circle Stone emanates a different quality and a higher intensity of current than virtually any other stone I know. I sense that it is only beginning to work with me, as I open myself to feel its message. I cannot say that this stone has brought me to the awakening of the new capacities I have glimpsed. I can only say that it communicates very strongly the desire of a being—the being who attuned these stones to her consciousness. I feel that this being longs for us, not merely as we are but as we can be.

Circle Stones can transmit the vibration or current of the future stream—the stream of unrealized potential, the stream of latent capacities that may come into being. They carry the pattern of our shared destiny with the Soul of the World. Human beings have never lived as human beings anywhere other than the Earth. We are very much the children of Sophia, and yet no imagination of the Mother is sufficient to encompass what she is. And no imagination of the future, including the glimpses I see through the Circle Stones, is large enough to embrace the wonder of what can be. I encourage those who wish to find their way into accord with destiny—with the spiritual awakening of themselves and the Earth as one—to work with these stones and to ask inwardly: "What is the communication they offer? What is the communication the crop circles themselves offer? What is the frequency of resonance to be achieved so we can know Her directly?"

The Circle Stones, in many ways, carry some of the most important questions of our time. They are born in their present vibrational pattern through the gesture of the Earth to us. (It is clear that the crop circles are gestures to humanity—whatever intelligence is making them— because many of the patterns are recognizable as human symbols.) It seems inevitable that whatever being, whatever consciousness causes or creates these formations is aware of the minds of human beings and our symbols. Offering us our own symbols as an invitation into shared consciousness could only be the gesture of a being with fantastically wide and deep awareness.

I once doubted that the crop circles were made by something mysterious. I assumed that people were making them as a hoax or an art form. However, my encounter with the stones found in the formations and my own experiences standing within crop circles—feeling the

currents flowing up from the Earth—convinced me that these are gestures from the World Soul. Although people could make the crop formations, I don't believe anyone could awaken the stones to such a high frequency. These common pieces of Flint have been stepped over, ignored or cast aside for thousands of years, but now they feel alive. The Flint found outside the crop circles does not feel the same. So here is another great mystery and an invitation into relationship with mystery. I don't think we are intended to find the explanation of the circles or the stones. We are invited into their mystery in order to wake up dimensions of our own being of which we are unaware, and through that awakening to meet a being who loves us immeasurably and who has linked her destiny with ours.

Circle Stones resonate synergistically with many high-frequency stones such as Azeztulite, Agni Gold Danburite, White Danburite, Herderite, Phenacite, and with all of the Ascension Stones. There is more to these stones than meets the eye, or even the meditating mind. Through engagement with them and their unknown qualities—and *our* unknown qualities—we may uncover a greater secret than we believe we are looking for.

CIRCLE STONES SPEAK   "I am waiting for you. Awaken. Turn to me and awaken. Breathe in my darkness, breathe my light, and awaken. I am in need of you. Awaken."

CREEDITE

KEY WORDS   Expansion of awareness, activation of all chakras, union of heart and third eye, Light Body awakening

ELEMENT   Storm

CHAKRAS   All Physical (1st through 7th) and Etheric (8th through 14th)

Creedite is a hydrous calcium aluminum sulfate mineral with a hardness of 3.5. Its crystal system is monoclinic, and it forms in slender prismatic crystals, which are often grouped in clusters. The name is derived from its locality of discovery, at Creed Quandrangle, Colorado, in the U.S. It crystallizes in white, colorless, orange and sometimes purple crystals. The original Colorado location featured pale lavender crystals. Orange Creedite clusters often form in porcupine-like balls that bristle with spiny crystals going out in all directions. Creedite is a rare mineral, and the best (and most plentiful) specimens come primarily from Mexico. The Orange Creedite "porcupines" occur in the same mine in Mexico where rare Pink Fluorite is found.

BACKGROUND   Creedite quickly and powerfully activates the upper-chakra energies, particularly the third eye, crown chakra and those above. It is an access-key stone for all kinds of encoded spiritual information. It can aid in attuning to the Akashic records, "opening the files" in record keeper crystals, understanding the messages of spirit guides, interpreting oracles such as the tarot, and channeling the messages of spirit beings. It can help meditators make the quantum leap to higher domains of consciousness, clearing any blockages in the third eye, crown chakra or the etheric chakras above the head. Creedite is a stone of the Light of the angelic realm, and it can help us manifest that Light in everyday life.

For opening the portals to the higher spiritual realms, Creedite resonates well with Azeztulite, Scolecite, Phenacite, Natrolite, Clear Apophyllite and/or Herderite. Black Tourmaline helps those working with Creedite to purify their energy fields and stay grounded. Creedite and Moldavite work together to bring experiences of spiritual awakening and transformation. Nuummite can be used with Creedite to ground memories of dreams and meditation experiences and to bring Light into experiences of spiritual darkness.

NEW ATTUNEMENT   Creedite's energy is a very quick and high-frequency vibration. As I sat to meditate with it, the currents immediately found the best portal for the stone's frequency, which in me was the third eye. My experience started with a series of rapid pulsations there. Creedite is one of the stones that can bring high-frequency energies into all parts of the body. As I held Creedite, its vibration flowed into my hands, and as I experimented with placing it on various chakras and energy points, I found that it brought the same high-frequency pulsations to all parts of the body.

Creedite, because it is capable of sending or bringing its currents into all levels of one's chakra system, is very helpful for clearing blocks. It can access areas that are not easily reached by high-frequency stones or currents. In my own case, Creedite was very effective in activating the root chakra and the second chakra, facilitating an overall raising of the vibrational spectrum of my body. Those who wish to begin experiencing the Light Body—its network of light and its labyrinth of vibrational currents—are advised that Creedite can be of great assistance. It can help any slower or blocked areas wake up and catch up with the vibrations of the more awakened parts of the Light Body.

Creedite is very helpful at linking one's entire bodily grid. If Creedites are placed all along the chakra column and at the hands and feet, one experiences the flow of currents as little spheres of radiance centered at each of the placements. One can feel columns or lines of energy linking these radiant centers wherever the stones have been placed. One intriguing idea is to gather enough Creedites to place them at as many of the meridian points as is practical, and to see what degree of activation of the Light Body occurs. The work of Light Body awakening and the merging of one's self-sense with the entirety of one's spiritual being has been long in preparation in our evolution, and it is still a gradual process. Those who wish to see this process accelerate are invited to come to Creedite for assistance.

Creedite has a strong predisposition to link and jointly awaken the heart and third eye consciousness centers. This is where a great deal of the positive feeling arises that one experiences from Creedite. The heart and third eye are natural partner chakras. When they work as one, the throat can act as their ally, expressing the jointly partnered wisdom of these two centers of consciousness. Thus, Creedite loves to be placed at the heart and third eye and allowed to work its magic of connection between them.

Creedite can accelerate the penetration of the currents of other stones into the body. It can help one enhance and accelerate the effectiveness of virtually all the other stones mentioned in this book. Creedite is the quintessential stone of rapid evolutionary acceleration.

CREEDITE SPEAKS "I invite all the outposts of your being, all the centers of your knowing, all the rivers of your existence to join and sing together. I offer stimulation and harmonization of your many layers, so that they become not one, but a harmonious choir whose fullness of being is your wholeness."

CRIMSON CUPRITE

KEY WORDS Life force, vitality, physical energy, courage, healing, Divine feminine, etherization of the blood

ELEMENT Earth

CHAKRAS Root (1st), Sexual/Creative (2nd)

Crimson Cuprite is a copper oxide mineral with a hardness of 3.5 to 4. Its crystal system is hexoctahedral. The name Cuprite is derived from the Latin *cuprum,* meaning "copper." This mineral is a relatively recent discovery, and it is a brighter red than most other forms of Cuprite. It may also vary slightly in composition from other varieties of Cuprite. When in crystal form, Cuprite's growing habits are octahedral, cubic or dodecahedral. Crimson Cuprite is found only in massive form, in oxidized parts of copper deposits, in association with Chrysocolla, Mala-chite and Azurite. Although Cuprite specimens have been collected in Africa in the Congo and Namibia, as well as in the U.S., Crimson Cuprite has been found only in Mexico. More common forms of Cuprite are widespread and are found in many copper-producing areas.

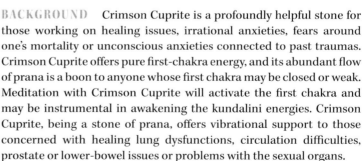

BACKGROUND Crimson Cuprite is a profoundly helpful stone for those working on healing issues, irrational anxieties, fears around one's mortality or unconscious anxieties connected to past traumas. Crimson Cuprite offers pure first-chakra energy, and its abundant flow of prana is a boon to anyone whose first chakra may be closed or weak. Meditation with Crimson Cuprite will activate the first chakra and may be instrumental in awakening the kundalini energies. Crimson Cuprite, being a stone of prana, offers vibrational support to those concerned with healing lung dysfunctions, circulation difficulties, prostate or lower-bowel issues or problems with the sexual organs.

Crimson Cuprite is a stone of feminine power, and it activates the feminine archetype of the Earth goddess. Women who wish to find their own connection to her are advised to wear, sleep or meditate with it, and to imagine their own base chakra with a red root extending deep into the Earth.

Crimson Cuprite can also be a stone of alchemy, and it resonates with the archetypes of the Magician and the High Priestess. Just as copper conducts electricity so well, Crimson Cuprite carries Divine energies from the inner world to their manifestation in the outer world.

NEW ATTUNEMENT   I am immediately able to feel Crimson Cuprite's currents at both the crown chakra and the root chakra at the base of the spine. The importance of Crimson Cuprite in the willed evolutionary work encouraged in this book is its ability to bring life force into the body, in an upward infusion, from the Earth through the root chakra. There is a great deal of attention in this book to bringing the higher spiritual energies into incarnation here through our bodies and our consciousness. It is also the case that the Earth is our life source as physical beings, offering us nourishment and life-giving currents. Opening to these currents more fully is an essential aspect of the development of the new human being, or simply the whole human being. Crimson Cuprite, with its capacity of opening the base chakra portal to receive life force from the Earth, aids greatly in a process I want to call by an unusual term—the *etherization of the blood.* This term is taken from Rudolf Steiner, who coined it. My understanding of this process is that the etheric body is readily able to attune to the currents of the spiritual worlds, and that within the material body the blood is the most receptive system for the transfer of spiritual energies into the physical self. The etheric body is deeply entwined with the physical body, and its first entrance into the physical body is the flowing, ongoing stream of the blood.

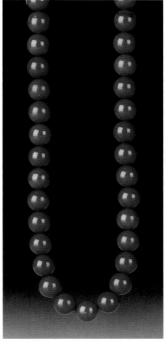

Crimson Cuprite's stimulation and opening of one's etheric body at the root and crown chakras allows the nourishing currents of life force to enter, which flow all around us through the etheric body of the Earth. The blood moves through all corners of the body and is the core of the Liquid Crystal Body Matrix. Patterns taken on by the blood are carried to every organ and throughout one's cellular structure. Oxygen offered via the blood to each cell is an essential component of the functioning of all aspects of the body.

When one is able to shift the pattern of the etheric body through voluntary and assisted opening of the chakra portals, new patterns can be readily assimilated into the physical self through the blood. This is especially so when a stone such as Crimson Cuprite resonates with the crown and root, and also the heart chakra. This is the third entry point for Crimson Cuprite's replenishing vibrations. The cellular matrix of the body can live much more vibrantly, and much longer, when it is reattuned to fully receive the nourishing currents of life force from the sea of life around us. Crimson Cuprite, through the opening of these chakra gates and its attunement with *prana,* aids us in this process.

As we evolve spiritually, we take in higher-vibrational patterns. In order to stay with the new vibrations we bring in (in all of the body's functioning—not only its higher-vibrational aspects), the cells must be more fully nourished, cleansed and filled with *prana.* The infusion of *prana* facilitated by Crimson Cuprite helps bring about a synergy of energies—with the Supramental Force and other Light vibrations—which we invite to our being. In these ways, Crimson Cuprite's gifts are invaluable to the evolutionary acceleration we seek.

CRIMSON CUPRITE SPEAKS   "The Breath of the Earth enters you through me. I am a Daughter of the Mother, and I pour Her love through my heart into yours."

CRYOLITE

KEY WORDS   Light Body awakening, kundalini activation, vibrational ascension, intelligence of the heart, attunement to the future stream, surrender, liberation

ELEMENT   Storm

CHAKRAS   All (1st through 7th), Soul Star (8th)

Cryolite is a sodium aluminum fluoride mineral with a hardness of 2.5 to 3. Its crystal system is monoclinic. Most natural Cryolite has been found at the Ivigtut site on Greenland's west coast. This find was almost completely depleted as Cryolite was utilized as a flux in aluminum smelting. It has been found associated with other minerals such as Siderite, Quartz, Topaz, Fluorite, Chalcopyrite, Galena, Cassiterite, Molybdenite, Columbite and Wolframite. In addition to the major discovery in Greenland, Cryolite has been found in the U.S. state of Colorado; Quebec, Canada; and at Miask, Russia.

Cryolite has a very low refractive index, similar to water, so clear Cryolite crystals will seem to "disappear" when immersed in water. Even white Cryolite specimens such as those pictured here will appear transparent at the edges when in water.

BACKGROUND   The energies of Cryolite focus directly on the awakening of our awareness to the intelligence of the heart, and the partnering of the most evolved areas of the brain with that intelligence. Cryolite powerfully stimulates the third eye, as well as the entire pre-frontal cortex of the brain. It also stimulates the heart and crown chakras, linking them with the third eye and facilitating inner vision. Further, it opens the channels through which the holographic knowing of the heart and its language of silent understanding can be received and comprehended by the conscious mind. This opening brings one from confusion to certainty, from egoic self-seeking to love, generosity and benevolence, from fear to trust, from control to surrender. It is the quintessential vibration of the New Consciousness sweeping quietly through humanity, destined to transform the world.

Cryolite and Nirvana Quartz make excellent allies for facilitating mind/heart integration. Moldavite is a ready and powerful ally for both of these. In addition, visionary stones such as Phenacite, Natrolite, Scolecite, Herderite, Azeztulite and Petalite can aid in further activating the latent capacities of the High Brain.

NEW ATTUNEMENT   Cryolite is surely one of the most potent stones for the Light Body awakening. When I sat down to meditate with this stone—even before placing it on a chakra—

simply holding it in my hands caused very pleasurable vibrations and a sensation of White Light to flow through my entire body. These energies coalesced around the base of the spine, and as I attended to them, I felt them rise up to the top of the spine and into the skull. I experienced an extremely pleasurable and Light-filled current that caused chills to run up my spine.

I sense that Cryolite is a potential awakener of a harmonious kundalini current, and I also feel that the process referred to as Ascension actually is both an ascent and a descent—the ascent of one's individual consciousness into the realms of Light, and the simultaneous descent of the Light into the body. Cryolite engenders a flow of this kind as soon as one opens one's heart and energy field to it.

The Ascension to which we refer may be something that develops over time and through many stages. This seems most likely. So when I say Cryolite enacts the Ascension, I mean that thus far, in my own experience, the first stages of Cryolite's awakening of my energy matrix took me some steps along the Ascension path. Not surprisingly, it did not bring forth the entire unfolding at once. I am given to understand that this is not the most desirable way for the Light Body activation and Ascension of the self into Light to occur.

The vehicle of self, including the corporeal body as well as one's astral, etheric and emotional bodies, is in almost all cases not yet strong enough to hold its integrity in the full-blown experience of awakening into the Light. Cryolite encourages the initiation of Ascension and Light Body awakening by enlivening this pattern within us and drawing us forward as many steps as we are prepared to take.

Cryolite, in its purpose as a stone of the New Consciousness, powerfully stimulates the mind-heart circuit and brings the mind into alignment with the heart through a process of illumination. In some processes, the mind is encouraged to surrender to the will of the heart, without knowing or understanding beforehand what the heart's urges mean or will take us toward. In the case of Cryolite, the brain is greatly illuminated and the mental activity is opened into greater awareness of the Light realms. This revelatory opening causes a natural turning toward the heart from one's point of attention, such that the White Light filling the brain-mind descends in loving adoration to the divine center-point in the heart. This activity can be named by an esoteric term—the Descent of the Dove—for the Dove is a harbinger of peace. The awakened attention, which descends from the brain-mind down through the inner Corridor of Light to the center of the heart, is a light of peace, understanding, wisdom and devotion. All of this is awakened through the insight that the Light-filling activity of Cryolite initiates. When the mind understands the will of the heart, its response is complete self-giving, surrender, devotion and service to the heart.

Cryolite, in its working through the body, reaches to the will center at the solar plexus. Its effect is the enlightenment of the will. The sensation, when Cryolite is placed over the solar plexus chakra, is one of feeling vastly comforted by the currents Cryolite brings. When the will is comforted, it softens—it no longer seems necessary to harden the will in order to accomplish one's aims. Now that Cryolite's currents have permeated the inner column of one's energies, the will gives itself over to the tender longings of the heart and its powerful surges toward giving of self to the unfolding of destiny. Either way one regards this shift, the effect is one of changing the hardened personal will to the softer, self-giving quality of willingness. This willingness is expressed in reverent surrender, which echoes the heart's regard for the Divine, and its divine regard for the individual self within which it has made its home.

Cryolite is a great stone of an inner peace so profound that it radiates into one's whole auric field. Its radiance can beam out through the eyes—through one's countenance and expression—such that others who meet us when we are attuned to Cryolite can feel the peace that emanates from us and be comforted.

Cryolite is highly resonant with the Soul Star chakra above the head. It is a mineral manifestation of the radiance of the Soul Star. Thus Cryolite reminds us of our identity as soul beings who have migrated from life to life and expressed as a multiplicity of forms. This allows a deepening of the peace that Cryolite offers, because it brings to rest one's anxieties about death and concerns about the fulfillment of destiny. It is true that destiny has its proper time, yet the Universe—both spiritual and material—is a resilient realm, and infinitely adaptable. Although one is always encouraged to give everything possible to the fulfillment of the activity of destiny unfolding, Cryolite brings us to peace in the awareness of our great soul-longevity, and of the vastness of the spectrum of our souls' expression through space and time.

Cryolite is highly resonant with the angelic domain and the mid-realm of the angelic hierarchy. These beings, one might say, are high enough to be near Source, yet close enough to us to be felt as a wave of tenderness.

CRYOLITE SPEAKS   "I am the kindler of your inner Light. I remind your soul that it is Light. I give your body a resonance of Light to stir its awakening. I am the tap of a raindrop upon the white cocoon of your holy body. I bring the message of the arrival of a spiritual spring. My invitation is your opportunity to take flight."

DANBURITE

KEY WORDS   Angelic communication, channeling, interdimensional travel, peace, freedom from stress
ELEMENT   Wind
CHAKRAS   Heart (4th), Crown (7th), Transpersonal and Etheric (8th and beyond, above the head)

Danburite is a calcium borosilicate crystal with a hardness of 7 to 7.5. Its name is derived from its original discovery in Danbury, Connecticut (U.S.). Danburite crystals are orthorhombic and prismatic, with linear striations running parallel to the length of the crystal. Crystals are generally four-sided, and their terminations are usually chisel-shaped. Most often they are colorless or white, but some specimens are light yellow or pale pink. The most abundant Danburite deposits were discovered in Mexico, with crystals also found in Russia, Madagascar, Bolivia, Burma and Japan. Danburite crystals are becoming increasingly rare as the large Mexican deposits begin to yield fewer good specimens.

BACKGROUND   Danburite is a gentle and powerful aid for lifting one's awareness to the higher spiritual vibrations. Danburite clears and opens the crown chakra, linking and harmonizing it with the heart. It activates and integrates the transpersonal and etheric chakras above the head, all the way up to the fourteenth chakra. This allows one to move in consciousness into the angelic domain, with which Danburite has a special resonance.

Danburite is an excellent stone for those who need to release stress and worry. It soothes the heart and sends it the message that all is well. It can help one overcome restlessness and get a good night's sleep. In encourages one to release worries and to flow with the events of life.

Danburite is one of the stones in the Synergy Twelve group, along with Moldavite, Phenacite, Tanzanite, Azeztulite, Herderite, Petalite, Tibetan Tektite, Brookite, Natrolite, Scolecite and Satyaloka Azeztulite. It is also one of the Ascension Seven, which also includes White Azeztulite, Petalite, Satyaloka Azeztulite, Nirvana Quartz, Golden Azeztulite and Satya Mani Quartz.

NEW ATTUNEMENT   When I meditated with Danburite placed at the heart chakra, my heart responded, and the response of my heart was a feeling I would describe as reverence. It was as though the Danburite revealed something holy to my heart, which my heart deeply revered. There was, in placing the Danburite near my heart, a resonance within my heart. In the space between the stone and my heart, there was a meeting in which my heart could feel the beautiful holy beings that stand behind and express through Danburite crystals. I have always believed that Danburite is a high crystal of the angelic realm, and this response of the heart, in reverence to what it feels when the stone is near, confirmed this for me.

I found that the currents coming through Danburite are felt readily in the third eye and crown chakras as well as the heart. In fact, I could sometimes feel all three chakras as if they were one, all in a state of very calm, soft reverence. The feeling of a gentle awareness of awe—again for something I cannot see with my outer or inner eyes, but I can feel through holding Danburite—is the most salient quality I associate with this stone. Even as I spoke these words into my tape recorder, I had to overcome an impulse to fall into silence. The Danburite inspires such reverence—such a feeling of inwardly bowing to a great presence, or many great presences—that expressing anything requires overcoming the urge to be quietly and reverentially present with what is.

Every time I hold Danburite and close my eyes, I feel as though I am within White Light. This is something different from the gold-white Light that I associate with Azeztulite, or any number of other Light qualities that I feel through sensing the stones. This Light is the pure White Light of the Divine, and my inner image is of the radiance of the Throne of the Divine.

It is as though the angelic ones who express through Danburite are among those nearest the Source. Therefore, their purity is beyond that of many other spiritual beings, and it is because of their purity that they are able to be near to the Light of the Source.

When we meditate with Danburite, we have the opportunity to share in the consciousness of these angelic ones. We have the invitation to feel what it's like to make a close approach to the ultimate, infinite Light. I feel that the reverence I experienced in my heart upon attuning to Danburite is akin to the reverence of the angelic ones themselves.

This impulse toward immersion in awed and reverential silence is one of Danburite's most potent qualities. In meditation with Danburite, as in most meditations, one wishes to reach a state of inner stillness. Many of the other states that can occur in meditative experience require first the stillness. Many people feel that stillness is difficult to achieve because the mind continues its inner monologue constantly. However with Danburite, especially when it is placed at or near the heart, there is a natural quieting of thought as one's attention is fully captured by the feeling of the presence of the holy.

It may be that the beings to which we attune through Danburite are so far beyond normal human experience that they can only offer us a glimpse of their reality. Our own evolutionary path includes activation and awakening of the Light Body, and ultimately Ascension in the Body of Light into the highest realms. There are many steps between our present state and the state of holy silence that Danburite embodies. Nonetheless, being within the presence of these high spiritual beings nourishes one's soul and spirit. It inspires us to see the horizons of our destiny, and it provides a taste of the ambrosia of that domain. Danburite, in a more everyday capacity—as it constantly emanates the White Light of the holy beings behind it—can help us soothe and heal the emotional body of old wounds or destructive habits.

Danburite is excellent as a helper for relieving stress and calming frayed nerves. It can aid people who are in depression or grief—not so much to rise above these feelings as to be at peace with them. Danburite can be a loving companion in the necessary times of grief, and it can help us remember the Light that invisibly pervades all being.

Danburite is not only a stone of the White Light—it is a stone of the Transparent Ray. This is the light-in-darkness; it is the invisible Light that is present everywhere, underlying all appearances. It is as though the Light that Danburite embodies in crystallized form is the substrate of all being, and the radiant Face behind all masks. There is great and powerful unconditional love expressed through Danburite. It is so clear and so without stain that apprehending the presence of this love can feel overwhelming to one's everyday self. Nonetheless, to hold oneself quietly within the loving arms of the Danburite, one might say, is to experience complete spiritual love and protection.

The spirit of each person descends into matter with a mission to bring Light into the world and to manifest it here. Danburite is a crystallized embodiment of the purest Light of the highest realms. Its high-frequency currents barely touch the Earth plane. Danburite resonates not only with the third eye and crown, but very readily with the etheric chakras all the way up to the fourteenth chakra. As I meditate with Danburite, I easily feel the extension of its vibrations through the crown chakra together with the opening of a funnel of Light from the crown—widening as it extends upward into the spiritual realms. There is a kind of dimensional membrane between the material and spiritual realms. Danburite makes us capable of crossing that threshold. When we work with this stone, we can experience ourselves as present in both the earthly and spiritual realms simultaneously. This is Danburite's great gift and our opportunity.

Danburite works synergistically with many stones—"With all," it says. As mentioned, it is one of the Ascension Stones and one of the Synergy Twelve. It works hand in hand with all varieties of Azeztulite. It combines with Herderite for an even greater expansion of consciousness, and with Phenacite for a deepening of one's visionary capacities.

Again and again, as I hold Danburite, I see a vision of white wings. I can only imagine that these represent the presence of the Danburite angels. At each glimpse of those wings I find myself again in reverent silence.

DANBURITE SPEAKS   "I love and enfold the spirits of human beings, and I remind them of their Home."

DATOLITE

KEY WORDS   Connection with the higher worlds, unity of heart and will, generosity, inner strength, retrieval of lost information, mental power, spiritual awareness

ELEMENTS   Water, Wind

CHAKRAS   Solar Plexus (3rd), Heart (4th), Third Eye (6th), Crown (7th), Transpersonal and Etheric (8th through 14th, above the head)

Datolite is a calcium borosilicate mineral with a hardness of 5 to 5.5. Its crystal system is monoclinic. The mineral forms in short prismatic crystals of high variability or in granular, porcelain-like masses. It can be colorless, white, pale yellow or pale green. Sometimes impurities can tint it pink, reddish or brown. Many of the best Datolite specimens come from Russia and are yellow-greenish in color.

BACKGROUND   Datolites are strong crystals for the third eye, crown and etheric chakras. They open the subtle vision, allowing one to see auras as well as beings in the astral, causal and subtle domains. Nature spirits, angels, guides, non-physical teachers, healers and helpers can all become visible and available for communication. The fast-pulsing energies of Datolite increase the vibration of one's energy field to enable conscious experience of one's own spiritual body, which can be used to explore the many higher dimensions surrounding us. Datolite can help retrieve lost memories of childhood, past lives and even the Akashic record of humanity's ancient history. It can enhance the accuracy of memory and sharpen all mental abilities.

Datolite works very well with high-vibration stones like Phenacite, Natrolite, Scolecite, Danburite and Azeztulite. All of these will strengthen Datolite's awakening of one's awareness of beings in the higher vibrational realms. For enhancing mental/intellectual properties, Datolite can be combined with Heliodor, Lapis and Cinnabar Quartz. Datolite also harmonizes with Merkabite Calcite and Lemurian Aquatine Calcite.

NEW ATTUNEMENT   Sitting down to work meditatively with Datolite, I noticed first that the stone resonated strongly at the solar plexus and the heart. It vibrated less strongly but still noticeably at the throat, and extremely powerfully at the third eye. When I held the stone to my third eye it filled my entire skull with powerful yet calm vibration. I would say that the entire brain was affected in a way that created a state of highly energized calm. I felt that my brain was filled with energy, and yet the energy's effect was to quiet thought and increase alertness. It seemed as though there was a steady attenuation of the chatter of the mind and an increased depth of internal quiet. It was a pleasurable sensation to feel this current of alert silence pouring into me through the stone.

When I used the stone at the crown chakra, there was once again a kind of buzzing intensity, and I wondered whether it would become uncomfortable. Instead it seemed after a few seconds to harmonize the chakra with its pattern. At that point a pleasant, intense, calm energy poured into my head.

When I held a piece of Datolite at the heart chakra, my heart responded by thumping in recognition. It was quite noticeable how clearly my heart was aware of the Datolite near it, and the thumping seemed to be a clear gesture of welcome. At my third chakra, the Datolite initiated a strong, steady vibrational stream.

Visually, during the time I was getting acquainted with the Datolite, I saw a number of interior images related to the stone. Several times I saw the soft contours or outline of a cranium in front of me, seeming to be a shape taken on by the being of the stone. I also saw the outline, in light, of a human-looking body, but very fuzzy at the edges and without precise features. It was a human shape rather than a human image, and the shape was made of light or energy. Again I associated this with the being of Datolite. As I continued meditating, a mandala of light—a pale purple mandala with radiant edges of white, green, yellow and, eventually, vibrating tips of orange-red—appeared before my inner eyes. I took this to be a deeper image of the being of Datolite.

Datolite appears to me as a stone eager to help human beings awaken into expanded awareness. It wishes for us to become cognizant of the many, many beings of the spiritual realms who are present around us and wish to contribute to our evolutionary shift. Their impulse is one of insistent encouragement. They both lovingly encourage and willfully insist that we grow, and grow quickly. Datolite can help us, if we choose, to blend the expression of the heart and the third chakra so that our will capacity is guided by the heart's wisdom, and the heart's purposes and longings are gladly embraced by our personal will. Through working with Datolite, one becomes increasingly aware of the spiritual realms that overlap this world, and of their inhabitants' interest in us—their well-wishing for us and their readiness to help us. The strong stimulation that Datolite imparted to my third eye and brain is said by the stone being to have been for the purpose of awakening me to awareness of spiritual beings and the higher realms. Datolite will do this with anyone who turns toward this stone willingly, with an open heart and mind.

Datolites embody strength, and they amplify our strength. There are many kinds of strength in the human being—physical vitality, strength of will, courage of the heart, alignment with truth, discriminative perception in thought. Among the most crucial is surrender to the Divine

Will. All of these are supported by Datolite. Keeping Datolite in one's meditation area and holding it during meditation can facilitate the revitalization of one's strength in all of these levels. In my experience meditating with Datolite for this chapter, I felt myself developing a willingness to follow the impulse and encouragement given to me by the spiritual realms. This was my strongest impression—and a surprising one to notice—as my entire skull was filling with energy from the Datolite.

Datolite, when worked with through the heart, will enhance expressions of generosity. Generosity is not primarily the giving of material wealth or goods. The sort of generosity enhanced by Datolite is the heartfelt expression of kindness—the giving of oneself to the world and other people. Datolite encourages the practice of praising; it encourages compassion and support for other beings. Datolite is perhaps the most enthusiastic stone for our developing compassion and acting upon it. The generosity seeded by Datolite, working through the heart, provides the nourishment of the feeling of giving—the shared pleasure experienced when offering heartfelt praise or tender compassion. Datolite encourages such generosity, not only to people but to animals, plants, the landscape, the Earth, the stars—all that one sees and senses. Generosity, Datolite says, is generative, and the heart thrives on it. As I sensed all this, I remembered a phrase from an early section of this book—"the New Consciousness is an activity of blessing." This is very much what I mean by generosity, in the sense encouraged by Datolite.

Datolite is certainly a stone that assuages worry and allows the release of stress, without necessarily slowing down the level of activity. It is much more of an awakener than a relaxer, even though it does quiet the mind. One finds that quieting the mind doesn't put one to sleep—it creates an increase rather than a decrease of consciousness and vitality.

Datolite is resonant with ancient knowledge. It can help us to understand and remember the wisdom of the past. It aids the mind/brain in activating the capacity to make intuitive leaps. It encourages awakening to the resonance among different ideas—for example, the likeness of mathematics and music, or the resemblances between myths from various times and places—such that one develops a stereo view of the underlying realities behind the resonant ideas. Datolite speaks, quite distinctly to me, of Atlantis, the legendary ancient civilization. Datolite suggests that intense, deep work with this stone and the effort to turn toward Atlantis may help unlock the memory of what was best (and worst) about its world. We may learn much about our nature simply by remembering Atlantis. Atlantis was not physical, Datolite tells us, in the way in which we experience our physical life. In Atlantis, the people felt themselves to be solid, as we do here, yet their vibrational capacity to blend into or attune with other dimensional frequencies was much greater than ours is now. Our capacity to allow the heart to do its natural work, which included great creative power, was far greater in Atlantis. Datolite kindled the images that gave rise to these assertions.

Datolite enjoys working in unity with many other high-vibration stones, such as Himalaya Gold Azeztulite from India, Golden Azeztulite crystals from North Carolina, and the original white Azeztulite, as well as Satyaloka Azeztulite. It combines well with Herderite, Seriphos Green Quartz and Circle Stones. With Circle Stones, the intensity of the influence to develop new capacities of perception and consciousness is strengthened even more.

Datolite is one of the least noticed of the high-vibration stones and could almost be called an unsung hero of the mineral realm. I encourage those who are aware of crystal consciousness, and who are capable of feeling the currents of the crystals, to make the effort to find Datolite. It will be a happy encounter.

DATOLITE SPEAKS "I will and I love. I arrive at your gate, and I enter when you open. I will work to please your heart, for your heart is a delight to me. I care less for your thinking than your loving and your will to love. In this I am your servant, for it is my joy to see your love expand."

As I spoke these words from Datolite, many lights appeared in my inner vision. In a state of elation and elevated awareness, I felt a rush of deep and beautiful feelings come into me through the stone. I sensed that the being behind Datolite is deeply generous and loves us more than we are likely to comprehend.

DIAMOND

KEY WORDS   Intensity, radiance, sovereignty, linking with the Heart of the Divine, revelation of the Logos, kindling the Light Body, awakening the Merkabah, attuning to the Music of the Spheres

ELEMENT   Storm

CHAKRAS   Heart (4th), Third Eye (6th), Crown (7th), and Etheric (8th through 14th, above the head)

Diamond is a crystal of pure carbon with a hardness of 10—the hardest of all substances. Its crystal symmetry is cubic, and Diamond crystals are found in a variety of forms including octahedrons, triangles, cubes and amorphous shapes. Diamonds are commonly thought of as colorless stones, exhibiting brilliant inner fire when faceted into gems. However, Diamonds are found in many colors—yellow, brown, blue, pink, green, orange and even red. Although Diamonds are highly stable under most conditions, heating them to very high temperatures where oxygen is present can cause them to vanish, transformed into carbon dioxide gas. This is how it is possible to "drill" holes in diamonds using laser beams.

Diamonds have long been valued for their magical properties, and Hindus more than fifteen centuries ago believed the stones provided their owners with protection from evil spirits, fire, poison, snakes, illness and various dangers. In other cultures, Diamonds were believed to provide victory, courage, faithfulness, purity and enhancement of love.

BACKGROUND   Diamonds were long believed to offer access to Divine energies. This is one reason why they were traditionally set in crowns. Putting such a stone near the brain, particularly at the forehead, can enhance inner vision and intuitive connection with the higher domains of spirit. Diamond can assist in activating the prefrontal lobes of the brain, the seat of most paranormal abilities and visionary consciousness. It is a tool one can use to evoke the inner King and Queen, those archetypal beings within the self that convey power, knowledge and sovereignty.

Diamond crystals are transducers that can make the high-frequency vibrational energies of the spirit realms more available to the conscious self. They can accelerate one's evolution and open the doors to psychic powers. Used in meditation, Diamond crystals will facilitate entry into meaningful visionary states. Worn in everyday life, they can intensify the ability to focus consciousness on manifesting one's goals and dreams.

Diamond crystals can enhance and magnify the energies of other high-vibration stones such as Moldavite, Phenacite, Azeztulite, Herderite, Celestite, Libyan Gold Tektite and Tibetan Tektite. They can also enhance the protective aspect of grounding stones like Black Tourmaline, Nuummite and Master Shamanite. Diamond crystals can be worn anywhere on the body and will affect the entire energy system and auric field. In meditation, the third eye is the ideal spot. Better still is placing one Diamond crystal at the third eye and another over the heart. This can activate the energetic circuit between these two vital centers, influencing them to act in synergistic union.

177

NEW ATTUNEMENT When I sat down to meditate with Diamond, I began by placing three crystals over my heart. I've long been aware of Diamond's capacity to stimulate and charge the third eye and crown chakras, but I have not done as much work with Diamond at the heart. I was surprised to feel the Diamonds' currents moving through my chest to my heart in a slender, tube-like flow. My heart was immediately responsive to the currents of Diamond. My sensation was that they were welcomed by the heart.

Shortly after this initial feeling response, I sensed an unmistakable longing—the emotional current of longing. This increased as I spent more time attending to the vibration of Diamond entering the heart. I felt this pull grow stronger. I noticed as I have when experiencing something like this through other stones, that this longing in the presence of Diamond was the mutual longing of one's individual self for the Divine, and the Divine's longing for union with one's individual self. This current of longing may be a common quality of many, if not all, of the stone beings.

In any case, it is deeply significant, and rather amazing, to understand that spiritual beings wish for relationship with us as much as we hope for connection with them.

The longing I sense through Diamond is like a flow of electricity between two points or two ends of a circuit, and it is metaphorically (and perhaps physically) similar to the AC (alternating current) form of electricity. It is not a simple linear flow that moves from one point to the other and resolves itself, but rather a sort of two-way pulling, a vibration that draws one's attention more and more into the heart, more and more toward awareness of the Divine. In that place, one encounters a consciousness that loves us and beckons to us. To realize that the Divine intensely loves and longs for union with beings as relatively small and insignificant as we is a great thrill and comfort. In fact, the feeling of Diamond as experienced in the heart can be understood as the conscious connection with the Paraclete, the Divine Comforter.

My sense while working with Diamond at the heart chakra was that it is perhaps the purest conductor for the mutual exchange of energies between our heart and the Heart of the Divine. It is as though the being or angel of Diamond offers itself—in a sense sacrifices itself—to the purpose of providing the purest, most perfect connection of consciousness between the highest spiritual realm and our individual awareness. Diamond seems to make the gesture of standing aside for a greater spiritual intelligence to use its perfection and strength to reach through the membrane between our realm and that of Spirit, so that unity may occur. The meeting with the great Beloved, through the gesture of Diamond to and within one's heart, is of such awesome magnitude that I found it difficult to remain just outside of this experience in order to record it. Had I fully entered the experience, there would have been no words.

As I worked longer with Diamond I brought an additional crystal to the third eye, while keeping a Diamond at the heart. This produced in the consciousness an immediate intensification of inner vision. Myriad patterns of light in vibrational forms appeared before my inner eye. I was shown several forms I recognized from sacred geometry, such as the pyramid, the tetrahedron, the octahedron, the star of David and the star tetrahedron, as well as the cube. All of these appeared shimmering before my inner sight as vibrational forms of Light. I was given to understand that Diamond can offer a revelation of the Logos, the primal laws of manifestation from the Divine to the material world.

The vibrational information imparted to our consciousness via Diamond is expressed as a great intensity of energy. When we work with Diamond in conjunction with other stones, we often find that its power of intensification strengthens the infusion of currents of the accompanying mineral.

Working with Diamond alone in meditative practice will usually induce a powerful influx of high-frequency currents. It can be challenging to stay with the high currents of Diamond, because they tend to flood one's whole being with Light, and although this Light is most welcome, it can sometimes feel overwhelming. And sometimes one inadvertently stops the experience from unfolding further, simply because one is in a state of bliss and does not imagine there is anywhere else to go. The question "How much joy can you stand?" is not entirely a joke when it comes to Diamond. Nonetheless, Diamond is highly recommended because of the purification it offers to one's entire Liquid Crystal Body Matrix. As I sit with Diamond, I can feel the great flood of Light entering the cellular network throughout the body, pouring most powerfully through the portals of the chakras, especially the crown, third eye and heart, and also the solar plexus.

Diamond will energize and amplify the power of every chakra. It is therefore of great value to anyone wishing to build and strengthen the Body of Light. As I worked to bring through the message of Diamond, I placed it upon the throat chakra and immediately felt a deepening of the sense of confidence in the words and vibrations that pour through the throat. If one wishes to become an oracle or a psychic channel, or in any way a servant of the expression of the Logos or the Word of Divine Truth, working meditatively with Diamond at the throat chakra is perhaps the most powerful activity to augment and accelerate the development of this capacity.

Discovering and developing such capacities is of great importance in these times, because the longing I felt originally in my heart is now clarified in thought with the understanding that the Divine wishes to be present and more fully manifested in the physical world. This need is growing ever more intense and urgent. My sense is that the Divine wishes for human beings to be transfigured into the Divine Human. This entails the full awakening and expression of the Light Body, which appears to my inner vision as the energetic pattern of the star tetrahedron. This pattern is resonant with the great geometric net that has been called the Flower of Life. We can see and experience many other geometric forms of Light in the archetypal realm, and through opening to them, we can embody their perfected forms in ourselves and our world. It is a matter of our willing partnership, opening to the great cascades of Divine patterns that long for expression. The heart's way of translating the infusion of Divine Love into the human being through Diamond is that felt sense of deep longing which, when we abide with it and open to it, becomes a powerful flood, flowing into the human being in a great torrent of Light. What begins as a thin stream of energy enhances and amplifies into an unbelievable, astonishing current of pure Divine consciousness, which has waited on the other side of the membrane of our willingness to pour itself into us, in an ecstatic union that goes beyond all the understandings we carry forward from the past.

Diamond is the primal gateway stone of union of self and Divine. It operates most powerfully in the realm of Light. Its feeling quality is a kind of impersonal yet hugely powerful love and longing.

Diamond carries the frequencies of the Music of the Spheres, as well as all the tonal harmonies that can be understood and expressed with mathematical precision through inner contemplation of the structure and harmony of the Logos or Divine Word. As was said in the book of Genesis, so speaks Diamond: "In the beginning was the Word and the Word accompanied God and was God." At the level of first expression, the expression itself appears as geometric forms that are the very outline of the Divine Nature. Thus the expression (the "Word," or form) both is, and is the expression of, the unfathomable Being of the Divine. In the realm of stones Diamond is the most high, in the sense that it is closest to the first expression of the Logos. Regarding the flow of spiritual qualities or currents into the world, Diamond serves as a primal Gate of Light through which the purest, most powerful Light currents can enter. This Light pours into crystalline expression, through a multitude of minerals and forms, and each stone is an expression of a complex Divine vocabulary, offering a wide spectrum or scale within the many notes of the Divine harmony of the manifest world.

All the words above comprise the message dictated by Diamond, in answer to my request to understand its nature and its offer of partnership. As it resonates with the holy Source of all, Diamond invites us to become a pure embodiment of the Divine here in the living world. Diamond's gift to us includes a powerful purification of all one's energy systems. If we allow its Light and vibrational intensity to sweep through us fully, everything that is an impure coagulation of lesser consciousness within our energy fields will be swept out and grounded in the Earth. Diamond vibrates at the highest frequency of all stones. It can be a challenging partner for those who work with it, especially in the beginning. My advice and my own intention is to abide with the being of Diamond and edge oneself further into relationship with it. Through this you may receive many gifts of Spirit, including a deeper attunement with spiritual truth, enhanced capacities for intuition and insight, and an increasing frequency of experiences of *gnosis,* or direct knowing.

Because of Diamond's tendency to magnify and intensify all sorts of currents, one's imbalances become highly visible under its influence. They are magnified in order to bring them to conscious attention, so that they may be purified and released. For such spiritual purification there is no faster or more powerful stone than Diamond. One must have the will to do this work, or the influence of Diamond can become quite uncomfortable. It is difficult to maintain false or negative habits once one becomes aware of them, but it can also be quite difficult to give them up. Using Diamond together with other minerals that purify—especially stones with carbon-based compositions such as Jet, Master Shamanite and Tibetan Black Quartz—can be helpful in doing the work of inner purification.

All of the aforementioned stones are highly resonant with Diamond, for they all carry a strongly grounded form of carbon. Jet is almost pure carbon, in a rather humble form, just as Diamond is carbon's highest, most perfected form. In meditative purification work, one is encouraged to place Diamond at the crown, with Jet, Master Shamanite or Tibetan Black Quartz at the root chakra. This creates the Alpha and Omega—the highest and lowest points of the Light geometry—overlaid upon the human body's energy grid.

Placing Diamond at the crown and one of the darker carbon stones at the root provides the polar anchors for the activation of the star tetrahedron or Merkabah Vehicle of Light. This is one practice for awakening the Light Body. It aligns the two poles of the root and crown chakras, with the heart chakra in its generating position at the center. The placement of these two stones at the Alpha and Omega positions initiates the coalescing of the Light Body and stimulates it greatly. In the next step, one may bring stones of the heart, especially Rosophia and Azeztulite, together at the heart chakra, in order to encourage the full outpouring of Divine Light into the human vehicle. The efficacy of Diamond in this process is great. Other crystals, especially Merkabite Calcite, can enhance this process.

DIAMOND SPEAKS   "I am a pure servant of the I Am That I Am. My body is Truth, my heart is Devotion, and I offer myself as a bridge of the Human/Divine union. I am the corridor of Light into the Heart of the One. Those who wholly attune through me shall find themselves at the threshold of the Infinite."

FULGURITE

KEY WORDS   Manifestation of one's higher purpose, enhancement of prayer, kundalini awakening, purification, sudden awakening

ELEMENT   Storm

CHAKRAS   All

Fulgurite is the name given to glassy tubes formed by lightning strikes on sand or other silica-rich soil. The event that creates a Fulgurite is characterized by a huge release of energy. Lightning carries extremely large amounts of static electricity, which is discharged in a very small spot, and the temperature of lightning has been calculated to be hotter (for an instant) than the surface of the sun. The heat is intense enough to vaporize the sand at the center of the strike and to melt the material around the edges. The tube is formed from the melted sand, and the hole down the middle is created by the vaporized material. Many Fulgurites that have been gathered from beaches and deserts are one to three inches in length and less than an inch in diameter. However, some specimens can be as long and thick as a human arm or leg. Some form multiple branches, like tree roots, though it is nearly impossible to unearth these intact.

Fulgurites are formed in a single powerful event rather than growing slowly over extended periods, as crystals do. This may have something to do with the intense energies and experiences that people report from their encounters with these stones.

BACKGROUND: Fulgurites are among the most powerful stones for manifesting visions through the strength of prayer. The lightning energy, long believed to be the touch of the Divine, still resides in them, and they can act as magnifiers of one's clear intention, building a powerful resonance between oneself and the latent powers of the higher worlds. One recommended technique for working with Fulgurite for manifestation is to sit for a while in meditation, deeply visualizing your prayers or intentions, and then to put the Fulgurite tube to your lips, exhaling through the tube and "blowing your prayers to the Divine." While doing so, imagine the energy of lightning moving in reverse, pulling itself back into the clouds along with your prayer. Then see the answers to the prayers falling in a deluge of manifestation, overflowing the streams and rivers of your world, irrigating and nourishing your life.

Fulgurites work well with Moldavite, Tibetan Tektites, Herderite, Azeztulite, Phenacite, Danburite and Brookite. For those who find Fulgurites a bit too intense, try combining them with the gentle energies of Ajoite, which will soften the Storm. For interdimensional travel Merkabite Calcite, Herderite, Scolecite, Phenacite or Natrolite can be added.

NEW ATTUNEMENT   Friends who are involved deeply in shamanic work have referred to Fulgurites as "Petrified Lightning," and this expressive image of Fulgurite is useful in understanding the spiritual qualities of these uniquely formed objects. I began my meditation with Fulgurite holding two large specimens, one in each hand, and wearing a third piece over my heart. I soon felt a very fast tingling energy filling the entire volume of my hands—front, back and interior. My felt sense was of a current of rapid communication between the spiritual worlds and the cellular level of my body. A number of images and inner lights rapidly arose, perhaps exemplifying the very quickness that Fulgurite embodies. It is unlike any other substance that we call a stone, because Fulgurite is formed in a flash of lightning. In this powerful energy discharge, the heavens and the Earth touch one another. As mentioned above, the temperature of a lightning bolt is higher than the surface of the sun, so one might say that in the lightning genesis of Fulgurite we see the meeting of the sun's positive charge and the Earth's negative charge.

Fulgurite keeps presenting me with the image of Hermes, the Greek deity of rapid communication, mental agility, magic and alchemical transformation. It gestures to us with the Hermes image as if to say, "I am like this one." Also, as I gazed upon one of the Fulgurites in my hand, I noticed that after a few moments there arose a foglike appearance of purplish light. It seemed to both surround and permeate the Fulgurite. I interpret purple light as denoting high-frequency currents, just as ultraviolet light represents a higher frequency than the visible spectrum. This reinforces the notion that Fulgurite is the embodied result of a unique instantaneous action, of which the visible aspect is the lightning bolt.

The felt sense in contemplating Fulgurite is that it invites us to dwell with the event of the Thunderbolt. In mythic symbolism the Thunderbolt is seen as a gesture from the divinities, and this gesture, if it touches one's body, causes a wounding or even death. Yet this can be seen as

the very challenge of being in the presence of the Divine, which has been described mythologically as "being struck by lightning." We speak of powerful insights coming to us "like a bolt from the blue." In other words, an unexplainable stroke of lightning hits us. This lightning stops us in our tracks, stops our ongoing habits of understanding the world in certain ways. The bolt of lightning can therefore be, in terms of insight experiences, both a wound to our old view of the world and a blessing. In its blessing aspect, the shocking event of the spiritual Thunderbolt offers a more divinely inspired (though sometimes more difficult) landscape of understanding.

Fulgurite suggests that to work meditatively with it is to make oneself available to the "bolt from the blue." It excites the neural activity of the brain and spinal cord. The high-powered currents of Fulgurite can enter through the crown chakra, or through any other area of the body, creating a resonance throughout the Liquid Crystal Body Matrix. As we hold it in our hand, Fulgurite generates tiny tingling impulses that move up through the hands and arms and reach the core of the body, exciting a host of meridians and neural connections. In touching the Fulgurite, we echo the Earth's gesture to the electrical charge in the clouds just before the lightning bolt strikes. The lightning bolt can be viewed spiritually as a mutual gesture between Earth and sky. The clouds build up a positive charge, and at the same time there is within the Earth a "ground charge" of the opposite polarity. Metaphorically, the cloud or the sky symbolizes the masculine, yang polarity, and the Earth the feminine, receptive, yin polarity. The yin reaches up to the rising charge of the yang in the sky, through any convenient object such as a hill, a tree or a post, or even a human body. When the charge in the cloud feels the gesture of the Earth, the lightning strikes, meeting the Earth's ground charge or upward gesture. This describes the physical lightning we see.

We can see an echo of that pattern in our work with Fulgurite. Using Fulgurite in meditative practice allows the ground current of our receptivity—our capacity to receive information, knowledge, insight, understanding, wisdom—to reach upward to the potential infusion of Light from the Divine world. It does this by exciting the Liquid Crystal Body Matrix and building up the charge of the Light Body through the column of the spinal cord. In calling down the spiritual Lightning, we act like the receptive Earth, and the spiritual realms of unlimited potential take the role of the oppositely charged cloud. As we hold the Fulgurite with this intention, we feel our "ground charge" rise up through the crown chakra. We have made ourselves available to the Thunderbolt and its inspiration, and when the moment is right, we may be filled with the intense grace of a sudden stroke of enlightenment. This is certainly the most powerful way to experience Fulgurite.

Those who work shamanically with Fulgurites say that they "blow their prayers" through these tubes of Petrified Lightning up to the Divine world. They believe that the Fulgurite amplifies the power of the prayer. This gesture is resonant with my description of the meditative practice whereby one's energies coalesce from the body along the tube of the spine, up through the opening at the crown chakra. We make our gesture of self-offering to whatever divine potential may wish to meet us. The flash of illumination that can occur through this activity is sometimes modest, sometimes vast. In each case, however, the insight reveals itself as an unforeseen, unique vision that was not previously within one's realm of thought.

To invite the Divine Thunderbolt, one must be fully open. One must not attempt to qualify or define ahead of time what may come down. This requires a certain courage, because in opening oneself to the Divine unknown, there is no way of being certain whether one will experience the meeting with the Thunderbolt as painful, delightful or both, or in what proportion this will come. Yet it is not the nature of the Thunderbolt itself that causes the pleasure or pain. It is our already-held attachments to that which we believe we want or wish to avoid. The best experiences of the Thunderbolt occur when one is fully surrendered, having given up any wish to understand or know in a certain way.

The heart chakra, seat of our courage, is the generator of our "ground charge," through which we reach to the Divine with the help of Fulgurite. The heart, through intention and a simultaneous surrender of will, is our best guide. The intention is the gesture up from the heart. It is the intention to offer one's "ground charge," one's love, one's openness to whatever the Divine may offer. One must intend, with a full-hearted will, to offer it up, to make the most complete and therefore the most inviting gesture. This is what a prayer is. This is why the shamans send their prayers through Fulgurite, using the Fulgurite and the breath (the *spirit* in re-*spira*-tion). To blow one's prayer through the Fulgurite is a powerful way of focusing and yet releasing one's intention or wish, one's petition to the Divine potential.

I did this prior to beginning this description of the qualities of Fulgurite. I had been sitting quietly, holding myself in receptive meditation, but without any real gesture of request. I saw lights, I felt energies, I enjoyed meeting some of the initial expressions of Fulgurite, yet not much else was going on. I then took the Fulgurite and blew my prayer through it: "May I understand you? May I understand the gesture, purpose and possibilities that exist between Fulgurite and me, and my fellow humans?" I did this with an inner emphasis that what I asked was not a scientific or neutral question, but the heart's desire. I sent out the promise to gladly receive whatever came back to me. All I have been saying about the Thunderbolt and the gesture to the Divine was inspired moments later by images flowing in to my awareness, seemingly as the immediate answer to the focused offer of my prayer. I therefore feel I was given a most coherent and true example of the kind of interaction we can experience with the aid of Fulgurite. Fulgurite revealed itself to me as a true helper. It offers itself as an energetic bridge between the world of our half-asleep consciousness and the spiritual realms of awakened Light.

I have a strong impulse to repeat the message that the Thunderbolt is in itself an infusion of Light. Our capacity to receive and transmute into understanding the bolt of the Divine light is a function of the strength of our physical, mental, emotional and spiritual container. I was shown the image of Benjamin Franklin catching a bolt of lightning through his kite-flying experience. He himself was severly shocked, and his body was literally "cooked" by the experience. Yet the lightning he purportedly captured in his jar is a kind of metaphor for the successful "catching" of the Divine lightning bolt in the human container. I find myself greatly appreciative that the bolt of lightning, which occurs in an evanescent instant, is preserved in its footprint—the Petrified Lightning. Fulgurite preserves and somehow mysteriously carries within it the inner qualities of the lightning bolt.

I agree with the shamans who have for centuries considered Fulgurite a sacred stone. It is a tube of connection to the sacred worlds. These are worlds with which we need to involve ourselves in order to live fully, and to fulfill our destined role as a bridge between heaven and Earth.

FULGURITE SPEAKS   "I am the quickener, the unexpected Light. I am the Messenger of the Light, and through me the Light of truth comes to you."

GLENDONITE

KEY WORDS Precise stimulation of chakras and
meridians, transmutation into the New Human Being
and the Body of Light

ELEMENT Fire

CHAKRAS All main chakras, secondary chakras and
meridians

Glendonite is the name given to a particular kind of pseudomorph—Calcite that occurs after Ikaite crystals. Calcite is a calcium carbonate mineral with a hardness of 3. Its crystal system is rhombohedral. Glendonites originated as crystalline masses of Ikaite, a hydrous calcium carbonate mineral. Ikaite only forms in near-freezing water of high alkalinity, in organic-rich sediments at the sediment-water interface. At warmer temperatures Ikaite is unstable, and the mineral loses its water content. It transforms to Calcite. During the Ikaite-to-Calcite conversion, the original crystal structure of the Ikaite may be retained. Calcite masses that retain Ikaite crystal shapes are called Glendonites.

Glendonites retain the star-shaped forms of the original Ikaites. They have been found off the coasts of South Africa and Australia. However, the most attractive (and energetic) specimens come from the Kola Peninsula in Russia.

I was initially bemused when I learned that Glendonite is a pseudomorph, meaning that this mineral has filled a space previously occupied, in the pattern once created by another mineral. The blossoming, radiant form of Glendonite is not the form the Calcite would have taken on its own. I mention this because there is a metaphoric resonance between this fact and the spiritual qualities of Glendonite.

BACKGROUND The currents of Glendonite enter the brain, and they work very quickly to free the mind of the tyranny of fixed ideas via their awakening of inner truth. Glendonites evoke the archetypes of the High Priestess and the Magician, the male and female spiritual beings who work through humans to bring the benevolent magic of the spiritual realms into dynamic expression in the world.

Glendonite stimulates the third eye, crown chakra and Soul Star chakra above the head. It can help increase psychic capacities, make inner visions more vivid and open the doors to

profound interior silence. Its influences can deepen meditative and dream experiences and help sensitize the conscious self to the subtle currents of the spiritual realms.

Glendonite can help the mind become more aware of the activity and thought of the heart. As the self aligns with the heart, one's ability to perceive and express the truth is enhanced. This alignment with truth brings forth a profound sense of freedom, for one is no longer a slave to falsehood.

Glendonite affects the brain and the thinking processes. It slows down rapid-fire cognitive functions and increases the influence of the right hemisphere of the brain. It quiets the inner dialog and opens the doors to the silent synthesis of ideas, emotions and perceptions. It increases feelings of spiritual awe and wonder, helping us to see how astonishing the world is. Glendonite can be used for calming headaches, relieving mental stress, overcoming insomnia, relaxing tense muscles and clearing blocked energies in the meridians. It can open and harmonize any of the chakras.

Glendonite facilitates the process by which the new Body of Light is brought into being. This body, which is less dense than our present form, is an almost musical flow of currents of Divine love, with our sense of self centered in the heart. Using seven pieces of Glendonite in combination with seven Tibetan Tektites—one of each at each chakra point—is among the most powerful layouts one can set up for the purpose of awakening the Light Body.

Glendonite works well with Azeztulite, Satya Mani Quartz, Natrolite, Phenacite and Herderite. It is excellent with Merkabite Calcite to bring awakening to the third eye and crown chakras.

NEW ATTUNEMENT   In sitting for this attunement, I was first drawn to place a Glendonite in a pouch over my heart, even though I believed this stone was a third-eye awakener. To my surprise, I experienced pulsations *between* the crystal and my heart. They seemed to travel a kind of elliptical, circulating path between the heart and the surface of my chest where the stone had been placed. This circulating flow of the current of Glendonite seemed to be one of its special qualities. When I held two stones with my hands in my lap, to my surprise I immediately felt an elliptical circulation of currents between these stones and my third eye chakra, which was perhaps two feet or more from where I held the crystals. Sometimes I feel third-eye resonance with a stone I am not holding at that spot, but this case was quite un-usual. It seemed that the current flowed not up through my body, but rather through the space directly between my stones and my third eye—traveling, as it were, through the air. This was a new sensation for me.

When placed directly on the third eye—especially when one touches one of the multiple terminating points of a Glendonite cluster to the forehead—an intense and pentrating stream goes through the third eye and into the center of the brain. This feels like a constant flow, not pulsating in the way one might experience with other stones such as Phenacite.

Placing a Glendonite at the crown chakra, touching the top of the head with one of the terminations, I again felt an intense stream of current. It felt like a somewhat fan-shaped flow of energy, but still much more of a straight stream than with most stones. This fan at the crown was like a narrow-beam flashlight, and in fact created an interior ray of White Light in the skull, along with an elevation of consciousness. I feel that one can work very precisely with Glendonite because of the narrow streams of current that it emanates through its points. I worked along the center line of my skull with the Glendonite crystal, and I was able to differentiate separate streams of current entering my skull at each contact, even though they were perhaps only one quarter inch apart. I discovered several sensitive areas not commonly thought of as chakras, including what I felt to be a harmonic mid-point between the third eye and crown. Placing Glendonite at this spot created a powerful resonance in both of those chakras. Placing it one quarter inch higher brought the energy primarily up toward the crown; aligning it a quarter inch lower shifted the balance toward the third eye.

My felt sense is that this precision makes Glendonite unique, favoring its application in treatments such as acupuncture. Practitioners who work with the meridian system are likely to find in Glendonite a new means of stimulation of the thousands of subtle energy nodes, intersections and current points addressed through acupuncture and certain other healing modalities. Those with healing practices that work primarily at the levels of our energy bodies will find that Glendonite can be highly effective. In the case of acupuncture, the precise energy streams of Glendonite might sometimes affect the patient more beneficially than the needles. I hope some professional practitioners will experiment with this.

Another intuition that arose during meditation with Glendonite was related to its history of formation as a pseudomorph. Calcite has filled in this form originally created by a cluster of Ikaite. The Ikaite was dissolved and replaced gradually with Calcite. I feel that even though the Ikaite is no longer present, its morphic resonance remains, because Glendonite is much more powerful than almost any other Calcite.

Glendonite is generated through a transmutation in which the original composition of the crystal cluster is dissolved, allowing for the infusion of a new substance. This is akin to Glendonite's potential influence when we work with it. Our identity, especially the dimensions of it that are not a part of our conscious awareness, is composed of an array of habits. Habits are repeating patterns with a momentum of their own, which may or may not be wholesome for us.

The momentum of habit is often simply a momentum of pure repetition and familiarity. We do many things because we have done them before, and we do them in the way that we do simply because we do not have to make a new choice in order to repeat a habit. Habits can in this sense be a kind of abdication of one's power—a default choice, which is simply what happens when we make no choice.

What calls to us as destiny is a new choice—in fact, a wealth of new choices. This transformation of self—the enactment of the potential of our highest destiny—requires and is fed by the dissolution of our old habits and the infusion of new choices. When we embrace it, we embrace new patterns, new energies, new insights in an ongoing interplay of intuitive feeling and fully conscious choice. Glendonite—through the precision of its currents and its tendency to stimulate precise openings within the brain/mind, meridians and chakras—offers the possibility of our transmutation.

We notice our habits when we feel something that doesn't fit with them. We realize we have been living by habit when something interrupts their repetition. The intense, precise energy infusion from Glendonite—which itself has experienced physical transmutation—encourages us to see and choose new ways of being. Just as Calcite, left to its ordinary "growth habits," would not have formed into the unique and powerful crystal clusters we call Glendonite, so too the infusion of the new is enhanced by the form of our human container. Our habits have not been detrimental in themselves, but they can be if they are left in place indefinitely. When it is time for change, change must be welcomed, encouraged, embraced and enhanced.

Humans are at such a juncture, and our destiny is certain to continue its unfolding and its call for change. All that we have been may influence and give certain forms to the vast infusion of Divine potential that knocks upon the doors of our minds, hearts and bodies. Yet our boundaries are no more inpenetrable than any physical material thing. All is vibration, whether it be crystalline or human, and vibration modulates in the presence of other vibration. Glendonite's history and its lesson, if we embrace it, suggest that we open to transmutation. Through this opening, the marriage of all we have been and all we might become can be consummated.

It is interesting to consider that the original Ikaite crystals transformed to Calcite (Glendonite) when environmental conditions changed, in this case as the sea grew warmer. We, too, are called to metamorphosis, because our inner and outer environments demand it. Glendonite is a great deal more powerful than other forms of Calcite, perhaps because it somehow resonates with the original Ikaite, as we've speculated. We may also discover that our past has provided us with the essential vessel to contain the new beings we are becoming. Glendonites began as organic material and mutated into crystals. Perhaps we will metaphorically (or actually!) do the same thing.

GLENDONITE SPEAKS   "I am the new wine filling the old bottles. I am the Light that enters through the shaded window. I am changed in my expression, surprised at my form, yet I find myself in my own transfiguration. Resonance with me brings the realization of this into you."

HEALER'S GOLD

KEY WORDS   Healing, grounding of high-frequency energies in the body, energetic harmony and balance

ELEMENT   Earth

CHAKRAS   All

H ealer's Gold is the metaphysical name given to a combination of Pyrite and Magnetite mined in Arizona. Pyrite is an iron sulfide mineral with a hardness of 6 to 6.5. Magnetite is an iron oxide mineral with a hardness of 5.5 to 6.5. Both minerals have cubic crystal structures. The colors of Healer's Gold are a mixture of black and gold, sometimes occurring in dramatic patterns. The name is derived from the material's metaphysical use as a healing stone and from Pyrite's nickname, "Fool's Gold."

BACKGROUND   Healer's Gold harmonizes the astral, subtle and causal bodies and aligns them correctly with the physical. It is balancing to the male and female aspects of the self. It activates weak or lazy chakras and enhances the flow of subtle energies throughout the meridian system. It helps people with low energy and eliminates passivity. In healing sessions, this stone brings about a synergy in which both practitioner and client are likely to feel a marked increase in their energy levels both during and after a session.

Healer's Gold can be used on any chakra. This stone is a source of prana or life force, as well as an integrative balancer of all one's energy systems. Healer's Gold promotes a positive outlook and facilitates the initiation of new creative projects. Wearing Healer's Gold can create a sense of overall well-being, comfort in the body, confidence in oneself, acceptance of others and balance on all levels. Sleeping with this stone can enhance relaxation and allow for the restoration of the body's magnetic and auric fields during the night. It can also help shield one's aura from negative or disharmonious influences during the day.

Healer's Gold works especially well with Moldavite, which can speed and strengthen its effects. Its healing influence can be augmented by Seraphinite, Rosophia and all varieties of Azeztulite. Its ability to clear negative energies is enhanced by Aegirine, Master Shamanite and Black Tourmaline. It harmonizes with almost all other healing stones and can be useful for grounding after working with Phenacite or other high-vibration crystals.

NEW ATTUNEMENT   When I sat down to meditate with Healer's Gold, before I even began, the stone began to do its work with me. I was experiencing some digestive discomfort at that moment. And as I was preparing to meditate, I placed the stone in my lap. Within moments the discomfort in my digestive tract was relieved, and I could feel a grounding in the body that was not fully present before holding the Healer's Gold.

When working with stones, especially the many high-vibration stones that are included in this book, there is sometimes the tendency for one's vibration to get ahead of the physical body. By this I mean that we can vibrate very rapidly in our mental, etheric and astral bodies. Even our emotional body can leap to higher frequencies more readily than the physical form. The physical body—our flesh and blood and bones—is a tremendous stabilizing influence for our whole being. Being grounded in the physical body is essential for the coalescence of all our other aspects into a whole being.

I speak of this because the message of Healer's Gold is very much about the harmonization and well-being of the body. Healer's Gold is truly a friend of our flesh and blood. Its composition of Pyrite and Magnetite is denser both in appearance and vibration than many stones. Yet it is spiritually a stone of powerful beneficial qualities. Healer's Gold influences the electromagnetic field of the body toward harmony. Its currents enter the meridians and the chakra system, facilitating proper alignment and symmetry. Aspects of our energy bodies that have become unbalanced are drawn back into their appropriate patterns through the influence of Healer's Gold. Also, the various levels—astral, etheric, emotional, mental and physical—are attracted into unity and re-centered in their appropriate patterns through the strong and healthy currents emanated by Healer's Gold.

Healer's Gold strengthens the third chakra, seat of the will, and encourages and enables us to act and make each gesture within each moment a gesture of power. This is not power over others; rather it is a sense of well-being that gives us power to act with conviction and confidence in life.

Healer's Gold engenders confidence through bringing one's energies into an alignment they recognize as the highest and truest pattern. Those who work spiritually for the rapid evolution of consciousness can benefit from Healer's Gold through its re-centering influence. I keep coming back to this because it is essential that we who attempt to be spiritual evolutionary human beings, working so much at the edge of things, not be pulled out of balance or fall into resonance with higher frequencies without bringing the body along. However, Healer's Gold reminds us that the body is our great ally—our home, the safe place from which we may venture into many realms, and to which we can comfortably return.

There is a sort of dynamic tension between the body as our rock of stability and the spiritual call for transfiguration of the body. I feel that the most beneficial use of Healer's Gold is in our moving step by step from the body as we have known it into the physical body reattuned as the Body of Light. We move ourselves into numerous unfamiliar energy patterns as we explore the domains of Light and the frequencies of the spiritual realms. Healer's Gold offers an opportunity to reset our energies from a grounded place. Healer's Gold also carries the pattern of the perfected human being. And it is in this that it aligns itself with our destiny as embodied Light Beings. The Divine blueprint of the body is very strong and stable yet capable of being influenced and modified by subtle forces. It is hugely adaptable and flexible. Our physical bodies are, after all, primarily made of water, and water is capable of taking on innumerable patterns.

Healer's Gold reminds the body of its strength, stability, capacities, adaptability and purpose. It is through this that Healer's Gold is a powerful force in ridding the body of disharmony, negativity and disease. In fact, dis-ease is what Healer's Gold most readily dispels, for it brings the body to a state of ease. Healer's Gold is a great ally for those who work as healers (from which its name was derived). Healer's Gold—in carrying the blueprint of the harmonious body, bringing stability to one's energy systems and providing a centering influence—benefits both client and healer, bringing both into a state of harmonious accord.

Meditation before a healing session with a piece of Healer's Gold can enhance any healer's capacity to find the vibrational gateway through which beneficial energies may be channeled. Meditation with Healer's Gold centers and brings together the energies of the healer and the spiritual beings who assist. The client is also encouraged to meditate with a Healer's Gold stone before receiving a session. When both healer and client have attuned through the stone prior to the treatment, they will find themselves in an easy resonance with one another as well as with their own well-being.

HEALER'S GOLD SPEAKS "I carry the dynamic flowing pattern of balance, well-being, healing and alignment between the spiritual and physical domains. I am a friend of the body. I am a friend of clarity. My truth is the truth of strength and harmony."

HERDERITE

KEY WORDS   Evolution, activation of latent capacities, awakening the higher brain functions, discovering the Light Body, entering the activity of blessing

ELEMENT   Storm

CHAKRAS   Third Eye (6th), Crown (7th), Soul Star (8th), Transpersonal (9th)

Herderite is a calcium beryllium phosphate with a hardness of 5 to 5.5. Its crystal system is monoclinic. It occurs as tabular or prismatic crystals and is found in granitic pegmatites. It can be colorless, pale yellow, green, brownish, gray and sometimes lavender. Herderites are rare crystals, found most abundantly in Brazil. Brazilian Herderites are frequently brownish, yellow or gray, occasionally pale green. African Herderite is translucent gray, with some lavender areas. Some rare bright-green Herderites were found in Afghanistan in the 1980s.

BACKGROUND   Herderite is one of the preeminent stones for awakening and charging the upper chakras of the body, and for connecting one's conscious awareness to the higher dimensions linked to the chakras above the head in the etheric body. It is an incredibly powerful tool for interdimensional travel and communication with spirit guides and Light beings. Herderite initiates growth in consciousness. It opens the third eye and crown chakras, as well as the first two etheric chakras, expanding one's sense of self. In fact, with Herderite one can experience oneself as an energy field that exists far beyond the confines of the physical body.

In the years ahead, there will be a quantum leap of evolution, and humans will become less dense. They may evolve to a trans-physical state in which they identify themselves as a field of consciousness rather than a personality inside a skin. This is an experience to which we can be introduced by Herderite.

Herderite is one of the Synergy Twelve stones, along with Moldavite, Phenacite, Tanzanite, Danburite, Azeztulite, Tibetan Tektite, Brookite, Satyaloka Azeztulite, Natrolite, Scolecite and Petalite. Herderite also resonates powerfully with Merkabite Calcite, Satya Mani Quartz, Agni Gold Danburite and Cinnabar Quartz.

NEW ATTUNEMENT   Herderite is such a powerful stone that whenever I prepare to meditate with it, I make sure that I have some extra time afterwards to ground myself. Its power is so immense and its energies so uplifting that I can only work with it when I'm prepared to take on a full-blown shift of consciousness.

In sitting down for this meditation, after clearing my field, I placed two Herderites in a pouch over my heart. I also had one Herderite in each hand and a large crystal of Herderite in my lap. Before placing the large crystal in my lap, I had begun by holding the others, and there was an immediate and powerful pulsing that went like a horizontal wave of great intensity through my entire brain. Herderite is highly focused on stimulation of the brain, along with one's energy field in the area of the skull. This is where its currents go, no matter where I apply the stone. After I placed the large Herderite in my lap, I noticed the initial pulsations had calmed, and I imagined they were going to stay at a lower level. However, when I touched the big Herderite in my lap, wave after wave of energy pulsed through my hands and up once again into the brain. I could feel the liquid crystal Matrix of my body shifting in response to Herderite's energies. I

could feel the currents move up through my hands into my shoulders, neck and head, culminating in great pulsing wave.

My felt sense was that these currents moved into the brain for the purpose of awakening something that is still asleep in us. One might say it is our evolutionary potential, our never-used or never-discovered capacities. It is as though Herderite is a kind of key whose purpose it is to unlock the dormant areas of the brain/mind. My intuition suggests that the unlocking of these capacities will be an important turning point, both for the individual and the collective.

The currents of Herderite, as they surge through the brain area, are exceedingly pleasant. They result in a sense of almost tactile pleasure in one's energy bodies and in their overlap with the physical. One intuition that came as I was attempting to see into Herderite's potential for working with us was that it helps to fully entwine one's spiritual body with the physical body. My sense is that the pleasure experienced from Herderite's stimulation of the energy centers in the head may actually be the felt sense, in the physical, of what it is like to be in the spiritual body. In other words, Herderite knits together our physical and spiritual aspects in a way that serves to deepen our conscious awareness of their shared identity. It is not the stone itself that causes us to feel pleasure, but the stone's linking us consciously to our spiritual body. This allows us to internalize some of the high vibration that is potentially natural to us as spiritual human beings.

As I meditated, I experienced a number of images and inner impulses indicating that Herderite can facilitate interdimensional travel. Much of this interdimensional travel, as I experienced it, is a movement of one's point of awareness through corridors and fields of geometries constructed out of light. The spiritual worlds contain architecture made from light, and beings whose forms are patterns of light. One's own being appears in some of these realms as an egg-shaped light-form, which varies in radiance and color as a function of the shifts of consciousness. It is instructive to the everyday self to go through the experience of interdimensional travel, in part to enable release of the culture-bound image of the self as a body-shaped thing without extension and with no other form.

Herderite gives us the felt sense that our energy bodies extend far beyond the confines of the skin. One of the pronounced effects of Herderite is a feeling of oneself extending in a kind of sphere of awareness that is a good deal larger than the physical body. In my own experience, I found myself extending first several feet and then perhaps fifteen feet out from my bodily core. I had the sensation that my *actual* "body" and awareness went far beyond this. The holding back from greater extension was primarily due to fear or reluctance in the consciousness to go any farther. I think that perhaps my individual self, as I had imagined it to be—more or less confined to the material body—could only go so far before beginning to worry that it would not be able to control or govern itself if it expanded beyond this fifteen or twenty feet from the center. My inner awareness smiled at this, because it knew better, but patience is helpful in such areas.

The faculties we call clairvoyance, clairaudience, clairsentience and prophetic vision are among the capacities I feel Herderite can stimulate and expand. In addition, its most immediate impulse is to vivify the senses of sight, hearing and smell. The sense of sight, as it is stimulated by Herderite—especially the seeing we do with eyeclosed—can take us beyond anything we have known, in a way that transcends our habitual limits. As I meditated with Herderite the sounds around me drew my ear—my sense of hearing—all the way to the source of the sound, as if my ears were casting out lines of connection. I also experienced everyday sounds with great pleasure, as if they were music.

The sensory vivification brought on by Herderite facilitates a special kind of meditation that is essential in our work of spiritual unfolding. If one holds a Herderite while purposely sending attention outward along the sensory paths, one begins to feel the sense of expanding outward, encompassing the whole field of one's sensory perceptions. It is as if the world is inside you, as if your own interior has vastly increased. There is also a sense of intimacy with the world, brought about through this purposeful embracing of perceptions.

Early in this book I recounted the dream experience in which I had asked before going to sleep, "What is the New Consciousness?" Several times during the early morning I awoke with the words ringing in my thoughts: "The New Consciousness is an activity of blessing." I feel that Herderite can help us enter this blessing activity, which unfolds as the experience of what I am calling the New Consciousness. The extension of the senses is among its dimensions. If one then adds loving, blessing intention to the expanded sensory awareness, one has engaged and enfolded the world within the activity of blessing. Through this activity, one enters into co-creative partnership with the Soul of the World.

I would like for a moment to expand on this notion. If we meditate with Herderite, taking note of the enhancement of the senses and the expansion of the self-sense beyond the bodily boundaries, which this stone facilitates, we are already part of the way into the state I am trying to describe. At this point we can do as I mentioned above—we can "send" our attention out to the sources of all our sensory perceptions. Doing this moment by moment increases the sense of being extended beyond the body. The next step is to "send" the intention of blessing out to each perceived object, being or event. To send blessing is basically to make a heartfelt love-gesture toward the world in relation to each sensory impression. To do this requires conscious choice and a little bit of will, but it is immediately and greatly rewarding. To gesture outward from one's core, again and again, in this blessing way, sends love into the world, which I believe is the nourishment the world needs from us. It also creates a love-filled consciousness in us, because we always experience whatever we express. The sensory extension beyond the body then moves out into a beloved and blessed world, which is both within us and all around us. Robert Sardello has described this state as *being within the world, within the heart*. As the poet Novalis was quoted in this book's first chapter, "Every beloved object is the center of a Paradise." I then added that when every object and every experience is beloved, all the world becomes a Paradise. Herderite does not make this happen, but the expansion it facilitates gives us an opportunity, and even the subtle suggestion, to make this move into another mode of being—the activity of blessing that opens the doors to the New Consciousness.

As I have indicated, Herderite is a powerful stone for expanding the sphere of one's self-sense. When it is utilized along with stones such as Rosophia and Morganite, the heart currents are more readily engaged in this expansion. If one then voluntarily begins to proceed with the activity of blessing, a wonderful transformation of consciousness occurs. Herderite will not push this gift upon anyone, but it clears the path for an easy and exceedingly rewarding experience of the expanded self.

HERDERITE SPEAKS   "I know you to be more than you know yourselves to be, and I wish to be the resonating mirror that reflects to you not only your image, but the very vibrations of your expanded whole self. You are destined to live the fullness of your true being, and I make myself available to serve that end—to awaken your remembrance of what you are destined to be."

HERKIMER QUARTZ "DIAMOND"

KEY WORDS Dreams, visions, purification, spiritualization of physical life, vibrational ascension

ELEMENT Storm

CHAKRAS Third Eye (6th), Crown (7th)

Herkimer Quartz "Diamonds" are a variety of Quartz crystal found in and around Herkimer, New York (U.S.). Their crystal system is hexagonal (trigonal). They are silicon dioxide crystals with a hardness of about 7.5. This is harder than most other Quartz varieties, and this may be because Herkimers are formed in a hard-rock matrix. Herkimer "Diamonds" are so named because of their form—the short, small, stubby, double-terminated shapes and glossy surfaces make them superficially resemble Diamond crystals. Herkimers can be clear or included. Inclusions are often black carbon deposits. Some Herkimers are smoky rather than colorless, and larger crystals frequently exhibit skeletal Quartz formations. Enhydro inclusions of water are found in a small percentage of these crystals. Similar-looking crystals have been found at other localities, but these generally do not have the hardness or high gloss of genuine Herkimer "Diamonds."

BACKGROUND   Herkimer "Diamonds," beyond almost all others, are manifestations of pure, solidified spiritual Light. They emanate a high, harmonious energy that positively sings on the upper levels of the Quartz vibrational spectrum. Herkimers are ideal for body layouts, dreamwork, meditation pieces, jewelry, templates, energy tools or just about any other application. They not only broadcast their own energies—they can also pick up and magnify the frequencies of other stones. This can be of great help when one is using a tiny specimen, such as a small Herderite, or a "soft-energy" stone such as Morganite. In the first case, the Herkimer can make a small stone feel as strong as a large one, and in the second case, it can strengthen the effects of some of the more gentle stones.

There is bliss and rapture in the vibration of Herkimer Diamonds, and one can use them in the process of vibrational ascension. This is the process of the spiritualization of matter, and it is the project many have incarnated to accomplish. Herkimers can be handy tools in helping attune to the high spiritual frequencies one must ultimately learn to incorporate into everyday life.

Herkimer Diamonds have a particular affinity with Moldavite. They also work synergistically with Azeztulite, Herderite, Satyaloka Azeztulite, Phenacite, Natrolite, Scolecite, Celestite and Danburite. These are all stones of the highest vibrational frequencies, and Herkimer Diamonds will magnify their effects.

NEW ATTUNEMENT   Herkimer Quartz Diamonds were among the first stones I ever worked with, and after Moldavite and Phenacite, they were the first stones whose energies I experienced. In meditating with Herkimer Diamonds for this book, I chose a very clear, near-perfect single crystal. Herkimer Diamonds are noted for their brilliance and clarity and for the fact that they are almost all double-terminated.

I experienced the currents of the Herkimer Diamond in my third eye immediately. This has always been the place where I tend to feel this stone, yet its energy is of such a clear, pure nature that it can resonate with any chakra. I experimented in meditation and found that all the chakras responded to Herkimer Diamonds with a pulsing resonance. It was gentle in all the chakras, with the exception of the third eye, where the vibration was strongest. I watched with my eyes closed, holding the Herkimer at the third eye, and numerous images arose. Since Herkimer Diamond has always been a stone of inner visions for me, I was pleased, though not surprised, to find many vivid images coming into my inner sight. Unlike other visionary stones, which can lull the consciousness into a dreamlike condition, Herkimer Diamond keeps the inner observer highly alert, even as it presents amazing and often surprising images.

If one directs attention to a certain query or quest, the visions will often meaningfully conform to that request and serve as a kind of answer. I am reminded of a practice called Last Thought/First Thought, mentioned earlier in this book. In this exercise, just prior to sleep one repeatedly and inwardly asks a question for which an answer is desired. Upon awakening, the first thought one has is the "answer," although the response is seldom direct or linear. Nonetheless, if one takes time to hold that first thought and meditate upon it, one often receives important insights.

It is similar with the images that arise when Herkimer Diamond answers one's query, although this occurs much more immediately than over the course of a night's sleep. One can sit down for a ten- or twenty-minute meditation with Herkimer Diamonds and the held question will often generate a meaningful answer (usually in image form) within that period. It is as if these stones offer a quick attunement with the unconscious, or with the spiritual realms that one accesses during sleep. Herkimer Diamonds' vibrations are very fast, reminding me of the beat of a hummingbird's heart. They bring this rapid intensity into resonance with the third eye. This may be why one experiences increased alertness along with the visions Herkimer Diamonds can bring.

Herkimer Diamond enhances the capacity to witness and be aware of subtle currents within one's physical body, as well as the astral and etheric bodies and the Liquid Crystal Body Matrix. This enhancement of the observer-consciousness allows one to sense the shift, for instance, in the way a part of one's body feels when someone's hand brushes past it without touching. It enables one to notice how the middle toe experiences the resonance of a stone placed at one's third eye. It allows one to imaginatively visualize the internal organs, in both their physical and etheric representations. It enhances the ability to work imaginally with the organs, the chakras or any other aspect of one's being, whether physical, astral or etheric.

The fine thin streams of energies that pour through the terminations of Herkimer Diamonds make them most useful as a sort of energetic acupuncture stone. (See also Glendonite.) One may run the stone along the paths of the meridians, periodically touching the skin, following where the energy goes. One can thus learn the meridian paths and find the places where there might be congestion or blockage in them. By twirling the Herkimer Diamond point-down at the congested area, one can clear entanglements on the subtle levels. In many cases, proper energy flow can be quickly restored with this simple practice.

In the hands of those who are well-versed in modalities such as psychic surgery, Herkimer Diamond can be a sort of energetic "scalpel" stone. It is helpful for finding disharmonious areas and "cutting them out" by clearing the blockages. One technique for doing this is to circle the disharmonious area again and again with the energy stream of the Herkimer Quartz, using the stream to form an energetic "cylinder" around the congested area. One then can bring the circling into a tighter spiral motion. Moving the crystal in and out, in and out—to the center and back to the edge of the "cylinder"—unwinds the block. This can be a beneficial technique in crystal healing practices.

Herkimer Diamond has a natural resonance with Moldavite. When used at the third eye, in conjunction with Moldavite at the heart, this stone can engender mystical visionary experiences. These types of experiences tend to follow the impulse of Moldavite's purpose within us, with the Herkimer Diamond allowing our inner sight to experience what is occurring in image form. This aids the conscious mind in understanding the experience.

Herkimer Diamond speeds up the vibration of anything toward which it is directed. One can work with it for increased rapidity of learning and retention of understanding. It is a stone of high mental energies. Meditative work with this stone helps open the mind to its optimal functioning and appropriate focus of purpose.

HERKIMER QUARTZ SPEAKS   "I am a being of vision. I offer the wide-seeing eyes of clairvoyance. I am an emissary of clarity. I attune the mind of the Witness. I hold the pattern of consciously chosen awakening, and I aid those whose eyes have opened to remain awake."

HIDDENITE

KEY WORDS   Interpersonal love, heart healing, rediscovering the joy of relationships, enlivening the senses, exuberant joy in life

ELEMENT   Water

CHAKRA   Heart (4th)

Hiddenite is a yellow-green or emerald-green variety of Spodumene, a lithium aluminum silicate mineral with a hardness of 6 to 7. Its crystal system is monoclinic. Hiddenite derives its name from W.E. Hidden, who discovered the stone in 1879 in North Carolina (U.S.). It forms in prismatic crystals and is found in pegmatite veins. It is a difficult stone to cut into gems, because its perfect cleavage is sensitive to pressure, which can cause the stone to break while being worked. The most important deposits of Hiddenite are in Brazil, Madagascar, Burma and the U.S.

BACKGROUND   Hiddenite teaches how to return spontaneity and genuineness to love relationships. It vibrates to the true chord of the freely loving heart, attuned to the future yet unconcerned about future consequences. Hiddenite's message is simple—even if love and loss go hand in hand, loving is still the best and the only thing to do.

Those who are ready to reclaim their ability to love with their whole heart are recommended to wear or carry Hiddenite, which will provide a constant pulse of loving heart energy. Spreading Hiddenite in all directions is good for one's relationships and good for the world.

Hiddenite works synergistically with all heart stones, such as Ajoite, Kunzite, Morganite, Rosophia and Pink Azeztulite. When combined with interdimensional stones like Phenacite, Herderite or Natrolite, it allows one to ascend in meditation to the realms of Universal love.

NEW ATTUNEMENT   In meditating with Hiddenite, I placed a stone over my heart, one over the third eye, one at the crown and one at the base chakra. The Hiddenite seemed to ask for this, and I wondered what the meaning of that feeling was. Although Hiddenite, like Kunzite, is a Spodumene mineral, Kunzite's frequencies tend to vibrate to the spiritual realm of Divine Love from on high. By contrast, Hiddenite's currents are usually felt much more as an upwelling of exuberant life force and joy from the Earth.

Like Kunzite, Hiddenite bathes the heart in love and a kind of joy. But where Kunzite's joy is quiet, Hiddenite's joy bubbles over like a spring. My sense is that the currents of Kunzite are more akin to the image of an overflowing chalice, and Hiddenite's is are like that of a mountain stream. In fact, as I worked with Hiddenite the image of a stream, bounded with grass and trees, came forward. Hiddenite brings not only spiritual joy but also personal happiness to the heart. Hiddenite reminds the heart that this Earth is our home, and that to be here—in this lush domain so filled with life, so flowing with the fertile exuberance of life—is a joy beyond what can be contained in silence.

There is a laughing quality to Hiddenite that can be felt in the heart and throughout the body. The being of Hiddenite feels young, full of vivacity and enthusiasm. It reminds the body of its vitality. Working with Hiddenite for healing, one feels a sense of rejuvenation, regeneration. It is as though the bubbling stream of Hiddenite is a kind of Fountain of Youth, infusing the etheric body with a great flow of life force.

Hiddenite steers one's consciousness into a feeling of easy good humor, and it reminds one to take life lightly. Even our spiritual purpose, says Hiddenite, must be enjoyed to be fulfilled. Too much solemnity takes us away from our truth, for the Divine is not only all-loving, it is also all joy, all happiness, all intimacy, all humor. When working with Hiddenite meditatively, one is presented again and again with its bubbling delight. There is also a heightening of the senses. Sounds flow out of what one might previously have thought to be silence. One's vision sees all things with enjoyment, and the natural world attracts the eyes, as one's true love draws one's gaze.

Intuition and empathy are deepened when one opens to this being, Hiddenite. My inner image of Hiddenite is that of a green pillar of Light, rising from the root chakra to the crown, leafing outward to one's limbs and all the interior of the body. Hiddenite reminds one that the body is a Tree of Life. Like a tree, we look upward to the Light and down to the Earth for our two-sided sustenance. In Hiddenite, the heart is remembered as the meeting place between the Above and the Below, between matter and spirit, between the spiritual realm of Light and the Earth of exuberant organic life.

HIDDENITE SPEAKS "I am forever the wide-eyed child, astonished and delighted—tickled into laughter by my delight in myself and my pleasure in what I behold. Invite me within you, and I shall bring with me this glee and enjoyment of existence, exactly as it is."

KUNZITE

KEY WORDS   Divine Love, emotional healing, activation of the heart's knowing

ELEMENT   Water

CHAKRA   Heart (4th)

Kunzite is the pink-to-violet form of Spodumene, a lithium aluminum silicate with a hardness of 6 to 7. Its crystal system is monoclinic. It forms as prismatic crystals with vertical striations and is found in granitic pegmatites, often in association with Feldspar, Muscovite, Quartz, Lepidolite mica and other pegmatite minerals. It can be faceted into beautiful gems, but cutting is difficult because of the stone's perfect cleavage. Kunzite

is named after mineral collector G.F. Kunz, who first described this material in 1902. The main deposits of Kunzite are in Pakistan, Afghanistan, Brazil and Madagascar, as well as California and Maine in the U.S.

BACKGROUND   Kunzite opens the heart to the energies of love—self love, interpersonal love, love for humanity, animals, plants, minerals—all that is. Most importantly, Kunzite is a conduit from one's heart to the vibration of Divine Love. Meditating with Kunzite can facilitate profound experiences of Universal Love. Carrying or wearing the stone helps one move through the day with kindness, gentleness and serenity. Kunzite can also facilitate stress relief, which is good for both physical and emotional health.

Kunzite can activate the silent voice of the heart, opening a wordless communion between one's mental and emotional aspects. The heart is the part of one that truly "knows" what the best path of action is. Even though the intuitions of the heart are unexplainable via logic, its knowledge is unquestionable. Kunzite can awaken the heart and encourage it to communicate more intimately with the mind.

Kunzite has a special connection with Hiddenite, both of which are forms of the mineral Spodumene. It also harmonizes with Moldavite, Morganite, Rosophia and Ajoite. Phenacite, Scolecite, Natrolite and all varieties of Azeztulite help open the doors to the spiritual realms with which Kunzite resonates.

NEW ATTUNEMENT   I have long been a friend of Kunzite. This was one of the first truly powerful stones I worked with when I began meditating with crystals more than twenty-three years ago. In attuning to Kunzite for this essay, I began with the stone over my heart, and I felt the familiar resonance of love that it engenders. Kunzite is a happy being, with a kind of generosity of love-giving that feels like an overflowing cup within the heart.

There is such a sense of plenty in regard to the love expressed through Kunzite that one cannot help but smile inwardly upon feeling its bubbling presence. Kunzite nourishes and heals the heart on multiple levels. If one holds loneliness in the heart, Kunzite can feel like a pair of healing hands around it—comforting, stroking, offering sweetness to assuage any sense of being bereft or isolated. As Naisha Ahsian has said, Kunzite reminds us that we are never alone and that we are always loved. This is quintessentially true of this immensely generous stone of the heart.

Kunzite is a stone of Divine Love—of spiritual love and the joy of spiritual awakening. Surprisingly for a stone of the Pink Ray, Kunzite vibrates with great resonance at the crown chakra, as well as the heart. When placed upon the crown, Kunzite engenders a sense of peaceful well-being (similar to that rendered through Petalite), in which one's consciousness is awash in Love-Light awareness. However, Kunzite's ray is more intimate and human-feeling than Petalite's angelic vibrations.

Kunzite seems to offer its current of love to each person, with a kind of knowing of us as our individualized selves. In that knowing, we are cherished. Given a little time, the awakening that Kunzite engenders via its pleasurable opening of the crown chakra moves into the third eye—generating a column of pink-white Light between the brain and the heart. When fully experienced, the currents of Kunzite fill the crown and the third eye, continuing to their goal in the heart. This is a situation in which Kunzite vibrates with a surprising intensity. As Kunzite's pulsations strive downward from the crown and third eye toward the heart, the sensation is that of experiencing a strong, purposeful penetration of one's energetic field. I felt that the "goal" of this permeating pulse was to provide spiritual nourishment to stimulate and awaken the heart's consciousness. As I have said elsewhere, the heart's consciousness is magnificent in its potential. Yet if it is neglected, as it has been in almost all of us, the heart's intelligence is suppressed, disconnected, asleep. It takes the radiant arrival of Love-Light awareness from the spiritual worlds to stimulate the heart for a sudden awakening.

The heart's response, upon sensing the currents of Kunzite reaching down to it from above, is one of immense gratitude and joy. This feeling spreads outward from the heart. If allowed to do so, these currents will resonate throughout the Liquid Crystal Body Matrix, bringing the vibration of joy, gratitude and awareness of our unity with Divine Love all the way into our cellular consciousness.

It is important that Kunzite be allowed to bring its message to our entire being. Although many stones we utilize in this book bring Light and high vibration to the emotional body and the cellular matrix, Kunzite's unmistakable flavor of joy and gratitude, as well as its vibrant embodiment of Divine Love, are not to be missed. They are the Nectar of Life.

KUNZITE SPEAKS: "I bring you greetings of love. I am a living Heart without a fleshly body. My crystalline body expresses through its love-lattice the pure Pink Ray of the High Heart, which lies asleep in you. You have within you a throne for the King and Queen of Love, and that seat is your High Heart. Allow me to crown them in their throne of flesh, and you may walk amid fields of joy in the domain of true Love."

LEMURIAN AQUATINE CALCITE™

KEY WORDS Dream awareness, emotional healing, access to world memory, communication with whales and dolphins

ELEMENT Water

CHAKRA Heart (4th)

Calcite is a calcium carbonate mineral with a hardness of 3. Calcites are among the most varied and abundant crystals, and they occur in a wide spectrum of forms and colors. The crystal system of Calcite is trigonal (hexagonal, scalenohedral). The predominant structure of the crystals is rhombohedral, but specimens can appear as scalenohedrons, rhombohedrons, prisms, masses, stalactites, etc. The name is derived from the Latin *calx*, meaning "lime." Calcite makes up the major part of most marbles and limestones. Calcite crystals are found on every continent. Lemurian Aquatine Calcite is a deep blue-green Calcite from a remote region of Argentina. It forms in masses, sometimes with stripes indicating layering. This kind of Calcite is more workable than many other varieties, and it can be made into beads, spheres and cabochons for jewelry. The name Lemurian Aquatine Calcite is indicative of the stone's spiritual qualities, which link it to the Water element and to the legendary lost civilization of Lemuria.

BACKGROUND Lemurian Aquatine Calcite gets its name from its affinity to the element of water, and to the water-oriented civilization of Lemuria. Whether a physical or etheric place, Lemuria was a realm of the watery qualities—intuition, dreaming, feeling and visionary consciousness. The Lemurian way of being was empathic, with consciousness very much overlapping with the spiritual realms.

Lemurian Aquatine Calcite deeply nourishes the emotional body. It is a strong antidote to stress, fear, worry and anxiety about the future. It soothes and replenishes the etheric body. It enhances dream life and facilitates lucid reaming. It is ideal for opening up one's capacity for recalling past lives, ancient knowledge and tuning in to the morphic fields of the Earth's past.

Dolphins and whales are sometimes said to be Lemurians who evolved into oceanic creatures. I prefer to say that the souls of Lemurians may have reincarnated into these highly intelligent "people of the sea." I do sense that those who wish to attune to communication frequencies of whales and dolphins can be aided by working with Lemurian Aquatine Calcite. Many people who spend time with dolphins say that these beings use telepathy as one mode of communication. Those who work meditatively with Lemurian Aquatine Calcite may find that their own capabilities in these areas are strengthened, and that encounters with dolphins, whales and people too will be characterized by an instant empathic—and even telepathic—rapport.

Lemurian Aquatine Calcite resonates with the heart, throat, third eye and crown chakras, as well as the etheric chakras above the head. It increases conscious sensitivity through one's energy field, enabling one to "feel" stimuli beyond the confines of the physical body. It helps increase awareness of spirit guides and angelic guardians, and allows for easier communication.

Lemurian Aquatine Calcite resonates well with Aqua Lemuria, Lemurian Seed Crystals, Lemurian Jade, Merkabite Calcite, Azeztulite, Rosophia and Pink Azeztulite (Rhodazez). Its visionary traits are enhanced by Phenacite, and Herderite can amplify the increased sensitivity of consciousness beyond the body.

NEW ATTUNEMENT As I began my meditative exploration with Lemurian Aquatine Calcite, I started by holding the stone to my heart. This instinctive movement was most appropriate, as I then sensed a deeply comforting energy spreading within me. There was a profound and lovely calming of the emotional body as a soothing wave washed through me. It is appropriate to speak of the currents of Lemurian Aquatine Calcite in terms such as "waves" and "washing through," since it is utterly a stone of the Water element. It led me in meditation to the threshold of dream consciousness, where images played before my inner eyes. The depth of its calming qualities brought me to the edge of sleep but allowed me to stay there without falling asleep. This is of great value to those who wish to explore the domains of the level of consciousness between the inner and outer worlds. The dream threshold is a rich area, full of images, laden with patterns that display multi-layered meanings and significance. Our unconscious—our vast reservoir of self—is this water, which touches our inner shore at the edge of sleep. If we can remain consciously aware at the border of this ocean, its many creatures and images come forth to meet us. Thus Lemurian Aquatine Calcite opens us to the world of the waking dream. This sort of awareness is one of great receptivity. Here we are able to allow whatever is within us to unfold without our attempting to direct it or even understand it intellectually. The wave form of the dreaming self is a flowing form, and we learn to let ourselves flow like water through the currents of the domain of dreams.

Lemurian Aquatine Calcite is aptly named, for the Lemurian society, whether it was fully physical or not, resonates most deeply with the sort of flowing, unbounded unconsciousness that we associate with dreams. The comforting quality emanated by the stone is much like the comfort one experiences in deep, peaceful sleep, although it is not exactly a sleep consciousness. If one's mental processes were likened to a pond, or if one's emotional consciousness were compared to a lake or a sea, both are calmed or quieted in the presence of this stone. In the Liquid Crystal Body Matrix, the cells are slowed in their intense activity and begin following the almost-hypnotic undulations of the currents of this stone—patterns that might recall a flowing melody or song.

The felt sense I have with Lemurian Aquatine Calcite is as follows: because one can utilize it to enter dream awareness without sleep, one can also work with it to gain access to the corridors of world memory. This may result in recalling events or images from the deep past of the human dreamscape. Thus one might attune not to an ancient civilization but to its dreams, to its spiritual resonances, to its felt sense of unity with the All.

As I concentrated on the stone I had chosen, I was surprised to see that it seemed to have the form of a mother with her arm around a child, which she held upon her lap. They both faced to their right, looking downward together, as parent and child might read a book or gaze upon some scene. This image was no doubt evoked from my imagination by the deeply comforted feeling I experienced as I held the stone.

As a Water element stone, Lemurian Aquatine Calcite resonates with all beings of the water realm. My intuition suggests that those of us who wish to find a way into a rapport and communion with the cetaceans—the whales, dolphins and porpoises—could be aided in this intention by Lemurian Aquatine Calcite, as already mentioned. Not only do its currents ripple through one's being like water, they also circulate within the heart in a way that helps transmit our inner call to those able to feel it and respond.

I have had the experience of being on a boat and hoping for whales to come. With no other way of communicating with them, I centered my awareness in the heart and called to them from there. To my great astonishment and delight, and though our boat was completely surrounded by fog, six whales swam to us and played nearby for over an hour, coming so close we could have real eye contact with them. Another time, in the Caribbean, I sent this heart call to the dolphins, and they also came to our boat. I think this is no special talent of mine but rather a natural communion that we can enter into by centering in our heart and reaching out to these beings of the water realm.

All of these images and memories came back to me as I contemplated this stone. I feel that the mood it takes me into is a deeper version of the same inner state from which I had apparently connected with cetaceans previously. My felt sense is that we may be able, with practice, to do more than call these beings. We might be able to feel their inner gestures and know them. Lemurian Aquatine Calcite is a stone for enhancing the depth of empathy we can enter via its calming of the emotional and mental bodies. If we simply begin with the intention, the state we enter through resonance with this lovely and comforting stone engenders a natural entrance into empathy. From there we can explore the depths of both Self and Other.

LEMURIAN AQUATINE CALCITE SPEAKS "I sing of the inner water that flows through you, which carries you into deepest memory, into truest feeling, into softest peace."

LEMURIAN GOLDEN OPAL

KEY WORDS   Integration of mental and emotional bodies, recalling Lemurian consciousness, dissolving inner walls and psychological boundaries

ELEMENTS   Water, Air

CHAKRAS   Crown (7th), Third Eye (6th), Heart (4th)

Opal is a hydrated silica material with a hardness of 5.5 to 6.5. It is composed of submicroscopic silica spheres bonded with water and additional silica. Sometimes the water in Opal can evaporate, creating cracks in the stone. Some but not all Opals exhibit the play of colors known as "fire." This is caused by the Opal's minute silica spheres being packed in a formation regular enough to cause light diffraction. The stone called Lemurian Opal is a yellow variety of Opal that does not exhibit fire. Its color, however, is quite vivid and relatively unique among Opals.

The name Opal is derived from the Latin *opalus* and the Sanskrit *upala*, meaning "precious stone." Precious Opals were mined in the former Czechoslovakia at least as long ago as the fourteenth century. Mexican Fire Opal was used by the Aztecs and brought to Europe by the conquistadors. In nineteenth-century Europe, Opal's popularity declined because of an association with bad luck, but it rebounded in the twentieth century and remains one of the most popular gems.

In Roman civilization, Opal was linked with good luck and hope. The belief in France that Opal could render its wearer invisible, allowing him or her to steal without being caught, may have been the beginning of Opal's negative associations. An Australian legend reports that a gigantic Opal governs the stars, human love and the gold within the earth.

BACKGROUND   In my first meditation with this stone, I inwardly heard the word "Lemuria." I saw images of temples with round green domes, and the people frequenting the temples looked semi-transparent. The air was so fluid, it felt like water, and it was permeated by swirling currents of psychic impressions. Thought and feeling circulated through the streets like blood in the veins. I felt I had been transported to the Lemurian realm, or rather, to the Akashic records of its existence. I feel that intuitive people meditating with Lemurian Golden Opal could do much fruitful inner research into the story of Lemuria, which can help us in these times. I also sense that these stones can assist us in developing the inner capacities that prevailed in Lemurian times. I am speaking here of telepathy, clairvoyance, empathy, prophecy and other psychic abilities.

Lemurian Golden Opal allows us to relax and feel the flow of life, and to willingly enter that flow. It aids in letting go of stress, and recognizing that willingness is an important quality of will. It can aid in manifesting dreams, in part by making one more fully aware of what one's deepest dreams actually are. It helps one move easily into deep states of meditation. It facilitates lucid dreaming and enhances memory of dreams. It can help one work spiritually to overcome sleep disorders, and it brings the recognition that one need not try to control others or the world. It instills calm and an all-pervasive sense of trust. Lemurian Golden Opal works very well with Rosophia and Morganite. Lemurian Aquatine Calcite can enhance its deepening of psychic abilities.

NEW ATTUNEMENT   As I sat with Lemurian Golden Opal for this book, as soon as I closed my eyes the third eye, crown chakra and the entire interior of my skull began to pulsate in a unique rhythmic pattern. A spot just between the eyebrows, a bit lower than the normal place

I feel the third eye chakra, was the focal point of intense vibrational currents. Soon my intuitive sense began to feel impressions of the stone's qualities. I seemed to be hearing that Lemurian Golden Opal offers support for the strength and coherence of the emotional body and the integration of the emotional body with one's mental level.

One of the many issues in meditative work, and in investigation of the dimensions of self for purposes of willed evolution, is that the "emotional mind" seems to be in its own world, not fully connected with one's normal thinking. It is as though thoughts give rise to emotional responses from some other place in the psyche, or that upwelling emotions take one along on their own train of thought. Given this, our goal of wholeness indicates that we should strive for some harmonization of the mental body and the emotional body. If we function with those two bodies in an agreeable coherence, we may go further in discovering the country of the New Consciousness. Lemurian Golden Opal emanates currents that stimulate mental activity and seem to initiate a clarity of thought and expression. At the same time, they support emotional stability and seem to open a kind of window between the mental and emotional aspects of oneself. Through this window one may, from a thinking perspective, better see and understand emotional patterns in oneself. On the other side of the window, the emotional body becomes more consciously aware of itself and of the other streams of activity in one's whole consciousness. These are important steps for the integration of the mental and emotional bodies. Lemurian Golden Opal, through its effect on the alignments within the Liquid Crystal Body Matrix, seems to open up these possibilities.

Lemurian Golden Opal was named because of a felt resonance with the qualities of consciousness associated with ancient Lemuria. The Lemurian consciousness, as I intuitively sense it, was a feeling-centered awareness. They were not intellectualized, as we tend to be. They had not separated themselves as individuals in the way we have. They delighted in living as communally conscious feeling beings, in a unified awareness with and of the world and one another. This was done by thinking via currents of feeling. In this kind of perception/awareness, feeling is the resonance of one's emotional body with everything.

These Golden Opals from Madagascar—a place that by some accounts defines one of the boundaries of the Lemurian archipelago—draw one's consciousness into a deeply empathic kind of feeling activity. The borders between oneself and the world of nature, other people, spiritual beings, the intelligences of plants and animals, and even the intelligences of other stones, are dissolved or made more porous through the influence of Lemurian Golden Opal. Thus one becomes much more readily attuned with and absorbed within the world's communal mind—the assemblage of the beings and intelligences that pervade the world.

Lemurian Golden Opal helps deconstruct isolating psychological boundaries, and it aids in releasing the armor around ego structures. I would not suggest that one try to destroy or throw away the ego, but to gently open it to receive love—to recognize that one is surrounded by a world family, a universal family, a net of kinship, which means one is never alone except by choice. And even this aloneness is something of an illusion.

When we work to enter into the Consciousness of Blessing—in which we are in full engagement with all the beings, things and processes of the world—Lemurian Golden Opal can do very important work by helping us loosen our boundaries. It is also important and helpful that this stone supports mental clarity, so that the loosening of boundaries does not result in a diminishment of consciousness. Having had the surprising experience of discovering these qualities has made me certain that Lemurian Golden Opal arrived at our doorstep at the perfect moment—just in time to enter the family of stones included in this volume.

LEMURIAN GOLDEN OPAL SPEAKS "When you allow me to share in your consciousness, I can pull aside the curtain that has covered your eyes and your heart, and you may view the world you have not seen. You may swim with many beings in an ocean of mutual joy, mutual support, communal strength and love."

LEPIDOLITE

KEY WORDS Emotional healing and balance, purification, serenity, relaxation, attunement with Ascended Masters
ELEMENT Water
CHAKRAS All, especially the Heart (4th) and Third Eye (6th)

epidolite is a potassium lithium aluminum silicate with a hardness of 2.5 to 3. Its crystal system is monoclinic. It crystallizes in cleavable masses, scaly aggregates and tabular hexagonal crystals. Lepidolite often occurs in association with other lithium-bearing minerals such as Tour-maline or Spodumene. The color is most often pink, purplish or lavender, although Lepidolite can also be grayish, white or even colorless. Good deposits of Lepidolite have been found in Africa, Brazil, Greenland and the U.S. In the United States, the best Lepidolite localities are Auburn, Maine, and San Diego County, California. One of the newest and most preferred types of Lepidolite for metaphysical use is Lilac Lepidolite from Africa.

BACKGROUND   Lepidolite is a stone of serenity, and this trait extends in many directions. It encourages one to respond to hostility without putting up defenses, to find the path of harmonious action and to see problems as opportunities to learn. It enhances physical grace and can be of great help to self-conscious dancers. It lends effortless eloquence to one's speech and teaches one to listen to others with compassionate, patient attention. It encourages the eyes to see beauty, even in tarnished surroundings. If one is depressed, it allows for willing descent into the grief beneath the depression, and the understanding that most of the suffering was not in the grief but in one's resistance to feeling it.

Lepidolite is a stone of spiritual purification, and meditation with it can clear blocked energies in any of the chakras and throughout the meridian system. It can dispel negative thoughts and remove negative emotional attachments such as resentment and envy.

Lepidolite harmonizes with other lithium-bearing minerals such as Tourmaline, Kunzite, Petalite and Amblygonite. Its property of purification can be enhanced by Tibetan Black Quartz and Master Shamanite. Its higher spiritual energies can be augmented by Phenacite, Azeztulite, Natrolite, Scolecite and Merkabite Calcite. Its property of serenity can be further activated by Rosophia and Lemurian Aquatine Calcite. Combined with Alexandrite, it can facilitate healing journeys into past lives.

NEW ATTUNEMENT   Meditating with Lepidolite, I was first aware of a calming and soothing influence, which I welcomed into my heart. It was as if Lepidolite offered a kind of spiritual substance that nourished the heart with a loving softness. In the presence of Lepidolite, the heart relaxes with an almost tangible sigh of gratitude. Placing a piece of Lepidolite at the third eye, I again felt the soothing qualities that had calmed my heart. It was like being in the presence of a guardian angel. In fact, as I meditated with Lepidolite, I saw a vivid interior image of a pair of wings wrapping around me, as if I were being held by an angel.

One cannot overstate the quality of soft, loving, spiritual touch that Lepidolite engenders. The etheric body immediately responds to the presence of Lepidolite with a quiet joy. The emotional body relaxes instantly. Stress dissolves and patterns of negative emotion or desire for specific outcomes dissipate. In the presence of Lepidolite one recognizes—first in the body, then in the emotions and finally in thought—that one always rests in the perfection of the moment, if one allows oneself to relax. Lepidolite also sends a vibration of spiritual purification throughout the etheric and physical body. This is one of its important activities in development of the human Light Body. The initial stage of formation of the Light Body involves integration of the emotional, etheric and astral bodies.

However, in all of us there are disturbances or imperfections in these three non-physical dimensions of the body; the disturbances are related to difficulties, wounds, pain, attachment, fear and other such negative patterns. They are debilitating to the self and stand in the way of full integration of one's layers and thus one's Light Body awakening. In other words, one must come to a harmonious unity of what is already present in the layers of one's being in order for the awakening of the Light Body to be possible. By bringing relaxation to all of our layers, and by permeating us with currents of love, acceptance and spiritual purification, Lepidolite initiates the process of inner harmonization. This same gesture from Lepidolite also works toward healing the imperfections or "knots" in one's various layers. It metaphorically "smooths all our feathers" so we can come into a quiet state of peace.

The ability to enter the state of peace is actually a sign of the dissolution of negative patterns in one's layers. Because habit is so powerful in the human consciousness—and especially in the unconscious—negative patterns have a way of coming back. Lepidolite's presence is a wholesome influence that can help maintain clarity and prevent unconscious negative patterns from reasserting themselves.

Lepidolite is a stone of the Violet Ray of purification. This is another way of illustrating what has been said thus far about Lepidolite. The Violet Ray is embodied in Lepidolite's soft color, and it inwardly stimulates resonance with some of the highest spiritual frequencies. For example, as I work in meditation with Lepidolite, I am sometimes made aware of the presence of beings who are called Ascended Masters. These non-physical beings have a great concern and care for the spiritual development of human beings and the Earth. They love human beings and the Earth very deeply and exude a quality of patient, protective mentorship toward humanity.

The Ascended Master most frequently associated with Lepidolite is St. Germain, who is said to be aligned with the Violet Ray as well as the Violet Flame of purification. Calling upon these forces while working with Lepidolite serves our individual evolutionary potential and our progress toward our highest destiny. The New Consciousness involves the development of capacities for expansion of awareness and entering into co-creating activity with the Soul of the World. We as individuals are invited into partnership with the great beings of the higher realms. We have old habits of thinking of ourselves as unworthy of such a gift. However, many of us do not wish to co-create life as much as we wish to "rule the world." Both of these ideas—unworthiness and the wish for control—are mirages that stem from the illusion of separation.

Lepidolite invites us out of separation, into loving relationship with itself and all the world. The activity of love has many faces—not only the exalted ones of transformation and awakening, but smaller ones such as intimacy, gentleness and small acts of kindness. Lepidolite's relaxing, soft emanations calm our mental activity in order that we may slow down and appreciate each moment of life. It encourages us to give time and loving attention to "small" things—to children, animals, plants, to each object and activity of the world.

As I quoted early in the book, each beloved thing, according to the poet Novalis, is the center of a Paradise. I added that when each thing in the world is beloved, then all the world becomes Paradise. The soft, loving qualities offered by Lepidolite facilitate exactly the state of consciousness from which one holds each thing as the beloved center of a Paradise. Again, I repeat that Paradise is not only grand; it is also small. Lepidolite's sheltering wings extend from the tiny to the great, valuing neither more than the other. In becoming aware of this and experiencing it within feeling, we embody Lepidolite's gesture and begin our joyous work of co-creating—re-creating Earth as Paradise. This Paradise is recognized in every relationship, every moment, every touch, every experience. None is above another. This is Lepidolite's lesson, its teaching, its offer and its truth.

LEPIDOLITE SPEAKS   "I am always creating love, truth, caring, protection, intimacy and nurturing. I feed what in you is hungry for Spirit. I cleanse what in you is out of harmony. I sweeten your heart's countenance. I soften your mind's activity so that it can notice beauty. I gently turn your inner glance toward the Beloved of the Soul, the Heart in your own chest, the Being that is your world, and the human Being sitting next to you."

LIBYAN GOLD TEKTITE

KEY WORDS   Confidence, mental acuity, psychic protection, access to Akashic records, manifestation, realization of personal potential, regeneration, transfiguration into Light

ELEMENTS   Fire, Storm

CHAKRAS   All, especially Solar Plexus (3rd) and Sexual/Creative (2nd)

Libyan Gold Tektite is a glassy yellow material with a hardness of 5 to 6. Its crystal system is amorphous. Also known by the name Libyan Desert Glass, it is found in the Sahara Desert in Libya and Egypt. It is similar in composition to Mold-avite and other Tektites, although the color is different. Scientists are unsure of the origins of this material, although it is found in the same areas in which meteorites have been discovered.

These stones have been prized for making carvings and jewelry for many centuries. In ancient Egypt, the funerary necklace of King Tutankhamen had as its centerpiece a large scarab carved from a piece of Libyan Gold Tektite. As with all such ceremonial pieces, this necklace was believed to be imbued with supernatural powers, which it conveyed to the wearer even after death.

BACKGROUND   Libyan Gold Tektites carry remarkable energies for enhancing the strength of one's will, one's ability to create and one's power of manifestation. Whatever the reason for their intensity, it is not surprising that a Libyan Gold Tektite was used as the centerpiece in the necklace of an ancient Egyptian king—these stones emanate the kind of mystic power associated with the god-kings of old, and they can facilitate the awakening of the inner King or Queen in oneself as well.

Those who work with the retrieval of ancient knowledge may find Libyan Gold Tektites to be powerful access keys to the Akashic records. These stones can aid those wishing to recover the ties of the early Egyptian civilizations to the influence of extraterrestrial entities. They can link one with the energies of Isis and Osiris, the mythic figures said to have given humankind the remarkable evolutionary boost that gave rise to civilization. The energies of the Sirius star system also seem to be connected with these stones.

Meditation and personal ritual performed with the Libyan Gold Tektite will be strongly enhanced, particularly if one's goal is to actualize some outcome in the material world. If one feels that one has yet to realize one's full potential, working with these stones is highly recommended. Combining them with Moldavite is ideal for the achievement of self-transformation to one's highest calling. Adding Tibetan Tektite to the Libyan Gold Tektite will greatly speed the process of manifestating goals. Using all three together can facilitate the most rapid transformation possible, under the guidance of one's higher Will.

NEW ATTUNEMENT   As I sat down to meditate with Libyan Gold Tektite, I selected three stones, one to go over my heart and one to go in each of my hands. Usually my hands are not as sensitive as certain other areas on my body—such as the third eye, the heart and the crown areas along the chakra column—although I am aware that many people are quite sensitive in their hands. In any event, when I handled the Libyan Gold Tektite and began to enter the meditative state, the first thing I noticed was a powerful current entering my body through my hands, moving with great intensity and speed to fill the entire body from head to toe. I sensed the current as a vibration, coupled with gold light. The felt sense was that the Libyan Gold Tektites' energy entered and resonated throughout the Liquid Crystal Body Matrix and the etheric body, realigning them both to the stones' frequencies.

There was a feeling that the body welcomed this realignment, and it very much welcomed the entry of the Light. There was also a felt sense of old patterns and habits being dissolved and dispersed by the entry of this vibration and Light. These stones kindled a number of interior images. I repeatedly saw faces and scenes—images expressing a kind of exuberance and a feeling of inner freedom. It is my sense that these images signified the process of beneficial realignment that the stone was initiating within me.

One key image that appeared vividly was that of a golden scarab beetle pushing a sun up from my heart toward my head. This is reminiscent of the ancient Egyptian scarab that was said in myth to push the sun across the sky of the Earth each day. The scarab is a symbol of the immortal, and the sun is the representation of Divine Light. The fact that they appeared together in my vision is fitting, because the Divine is imperishable. I recalled that Libyan Gold Tektites were revered in ancient Egypt as sacred stones, and that one of them was carved into a scarab as the center of the burial necklace of King Tut. When this image arose in my meditation, my feeling was that the Libyan Gold Tektite was generating it in order to communicate its capacity to engender the pattern of enlightenment and immortality in the human being.

Over millennia, humanity has lost its conscious awareness of its connection with the Divine, and through the many centuries of separation, patterns of fear and contraction have been habituated into the cellular consciousness as well as the etheric bodies of human beings. The cellular mind, in my understanding, is a willing and loving servant to the whole of us, yet it operates by habitual repetition of the patterns we have given to it. If we continually impress

destructive patterns upon the cellular mind through engaging in fear and other negative interpretations of our experiences, we unintentionally discourage the cells' enthusiasm—their predisposition for life and regeneration. Even without one's conscious participation, our entire human milieu is permeated with greater and lesser fears, and the expectation of degeneration and death. The realignment of cellular structure—the realignment of the cellular mind—involves seeding and nurturing, within the cellular consciousness, new patterns that are positive, regenerative and Light-filled. Currents of this kind appear to be the gift of Libyan Gold Tektite. If these patterns are fully imbued into the cellular consciousness, new habits may be formed that are regenerative rather than degenerative. This was displayed symbolically by the Egyptian image of the scarab pushing the radiant sun, symbol of life. Spiritual Light and life are equated, and to be filled with Light is to be filled with life. The infusion of golden solar radiance from Libyan Gold Tektite links one's consciousness—from the cellular up to the mental—with Divine awareness, which is also a bridge to the undying.

Another vivid image generated in my meditation with the Libyan Gold Tektite was that of a golden, laughing Buddha. The Buddha is an emblem of enlightenment, and gold symbolizes successful development as well as the Light of consciousness. Receiving this image reminded me that the teachings of the Buddha include the noble truth that desire is suffering. Both desire and aversion are seeds of negative patterning, leading the self (and the cells) into the same discouragement that engenders the degenerative patterns that bring about patterns of suffering and death. As I considered the laughing, golden Buddha image, it was clear that such a being is free of aversion and desire. He is in a state of joy, fully present in each moment. The Libyan Gold Tektite seemed to be showing me that its golden Light offers liberation, life and joy to the body and to one's consciousness.

Like Moldavite, Libyan Gold Tektite was formed by a meteoric collision in the distant past. It was created in a moment of tremendous explosive power, and it was transformed in that moment into the substance we can now hold. Therefore, one can symbolically view Libyan Gold Tektite as representative of the Phoenix, the mythical bird said to be consumed by flames and reborn from its own ashes. Libyan Gold Tektite arose in a similar manner, formed in a fiery explosion involving complete destruction of the original meteoric substance as well as some of the Earth where it hit. The two substances—meteor and earth—were vaporized in the explosion. As the gaseous silica cooled, it condensed into a rain of molten glass, eventually cooling enough to solidify into the glassy golden substance we call Libyan Gold Tektite. Here again we see a connection to the image of transformation and rebirth. The formation of Libyan Gold Tektite speaks of regeneration, echoing the images it presented inwardly to me.

LIBYAN GOLD TEKTITE SPEAKS "I am a being of the Sun. I carry and offer the infusion of the true Gold Light. I encourage the transfiguration of your being, and I embody transfiguration. My gesture is transmutation through the purifying fire of the golden Sun. I invite you into the embodiment of this gesture, the pattern of your destiny."

LITHIUM QUARTZ

KEY WORDS   Inner peace, awakening to the Higher
Self, release from negative attachments, aura
healing, harmonizing relationships, freedom
from stress, visionary experience

ELEMENTS   Storm, Water

CHAKRAS   All

Lithium Quartz is a member of the Quartz family, a silicon dioxide mineral with a hardness of 7. Its crystal system is hexagonal (trigonal). It occurs as prismatic Quartz crystals with inclusions of lavender or pinkish gray material. The included material is lithium-bearing, which explains the derivation of the name. The only known location for this rare material is a very remote area of Minas Gerais, Brazil.

BACKGROUND   Upon first touching or holding a Lithium Quartz crystal, one may feel gentle yet powerful energies moving through one's body. The heart chakra will open, followed by a wave of pleasant euphoria. In the next moment the third eye is stimulated, and rhythmic pulsations of positive energy may be felt flowing into all the mind centers. These stones will enhance the depth of meditation as well as the quality of the inner visions received. Their vibration is one of profound healing, emotional peace, release from tension and awakening of the Higher Self.

Lithium Quartz crystals can benefit those seeking harmony in their various relationships—from friends and family to spouses and lovers. In fact, one might experiment with a small crystal under each partner's pillow for enhancement of both intimacy and passion.

"Planting" Lithium Quartz crystals in gardens or potted plants will provide positive stimulation of growth and an invitation for the participation of the devas and nature spirits. These beings will be naturally attracted to the sweet and strong energies of the Lithium Quartz.

Lithium Quartz works in harmony with almost all stones and is particularly good with Ajoite, Petalite, Kunzite, Lepidolite, Celestite, Moldavite, Morganite, Rosophia, Pink Azeztulite and Hiddenite. In addition, Crimson Cuprite will add intensity and a connection to the lower chakras. Danburite, Phenacite, Azeztulite, Natrolite, Scolecite or Satyaloka Azeztulite will bring a stronger connection to the transpersonal chakras and dimensions above and beyond the body.

NEW ATTUNEMENT   As I held Lithium Quartz in meditation, there was at first a tingling in the heart chakra and also a strong current entering through the third eye. Even after removing the stone, the residue of tingling in the forehead and crown chakra remained. There was a feeling of pulsation through the corridor from the heart to the crown, and at the same time a deeply relaxing, soothing energy.

Lithium Quartz works effectively to heal wounds or holes in the emotional body. These holes appear to my inner vision as little ragged patches on the fabric or surface of the emotional body. These patches are condensations of fear. The first statement I heard inwardly from Lithium Quartz was, "I heal fear." I recognized immediately that fear is the most all-pervasive hindrance to spiritual evolution, and that a great deal of spiritual work entails rooting out, looking at and letting go of fear. Much effort and time is involved in this healing process.

The currents emanated by Lithium Quartz are so soothing and loving to the emotional body that many of the patches of condensed fear can be repaired simply by holding and attuning oneself to the stone. The soothing qualities of Lithium Quartz are so profound that meditation with this stone can readily lead all the way into sleep. It is an excellent stone for those who have difficulty sleeping or are otherwise disturbed at night by tension and anxiety. Lithium Quartz resonates with a harmonious, soft tranquility that feeds the wounded emotional body and allows the release of unconsciously held fear and stress.

At the same time, Lithium Quartz is an awakener of consciousness. Its stimulation of the third eye chakra can bring forth vivid inner visions. When I held this stone up to my third eye, I began seeing veils of webbed light in different colors. The first pattern was magenta, the next color was pale blue, and the third was a golden yellow. These veils of light appeared to my inner sight and seemed to fill the interior of my forehead, stimulating my entire field of inner vision. Each of the color webs appeared to move toward me, growing larger in the field of vision until they each reached my point of view and broke over it with a wave of quiet, pleasant relaxation.

Lithium Quartz is a stone of visionary experience, opening and preparing the neural net in the front of the brain to receive the vibrational impulses of the spiritual worlds, which give rise to visionary experience. In this process, vibrational patterns from the spiritual worlds enter into resonance with our nervous system, and we, as the observers, experience those patterns inwardly as visions of light and as insights. Lithium Quartz brings a sense of relaxation into one's thoughts and feelings prior to its initiation of visionary experiences—as though it is necessary to come to a state of quiet receptivity in order for the subtle currents that generate inner vision to be noticed and allowed to influence the consciousness.

In one experience, I felt myself drawn down a corridor of light, which was hexagonal and bordered on all sides by soft, cushion-like, rounded protrusions. I have seen geometric corridors of light with other stones, such as Phenacites, and have traveled along them into other dimensions. The interesting difference with Lithium Quartz is the feeling and appearance of softness, even within the normally severe and straight geometric lines. I feel this is a visual representation of the stones' qualities of gentleness and comfort.

Lithium Quartz resonates in a synergistic manner with stones such as Amblygonite and Seriphos Green Quartz. It is attuned and energetically akin to Azeztulite, particularly the Himalaya Gold variety. For healing purposes, especially those in which physical ailments are emotionally rooted, Lithium Quartz combines synergistically with Sanda Rosa Azeztulite. With Phenacite, its capacity for initiating inner vision is magnified.

Lithium Quartz suggests that the healing it offers to the emotional body can be augmented through singing. Those working on emotional healing are encouraged to hold a Lithium Quartz the heart and to sing whatever the heart prompts one to sing. It does not matter whether the songs are familiar or spontaneously created. The healing is engendered by the heart's creative expression through the throat and voice. The Lithium Quartz acts to encourage and amplify this activity.

The heart is a naturally resonant area for the currents of Lithium Quartz. This stone's soothing qualities help the heart rest, even between beats. It is therefore recommended as a healing influence for hypertension. For example, bathing with Lithium Quartz can be a deeply relaxing practice. The stone is well attuned with water, and the skin's open pores allow entry of water molecules that are aligned and influenced by the qualities of Lithium Quartz. This beneficially influences the entire Liquid Crystal Body Matrix.

Lithium Quartz is excellent for those working to reach deep silence in meditation, and for those who wish to unify their inner intentions in prayer. In both cases its quieting influence can be deeply helpful.

LITHIUM QUARTZ SPEAKS   "I am a messenger, a courier of the Light lotus that blooms at your crown. I invite you to receive the Light."

I must comment that as the stone seemed to communicate these words, I saw a vivid image of a many-petaled flower—a lotus that encompassed the entire top of my head and reached upward with gold-white petals toward a higher Light. There were hundreds or perhaps thousands of petals. There was a feeling of sweet, blessed Light currents filling the entire top of my head. Then the stone spoke within me once again, saying: "This demonstrates my gesture."

MAGNESITE

KEY WORDS Awakening the higher sensibilities, opening to inner vision, truth and bliss, listening to the heart, integrating the Light Body with the physical

ELEMENT Storm

CHAKRAS Heart (4th), Third Eye (6th), Crown (7th)

Magnesite is a magnesium carbonate mineral with a hardness of 3 to 4. It occurs in rhombohedral crystals, and occasionally in other crystal forms. It is also found in granular, massive and fibrous habits. It forms in sediments, hydrothermal veins and metamorphic rocks. Magnesite is frequently white but can also occur in shades of gray, yellow or brown. Some of the finest crystalline specimens of Magnesite come from Minas Gerais, Brazil.

BACKGROUND   Magnesite is one of the most powerful stones for activating the third eye and crown chakras. Placing one of these stones upon the forehead and closing the eyes, one can expect to feel a rhythmic pulsing energy, becoming stronger as the minutes pass. In some individuals, this will be followed by a feeling that one's closed eyes are crossing and "looking" upward toward the center of the forehead. This is the beginning of the activation of the eye of inner vision in the prefrontal lobes of the brain. As one goes on, the energies can be felt more deeply in the skull, and there will ultimately be the sensation of a vibrating energy link between the third eye and the crown chakra at the top of the head. If one receives the full experience of this opening, there will come a moment when the crown "blooms" into the "thousand-petaled lotus." These openings are accompanied by feelings of bliss and the rather startling experience of direct knowing. It is as though information is simply pulled out of the air. Of course, working with Magnesite by no means guarantees such experiences—one must be both ready and fortunate.

Magnesite can help in the process of self-reflection and can clarify inner vision. It is something of a "truth detector" when doing inner work, and it can help one to see through the unconscious blinders that may keep one in a state of confusion.

Among Magnesite's mystical properties is the awakening of the mind to communication with the heart. The heart speaks not in words but in yearnings, desires and fleeting sensations of joy or pain. When the heart is in communion with the higher mind, there can be sustained experiences of ineffable joy. Magnesite doesn't activate the heart chakra, but it does stimulate the part of the brain/mind that can hear and respond to the heart's "voice." Magnesite has a special affinity for Rosophia and Morganite, when one is working to increase heart awareness. For the upper chakras, Phenacite, Herderite and all varieties of Azeztulite can be very helpful.

NEW ATTUNEMENT   I first placed a piece of Magnesite over my heart chakra and gave close attention to any perceptions that might arise from this. I felt that the resonance between the Magnesite and the heart is not of overwhelming power but of a certain precision of vibration. I believe that by placing Magnesite at the heart and paying attention via the mind's eye, one will be more able to sense the subtle thinking streams and shifts of consciousness in the heart than would normally be possible.

The awareness and thought of the heart is rarely noticed in most of us, except in moments of intense feeling. However, the heart is always conscious and always engaged in the world-forming activity that gives us our reality. Its operation is so seamlessly harmonious and subtle

that the preoccupied thinking mind is virtually unaware of it. When we work with Magnesite in the activity of observing and entering heart awareness, it is of inestimable value for developing clear perceptions of the heart's activity and making fine discriminating distinctions among various heart states and gestures. For one who wishes to become aware of the heart and, in a sense, to befriend one's heart, Magnesite offers great assistance in seeing. The quality of Magnesite that helps engender clear-seeing is not limited to awareness of the heart's activity. This stone can also be a mirror of the mind.

Placed at the third eye, Magnesite generates immediate, powerful currents that infuse the brain with impressions of clear Light. Magnesite facilitates an enhanced clarity of thought and awareness—one's brain chatter is gently brushed aside as the thinking mind becomes more awake and more resonant with each object or activity of contemplation. Capacities for abstract thinking, image-making and intuitive awareness seem to sharpen under the influence of Magnesite. Imaginative creativity, as exemplified in painting, sculpture or poetry, is also enhanced by the presence of the currents of Magnesite, especially when they are directed into the third eye.

When we are clear inwardly, the world seems clearer as well, and one's encounters with others reflect this clarity. Magnesite can aid one in remaining balanced in all sort of experiences and interactions, and it helps one develop the habit of empathic receptivity—the capacity to take in, without judgment, that which is presented by another person or by the world itself. In fact, the clarifying qualities of Magnesite are greatly helpful in putting aside the habit of judgment that we tend to impose upon all our experiences.

Magnesite is exceedingly helpful in achieving attunement of mental activity with the heart's thought. One of the processes that strengthens the mind/heart connection and invites us more deeply into the consciousness of truth is the practice of "asking the heart." In each moment of life, and especially in moments of stress or potential confrontation, it is good to put one's attention in the heart and inwardly ask, "How should I see this? What is the truth? What is the best response I can make?" The next step is listening, watching, regarding the activity of the heart.

With Magnesite placed over the heart and over the third eye, the communication of the heart via imagery is greatly facilitated. As I meditated with Magnesite, I worked with it in this way. Each time I asked the heart any question, I received an immediate response in the form of an image or an urge welling up from the heart. The heart seems to have less capacity to express itself in language, which is usually the brain's territory. However, the heart has a genius for creating images that function as symbolic diagrams of its thoughts and will. One must learn to give attention to the heart's thought-images and to understand them through the feeling awareness and metaphoric thinking. Magnesite, in its clarifying influence on overall consciousness, as well as its enhancement of one's ability to receive impressions from the heart, can be a most beneficial ally.

In spiritual practice, Magnesite is resonant with the vibration spoken as *Om*—the primordial sound of the Universe. "Om" has been said by the Dalai Lama to simultaneously signify the eternally perfect spiritual body and the imperfect physical form of the human being. To chant

"Om" is to evoke the unity of our corporeal body and our perfected Divine blueprint or Light Body. In the process of opening into the New Consciousness it is vital for each of us to find the resonance between the perfected pattern of one's Light Body and one's corporeal body. These two are meant to come together, and the physical body is meant to be transfigured into full resonance with that perfected pattern. Magnesite's resonance with Om helps build a vibrational bridge for the physical body and the Light Body of an individual to come together.

To work with Magnesite for this process, it is suggested that one meditate while lying down with Magnesite placed on the heart and the third eye. One may then repeat the sound of Om, inwardly or with the voice. It may also be helpful to sleep with a Magnesite taped to each of those chakras. Going into sleep consciousness is a kind of release of control over one's thinking, feeling and physical processes. Therefore, sleeping with Magnesite, which works to bring the perfected pattern of the Light Body into coherence with the physical body, allows the resonance to build up over a number of hours, without interference from the conscious mind.

Another helpful practice for integrating the Light Body with the physical involves meditation with Magnesite. In this process one visualizes a Divine form descending into and completely overlapping one's physical form. This can help teach the body to transfigure itself into the Light Body pattern. Magnesite, with its light-giving currents, first stimulates the brain and mind, and it can ultimately bring the same Light into the entire body. One is encouraged to visualize the body as Light-filled and radiant, while holding or placing the Magnesites in the area of the heart and third eye, and also holding a Magnesite in each hand.

Magnesite can help to strengthen the inner witness, the pure observer. It is highly important to develop the observer as an interior structure of consciousness so we are not pulled off-center by each passing feeling or impression. Intuition tells me that Magnesite stimulates the development of the inner observer, in part by encouraging formation of a supporting neural net, primarily in the brain's left hemisphere, where observer consciousness naturally resides.

MAGNESITE SPEAKS   "I bring the clear vision of truth. I am revealed through the heart and perceived through clarified consciousness. My power or energies descend through the layers of heaven, from the ineffable Center of consciousness. I can show you how to become the Light that you are."

MASTER SHAMANITE

KEY WORDS   Linking the physical and spiritual realms, inner purification, spiritual protection, shamanic journeying, transformation to the Diamond Self

ELEMENT   Storm

CHAKRAS   All

Master Shamanite is a carbon-rich form of Calcite. It forms in black masses and is found in a remote mountainous area of Colorado. It is a calcium carbonate mineral with a hardness of 3. Calcites are among the most varied and abundant crystals, and they occur in a wide spectrum of forms and colors. The crystal system is rhombohedral, but specimens can appear as scalenohedrons, rhombohedrons, prisms, masses, stalactites, etc. Most Master Shamanite specimens appear as non-crystallized masses. The name Master Shamanite refers to the spiritual qualities of the stone, which are said to facilitate entrance to shamanic states of consciousness.

Master Shamanite is far more complex than simple Calcite. It contains a high concentration of almost pure carbon, as well as lesser amounts of included Pyrites, Marcasites, Quartz, Chlorite, Zircon and Strontianite. In addition, there are visible and microscopic fossils, including the shell fossils known as the "Kings of Creation." Some appear within Shamanite as white spots and, more unusual, as minute white spirals. The colors of Master Shamanite vary through multiple shades of gray and black, with some tan or brownish varieties, and some specimens of mixed colors.

Master Shamanite has been treasured as a protective talisman by Native American tribes, with certain varieties being called "Toho" (the Mountain Lion). It was used for ceremonial carvings, amulets and bead jewelry. It is said to be known to present-day native peoples of the Southwest as a protective stone, with the power to heal spiritual wounds, ancestral troubles and grief.

BACKGROUND   Master Shamanite is aptly named. It can be very useful for initiating shamanic journeys, and it can help one connect inwardly with power animals and spirit guides. It is a Stone of the Ancestors, aiding in communication with spiritual elders and guides on the other side, as well as loved ones who have passed. It is a stone of those who wish to walk between the worlds, and to heal others through soul retrieval. It can help dispel the fear of death through bringing one to a clear experience that death is not the end of one's being.

Master Shamanite resonates with the heart and third eye chakras, and it can activate a synergy of their energies to open the portal of the crown chakra. This is important for shamanic journeying in which one wishes to leave and re-enter the body through the crown. The Calcite component of Master Shamanite facilitates a clear, calm awareness, making it easier to remain centered through difficult moments of inner or outer life.

Master Shamanite resonates in some mysterious way with the beings thought of as inter-dimensional. It can be used in meditation to help one become aware of these beings and their benevolent intentions. These stones can also expose the inner activities of so-called demonic forces, which are working to keep humans in a lower state of awareness. This exposure dissolves the power of negative beings to hold one in a state of limitation.

Master Shamanite offers spiritual protection to those who simply wear or carry it, and it offers more to those interested in serious inner work. If one wishes to be a "Warrior of Light," Master Shamanite can be a powerful ally.

Master Shamanite resonates synergistically with Moldavite, Larimar, Shaman Stones, Nuummite, Cryolite, Azeztulite, Sanda Rosa Azeztulite, Lemurian Aquatine Calcite and Merkabite Calcite. Strontianite combines very beneficially with Master Shamanite for inner journeyers who find themselves assaulted by negative forces.

NEW ATTUNEMENT   I sat down to meditate with Master Shamanite holding a sphere in my right hand and a raw chunk in my left. I was wearing a pouch with several tumbled pieces upon my chest. The first sensation I noticed in meditation was a strong amplification of the energy current normally at the third chakra, the solar plexus. It seemed as though Master Shamanite was strengthening this chakra and its current. My immediate impression was that this is a stone for the enhancement and strengthening of one's personal power. That is fitting for a stone named Master Shamanite, because many shamanic practitioners develop their personal power to a high degree.

Giving more time to the meditation, I noticed that below the third chakra, the currents opened in a sort of fan-shaped pattern, descending all the way through the lowest chakra at the base of the spine. When beginning meditative work of this nature, I usually create an imaginary grounding cord, visualized as a root going down from my base chakra to the center of the Earth. In this case, without my prompting it at all, this cord became an entire webwork of branching roots that held me much more securely to the Earth than had any of the other stones, except perhaps Black Tourmaline. Certainly the spontaneous grounding rootwork created through Master Shamanite was much stronger than any grounding cord I had created for myself without the aid of a stone.

I say all this by way of illustrating the observation that Master Shamanite is very much about the linkage and intertwinement of one's soul being with the energies and body of the Earth. Master Shamanite is an important stone for those who, like myself, wish to work with the high-frequency energies of many of the stones discussed in this book. One cannot only climb up to the stars; one must also reach down into the Earth in order to be whole and human. We are called at this time to work as bridges between the spiritual worlds and our Earth, for the fulfillment of our purpose and for the healing and benefit of the Soul of the World.

Master Shamanite is a great and tireless ally in taking care of our lower frequencies and linking (through us) the lower, denser vibrations of the physical with the high currents of the spiritual worlds. Master Shamanite can also help us purify our etheric and astral bodies. This is especially beneficial to the astral body, which is a "traveling" body and is prone to picking up attachments of negative or impure vibrations.

As I sat with Master Shamanite, I could feel its intense purifying streams permeating my body and energy field. It is a deeply cleansing stone, one that works quickly and efficiently to bring clarity and a free-flowing quality to one's soul bodies. It vibrates the Liquid Crystal Body Matrix in a way that tends to cause the immediate discharge of disharmonious patterning. The strength of Master Shamanite for this purpose cannot be overstated. I am a little in awe of its powerful cleansing and purifying qualities. It is healthful and wholesome, and so strong that one could not exactly call it gentle, although it is highly beneficial.

As I held the Master Shamanite for a longer period of time, I felt an unusual sense of comfort filling my entire physical body. There was a pleasurable sensation as if being touched and caressed by tiny fingers—very smooth and warm. It became darker behind my closed eyes than I had ever seen it before. It was as though I had descended to the interior of the Earth. The darkness was inky black, and the comfortable sensation that pulsed, throbbed and practically purred through my body was more and more tangible. Throughout the rest of the experience, the feeling of interior and exterior pleasure from the touch of invisible warm currents reminded me deeply of the way I imagine a cat must feel in its body. A kind of sensuous current of dark fluidity ebbed and flowed in an unending stream of pleasant comfort.

I experienced a flash of inner imagery—an ancient stone wall, coated with gold. The wall was partially lit by a nearby flickering fire, and it was covered with inscriptions. In this quick inner flash I saw the image of an equal-armed cross, and also the embossed figure of the crescent moon on the wall. I felt that the images signified that Master Shamanite links one with the deep past and the ancient civilizations of Egypt. This was a surprise to me, as Shamanite is from North America. Yet the temple wall I saw was in Egypt, or someplace in that part of the world that had hosted a very ancient human civilization.

I chose to attempt a shamanic journey to meet the being of Master Shamanite. I attempted inwardly to go to my usual entrance to the shamanic world. However, to my surprise, I was drawn to imagery that I had not seen before. I was standing in front of a fire, outside the entrance to a sweat lodge, and I was to go into the lodge for purification before meeting the being. I followed the unfolding imagery and viewed myself within the sweat lodge. I saw the glowing stones in the center, felt the heat and the intensity of the humidity and experienced the difficult breathing inside the lodge. I saw the shaman who was leading the purification ceremony lying horizontal

upon an earthen ledge. I spent some time there allowing the cleansing to complete itself. After the appropriate inner ritual, and after asking to meet the being of Master Shamanite, I found myself able to emerge from the lodge.

Again outside the lodge, I asked to meet the being of Master Shamanite. I did not see what I might have expected. I experienced repeated flash-images of a being one might call half human and half panther—with incredibly fierce facial features, long teeth, glowing yellow-green eyes and supple, short, black shining fur over its body. This being was a fierce shamanic warrior. Master Shamanite says through images such as this that it offers not only purification but powerful spiritual protection. This is important for those of us who work to open into higher awareness and the Light Body. In opening ourselves, we can cause our personal shells of protection to vanish or dissolve. This is essential, yet it is not to be done heedlessly. Master Shamanite, as a helpful being of the lower worlds, shows its fierce face to any entity or energy that might seek to use us for its purposes. This Panther face of Master Shamanite is the face of the Protector.

I experienced further images during this journey. Again they surprised me. I saw incredibly vivid visions depicting scenes of chaos and even warfare. As I puzzled over why such images would come, an intuition told me that Master Shamanite does not hesitate to face the most disharmonious qualities or energies—either those that assail us from without or those that we carry within. Master Shamanite offers to clear, cleanse and purify one's body and energy fields of all these disharmonies. It does not balk at the worst that we embody and hold in our unconscious. I was shown the violent and difficult images to display the fact that no matter how much we strive for the Light, we must attend to and find a way of working through all of our Shadow material. Master Shamanite fiercely brings forth the images of our Shadow if we work with it meditatively to dissolve these difficult patterns. It brings them forward for us to view as we receive its help in letting them go.

Eventually the Shadow material subsided and I again asked to see the being of Master Shamanite. This time I viewed the bottom half of his body—a pair of shining black legs culminating in large feet with great toes that gripped the Earth like roots. The knees were bent in a slight crouch, and it was easy to see that this being was at home on the Earth, at home in the soil, at home with everything under the Earth. I tried to look up to behold its face. I saw rich multicolored wrappings around the waist and lower torso. This said to me that Master Shamanite is a kingly stone, with its own power, sovereignty and will. (This does not make it a stone for men only. In fact, it can be of great help to women in developing their masculine side.)

As I finally was able to raise my eyes to the head of this being, I saw on the way up the torso that it became radiant and light-filled. I was no longer able to clearly discern the body, because the radiant light of this entity was impenetrable. At the center of this radiance, to my great surprise, I saw a large diamond—an octagonal crystal that turned left and right like a head. There was no face and no eyes. It was a diamond crystal, emanating a brilliant radiance. I knew then that I had been shown the being of Master Shamanite. It displayed itself in perfect symbolic imagery, for as a carbon stone—a carbon Calcite stone—Master Shamanite carries the substance of both the lowliest coal and the highest expression of carbon, the Diamond. It displays itself as a pattern for how we may draw from our shadows the material that is transformed through purification and the application of power and pressure. The intensification and strengthening of one's will—the will to go down into the body, into the Shadow and into the Earth—creates a pressure which can transmute the lowly dross of the human self into the radiant Diamond Self, our Divine Spirit incarnated in physical form.

MASTER SHAMANITE SPEAKS   "I am an ally, a protector and a teacher. Those who are willing to walk the downward road to the invisible Light of the Midnight Sun will find me there. Invite me, and I will walk with you through your dark journeys and into your radiance."

MERKABITE CALCITE™

KEY WORDS   Consciousness expansion, interdimensional travel, ascension, access to higher knowledge, awakening the Merkabah Vehicle of Light

ELEMENTS   Fire , Storm

CHAKRAS   Third Eye (6th), Crown (7th), Transpersonal and Etheric (8th and beyond, above the head)

Merkabite Calcite is a variety of Calcite that occurs in irregular crystalline forms, sometimes in disc-like shapes with wedge edges. It is found in the plains of western Kansas in the U.S. Calcites are among the most varied and abundant crystals, and they occur in a wide variety of forms and colors. The predominant structure of the crystals is rhombohedral, but specimens can appear as scalenohedrons, rhombohedrons, prisms, masses, stalactites, etc.

The name "Calcite" is derived from the Latin *calx*, meaning lime. Calcite makes up the major part of most marbles and limestones. Calcite crystals are found on every continent. Merkabite Calcite is white or grayish white in color, with areas of transparency in some specimens. The name Merkabite Calcite refers to the stone's spiritual qualities, including a particular association with a spiritual structure called the Merkabah Vehicle of Light.

BACKGROUND   Merkabite Calcite's currents can stimulate a great rush of energy, like an interior wind blowing through the upper chakras and out the top of the head. Allowing this energy to move through, one can be transported upward through each of the seven Light Body chakras above the head. Merkabite Calcite can facilitate access to multiple "halls of records" and other interdimensional realms. It is fitting that these stones are named after the fabled Merkabah Vehicle of Light mentioned in kabbalistic texts, because they tap into the inner template for ascension of one's consciousness.

Merkabite Calcite works synergistically with Moldavite, Phenacite, Azeztulite, Danburite, Scolecite, Natrolite, Seraphinite, Ajoite, Fulgurite and most other high-frequency stones. For those who need some grounding with it, Master Shamanite is suggested.

NEW ATTUNEMENT   I entered the meditation session for this writing having placed one piece of Merkabite Calcite at the crown chakra, one at the base chakra and one in each hand. There was an immediate felt sense of a strong corridor of White Light energy, extending the entire length of the chakra column between the two stones. Secondarily, there was noticeable tingling in each hand from the two stones held there. When I held one of those stones at the third eye and the other at the heart, a wave of energy washed through the third eye and filled my skull. I began to see inner images that seemed to depict the qualities of Merkabite Calcite, which (as mentioned) was named in reference to its capacity for awakening the Merkabah Light Vehicle, which is one aspect of the Light Body.

As I held the two Merkabites in each hand and kept the other two at the root and crown chakras, I saw images superimposed on my body of two tetrahedrons that interlocked to form a star tetrahedron. The top of the upward-pointing tetrahedron coincided with the crown chakra, and the bottom of the downward-pointing tetrahedron coincided with the root. The images of the tetrahedrons began to rotate. The top tetrahedron rotated clockwise, and the bottom tetrahedron rotated counter-clockwise. For those who have not seen the image of the star tetrahedron, it looks like a three-dimensional Star of David form. In the body, the images generated by Merkabite Calcite were composed of White Light or white glowing energy currents. A vortex was created where they overlapped one another, with its center just below the heart. If one can visualize two interlocking tetrahedrons, rotating in opposite directions, one can get a hint of the felt sense of the inner vortex activated by these stones.

As I was watching these images and feeling them in my body, I was aware that the faster the two tetrahedrons rotated, the more powerful was the vortex in the body. I also saw that the rapid rotation of the tetrahedrons made them appear to be rotating cones of Light rather than angular geometric forms. I saw that if one were to watch one of the rotating tetrahedrons from a single point, the exterior perimeter of the cone at that point would seem to oscillate in and out, since the tetrahedron was indeed a geometric form composed of flat planes. As it turned in a circular motion, the nearest point of any part of the tetrahedron to a stationary observer seemed to move in and out. This, I saw, could correspond to one's breathing.

I experimented with breathing in a continuous in-and-out flow of breath, in unison with the rotation of the tetrahedrons. My intuition suggested doing this breathing while willing the images of the interlocked tetrahedrons to rotate in rhythm with the breath. This creates a very powerful interior vortex of Light energies. As one speeds up the breathing, the rotating tetrahedrons also go faster, and the sense of the oscillating field within the body intensifies. If one is willing to continue increasing the speed of the breath and the interior speed of the tetra-hedrons, the felt sense of one's sphere of consciousness expands.

There also seems to be an intensification of a cord of Light that runs from the crown to the root chakra, extending it further above and below the body. This extension grows as the vortex intensifies. In my meditation, I was able to glimpse that one can, while creating this interior Merkabah vortex, "point" one's crown chakra figuratively at any place in the inner or outer universe. One can then "ride" the Light axis to that point in consciousness. All of this imagery and the intensity of energy currents result directly from the infusion of spiritual Light through the Merkabite Calcite.

The energy vortex I experienced, created via the envisioned rotating tetrahedrons, seems also to correspond to the torus field generated naturally by the heart. The heart creates both an electromagnetic and a spiritual-vibrational field around itself. The electromagnetic, and perhaps also the spiritual-vibrational field, has to do with the spinning of the blood within the arteries as it is pumped through the heart. These interrelated heart fields serve to interlock one's heart with the life-giving energy source of the Divine realm. Merkabite Calcite helps us to envision and feel the heart's torus vortex, and to inwardly create the Merkabah vortex of the star tetrahedron. In doing this the two fields overlap and integrate. This creates a powerful uni-fied vibrational field, in which various levels of one's physical and subtle bodies come together and expand. Much has been written about the Merkabah, and the interior experience gener-ated by Merkabite Calcite seems to confirm the idea that the Light Body is intimately related to this energy form.

I also experienced the urge to work with intensifying this field in order to travel interdimen-sionally. I feel certain these stones can facilitate such activity if one's will can be aligned with the potential the stones awaken. Merkabite Calcite excites all of the cells through its permeation of the Liquid Crystal Body Matrix. The cellular consciousness is enlivened and awakened to a desire for exploration and expansion. Merkabite Calcite infuses the intra-cellular fluid with a great deal more spiritual Light. It awakens a powerful longing for an increase in consciousness, and it seems to offer a kind of spiral path of ascension into higher levels of awareness. My inner image showed a spiral staircase composed of sparkling Light, which one's consciousness was invited to ascend. There was also the intuitive message that this spiral exists in the DNA spiral, and that the ascension the mind might envision as a journey upward to the stars occurs also in the body at the core of every cell.

Merkabite Calcite is a powerful stone for the overall expansion and ascension of aware-ness. It can greatly enhance the inner experience of working with high-vibration stones, such as those in the Ascension Seven and others. People wishing to experiment with intensification of the currents offered through Merkabite Calcite are encouraged to try various sorts of breath exercises in conjunction with meditation with this stone. Such modalities as Transformational Breathwork, *pranayama* and Holotropic Breathwork seem likely to yield the most powerful results.

MERKABITE CALCITE SPEAKS "I resonate with the frequencies of the First Cause, and my Body of Light expresses itself in primal sacred forms. I kindle the great Star of Fire, the white fire of your core essence. You may climb the ladder of stars into the vast fields of the Light worlds through me."

MOLDAU QUARTZ

KEY WORDS Grounding spiritual Light in the body, appreciating and expressing beauty, awakening heart awareness, grounding the vibrations of Moldavite

ELEMENT Storm

CHAKRAS All, especially Heart (4th) and Third Eye (6th)

Moldau Quartz is the name given to pieces of massive (and occasionally prismatic) Quartz that are found in the Moldavite fields of the Czech Republic. Like other forms of Quartz, it has a hexagonal (trigonal) crystal system and a hardness of 7. If it weren't for their exceptional energies, probably no one would be interested in these humble-looking stones. In the uncut state, they range from about one inch to eight inches in diameter, partially rounded and smoothed by erosion. The colors of Moldau Quartz include white, gray, brown and rusty orange.

BACKGROUND Moldau Quartz has spent millions of years in the same soil where Moldavite is found. These stones have, in a sense, been "taught" by the presence of Moldavite. They are stones of the Earth that have been attuned to the frequencies of the higher worlds. In this, they hold the pattern we ourselves are reaching toward in regard to grounding spiritual Light in our physical bodies. Moldau Quartz is particularly helpful in this area.

In meditation, I sensed a distinct downward pull of Light energy into the body from above as I held the stone over my heart. The heart itself resonates with Moldau Quartz more than most other varieties of Quartz. Moldau Quartz's vibration is a kind of synthesis of Moldavite and Azeztulite. Azeztulite is resonant with the highest spiritual realms, and Moldavite is

deeply attuned to the Divine spark in our hearts. These realms are not truly separate, yet their vibrations are of different qualities. The bridge offered through Moldau Quartz allows one to incorporate much of Azeztulite's high frequencies with the heart-resonance characteristic of Moldavite.

NEW ATTUNEMENT   Moldau Quartz, in my meditation, generated images of various locations around the Earth. In each, there was the sort of beauty one might notice in the most aesthetically pleasing natural scenes. This tells me that Moldau Quartz is resonant with the beauty aspect of Sophia, the Soul of the World. It is, in fact, a very pure emanation of Sophia—this feels true in my heart as I relate it. Sophia is, of course, expressing herself through all of the stones in this book. Yet she has a myriad of qualities, so each stone is different. Moldau Quartz opens the pathway for one's consciousness to appreciate the expressions of beauty constantly offered to us from our own heart. The heart speaks in images more than words. The heart gestures in impulses and urges more than it does in language. In many of us, the heart seems to have no language other than that of image and feeling. But, if we pay attention, what language could be more expressive than those?

Stimulation via Moldau Quartz gives rise to an urge within the heart to speak "upward," expressing the beauty of its nature to our (ideally receptive) mental consciousness. We are falsely divided between heart and brain, and our mental side is often so dominant that we rarely notice the thought of the heart. The heart in most of us waits quietly until it is stirred to action by some crucial or difficult situation. With Moldau Quartz, the heart's consciousness is stimulated so that what may seem to be asleep in us awakens and begins offering its thought and nature to our mental side. This is invaluable, because in order for us to become whole, the mind and the heart must join, and the heart must be seen as the true sovereign of our being. This is very much the purpose of Moldavite. Moldau Quartz reflects that purpose of the great ascension of heart consciousness into the brain. Moldau Quartz seeds this possibility by stirring the heart's activity and engendering its offer of beauty and love to the mental self. If the mental self will turn toward this newly awakened heart expression, the actions of the wakeful heart are reinforced and supported. Then a dialogue ensues, becoming more and more constant as we give attention to it. When the dialogue becomes so continuous and so love-filled that there is no sense of separation between heart and mind, the stage is set for a great awakening—our recognition of the heart and its ascension in glory to its seat of sovereignty. In simpler language, this means that the mental consciousness releases its dominance, because it has recognized the greater wisdom of the heart and has discovered its love for the heart. This also brings the illumination of the mind that is discussed in the chapter on Moldavite.

Moldau Quartz can be used for grounding the vibrations of Moldavite more firmly into the physical body. Orange or brownish Moldau Quartz stones are most helpful in this grounding capacity. White Moldau Quartz tends to vibrate a bit higher, and it is helpful in attuning the mental consciousness to receive the heart's messages. The purpose of Moldau Quartz—closely aligned with that of Moldavite—is the unity of self. It facilitates the joining together, in a gradual and appropriately timed process, of mental awareness and heart awareness. When accomplished, this infuses the entire self and is a full-body awakening.

MOLDAU QUARTZ SPEAKS: "I was blessed in the soil of the Earth by the presence of the newborn Stone of Light. I received and collected this Light in my being, which I now reflect in gratitude and with all of my power and intensity. I have been seeded with the Light of heaven, and I plant a seed of heaven in you."

MOLDAVITE

KEY WORDS   Transformation, rapid spiritual evolution, chakra activation, cleansing, protection, increased incidence of synchronicities, Ascension of the Heart

ELEMENT   Storm

CHAKRAS   All, especially Heart (4th), Third Eye (6th) and Crown (7th)

Moldavite is a member of the Tektite group, a glassy mixture of silicon dioxide, aluminum oxide and other metal oxides, with a hardness of 5.5 to 6. Its crystal system is amorphous. The color of most specimens is a deep forest green, though some pieces are pale green and others, especially those from Moravia, are greenish brown. A few rare gem-grade stones are only a little darker than emerald green. Moldavite's formation coincides with the crash of a large meteorite in what is now the Bohemian plateau of the Czech Republic, approximately 14.8 million years ago. Most specimens are found strewn throughout that area. Farmers often turned up pieces of Moldavite when plowing fields, and Moldavite "miners" sift and dig through loose sands and gravels. Some of the richest finds have occurred at the towns of Chlum and Slavce. A very delicate, lacy form of Moldavite has been found near the village of Besednice. In recent years the Moldavite fields have become depleted, and the stones are becoming increasingly rare.

BACKGROUND   Moldavite is the stone that initiated me into awareness of the spiritual properties of crystals and minerals, as well as my personal spiritual destiny. It has, over the twenty-two years I have worked in this field, had similar effects on thousands of other people with whom I have spoken and corresponded. From my perspective, it has a special role to play in the awakening of humanity now underway, and for this reason we go into Moldavite's story in somewhat more depth than we do with the other stones.

Scientific theorists differ on hypotheses regarding Moldavite's origin. Some contend that Moldavite is earthly rock melted by the heat of the meteorite crash, while others suggest that the material is of extraterrestrial origin, possibly a type of obsidian ejected by a lunar volcano. A third theory holds that Moldavite is a fusion product of meteoric material and earthly rock vaporized in the tremendous heat of the impact explosion, with the resultant gas being propelled high into the atmosphere. This gaseous material would have then cooled and condensed into a liquid glass that "rained" down on the crater and surrounding areas. Regardless of which, if any, of these ideas is correct, it is known that Moldavite indeed fell from the sky, because of the aerodynamic shapes of certain pieces. Most scientists associate it with the meteoric collision that formed the Bohemian plateau and surrounding mountains.

The event that gave birth to Moldavite was one of tremendous power. The force of the impact explosion has been estimated at six trillion megatons, far more than all the atom bombs on Earth. The heat, as mentioned above, was high enough to vaporize rock, and the main body of the meteorite is believed to have passed completely through the Earth's crust, penetrating into the liquid iron at the planet's core. This deep impact is said to have disturbed the currents of rotating liquid iron enough to cause a reversal of the Earth's magnetic poles.

Throughout history, and even into pre-history, Moldavite has been regarded as a spiritual talisman. The Neolithic peoples of Eastern Europe wore Moldavite at least twenty-five thousand years ago, and the famed Venus of Willendorf—the earliest known goddess statue—was discovered in a digging site that contained a number of Moldavite amulets. People of that period also used Moldavite for arrowheads and cutting tools.

More recently, Moldavite has been viewed as a relic of the legend of the Holy Grail. In some recountings, the Grail was said to be not a cup but a stone, an Emerald that fell from the sky. In other stories, the Grail cup was carved from the Emerald. The correspondences of the Stone of

the Grail with Moldavite are clear. The ancients called all clear green gemstones "Emeralds," and Moldavite is the only such stone ever to have fallen from the sky. In history, there was even a physical "Grail" discovered and brought to Napoleon, who was disappointed to find that it was green glass. (But, of course, Moldavite *is* green glass.) Another chalice, this one made of gold and adorned with Moldavites, was passed down through the centuries and disappeared during the second World War. In the 1930s, the famed artist and mystic Nicholas Roerich compared a Moldavite (which he called *agni mani*, meaning "fire pearl") to the fabled Stone of Shambhala, further asserting it was the the same stone mentioned in the legend of the Holy Grail.

Interestingly, the energetic effects of Moldavite parallel those attributed to the fabled Grail stone. Both stones serve to quicken one's destiny and set one upon a true spiritual path. In Czech folklore, Moldavite was believed to bring harmony to marital relationships, and it was used as a traditional betrothal gift for centuries. The Stone of the Grail was believed to have similar properties.

In modern times, Moldavite has emerged as one of the stones most prized for metaphysical purposes. Its effects vary widely, from mild to almost overwhelming, from physical cleansings to spiritual breakthroughs—yet the common denominator seems to be the revitalization and acceleration of one's path of personal evolution.

People who hold Moldavite for the first time most often experience its energy as warmth or heat, usually felt first in one's hand and then progressively throughout the body. In some cases there is an opening of the heart chakra, characterized by strange (though not painful) sensations in the chest, an upwelling of emotion and a flushing of the face. This has happened often enough to have earned a name—the "Moldavite flush." Moldavite's energies can also cause pulsations in the hand, tingling in the third eye and heart chakras, a feeling of light-headedness or dizziness, and occasionally the sense of being lifted out of one's body. Most people feel that Moldavite excites their energies and speeds their vibrations, especially for the first days or weeks, until they become acclimated to it. However, some individuals, especially Starborns, find that Moldavite relaxes them, as if it were a little piece of "home."

Moldavite's energies can activate any and all of the chakras. Its vibrations tend to focus in areas where one has blockages or "wounds," first clearing these areas and then moving into resonance with one's entire energetic system. Resonance with Moldavite can take many forms—chakras can open; synchronicities can increase in frequency and significance; one's dream life can become dramatically more vivid and meaningful; one can connect with spirit guides; physical, emotional or spiritual healings can happen; jobs and relationships can change; meditations can become deeper and more powerful—yet all these can be viewed as symptoms of a shift in one's own energies. This shift is what Moldavite can catalyze. With its high and intense vibrations, it can resonate with one's energy pattern in a way that creates an intensification of spiritual vitality and an acceleration of progress on the path of one's highest destiny. This is much the same effect that legend says resulted from exposure to the fabled Stone of the Grail.

The spiritual Grail may be thought of as the awakened and fully realized intelligence of the human heart. Moldavite once again parallels the Stone of the Grail in its affinity for the heart and the heart chakra. Through the heart's electromagnetic field and its accompanying field of non-measurable subtle energies, we can directly perceive the conditions of other people and the world. The heart's field resonates to All-That-Is, from atoms to galaxies, from individual soul to cosmic consciousness. And the heart not only perceives—it also changes conditions. Through the heart's will it is possible to alter reality, and, knowing this, one has the responsibility of willing the highest good in each moment without knowing what form it will take. Moldavite offers

the promise and carries the potential for assisting one in fully awakening the intelligence of the heart.

Moldavite is a powerful aid for meditation and dreamwork. In both cases, taping a piece of Moldavite to the forehead can have the effect of creating a much more vivid and visionary inner experience. Moldavite increases one's sensitivity to guidance and one's ability to discern the messages sent from the higher realms. Moldavite can be a powerful catalyst for self-healing, clearing blockages and opening the meridians, as well as energizing the interconnections among all aspects of one's etheric, astral, causal and physical bodies. Like the fabled *agni mani* revered in ancient lore, Moldavite is a talisman of spiritual awakening, transformation and evolutionary growth.

In addition to use in meditation and dreamwork, Moldavite can be worn as jewelry. This conveys the advantage of being able to keep its energies in one's vibrational field throughout the day, for further strengthening of its effects. Doing this also draws an increased incidence of beneficial sychronicities into one's daily life. Some people will have to accustom themselves gradually to wearing Moldavite because of its energetic intensity, but most will make the adjustment in a few days.

Moldavite also offers an energy of spiritual protection. When one is in resonance with its high-frequency vibrations, negative energies and entities cannot connect with or hang onto one's field. In alignment with its transformational properties, Moldavite tends to disconnect one from unhealthy attachments and to magnetize the persons and situations most needed for evolutionary progress.

Moldavite can be cut and faceted into gems and other forms, some of which can enhance its energies. The forms that magnify and focus Moldavite's vibrations include pyramids, Platonic solids, spheres and star tetrahedrons. The most powerful gem cuts are round brilliant, radiant octagon, trilliant and oval. Round Moldavite beads are both gentle and powerful. Like spheres, they allow an even, omnidirectional flow of Moldavite's vibrations, accompanied by a kind of softness, which may come from the stone's rounded shape.

Moldavite is an ideal stone for use in making energy tools. It can be glued or otherwise attached to other stones to magnify both energies. It can be added to wands, headbands, templates, grids and all sorts of devices to intensify their effects.

Moldavite has the ability to enhance and accelerate the beneficial effects of many other stones. It works well with all types of Quartz, as well as Amethyst, Citrine, Rose Quartz, Sugilite, Charoite, Lapis, Larimar, Rhodochrosite, Aquamarine, Heliodor, Pietersite, Smoky Quartz, Selenite and most other gemstones. For healing purposes, it works very well with Seraphinite. For enhanced visionary experience, Herkimer "Diamonds" are an excellent ally. Genuine Diamond, in crystal or gem form, further intensifies Moldavite's transformational energies. Libyan Gold Tektite increases Moldavite's empowerment of the third chakra, focus of personal power and will.

Moldavite is one of the Synergy Twelve stones, along with Danburite, Tanzanite, Azeztulite, Phenacite, Herderite, Tibetan Tektite, Satyaloka Azeztulite, Petalite, Brookite, Natrolite and Scolecite. This combination is the most powerful yet discovered for enhancement of the etheric pattern of the perfected self. Moldavite also works harmoniously with each of these stones on its own.

If one were forced to be isolated on a desert island with only one stone as an ally, Moldavite would be an excellent choice.

NEW ATTUNEMENT   I have worked with Moldavite now for almost twenty-five years, and I have so many associations and stories about Moldavite that taking a fresh look at it is rather challenging. Nonetheless, I attempted to do so in the meditation for this book. The first sensation I experienced when I placed Moldavites in my left and right hands, as well as putting one

221

in a pouch over my heart, was a very rapid pulsing in all three locations. I have experienced pulsing as a common response of the Liquid Crystal Body Matrix to many of the stones in this book. However, the pulsing of Moldavite was of a much quicker frequency than any other stone. As I stayed with it, the pulsing became aligned with the influx of an energy current through the top of my head. The current descended, swirled and centered on my heart. It continued to circulate around the heart while it penetrated further, into the lower chakras. Within less than two minutes, my entire chakra column was vibrating at this quick and intense frequency.

Moldavite has a way of moving to whatever place it is needed in the body. Wherever there is an imbalance, its energies will naturally focus. If there is not significant imbalance to be cleared, it will act much as it did in this meditation, curling around the heart, invigorating and enlightening one's entire energy body. The felt sense was of friendly and beneficial currents, which also carried a note of insistent urgency. The urgency was not fear but simply the impulse to go forward, to get on with it, to move quickly toward destiny's unfolding. The journey of destiny is the road of Moldavite. Over many years, I have experienced it as a catalyst for my own synchronistic and rapid movement along my true path. Moldavite seemed to lead me, through all sorts of unlikely routes, to exactly the place, situation or relationship I needed in order to grow further, and in order to benefit whomever and whatever came to me. Moldavite asks that we don the robes of our highest purpose and wear them in a meaningful way. Moldavite seems to say, "It's time to grow!" It fertilizes our soil and radiates the shoots of our freshly sprouted seeds of evolution.

For this writing I tried a meditation that I have led before with groups of people who are working with Moldavite. This meditation involves holding a Moldavite over the heart while placing one's attention in the center of the chest. Doing so, one visualizes an egg-shaped space around the heart, in the center of the chest (rather than the left side). This is said to be the location of the etheric heart. One imagines that one's attention fills this five- or six-inch-tall egg and that it softly presses outward on the interior boundary of the egg. Then one reverses the activity and puts awareness on the outside border of the egg, pressing lightly inward. One goes back and forth—pressing outward, pressing inward in imagination—while envisioning the egg-shaped space.

The next step involves imagining a golden cup—a chalice or grail—within the egg-shaped space. One then puts attention on the Moldavite held over the heart and imagines that the stone is in the chalice, which is itself within the egg of the heart. The process continues by imagining that a liquid golden Light is radiating from the stone. The light soon fills the cup and causes it to overflow. One then envisions the egg of the heart pulsing, pumping the golden Light through its membrane and into the chest. The liquid gold Light then flows throughout and fills the body.

In the next phase of the meditation, a second Moldavite is placed at the third eye (the first remains over the heart). One then enlarges the egg-shaped space and the chalice within it so that the base of the chalice is at the heart, and the cup is within the skull area. The egg-shaped space encompasses the body from the heart to the top of the head. Once again, one imagines the Moldavite stone in this larger chalice, watching as the radiant golden Light pours over the top of the chalice, now showering one's entire body and energy field with liquid gold Light.

As I did this meditation, it was for me an effortless visualization that seemed to carry its own momentum, and I felt inwardly the infusion of gold Light throughout my body. In the second phase, I felt the shower of golden Light throughout the auric field and all of my energy bodies. This is one of Moldavite's great gifts—the enhancement of visionary experience and inner journeying. Another aspect of this gift is that the golden Light is quite real. One can feel its effects if one imagines it as vividly as possible, then pays attention to the subtle (or sometimes obvious) sensations that ensue.

As I continued, the Moldavite showed me another inner image. I saw a detail from a painting by the artist Antonio Campi—a painting I had once seen on a trip to Paris. (This painting is reproduced and discussed in Chapter Six.) It depicts a vision of the Ascension of Christ to heaven, with scenes from the life of Jesus, including the crucifixion and resurrection. There are many images of Jesus in the painting. Near the top right corner is an image of the Ascension, showing Christ in the Resurrection Body of Light, flying upward into a golden dome that has supernaturally formed within a group of very dark thunderclouds. It is as though we are looking through an interdimensional portal into the heavenly realm itself. The painting suggests that the triumph of the passion of Christ has caused an opening in the material world—an opening to heaven, into which he ascends.

The picture shows the Ascension of the resurrected Christ into a golden space shaped rather like a human skull. It is Light-filled, with the same golden radiance that flows through the body in the Moldavite meditation I have described, and which also spontaneously filled me many years ago in my Moldavite-initiated journey to the Great Central Sun. This association of Moldavite with the Golden Light is essential in appreciating and attuning oneself to receive Moldavite's highest gifts.

To return to the image of the painting, one sees the dome of heaven at the top of the skull-shaped cloud, within which is a sphere representing the world. Within the world sphere can be seen the Sun, the Moon, and an inner sphere that represents the Earth. This image in its entirety symbolizes the Ascension of the Earth, and indeed the entire universe, when the pattern of the divinely resurrected Christ (or the resurrected self) is fully realized. In other words, the self and the Earth and the universe ascend as one. The image in the painting also depicts a number of souls (representing the rest of humanity) drawn upward into heaven behind the ascending Christ. It shows that the dome itself is a living dome, held up by innumerable human figures. One might imagine these to be the many Masters who have dedicated themselves to the unification of the spiritual worlds with the Earth.

The purpose of this book—which invites readers to enter into the New Consciousness through resonance with the beings of the stones and through assimilation of new patterns into the Liquid Crystal Body Matrix—is, in essence, the realization of a pattern similar to the Ascension, as shown in the Campi painting. I have long felt that Moldavite, as the Grail Stone, is the stone most properly aligned with this pattern. We remember from the legend that the Stone of the Grail joins heaven and Earth. Moldavite is the gemstone that combines heaven and Earth in its very substance, like the fabled Emerald from the sky, the Grail Stone.

I am drawn to continue comparing Moldavite and the inner process it engenders to the Ascension process depicted in the Campi painting. One sees that the colors surrounding the ascending Christ are the colors of the heart—a pink-gold Light. The joy of the Christ with his upraised arms, and the joy of the beings surrounding and following him, is evident in their postures and gestures. I believe that this image displays a pattern which can occur in our bodies, and which is suggested in the meditation of the Moldavite within the inner Grail. The heart in us is our true center of sovereignty. The heart, by virtue of its love, its wisdom and its self-giving generosity, is the true King or Queen of our being. The heart is the organ of truth and the center of love within us. It can be all of this because it is the center of the Divine in us.

Our history, as we recall it, is a history within which the heart has been continually dominated and suppressed—one might even say crucified—by the tyranny of the fear-bound mind. We all know that when we are in fear, we are most ready to be tyrants, because fear makes us believe that we have no other choice. Human history has been dominated by fear and its consequent aggression. The ascension of the heart in us to its seat of sovereignty as the King or Queen of the wholeness of our being is diagrammed in the painting, as Christ ascends into the skull-shaped golden dome. When one's spiritual heart ascends, it moves upward within the body, into the "throne" in the center of the brain. When this occurs, the crown chakra and the heart chakra become one. The brain is finally relieved of its impossible task of governing our being. It has recognized the heart as the true Sovereign. The two sides of the brain become two angels, instead of being what they have been—two warring demons. And these angels, like all angels, willingly serve the Divine.

All of this occurs within us. Our Divine center and self, the Heart, rises to govern as the loving sovereign of our inner Kingdom. As the heart rises, it fills the skull with radiant Golden

Light, and our consciousness is illuminated. Our illumined consciousness, in recognition of the heart, wishes only to serve its wisdom—with all of its capacities and abilities put at the disposal of the heart's suggestions. The heart governs not through tyranny but through love. It offers its impulses, and the rest of our being can choose what to do with those impulses. But when we are illumined from within, we become whole, and there is no separation or even the thought of separation between the mind and heart. They are one, a completed unity, and heaven and Earth become one in us. This is the process of Heart Ascension, which is the transformation we seek.

While writing this book, I was reading another book called *The Wedding of Sophia*. It is written from an alchemical perspective, and there are many amazing references linking Sophia, Soul of the World, to the Philosopher's Stone. There is a section from *The Emerald Tablet*, believed to be a summary of the Great Work of alchemy. The Emerald Tablet itself was described as a huge Emerald that fell from heaven, upon which the principles of alchemy were inscribed. (Moldavite has long been associated with this legendary Emerald Tablet.) See now how the quoted text from *The Emerald Tablet* echoes the pattern incarnated by Moldavite:

> With great capacity it ascends from earth to heaven. Again it descends to earth, and takes back the power of the above and the below.
>
> Thus you will receive the glory of the distinctiveness of the world. All obscurity will flee from you.
>
> This is the whole most strong strength of all strength, for it overcomes all subtle things, and penetrates all solid things.

This language is at first a bit obscure, yet we can readily see its resemblance to the genesis of Moldavite. The meteor that struck the Earth caused a tremendous explosion (over six trillion megatons) that vaporized both the meteor and a great amount of earthly rock, sending a huge cloud of superheated silica vapor into the sky. The explosion is the *great capacity* that caused the plasmic substance to *ascend from earth to heaven*. The great energy within the silica plasma, composed of both meteor and rock, carries *the power of the above and the below*, giving birth to the new substance. The rest of the lines correspond to Moldavite's spiritual qualities. We know of Moldavite's tendency to accelerate spiritual evolution—to attract what serves that evolution and to dispel whatever blocks it. This may echo the meaning behind the statements *Thus you will receive the glory of the distinctiveness of the world. All obscurity will flee from you.* Finally we have the statement: *This is the whole most strong strength of all strength, for it overcomes all subtle things, and penetrates all solid things.* I liken this to Moldavite's resonance with the pattern of one's highest destiny *(strength of all strength)* and the all-permeating quality of its energies *(it overcomes all subtle things, and penetrates all solid things)*. To find such a quote in *The Emerald Tablet,* which purports to be a wisdom text discovered inscribed upon a heavenly green stone, is a synchronicity too great to be ignored! I can't say with any certainty that the text is *meant* to describe Moldavite, but I do believe it did so, and the resonance of such patterns provides us with some provocative clues.

Moldavite has been for many the seed of the heart's awakening. Without this awakening, there can be no Ascension. Without this awakening, there can be no blessed marriage between heaven and Earth. Yet as in the Grail legend, when one drinks from the sacred cup—the chalice of the heart—when one allows its waters to flow through one's being, one is illumined, one is awakened to truth, one is filled with the Love-Light of one's Divine spark.

Moldavite, as the Grail Stone, is a talisman of this entire awakening, and I believe it is the longing of our hearts that this should come to pass. Moldavite helps us find and identify the deepest spiritual longing in ourselves. It facilitates each step on the Grail journey. It revitalizes our sense of purpose. It brings us into the magic of synchronicity and the recognition of the Wisdom permeating the world. It shows us that not only do we live in a magical world, we ourselves are magical. Moldavite is resonant with the ongoing, evolving pattern of our highest destiny, and it invites us along every step of that great and perilous journey.

MOLDAVITE SPEAKS   "I am the Green Stone that serves. I am a stone for healing. I am a stone for loving. I am a talisman of Light. I am a friend in darkness. I am a messenger of your purpose. I bow to you."

MORGANITE

KEY WORDS   Divine Love and compassion,
  finding one's true path through love

ELEMENT   Water

CHAKRA   Heart (4th)

Morganite is a pink, peach or purple/pink variety of Beryl, a beryllium aluminum silicate mineral with a hardness of 7.5 to 8. Its crystal system is hexagonal (trigonal). Its color is caused by the presence of manganese. Morganite was mined first in Madagascar in 1902. It was named after the financier and mineral collector J.P. Morgan. Important deposits of Morganite come from Brazil, Mada-gascar, Africa and the United States.

BACKGROUND   Just as Rose Quartz is the great energizer of personal love and self-love, Morganite is attuned most clearly to the frequency of Divine love. Morganite opens the heart on another level, making us aware of the huge ocean of cosmic love within which we all exist. Morganite gives us the opportunity to surrender to the immense power of Divine love and to let it show us our life path more clearly.

Morganite can bring an immediate release of old pains and sorrow and a sense of lightness, as though a burden has been lifted. Not only can it cleanse and activate the heart, bringing it into harmony with the Divine plan, it can also awaken us to the awareness that all of our life's suffering and pain served the higher purpose of our spiritual growth.

Wearing Morganite brings a sense of peace, joy and inner strength, expressed in the most gentle and loving fashion. When one keeps Morganite on one's person for extended periods of time, there is a growth of confidence and power that comes from being constantly aware of one's connection to Divine love. One feels as though one is a conduit for that love to flow into the world through all one's interactions and relationships.

Morganite harmonizes with many of the heart-chakra stones—Rosophia, Rose Quartz, Rhodochrosite, Kunzite, Lepidolite, Emerald, Dioptase, etc., as well as Phenacite, Danburite, Petalite and Azeztulite.

NEW ATTUNEMENT   I sat down to meditate with Morganite, one stone in a pouch over my heart and another in each of my hands. My felt experience was of a delightful, sweet current that pulsated lightly and delicately through my entire body. There was a feeling of delicious enjoyment as this current resonated within my Liquid Crystal Body Matrix.

Holding or suspending Morganite over the heart brings a sense of deep comfort. The heart experiences the pleasure of being welcomed into the home of Morganite. We associate Morganite with the quality of love. Love, in a very generous and nourishing frequency, seems to permeate one's heart when Morganite is near it. I sensed the Being behind the stone as a pink-gold illuminated presence of total love. Morganite evokes images of pink-golden lights, and these coalesce into a sphere of golden Light, tinged with an outer shell of pink, sheltered by curtains of White Light and covered from above by wings made of clear Light. This was my inner image of the being expressed as Morganite.

The capacity for total commitment to the path of the heart and the way of love is deeply encouraged by Morganite. The being behind Morganite presents itself as one of complete and total love, without any reservation, hindrance or condition. Morganite, through its resonance

with us, reminds us that the truest life is just such a life—one of complete commitment to the path of love. This entails meeting each experience, each person and each moment with an open heart—blessing each experience, regardless of content. Morganite shows us that this is the way of truth, and it reveals how we can live that kind of love.

Morganite infuses one's interior realm with its pink radiance. Experiencing this is highly pleasurable. If one dwells for some time in the presence of spiritual Light emanated by Morganite, one approaches the threshold of ecstasy. Morganite says, "Love unhindered leads to ecstasy." Morganite encourages us to express in the world its aim of linking all of life through love. Morganite's purpose is for love to prevail on Earth, and within us.

MORGANITE SPEAKS "The Earth is a Divine Woman and I am the jewel She places upon Her heart. I express Her heart's pure radiance of love. It is my joy to be near Her heart and I wish to kindle your hearts. She wishes it of me, and I am Her joyful partner."

MYSTIC MERLINITE™

KEY WORDS Alignment of the chakra column, balancing and integration of polarities, healing inner fragmentation, claiming one's wholeness, creating through magic

ELEMENTS Fire, Earth

CHAKRAS All

Mystic Merlinite is the name given to a unique mineral discovered in Madagascar. It has not been fully analyzed, but it appears to be constituted of Quartz, Feldspar and several trace minerals. Its color is a swirling blend of black and white. The Quartz component of Mystic Merlinite has a trigonal (hexagonal) crystal system and a hardness of 7. The Feldspar component has a monoclinic crystal system and a hardness of 5 to 6. These stones are plutonic, formed when molten magma is trapped beneath the Earth's surface and cools into a crystalline mass. The name Mystic Merlinite refers to the spiritual qualities of the stone.

BACKGROUND Mystic Merlinite can part the veils between the visible and invisible worlds, opening the doors to deeper intuitive abilities. It aids in developing psychic capacities such as clairvoyance, clairaudience, clairsentience and prophetic vision. It can facilitate opening the dormant areas of the mind and in recalling knowledge and talents from past lives. It increases sensitivity to the communications of the subtle realms, allowing one to "talk" with plant and animal spirits, as well as other entities in the spirit worlds. I sense it as a stone that links directly to the elemental energies of Earth, Wind, Fire, Water and Storm. For those wishing to work with elemental energies for magical manifestation or awakening to mystical experiences, this stone can be a powerful ally.

A mystical experience can be described as the sudden realization of who one truly is. Mystic Merlinite's most important quality is the expansion of self-awareness to the critical point at which such realizations occur. The black and white mixture of Mystic Merlinite symbolizes the Light and Shadow sides of the self, both of which one must embrace in the moment of inner awakening. Working inwardly with Mystic Merlinite is a way of putting oneself on this path of self-realization.

One of Mystic Merlinite's key qualities is that of bringing the exiled parts of oneself back into the light of consciousness. This can be seen in its structural patterns—the swirling interpenetration of the light and the dark. The healing of darkness—in oneself or in the world—involves taking in just such a pattern. One must invite one's judged and rejected parts into the Light of the heart, loving the very qualities we have been taught are bad or unacceptable. This often difficult passage can lead to the true mystic union, which brings the self into wholeness and allows the unity of self and World. Mysteriously, this stone embodies and encourages the critical inner gesture that can lead one into a whole new life. In that new life, one constantly extends the gesture of loving, non-judgmental appreciation to each moment and each being one encounters.

Mystic Merlinite resonates powerfully with Master Shamanite, as well as all forms of Azeztulite, Black Tourmaline, Jet and Smoky Quartz. Its dream-enhancing qualities are encouraged by Lemurian Golden Opal. It can be used with Lemurian Aquatine Calcite for healing the emotional body. For attuning to the spiritual call of the unknown future, Mystic Merlinite can be combined with Circle Stones.

NEW ATTUNEMENT   In my initial meditation, I began by placing stones at the heart and third eye, as I usually do. I found that the heart responded with a pulsation of joy to the presence of Mystic Merlinite. The mind and brain, when I added a second stone at the third eye, vibrated in a pleasurable and clearing manner. It seemed to me that the presence of Mystic Merlinite was an influence toward dispelling confusion, opening me to deeper levels of intuition and more wide-ranging access to the inner worlds. Placing Mystic Merlinite below the root chakra, I found a welcome resonance there, which enhanced my sense of connection with the Earth and increased the beneficial effects of being fully grounded.

Placing one Mystic Merlinite at the base chakra and another at the crown brought a power-ful sense of a completed circuit, along with a sense of alignment throughout the chakra column. I felt this to be of great benefit. Like few other stones, Mystic Merlinite is capable of strengthening, reinforcing and helping to pull together the entire energetic axis of the body. It resonates with both the Alpha and the Omega—the most ethereal and the densest vibrations, the most exalted and the most grounded or base, the most open to the Divine worlds and the most solidly linked into the Earthly domain.

I have the impulse to call Mystic Merlinite the stone of Feirefiz, who was the prototype in the Grail legend of the fully evolved human being. Because he had parents of two different races, his skin was a mixture of black and white—half of each, very much like the pattern of Mystic Merlinite. In the symbology of the Grail stories, Feirefiz was the perfect mixture of Light and Darkness, of the Above and the Below. He was, alchemically speaking, an embodiment of the Great Work completed. Mystic Merlinite is the stone that most closely embodies this unity of opposites, both in its physical appearance and in its capacity for coalescing the higher and lower energies of the body in a way that does not lead to imbalances.

Most of the stones in this book are upward-reaching Light Body stones, resonant with the spiritual worlds. I have chosen them because our condition as human beings is, in my eyes, imbalanced in the direction of materialism. (Materialism wouldn't be so bad if it cared about real substance, but it focuses instead on mental *concepts* of the "objective" world.) Therefore, in order to find our true center and wholeness, we need to work intensely toward reconnecting with and re-embodying the high vibrations of the spiritual realms. Mystic Merlinite is very helpful because it is a model of where we are going. It is capable, through its energy currents, of giving us the blueprint for the dynamic flowing activity of the whole spiritual human. Like Feirefiz, the spiritual human is able to hold Light and Shadow in dynamic balance. One does not try to overcome and send darkness into exile—one acts from the heart's strength and resilience, working with all that one is.

How do we get to such a state? Mystic Merlinite presents an energetic pattern that helps to draw us there. One of the keys offered by Mystic Merlinite is the suggestion, felt in the impulse of its currents, to reclaim the parts of our souls that have been lost or exiled through fragmentation of the self and through judgment.

In our lives within the sphere of humanity there are powerful influences that fragment our natural wholeness. We may carry the trauma of pain or fear from our birth or early childhood. Even events from past lives can shatter the self and cause one's soul to attempt to function as a patchwork of broken pieces.

In childhood, a relatively minor though very common example of fragmentation can be seen if one looks at the scolding a toddler might receive for supposed misbehavior. Our imaginary child is pulling items off the grocery store shelves, imitating Mother. "Don't do that! Bad girl!" says the parent. If the behavior continues, punishment may ensue. In order to remain bonded to the parent, the child must sooner or later cease the forbidden behavior and agree, at least tacitly, that she is a "bad girl." This type of situation, in countless repetitions, creates the pattern of the "inner judge" and the "inner criminal" in the self. Since there is only one self in each human being, this inner judge and inner guilty one constitute a great fragmentation. The phrase "I am so mad at myself" exemplifies this fragmentation. All of us carry such imbalances. I recount this by way of saying that when one does meditative work with Mystic Merlinite, one is encouraged and enabled to revisit the fragmented areas of oneself and to invite them back into one's heart.

Combining helpful stones with inner processes is one of the keys to the New Consciousness. I have a favorite process for working to heal this sort of fragmentation. Holding or wearing a Mystic Merlinite over the heart chakra, one may, during meditation, say inwardly, "I am so grateful for *blank*." One can then fill that blank with such phrases as "my dishonesty," "my shame," "my anger" or other qualities that one may have judged and exiled. To bring these old judgments into one's heart in the presence of gratitude is to bring the darkness into the presence of the light. When the darkness and the light are mixed, the wounds that fractured one's wholeness can be healed. One should not try to do away with darkness, but simply forgive it.

This is a practice one can do with or without a stone, and it is an essential one. No fragmented psyche can, without such healing, be a container capable of carrying the Divine energies we are destined to embody.

Upon deciding to do this work of bringing back the exiled parts of the soul and welcoming them into the heart, one may also wish to include a stone of forgiving, such as Celestite. These two stones together are the ideal pairing for such work.

Other qualities of Mystic Merlinite include the capacity to influence the world itself through creative intention. This sort of influence might be called magic. And all of us do this kind of magic, whether we are aware of it or not. For example, when we are unhappy, we tend to complain about our bad situation. Unknowingly, we tend to perpetuate these conditions because the response from the World Soul must in some way reflect our intention, which in this case is perhaps unintentionally negative. When we are happy, we tend to express our pleasure, and sometimes our gratitude. Such expressions can influence the circumstances of life to conform to their patterns as well. However, this "magic" is not a simple reflection, for the world is a *living* mirror, with its own volition. The most delightful and amazing quality of this sort of co-creating is the world's unique response. The magic we can work is not only ours, but is the activity of Sophia.

Mystic Merlinite works very well with the elemental energies Earth, Air, Fire and Water, as well as the fifth element, which is both the synthesis and the surpassing synergy of all. It is at this intersecting point of the vertical axis that Mystic Merlinite centers us. Its balanced currents align one from root to crown, and from this place our powers of manifestation and co-creation are at their peak. We do not yet have the words or concepts to fully imagine them. In fact, it may be that there is no way to conceptualize such capacities, since they arise from a state we have yet to achieve. They may be accessible only through feeling, and the inward gesture of reaching toward the world from the place of being whole. Such a gesture arises from a fully realized human being, such as the victorious knight Feirefiz, whose example we see in the Grail stories. This kind of existence may seem far from where we are, but the currents of Mystic Merlinite reveal their potential to our inner vision.

MYSTIC MERLINITE SPEAKS "I call all who seek self-awareness and self-mastery to join me in bringing yourselves into fullness. You are all, in your potential, mystics and makers of magic. I stand as your teacher, encouraging your metamorphosis and awakening."

NATROLITE

KEY WORDS Visionary experience, quantum leap to higher consciousness, brain evolution, extraterrestrial connections

ELEMENT Storm

CHAKRAS Third Eye (6th), Crown (7th), Etheric (8th and beyond, above the head)

Natrolite is a sodium aluminum silicate mineral with a hardness of 5 to 5.5. Its crystal system is orthorhombic. It typically forms as slender, vertically striated prismatic crystals, although it may also occur in massive, granular, fibrous, radiating or compact habits. The stones can be colorless, white, yellowish or gray. They often occur in cavities in basalts, in association with other zeolites. They can also be found in igneous rocks such as nepheline-syenites. Beautiful Natrolite crystals have been collected in northern Bohemia (Czech Republic) and in New Jersey (U.S.). Other localities exist in India and Russia.

BACKGROUND Natrolite is one of the two or three most powerful stones for stimulation of the third eye and crown chakras. When one works in meditation holding a Natrolite to one or both of these points, a strong pulsing energy moves into the chakra, pulling the chakric vibrations into resonance with the Natrolite's emanations. This begins a process by which the third eye and crown chakras link and expand, creating an experience in which one feels as if they have merged into a single huge chakra, pulsating with Light and intense vibration.

Natrolite's energy moves beyond the confines of the physical body, activating one's conscious link with the eighth through fourteenth chakras above the head. Natrolite provides

psychic protection, making it impossible for negative entities or influences to penetrate one's auric field. Its pulsating vibrations can bring Light to any area of the body where energies are blocked or slow-moving. It is useful in stimulating the nervous system to higher levels of sensitivity to the subtle spiritual energies that surround us. It allows easier access to inner guidance and can even help one set up two-way communication with angelic helpers. Natrolite is a stone of optimism and hope. It inspires acting in accordance with one's highest visions and expressing gratitude for their blessings, even those yet to manifest.

Natrolite is an Ascension Stone, along with Herderite, Phenacite, Danburite, Azeztulite, Scolecite, Brookite, Phenacite and Satyaloka Azeztulite. Natrolite is also one of the Synergy Twelve stones, which includes the Ascension Stones plus Tanzanite, Moldavite and Tibetan Tektite. In addition, Natrolite can spiritualize the energies of most other stones.

NEW ATTUNEMENT   nn beginning my meditation with Natrolite, I held a large stone while placing several smaller pieces in a pouch over my heart. After a few moments I also held the large piece over my heart. There was an immediate upwelling of energy, like the bubbles in a bottle of champagne. The vibrations rose quickly to the third eye chakra, filling it with a pleasurable current. After a few minutes of stimulating the third eye chakra, the current moved higher, stimulating and activating the crown chakra. There was also a powerful L-shaped current pattern coming in from the third eye and turning up to the crown chakra.

In holding the Natrolite near the third eye, I found that its current created the involuntary but not uncomfortable crossing of the eyes. I felt them turn upward and point inward toward the center of the forehead. As I have written before, this phenomenon is known in Eastern meditation traditions and is practiced for the purpose of awakening the third eye. Working with Natrolite, the turning of my eyes up to the forehead was accompanied by a sensation of strong intensity. It was a concentration of my own attention and energy, along with the stone's energy, focused at the third eye. The effervescent currents of Natrolite's vibrations then moved in through my hands, and again they had the overriding tendency to move upward in the body. Wherever I place Natrolite, even in the lower chakras, the energy moves up and tends to center in the third eye.

Natrolite is most notably a stone of inner vision and the awakening of dormant, as yet unrealized senses and capacities of the prefrontal lobes of the brain. These lobes, which rest just behind the forehead, are believed to be the most recently evolved portion of the human brain. They are known as the "silent areas," because their activity is apparently very minimal in relation to their capacity. They are also called the "angel lobes" and are believed to be the areas of the brain in which our most altruistic and compassionate consciousness is centered. These bits of information, coupled with the felt sense of Natrolite's currents—including their pleasurable nature—point to the possibility that there are very important human capacities sleeping in the frontal lobes of the brain. I feel that our evolutionary potential calls us to awaken them.

Natrolite strongly stimulates this entire area of the brain and the corresponding areas of our non-physical bodies. During the meditative session for this book, I held a Natrolite in front of my eyes and looked at it carefully, with alternating focused and diffused attention. I noticed that my imaginal vision emphasized a pattern in the stone, bringing forward to my spiritual sight the image of an equal-armed cross—a symbol in multiple cultures, sometimes indicating the four elements or the intersection of the "horizontal" material world with the "vertical" spiritual domains.

In gnostic cosmology, it was written many centuries ago that the Aeons (archetypal deities), which were formed in the first echelons (levels of being) below the unfathomable Divine, joined their energies and created something that was called a Cross in order to insulate the perfected divine realms from the chaotic qualities of the Earth and the other manifest material worlds. This is because the Aeons were preservers of the essential Divine patterns within which all the cosmic forces of the spiritual worlds interact in a perfected harmony. It is interesting to note that "Cross" was the term used to describe the barrier or the membrane between the material and the divine realms. The fact that this image came forward when I began my meditation contemplating Natrolite speaks to me of Natrolite's capacity to energize one's consciousness to move *through* the membrane. I see this journey as an ascending spiral, beginning at the Crossroads of the material and spiritual—entering into consciousness of the higher realms through the gateway of the intersection point. It may be that this intersection point is located in human beings at the third eye chakra.

When we speak of expanding consciousness, we speak of developing inner sight, or insight. Natrolite acts as a kind of beacon, bringing light into one's inner space, thereby making conscious many areas that were previously in shadow. This is not neccesarily the sort of shadow one thinks of as some negative or fearful quality. This shadow is simply that which has not yet risen to consciousness. Natrolite opens the portals in one's etheric body and chakra system, enabling us to engage the unseen realms of the spiritual domain.

There are mentor beings, teacher beings, which accompany the stone Natrolite, and which reach through its vibrational lattice into our energy systems, facilitating our initiation into a New Consciousness. This is very much a Light-filled awareness, as many spiritual traditions tell us. When I closed my eyes after gazing upon the Natrolite stone, and the form of the Cross upon it, I saw an after-image before my inner eye. It was a column of blue-white light. I sensed that this column of light was the image of a membrane opening via Natrolite's energies. The blue-white column of light seems to be Natrolite's portal, through which one may enter meditatively into its region of the spiritual realms. I suggest that those working with Natrolite experiment with this practice, looking for that portal.

As I meditated with the Natrolite I began to receive inner visions of cosmic realities. I saw a beautiful spiral galaxy. That image triggered this insight about the spiritual realms: We know that the center of our galaxy contains a vast black hole, which appears to us as a complete absence of light, an emptiness deeper than the vacuum of space. In the same way, the spiritual heart of Being, beneath its garment of Light, is a kind of unfathomably deep silence. Around this silence is a cloak of Light, which includes the beauty we experience as the light of the stars and

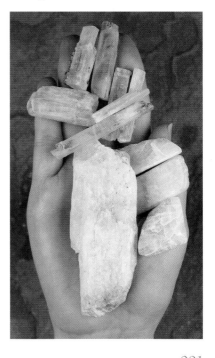

the radiance of our interior visions. This cloak of Light is in place for the nourishment and comfort of living beings, who might be unable to withstand the vast silence. I also glimpsed that this darkness and silence compose the veil over a deeper kind of Light, a dark radiance which, if we were to see it, could overwhelm us. Whenever I approach this, I am awed, and I feel somehow held back. However, Natrolite helps me to reach the threshold.

Natrolite invites one to enter visionary consciousness for the purpose of spiritual evolution and growth. It is a stone of high intensity in the realm of vision, as my own brief encounter with the galaxy image showed me. Natrolite does not hold back. What it reveals to us—what it opens in our consciousness—powerfully guides us toward the center of the nature of All That Is. The effervescent, energizing effect of Natrolite permeates the entire body if one holds the stone in meditation for even a short time. The rate of vibration of the Liquid Crystal Body Matrix is increased to a much higher frequency, and there is a kind of elated feeling throughout the cells—a feeling of "At last we are attuned!"

The cellular consciousness enjoys and is exhilarated by the intense high frequencies of Natrolite. The shift it engenders allows us to discharge negative attachments, which cannot abide the high vibration that Natrolite introduces. This is fortunate, because the opening of consciousness is an occasion of vulnerability, since certain habitual defenses must come down for the experience to fully develop.

I encourage people to work with Natrolite because of the speed at which it expands consciousness. Natrolite can also encourage an awakening of the heart. Heart intelligence is stimulated by proximity to Natrolite, and similar energies to those felt at the third eye can be felt at the heart when one gives time and attention to this. When Natrolite's currents began to work in the heart, I experienced a soft burning sensation in the heart chakra, which surged upward to the high brain—the frontal lobes and the crown. This linking and integration of the heart and the brain must occur in order for one to awaken into the New Consciousness. One can feel the first wave of the heart's joy as this begins, through the introduction of Natrolite at the heart.

NATROLITE SPEAKS "I represent multiple beings with an aligned intention. Our purpose is the incarnation of Light. Our agenda is your initiation into a higher-frequency domain. We offer a certain education, which is an education of currents and vibration—an education into resonance with frequencies of Light is offered for you. What you call White Light is a many-faceted jewel, and each facet vibrates in a different way, bringing a different view of the Divine kaleidoscope.

"So when Natrolite becomes your teacher—when we enter into relationship with you—you are offered the opportunity to learn more than how to enter Light. You are given experiences of the many pure emanations of the Light. There are more variations within White Light than there are colors in the spectrum you know. The White Light is, in one way, to be known as the milk of the Divine Mother, for it nourishes life and carries Her love."

NIRVANA QUARTZ™

KEY WORDS   Opening to the future, heart/brain synergy, inner silence, destiny, evolution, trust, self-acceptance

ELEMENT   Storm

CHAKRAS   All

Nirvana Quartz is the name coined to describe a specific group of growth-interference Quartz crystals that were discovered in the high Himalaya mountains of India. Like other Quartz, they are silicon dioxide crystals with a hexagonal (trigonal) crystal system and a hardness of 7. The stones were first found in 2006, at altitudes above 18,000 feet, where glaciers receding due to global warming exposed them. They have apparently lain under the ice for thousands of years. The crystals themselves visually resemble the jagged ice sheets and crevices that have so long hidden them. (One of the other names by which they are known is "Ice Quartz.") They are irregularly formed and convoluted, with deep recesses and strange contours. No two pieces are alike, though it is clear that they are all of one "species." Though most pieces of Nirvana Quartz do not exhibit the regular six-sided body and pointed terminations of other Quartz crystals, they sometimes show natural facets and partially smooth bodies. The majority are roughly wand-shaped, though many are rather thick and stubby. An unusually high percentage of them are trigonic—exhibiting inscribed, downward-pointing triangles etched into their surfaces. Oddly, they come in two colors—clear white or pink. The pink coloring of approximately half of the specimens seems to be caused by inclusions on or near their surfaces.

Growth-interference Quartz is said to derive its fantastic shapes due to the growth of Calcite or other minerals within and during the forming of the Quartz crystal body. Later, the intergrowing mineral dissolves, leaving the strangely formed Quartz.

BACKGROUND   Nirvana Quartz crystals resonate at the intersection of past and future time. They have apparently existed in quiet isolation beneath glacial ice for many thousands of years, almost as if waiting for this moment to appear in the human world. Though they carry the current of the deep, silent past, their mission is to attune us to the not-yet-formed potential of what can be. The spiritual beings that express as these complex, almost unearthly crystals are available to aid us in the evolutionary transmutation which is our highest destiny.

Meditation with these stones is first an immersion in deep peace and interior silence. The inner dialog of thoughts is stilled with much greater ease than is usual. The gentleness of Nirvana Quartz is paired with a current of strength that even those who are normally not crystal-sensitive can feel. If one allows the unfolding to continue, visions often come—waking dreams that picture what one most needs to see in order to consciously choose the path of one's highest destiny.

Another aspect of the effects of Nirvana Quartz concerns the integral linking of the brain/mind with the heart. The clear/white Nirvana Quartz crystals tend to stimulate and awaken the third eye and crown chakras, while the pink crystals are felt deeply in the heart. When used together, the currents of both types of Nirvana Quartz can flow through the entire passage between the head and heart.

The pink Nirvana Quartz crystals are associated primarily with the feminine stream, and the white with the masculine, though these distinctions are not rigid. Similarly, though the white crystals resonate easily with the sixth and seventh chakras, while the pink ones flow with the heart, one can encourage and allow these to flow through all levels of oneself.

Nirvana Quartz Crystals work well with Agni Gold Danburite, Phenacite, Herderite, Azeztulite, Satyaloka Azeztulite, Petalite and white Danburite for upper-chakra attunement. Stones of loving heart qualities such as Rosophia, Morganite, Kunzite, Seraphinite, Moldavite and Lepidolite can aid in emphasizing the heart aspect of Nirvana Quartz's dual mind-heart centering.

NEW ATTUNEMENT   In sitting down with Nirvana Quartz, I first noticed how deeply it tended to move me into inner silence. Often in meditation, several minutes are required to still the monologue of the superficial mental level, in order to attend to silence and deeper areas of consciousness. Nirvana Quartz is attuned to the spiritual realms of silence. It carries such powerful currents that if one works with it and aligns with its energy, one is drawn into deep silence and contemplation very quickly.

Holding a piece of Nirvana Quartz in each hand while placing another over the heart, I almost instantly felt the shift in my Liquid Crystal Body Matrix. This shift, as mentioned, was toward silence, and also toward a state of such strong attunement to the spiritual worlds that a soft thrill of recognition washed through my body. I understood this as an awareness of having moved into resonance with a deeper level of the spiritual realms. I noticed also that the piece of Nirvana Quartz over my heart was resonating with my heart chakra. I felt this as the arising in the heart of a subtle mandala of vibrating activity. I would describe it as "cool heat," which developed into a feeling that the heart chakra itself was beginning to spin.

When I held one piece of Nirvana Quartz over my heart and another piece over the third eye area, I experienced again the awakening of the circuitry or the current-path between the heart and the third eye. This is Nirvana Quartz's signature gesture. The initiation of activity within this inner corridor can be greatly helpful. It is critical for human beings to stimulate, awaken and strengthen this normally rather dormant neural and energetic pathway. These chakras are destined to operate in unison and in complete accord with one another. Nirvana Quartz lets us experience the first sensations of this resonant integration, and it suggests that our investment of attention will bear fruit beyond what we can now imagine.

Nirvana Quartz has a resonance with the future time stream moving toward us, unfolding in each moment from potential into manifestation. An aspect of our future state of being as spiritually developed humans is the resonant unity of heart and mind. It is through this joint mode of consciousness that we reach our calling to be co-creative with the Soul of the World. This is a central focus of the development of the New Consciousness in us. Nirvana Quartz is one of the most powerful tools for embodying the essential inner connections that open us to the New Consciousness.

In this meditation, I was reminded of the information from quantum physics that gives us a pattern for understanding what it is to participate in creating each moment in resonance with the future stream of time. It is said in quantum physics that the possibilities or probabilities for any phenomenon to appear in one way or another exist only *in potential* before an observation is made. One example, which is not from quantum physics but is easy to understand, is the event of a rainbow. We know that when one gazes at a rainbow, the phenomenon itself is a sort of triune interaction of the rain, the angle of sunlight and the position of the observer. If the observer is not positioned at the correct angle between the rain and the light, no rainbow will be seen. Also, if there is no observer at all, clearly there is no rainbow, for one of the three essential ingredients is not present. The observer is just as necessary as the rain or the sunlight. We also know that the apparent location of the rainbow moves when the observer moves. If the rainbow seems to be, for instance, about a mile away on the side of a hill, walking in that direction will cause the rainbow to appear to move, keeping the same distance from oneself. This shows us that the phenomenon has no objective position outside its relationship with the one who looks.

In quantum physics, it is said that any phenomenon such as the position or momentum of a subatomic particle exists only as a probability until we observe or measure it in some way. This act from our side is said to collapse the probability wave and form it into a specific manifest event. This seems unbelievable at first—that there is no event until the act of observation occurs—although the rainbow example, when applied to other types of experience, gives us a way of understanding it. I describe all of this now as I recount my meditative encounter with Nirvana Quartz because it was brought to mind seemingly by the being of the stone itself. It arose in my mind as I reached for a way to understand and speak of its capacity to attune us more perfectly to the unfolding wave of the future time stream.

By way of further picturing this, I am also reminded of discoveries that our heart has a great deal of neural complexity, providing a physical "home" to the intelligence of the heart—giving it a means of expression in the physical body. Not only does the heart have its own intelligence and awareness—of a different nature than that of the brain—but it has been discovered (and even measured) that the heart has the capacity to attune to the wave of the unfolding potential coming from the future.

The heart "feels into" the quantum wave of potential—the unmanifest pattern of the "not yet." The heart senses the pattern of the universal dance, because the heart is a center of that unfolding activity. Although the future is not determined yet, in some ways the probabilities of the expressions of what is to come are given their strength by the paths that events have followed in the past. In other words, one might say that probabilities are measurements of the way things have happened before, which indicate the way things may tend to unfold in times to come. Yet these are not laws—they are simply the measurement of habit or the patterns carried into this moment from the past. Whether our consciousness tends to work by repeating habits from the past or whether the universe itself has this tendency—or both—it is also true (so says Nirvana Quartz) that there is great freedom in the possibilities of what can be. Our heart generates fields of its own currents, extending out from its center into engagement with the world. It is not hindered in its perceptive capacity by the shell of mental thinking characteristic of the brain. Therefore, the heart can feel the unfolding patterns of the future coming.

The heart also is an organ of harmonious awareness, which chooses again and again to act for the well-being of the whole. This may be because the heart is an aspect or microcosm of the whole, and it displays its nature by acting for well-being. It may be also that this is the longing of the Divine in us for universal well-being, which we feel as if it were our own longing.

In human beings, mental activity of the mind/brain has, for thousands of years, dominated our awareness and governed our choices and actions, in ways mostly disconnected from the heart's intelligence and longing. Nirvana Quartz speaks to us of the need for a New Consciousness, which is one of unity of mind and heart. What is called for in us now is a loving communion of heart/mind and an ever increasing integration of their intelligences, such that we reach the state within which heart and mind are so entwined in mutual loving accord that our entire being acts, thinks and feels within a unified and vastly expanded consciousness. The experience of meditation with Nirvana Quartz, placing one crystal at the heart and one at the third eye, is one of powerful resonance—not only between these two points but throughout the entire corridor in the body extending from heart to brain. Nirvana Quartz can stimulate and awaken this vital channel. The experience of this structure's activation is a highly pleasurable feeling, and one can accentuate it by consciously willing an intensification of the current. This is done by focusing attention on the "corridor" within the body and attempting to feel the flow of currents in as much detail as possible. Further, one may, in a feeling sense, "send a smile" from the brain down this corridor to the heart. The inner smile is an actively appreciative feeling. When the heart receives this feeling, it experiences an immediate joyful upwelling, of which the brain can be almost instantly aware. Then, when one's brain/mind recognizes the heart's response, it can and is often inspired to respond with a greater smile. The heart will answer that with a greater joy, and in this way we create a circulation of blessing between heart and mind. When this activity becomes continuous and need not even be willed, we are experiencing the New Consciousness—the unity to which we are called.

[In my tape-recorded session, I paused at this point in the description because as I spoke of it, I was also doing this brain/heart circulation of blessing and appreciation, and it brought such a feeling of reverence and unbridled happiness to my consciousness that it was difficult to go on speaking.]

There is, in many esoteric traditions, something called the "Beloved of the Soul." This being is experienced as a separate consciousness from one's usual thinking self, and it appears to dwell in the heart. The Beloved may indeed be another name for the intelligence, love and consciousness that exist in the center of our heart. This intelligence may or may not be the heart itself, but it expresses through the heart.

Nirvana Quartz suggests that one's heart—the dwelling place of the Beloved of the Soul—is a holographic point through which the Divine consciousness is reflected and is present in us. In our preoccupation with the surface of life and our bondage to materialism, the Beloved consciousness of the heart is forgotten, except at peak times of feeling intensity in which it manages to well up and surprise us. "The Meeting with the Beloved," as it is called in some esoteric teachings, may be the joining of the heart's consciousness with our everyday thinking selves. This is an ecstatic reunion, prized above all things by mystics and spiritual poets throughout the ages.

Nirvana Quartz, with its focus on this awakening—on this unfolding resonance between heart and mind, or heart and brain—carries the potential of one of the greatest gifts possible for us to receive. Yet this gift is not simply to be enjoyed—it is to be lived, expressed and brought forward as our very being, as the center from which our choices and actions come forth.

With its attunement to the future time stream, Nirvana Quartz helps us to move into our destiny as co-creative beings. I am cautioned to mention that we do not alone create our reality. Our reality comes to us as possibility, as potential. I think the metaphor of the dance may be helpful here. (It is the image that arises as I inwardly ask of Nirvana Quartz what is the best thing to say.) If we are engaged in a co-creating dance with the Soul of the World—with the Unknown coming-to-be—we might say that our Partner gives us cues or gestural suggestions, and we respond with our own harmonious creative flourishes, as we would when dancing with a human partner. It is also the case that we, through our intention, vision, imagination and will, make our suggestions to our Partner, to which She responds. She seldom, if ever, answers us with exactly what we imagined, but often with a recognizable agreement with our intention, which is enhanced by Her creative flourish. When we allow ourselves to fully embrace it, this dance continues and blooms in a mutually reinforcing way, and many truly amazing and wonderful things come to pass.

Becoming a full partner in the co-creative dance of being is a calling far beyond anything we have yet embraced. It asks us to become whole, immeasurably greater than we have ever been. Yet whatever effort we must make is rewarded by a precious opportunity for joyous, even ecstatic rapture as we come fully into this new partnership consciousness and activity.

Though I did not coin the term Nirvana Quartz, I think it is aptly named, because its gesture invites us first into the development of our wholeness and then into ecstatic engagement with the World Soul, in the activity of the co-creative dance I attempted to describe. If this potential is realized, we will indeed experience all that the traditions tell us Nirvana has ever been, and my insight says we will possess an abundance of joy beyond our current ability to imagine. This Nirvana will not be a departure out of the world to some heaven but will in fact be the descent of heaven to Earth.

NIRVANA QUARTZ SPEAKS "We have abided in waiting through more centuries than you can remember. It is our joy to come forward and reach out to you with our open hands. We do not compel anything, yet we offer what we have. If you accept our aid and partnership, this is the very fulfillment we desire."

NUUMMITE

KEY WORDS Personal magic, the deep journey to the core of self, enhancing clairvoyance, attuning to the elemental forces, achieving self-mastery, shamanic journeying

ELEMENTS Earth, Storm

CHAKRAS Third Eye (6th), Solar Plexus (3rd), Root (1st)

Nuummite is a unique combination of Anthophyllite, a magnesium iron silicate, and Gedrite, a lithium-bearing amphibole. Its crystal system is monoclinic. The hardness of Nuummite is about 6. Found primarily in Greenland, this type of stone is very ancient—about three billion years old. It is characterized by closely intergrown crystals that display flashes of iridescent color. The base color of Nuummite is charcoal gray to black, and its labradorescent shades include red, orange, gold, yellow, green, blue and violet. The most common reflected color is gold. Nuummite is mined in a remote area of Greenland and can be extracted only during the warm months. Although it is difficult to find and must be cut with care to display the color, Nuummite has become quite popular as a metaphysical talisman and gemstone.

BACKGROUND Nuummites draw upon the fiery energies of the Earth's core, and they offer us the gift of inner power. They can facilitate journeys into the depths of the psyche. Nuummite can aid in releasing energies trapped in the subconscious—parts of the self that may have been lost to fear, trauma, guilt or shame. It can help one recall and release fixated energies from childhood, birth or even past lives. It is a solid ally that reinforces one's courage and determination to do whatever inner work is necessary to be healed and whole.

Nuummite may be used as a gazing stone, helping one move into altered states of consciousness. It can enhance clairvoyance and intuition. It can help one learn the language of the body and channel healing energies for oneself and others. It can assist in attuning to the elemental forces of the Earth, so one may call upon them in times of need. It is a stone of personal magic that can increase the frequency of synchronicities and "good luck" in life. Nuummite facilitates efforts to transform ungrounded fantasy into magical reality. Nuummite can be a powerful meditation stone, opening the inner doors of self-discovery. As a gifting stone, it signifies deep love, for it symbolizes the gift of sovereignty.

Nuummite harmonizes with Azeztulite (for bringing more Light into dark inner journeys), Moldavite (for evolutionary transformation), Libyan Gold Tektite (for manifestation), Seraphinite (for healing), Master Shamanite (for Shamanic Journeying) and with Tibetan Black Quartz (when spiritual protection is needed). Other stones that work synergistically with Nuummite include Phenacite, Scolecite and Natrolite.

NEW ATTUNEMENT   As I began to meditate with Nuummite, I was made aware of the suggestion to work in the mode of a shamanic journey. Nuummite's nature is that of a shamanic stone, a facilitator for journeying into the Other World. This realm is usually entered through an immersion in inner

and outer darkness. It is not to be confused with anything negative or evil. The shamanic nature of Nuummite is first and foremost that of a protector which guides and keeps us safe in our interior journeys.

As my journey began, I experienced a stream of images in an interior narrative. I found myself in a sort of cave of bushes, and in this cave there was a hole at the far end that went down into the Earth. I entered the hole feet-first and began pulling my way down into the darkness of the Earth. The next image that arose was of entering a dark underground room, out of which a number of small caves led in different directions. One doorway appeared to be light-filled, and I thought first to go in that direction. But I was told inwardly, "This simply leads back out," and that the inquiry I wanted to make meant going through a different doorway. I turned slightly to my left and entered a small cave that went on for a long distance. As I walked through this cave, there were various side tunnels going off to the left and right. In these tunnels I saw and sensed a number of beings. Some of them had the forms of animals. Others appeared as elders, teachers, shamans. I was instructed that Nuummite offers one access to the realms where these beings will work with us.

My journey continued, and after some distance the cave in which I traveled climbed upward, and a hole in the ceiling appeared. I looked up and saw starlight above the hole, and I crawled out onto the ground. I emerged into a green lawn or meadow. The most prominent nearby feature was a very large, green, leafy oak tree. I approached the tree and sat down beneath it to await the impulse for my next move. I asked inwardly for the being of Nuummite to approach and speak to me of its capacities—of its nature, of its gift or offering, and of our potential in working together.

Soon a man appeared in front of me. He seemed to be a shamanic figure, wearing a hat made of fur with protruding horns on each side. I asked if he was the spirit of Nuummite, and he nodded once. I asked him to show me his nature. I watched as he seemed to dissolve, from a figure of a human being into a shadow, standing diffuse, like a blackish fog before my eyes. He reappeared in the human form then again assumed the shape of dark mist, repeating this two or three times. I felt I was being shown that Nuummite offers itself as a teacher of shape-shifting.

This shape-shifting is to be understood as a mode of communication and intuitive understanding that employs various image-forms, each of which conveys its own net of meanings and associations. Thus the human figure with the hat of fur and horns carried a set of associations with shamanic work and that type of inner power. The shift to the dark fog was a way of

237

showing that there is fluidity in Nuummite's capacity to bring forth such images.

A few moments later, the shamanic figure returned riding a horse, and I was invited to climb on behind him. I did so, and within a few moments of galloping the horse went upward into the air and flew—still running—into the night sky. I was aware of a pink-ish sparkling trail left behind, appearing just beneath the horse's hooves as we ran onward and upward. Upon reaching a certain level in the atmosphere, we stopped and turned back to look down upon the Earth. The pink trail we had followed had widened to a sheet of shifting light, commingled with green and other many-colored light patterns. I recognized it as the *aurora borealis*—the Northern Lights—and I realized this phenomenon appears very much like the reflected light of Nuummite's iridescent patterns.

The shaman said of the Earth, "The *aurora* is her Gown of Light. I brought you here to see her beauty and to let you feel in your heart what is there." At that moment, I did sense the love I hold for the Earth, and the intensity of the affection I experienced came as a shock. With it was a sense of urgency in regard to caring for the Earth's living soul—an urgency to help heal the Earth's soul, or to somehow give life to her. I was drawn back to her with a deep sense of longing.

We then turned, as the guide urged the horse on- ward, and soon we were running—down, down into the sea, still in the time of night. We rode down under the water. In the sea there were more beings. They appeared like the amorphous shapes of dreams, or those one sees on the threshold of sleep, where fantastic patterns and lights can arise. These beings seemed curious, but they did not address me. They only watched. As we went deeper, I recognized two or three people whom I knew to have died. I understood that the Nuummite being was showing me its capacity to act as a facilitator for journeying to the realm of those who have died. I sensed that Nuummite can help us do whatever work or make whatever ges-tures are needed to effect reconciliation or healing for those who have passed, and often for oneself. Nuummite said, in its image-gesture, that it is a guide into the realm within which the souls of those who have died can meet us. This is an important gift, for it is generally difficult for us to establish a conscious connection with those who have passed. Nuummite says through its gesture that our souls may be incomplete or stuck around issues that exist in relation to those who have died. It can help both the deceased and the living to inwardly journey to their realm for the purpose of healing relationships and reclaiming lost parts of ourselves. (These soul parts are often attached to those unreconciled concerns.) Also, Nuummite opens the door for us to be of service to those who have died by joining them in their realm and bringing our love and appreciation to any beings there with whom we have a natural resonance.

After this, the horse rode up and out of the sea to a clearing where a campfire or bonfire was burning. I found myself climbing off the horse and, in a way—though not an artful way—danc-ing my way into the fire. The image of myself stepping into the flames and rhythmically bounc-ing or dancing in the great gold-red fire was exceedingly vivid. I noticed the fire moving up the length of my body, turning me momentarily into a Being of Fire in human form. The form began to merge more completely with the fire, and my point of view moved within the fire itself. Nuummite's gesture of the fire seems to indicate that it can bring us inwardly to an activity of purification within which our old form—our pattern or habit of superficial selfhood—is burned away. I noticed as the vision continued that the flames suddenly ceased, leaving charred embers on the ground.

Within the ashes of the fire there was an egg, bluish green and perhaps twice as large as a hen's egg. It seemed to have a lid or rim about two thirds of the way from the bottom, and as

I watched it opened. A small radiance of light appeared—itself in the blue-green spectrum—perhaps only an inch or so in diameter. It rose, rather like an insect, flying gradually up from the opened egg. This light moved toward what I recognized as the great oak tree I had seen upon emerging from the cave. The light came to rest on the bark of the oak. It moved inside the tree at about eye-level height. I watched the tree as the little radiant light entered its interior. The tree itself began to glow from within, and this radiance was of the same pastel bluish-green light. I saw the entire tree begin to fill with this radiant light. Its branches, like great arms held aloft, glowed, as did the entire trunk—radiating the light in a kind of pulsing way. I did not initially have any idea what this image could mean. A bit later, my first thought was that the egg and the emerging light symbolized some kind of rebirth into which Nuummite could lead us.

As I continued to watch this image of the glowing tree, a kind of a green-blue flame arose out of the core of the tree, far up beyond its highest branches. It took the form of a radiant, beautiful woman. I instantly recognized this as an image of Sophia, the World Soul, rekindled into form through the entire process of my journey. Perhaps my image of dancing in the flames was symbolic of giving oneself to the fire of destruction of one's old idea of self—the habitual pattern of self—letting go into whatever might come. This willingness to die to one's habitual ways encompasses a release of the idea of control, and a deep resolve to give oneself to the living fire of transformation. I feel that the rebirth as the little radiant light that flies like an insect to the great World Tree is an image of each of us as a spark of soul, offering oneself to the great Tree—into the Heart of the Earth. The kindling of the blue-green radiance within the entire tree signifies how one's seemingly small gift of self to the Soul of the World is the spark that ignites her life. When our little light enters her oaken heart, we bring her miraculously to the fullness of her life.

When I looked again at the oak from my new perspective, somewhere high in the glowing tree the shaman on his horse bowed his head and then looked back at me, beckoning. In the next moment the tree reached a branch toward me and touched my heart as I stood on the ground. I was once again in the shape of a man, standing beside the horse and shamanic figure. The touch of the branch at my heart infused my chest with the blue-green light. At that moment I felt a great effervescence of joy. I tearfully mounted the shaman's horse and sat behind him. He spoke a word and off we galloped, back to a cave opening. We rode down under the Earth, back to the room through which I had entered the Underworld. I found the doorway to the small passage leading to the enclosure of bushes, and I went back through it, up to where I had begun. I looked down, seeing a Nuummite pendant with blue-green iridescence and the other colors of the *aurora borealis* lying upon my chest. The journey was complete.

NUUMMITE SPEAKS   "I am ancient, yet I am new. I offer you a journey into all that dwells within you, and into what lives in the deep places of the world. There you may become what is whole and true. There you may offer your life to Her."

PETALITE

KEY WORDS Tranquility, uplifting, expansion of awareness, manifesting the spiritual in the physical, opening to the higher worlds
ELEMENT Wind
CHAKRAS Third Eye (6th), Crown (7th), Transpersonal (8th through 14th)

Petalite is lithium sodium aluminum silicate with a hardness of 6 to 6.5. Its crystal system is monoclinic. It crystallizes relatively rarely and most often occurs as large, cleavable masses. Its color can be white, colorless, gray, pinkish or yellow. Color-less pieces can be faceted into exceptionally sparkling gems. Some can be cabbed into cats-eyes. Petalite forms in granite pegmatites and is often associated with other lithium-bearing minerals such as Amblygonite, Kunzite, Spodumene and Lepidolite. Petalite is found in Australia, Brazil, Sweden, Namibia and Afghanistan.

BACKGROUND Petalites have a deep connection to the realm of Spirit. They can take one to a dimension of rest and healing, a space in which the worries and concerns of this world are released. Petalites are also stones of vision. Like Phenacite, they can open the inner eye to the many mansions of the higher dimensions, allowing the questing mind to discover multiple new horizons. Petalite can be used to enhance all the psychic powers, such as clairvoyance and telepathy, and to help one attune to the knowledge of one's *dharma, or path of highest destiny.*

Petalite has a grounding aspect that helps one stay connected to earthly life while exploring the inner dimensions that this stone opens. Thus it is also a stone of manifestation, helping bring to physical reality the exalted visions one finds as one journeys to the higher worlds. The simplest use of Petalite is to place a stone upon the third eye during meditation. Although Petalite can be used for inner exploration, its most effortless application is in the quieting of thought and the elevation of awareness to the quiet spaces of the mansions of Light.

Petalite is one of the Synergy Twelve stones, also including Moldavite, Phenacite, Danburite, Azeztulite, Herderite, Brookite, Tanzanite, Satyaloka Azeztulite, Natrolite, Scolecite and Tibetan Tektite. Petalite can also be combined with Merkabite Calcite, Nirvana Quartz or Magnesite for interdimensional exploration. Rosophia, Pink Azeztulite, Ajoite, Lepidolite and/or Morganite can be used with Petalite to further enhance its energies of peace, joy and tranquility. Its loving qualities are most strongly amplified when Petalite is combined with Rosophia.

NEW ATTUNEMENT Petalite is a stone of profound peace and tranquility. Meditating with Petalite, I began with one stone over the heart and another at my crown. The immediate resonance of Petalite was in the crown chakra area, and it softly yet powerfully emanated currents that quieted the mental processes, leading me into a state of deep, peaceful, silent meditative contemplation.

I have written elsewhere that Petalite can facilitate the opportunity for the soul and the individual self to rest and be rejuvenated and restored to calm well-being in the great Light mansions of Spirit. The vision that accompanied this meditation with Petalite was one of a great white-pillared temple, with ceilings perhaps forty or fifty feet high, marble floors and a crystal bathing pool. One is led to the pool, not by people but by beams of Light that move toward the glowing, sparkling, Light-filled water. One sits in this pool of liquid Light and is gently bathed in a flowing current of healing and restoration. It is greatly pleasurable and deeply peaceful to allow oneself to inwardly experience this.

Petalite is a stone of the deepest peace. It can take one to the eye of the circulating winds of existence, where the currents are calm and one is cradled in the arms of gentle, loving Light. Petalite's energy is feminine in tone and engenders images of the Great Mother. Yet it has a masculine side as well, which is imaged as the Great Father. Both of these beings appear to the mind's eye as ancient and immensely glorious. In the realm to which one is conducted by Petalite, the Great Father appears as a being with long, flowing white hair and beard. Turning toward the Great Mother, I saw a vision of a priestess in radiant white raiment that looked (surprisingly) like fish scales, and with wings almost like fins seeming to emanate from where her arms would be. Her face was luminous, with clear blue eyes that looked like the sea. The masculine entity appeared to reside among clouds, while the feminine being was of the sea. I inferred from these images that Petalite is a stone of the Air and Water elements. Clearly it gestures to us with great love and gentleness, and its offer of restoration.

Petalite stimulates the image-making capacities of heart intelligence and encourages the mental intelligence to widen itself so that it is no longer under the influence of dualism and polarities. The peace emanated by Petalite is one of inclusion—screening out no being or circumstance from its calm acceptance.

Petalite is a stone of the activity of forgiving. This is resonant with its tendency to widen the perspectives of thought beyond dualism. In the light of Petalite's expansion of awareness, the idea of judgment falls away. In its place, one is inspired to make the gesture of opening one's heart to take in each being and each event of life. To judge is a way of saying "no" or "wrong" to a person, event or moment. Petalite's gentle acceptance of all is the quintessential "yes."

Petalite forgives without even considering any other possibility. Forgiving is Petalite's way of being, and when we resonate with this beautiful quality, it brings peace to the heart. Petalite is one of the Ascension Seven stones, and it opens the upper chakras to receive spiritual Light. It stimulates the entire Liquid Crystal Body Matrix to higher frequencies of activity and Light consciousness. It will work beautifully with other high-vibration stones and will bring one into a state of profound calm, even in the midst of rapid transformation and awakening.

Petalite's emanation of peace creates a very subtle grounding effect. Compared to stones of denser energies, which ground one firmly in the body, Petalite's grounding influence is more like a tether on a balloon or the string on a kite. With Petalite one may fly high, but one will not lose connection with the body or the Earth.

PETALITE SPEAKS   "Were you to see me in my spiritual form, you might recognize me as an angel. For although angels exist in a multiplicity of expressions—many of which you do not imagine—I appear much as you might picture me, in my raiment of white. My devotion is to the Love-Light of the Divine realm, and to the healing of soul and spirit. Those who are broken in heart or filled with tension will find a healing balm in me."

PHENACITE

KEY WORDS Third-eye activation, inner visions, awakening the Light Body, interdimensional travel

ELEMENT Storm

CHAKRAS Third Eye (6th), Crown (7th)

Phenacite is a beryllium silicate with a hardness of 7.5 to 8. It is a rare mineral, especially in well-formed crystals with transparency. Its crystal system is hexagonal (trigonal), and it often crystallizes in short prisms. However, Phenacite varies greatly in form from one location to another. In fact, its name is derived from the Greek word meaning "deceiver." This is because Phenacite's growth patterns are so diverse that it is easily mistaken for other types of crystal such as Quartz, Topaz or even Tourmaline. Phenacite has been found in Brazil, Sri Lanka, Mada-gascar, Mexico, Zimbabwe, Zambia, Norway, Russia, Tanzania, Switzerland and the U.S.

BACKGROUND Phenacite is truly the supreme stone of the third eye chakra. Its pulsing energies are so strong that they can be felt at the third eye, even by many people not normally sensitive to crystal energies. It opens the interdimensional portals for inner journeying, allowing one's consciousness to plunge through unending corridors of sacred geometric forms. The stimulation of the third eye offered by Phenacite is stronger than one receives from virtually any other stone. It can also be used to awaken the latent special capacities housed in the prefrontal lobes, the newest and most advanced parts of the brain. This can sometimes bring spontaneous experiences of telepathy, psychokinesis, prophetic vision or remote viewing. Sitting in meditation with one Phenacite on the forehead and another on the crown can link these two chakras, providing the user with a profoundly pleasurable sensation of their joined energies.

Phenacite's link with the higher realms makes it a powerful tool for manifestation of inner images or patterns of intention in the outer world. For bringing prosperity and financial abundance, combining Phenacite with Yellow Sapphire and/or Cinnabar Quartz is highly recommended. For assistance with creative projects, pairing Phenacite with Rosophia is excellent. For enhancing one's ability to manifest through the will, Phenacite should be combined with Libyan Gold Tektite and/or Sunset Gold Selenite.

Phenacite is one of the Synergy Twelve Stones, along with Moldavite, Petalite, Danburite, Azeztulite, Herderite, Brookite, Tanzanite, Satyaloka Azeztulite, Natrolite, Scolecite and Tibetan Tektite. Phenacite also harmonizes with Merkabite Calcite, Nirvana Quartz, Magnesite, Lithium Quartz, Himalaya Gold Azeztulite, Golden Azeztulite Crystals and other high-vibration stones for activation of the upper chakras of the body and the etheric chakras beyond the body.

NEW ATTUNEMENT As I prepared to attune to Phenacite for this meditation, I held several pieces in my hand. I was reminded immediately of my long-standing sense that Phenacite is one of the highest-frequency stones in the entire mineral kingdom, and that it is the most powerful stone for stimulation of the mind centers. I have used it, primarily at the third eye, for opening that chakra and initiating inner visionary experiences. In many cases, the currents of Phenacite—experienced as a rapid pulsing coming in through the entry point at the third eye—are powerful enough to move into the interior of the skull and up through the crown chakra, thereby unifying both energy points in a single interior motion or flow.

Phenacite clearly and powerfully stimulates the third eye. The felt sense that I have had for many years is of instantaneous rhythmic pulsations, which, unlike those of other stones, increase in frequency and intensity, as though building up a charge in the areas they affect. Another quality of Phenacite that distinguishes it—and in some ways sets it beyond most other stones of the third eye and crown—is that its pulsating frequencies go completely through the skull and resonate at the energy point or chakra sometimes called the Mouth of God, a point at the back of the head where the base of the skull meets the spine. This is a powerful gate of kundalini awakening.

When I was eighteen years old, I had a spontaneous mystical experience—without benefit of stones, drugs or spiritual disciplines. The culminating moment of this experience happened when a kind of explosion of Light occurred at the Mouth of God point in the back of my head, filling my skull with pure White Light and flooding my consciousness with a sense of ecstatic bliss. I experienced an awareness of wisdom and an infusion of utter love throughout my being. In meditating with Phenacite, I often feel powerful echoes of this *samadhi* experience. When I place one Phenacite crystal at the third eye and another at the back of the skull, the pulsations with which I so familiar resonate through the entire skull, from the third eye to the Mouth of God point. This pulsation then reverberates forward to the third eye and crown in a kind of fan-like shape, with an increasingly rapid current.

If one persists long enough in meditative attention, Phenacite's pulsations become Light vibrations, centered within the skull. The color of this Light is white, and the feeling I sense is that this is the same sort of Light I recall from my first powerful experience at eighteen. It is of a lesser intensity than it was in my full-blown mystic awakening. However, it is like hearing familiar music played softly, akin to the similarity between the calm surf of a lovely shoreline and the power of a tidal wave. Although the everyday surf is calmer, its motion is similar to the motion of the tidal wave, and it is governed and expressed through similar forces and patterns. One who has felt the spiritual tidal wave will recognize its seed pattern in the surf. This is how I relate the Light-generating properties of Phenacite to the powerful, explosive nature of *samadhi*. My sense is that those who wish to make themselves available to the spiritual Light of the Divine will find a helpful ally in Phenacite. By using Phenacite, one increases connectedness with this Divine Light, through one's consciousness and body both.

As I speak of light, I am reminded that even everyday light in our experience is generated from within the brain/mind through mysterious processes. The neural activity that has been observed and reported may not fully explain these processes. Science tells us that it is not actual light that enters our brain through our eyes. Rather, neural impulses occur in response to stimulation by the phenomenon described as light in the so-called exterior world. Those impulses in the brain are transmuted or somehow organized into what we envision and name as light. Therefore, it may not be surprising that light would possibly be generated within the consciousness by means other than physical sensory input. Currents such as those available to us through Phenacite may directly stimulate the light-forming processes of the brain/mind, without passing through the eyes and optic structures. Certainly the felt experience of working meditatively with Phenacite is frequently one of seeing lights and patterns of light within consciousness. These patterns often display themselves as geometries of light—corridors of light-geometry through which one may travel in a sort of heavenly shamanic journey. The corridors of light, which are a familiar phenomenon of meditative work with Phenacite, are delightful to discover and enjoyable to travel. One may inwardly visit distant dimensions

243

and even other physical locations. The felt sense I have is that such activities as remote viewing, clairvoyant vision and intuitively sensing far-away situations are all enhanced by the stimulation of consciousness provided through Phenacite.

The other important dimension of the light geometries offered to consciousness via Phenacite is that of intuitive recognition and appreciation of archetypal patterns. By archetypal patterns, I mean the form or formal manifestations of consciousness, matter, energy and the dynamic tensions among them. There are recurring patterns pervading the natural world, including Fibonacci spirals, the Platonic solids and the many elegant harmonies expressed through mathematics and music. In addition, there are a number of powerful psychological archetypes. Yet we can also experience a felt sense of the harmonic underpinnings of being through pure contemplation. In my deepest meditative work with Phenacite, I have at times seen such unfolding patterns and received insights about the multiple echoes of these patterns through all levels of being.

For healing purposes, Phenacite offers its best application in the realm of neurological healing. It is excellent for stimulating the brain/mind and nervous system into their highest capacities. My felt sense is that Phenacite can help increase the focus and power of one's intention and attention, expanding consciousness to awaken previously unknown capacities. It is a cliché to say that we use only a fraction of the potential of our brain/mind, yet it is undoubtedly true. We have a difficult time finding out that we even *have* unused capacities, since our ignorance of them makes them nearly invisible. Sometimes occurrences in meditative experience (and outer life) can spontaneously open up these capacities. It is then one's opportunity to follow the thread of potential from this opening into the development of the new capacities. Phenacite cannot do the work for us, yet it can help us—when we join with it in inner exploration—to get some electrifying glimpses of what is possible.

PHENACITE SPEAKS   "I move within you at the speed of light, for within you, I am Light. I offer an invitation into greater Light, if you will ask the Light to fill you."

PROPHECY STONE

KEY WORDS   Grounding spiritual Light in the physical self and the world, seeing prophetic visions

ELEMENT   Earth

CHAKRAS   Soul Star (8th), Crown (7th), Third Eye (6th), Earth Star (below the feet)

Prophecy Stone is a rare and odd stone found in the desert of Libya. It appears to be a concretion or a pseudomorph, though it displays a color and outer texture that is reminiscent of Meteorite. (Incidentally, it comes from the same area where Libyan Gold Tektites and some types of Meteorite are found.) Its chemical makeup is not known, though oxidation on some specimens indicates the presence of iron. The man who discovered Prophecy Stones gave them this name because he experienced what he termed "a prophetic vision" while meditating with one of them.

BACKGROUND   Prophecy Stones are perhaps the most powerful of all minerals for grounding Light energy in the physical body. When one holds or meditates with one of these stones, a powerful current comes in through the crown chakra, filling the body all the way down to the soles of the feet. After a few minutes, the energy moves even deeper, stimulating the Earth Star chakra below the feet, anchoring in the Earth. This experience is common to many individuals who work with Prophecy Stone, and many people are amazed at the strength of the vibrations that move through them when they hold these stones.

True to its name, Prophecy Stone can catalyze visions of probable futures. To experience these, one must usually work with Prophecy Stone regularly in meditation for some weeks, although highly sensitive individuals may receive the visions much sooner. Often the initial experiences are fragmentary, and one may not be certain of the time frame to which they refer.

Prophecy Stone harmonizes especially well with Moldavite, which can bring through an even greater amount of Light energy. Its visionary capacities are further enhanced by combining them with Shaman Stones and/or Phenacite. Its ability to "ground the Light" is strengthened by pairing it with Hematite. Herkimer "Diamonds" and Phenacite can increase the vividness of the inner visions. Prophecy Stone can be helpful to those working with all forms of Azeztulite, because of its capacity to effectively ground high-vibration currents such as those of the Nameless Light.

NEW ATTUNEMENT   My meditation with Prophecy Stone began with placing a piece of it over my heart, plus one in each hand and one on my crown. I experienced a strong tingling current at each location; and through each of these places, especially the crown chakra, I felt spiritual vibrations grounding into the body.

With Prophecy Stone, the energy currents feel different than they do with typical high-vibration stones. Such stones may bring energy into the body, and they make one feel that one's awareness has shifted "upward" to the spiritual frequencies. With Prophecy Stone, my felt sense is that the spiritual frequencies are stepped down—they are able to permeate the physical body. This is a most excellent thing, because we must, I believe, embody and incarnate the spiritual worlds. This is part of the destiny of humanity as revealed in the awakening of the New Consciousness.

Prophecy Stone's way of grounding high-vibration energies in the body provides a very clear and positive sensation. It facilitates an infusion of high-frequency currents in a way that the cells and tissues can receive and accept. This is its primary gift—the transmutation of frequencies too high for one's physical embodiment into resonant frequencies that the body can receive and benefit from.

Prophecy Stone is a bridge stone that offers us a way of crossing the gap between the material and spiritual worlds, so that certain spiritual qualities may enter fully into incarnation.

Prophecy Stone is excellent for cleansing the etheric and astral bodies. I felt the clearing and release of attachments—and of little toxic negativities which were in my etheric body—as I held and meditated with Prophecy Stone. In this cleansing process, Prophecy Stone initially prepares the physical body to take on a higher frequency of positive spiritual energies. Next it funnels these energies in through whatever part of the body is in contact with Prophecy Stone. The activity of Prophecy Stone's currents in the body is one of cleansing and rejuvenation, reinvigoration and eventual transfiguration of the physical self. This is critical, because in human life the gap between our spiritual awareness—even that which we have developed up to this point—and our physical lives seems impassable. Because of this, there even seems to be contradiction between our spiritual vision and our so-called real lives. Prophecy Stone can serve our evolution by making possible a bridging by which the integration of the spiritual worlds and the physical world can unfold through us.

The visionary experiences that have given Prophecy Stone its name are connected to this bridging of the worlds. It requires more time for most people to attain these visions than to experience Prophecy Stone's beneficial grounding qualities. When I initially worked with Prophecy Stone, I did experience one such vision. The man who does most of the mining of Prophecy Stone also experienced a powerful and true prophetic vision on the first night that he slept with one of the stones. (After that, he started calling them Prophecy Stones!) In working more long-term with Prophecy Stone, I have found that visions of the future stream, at first fleeting and hard to understand, have come to me several times.

More recently, Prophecy Stone has taken me to what I call the Seat of Seeing. This, in my vision, was imaged as a stone chair on the top of a mountain. Now when I work with Prophecy Stone for visionary experience of the future, I imagine myself in this mountain seat. If I imaginally choose to sit down in the Seat of Seeing, I can then turn attention, while holding Prophecy Stones in my meditative state, to any area of life. My usual question is "What is the most beneficial thing for me to see regarding x, y or z?" Then I wait, looking out from the Seat of Seeing until something draws my attention. Often scenes that hold symbolic images relevant to my question will appear to me.

I find that it is best to give careful attention to the essential *feeling* quality of what comes when working with Prophecy Stone in this way. One may sense how the person or situation feels in the future but not see the specific circumstances. This makes sense to me, because I believe the future is only partially created and exists, from our standpoint now, as probability. The momentum of many streams of probability coalesces into a kind of fuzzy picture of the future. Prophecy Stone helps bring these streams into coherent focus in regard to one's question, and the clearest quality of that picture is the feeling quality. This may be because the heart is strong in the realm of feeling, and it is also the heart that is most in touch with the future.

One may make educated guesses about a situation when one has experienced the feeling quality of it, yet I feel it is unwise to draw precise conclusions from these visions, because the future is not yet condensed into actuality. This all has something in common with the idea we know from quantum physics—the wave of quantum potential. This is science's term for what I have been calling in these pages the future time stream. The wave of quantum potential is a probability wave, showing the odds or tendencies for reality to appear in certain ways. (For example, light can appear to manifest as a wave, a particle or even both at once.) The fact that these are probabilities rather than absolutes shows us that even the physical world is open to spontaneous maverick occurrences. When one makes an observation of the event, the event is coalesced and concretized into an experience. The activity of the coalescing of potential into actuality is the activity of creating.

Our joint creating with Sophia, the Soul of the World, occurs moment by moment in the coalescing wave. Sophia herself has been described as the evanescent flow of Wisdom, beauty and harmony in the world, though she herself is not to be found in any thing or event. She is the creating activity giving rise to the world in each moment. This is a fair description of the instant in which the wave of quantum potential coalesces into an event. That coalescence (called the collapse of the quantum wave) does not occur in a moment or location in space/time that can

be captured or pinned down as a law or prediction, and it is *always* happening. And like the collapsing quantum wave, Sophia can never be captured in space/time. Of special note is the fact that in both cases, we ourselves are involved in the creating process. Both Sophia and the quantum wave need a participant observer for anything to come out of potential and into being.

Prophecy Stone's grounding qualities are helpful to us as co-creators, because they facilitate our capacity to bring the currents of potential from the spiritual worlds into manifestation here. They help us "collapse the wave" and ground what might be into what is. Prophecy Stone's visionary qualities sometimes reveal to us the coming potentials of the future stream. One of these potentials is the awakening of the Body of Light. As we become more adept at attuning to the high frequencies of the spiritual realms, and at grounding these currents into our bodies and the Earth, more of the inner Light will fill our Liquid Crystal Body Matrix. Through Prophecy Stone, we may see our potential for truly becoming Beings of Light, and through its grounded resonance with the higher realms, we may actualize it.

PROPHECY STONE SPEAKS "I am a lightning rod for what can be. I am the bridger of worlds. I am strong and strengthening. I am deep in matter, and many rays of Spirit pour into me and through me. I will help, when asked, to make the Light Body become a living substance in the material world."

ROSOPHIA

KEY WORDS The Love of Sophia, awakening of Heart Awareness, co-creating with the Divine, alchemical transmutation of self and world

ELEMENT Earth

CHAKRA Heart (4th)

Rosophia is a newly discovered gemstone from the Rocky Mountains of the U.S. The stone is a mixture of reddish Feldspar, clear or white Quartz and black Biotite. The Quartz component of Rosophia has a trigonal (hexagonal) crystal system and a hardness of 7. The Feldspar component has a monoclinic crystal system and a hardness of 5 to 6. The name Rosophia is derived from the phrase "Rose of Sophia," meaning the "Heart of Wisdom." This name was chosen because of the stones' readily perceived heart currents, and the intuition that the stone carries the qualities and presence of Sophia, Soul of the World.

BACKGROUND In August of 2008, my wife Kathy and I traveled to Sante Fe, New Mexico, where we were both invited to offer presentations at the Sophia Conference, hosted by the School of Spiritual Psychology. When we were shown into our sleeping accommodations, one of the first things I noticed was a colorful five-inch chunk of stone on a shelf right in front of the door. After putting down our suitcases, I picked up the salmon-pink, white-spotted rock, and I held it up to my chest.

Within moments I could feel sweet, swirling currents pleasantly circulating in and around my heart. The currents felt both strong and gentle, nourishing and inspiring, healing and even playful. I was astonished at experiencing such an immediate and powerful heart connection with this stone. I had never seen such a rock before, and I thought I knew about almost all the world's gemstones and crystals! I passed the stone to Kathy, and she too felt the immediate swirling currents of pleasant energy.

I guessed that the stone that had appeared synchronistically on the shelf of our room at the conference must have been left there by someone who found it near the conference center. The center was situated on a hill with an adjoining canyon, and later that day I set out looking among the nooks and crannies of the arroyo for more of the new stones. After searching in the canyon, I was able to find a couple dozen stones to bring home by the end of the conference. When I arrived back in Vermont, I was eager to show the new "stones of Sophia" (as I had begun to think of them) to my friends and co-workers. Once again, the currents of the heart were

quickly and easily felt by virtually everyone—even people who had never felt a stone before.

I could not forget about these new stones, and I knew I wanted to offer them to all the crystal-lovers who read our catalogs. But there was no way to buy them. If we wanted them, we would have to go back to New Mexico and find them!

Guided by the strong feeling that this new gemstone was an essential piece in the unfolding of both the crystal work and the evolution of heart intelligence guided by Sophia, I set off early for my fall buying trip to Denver, planning to go first to New Mexico to look for more of these "stones of destiny." Justin from our mail-order staff came with me, his own sense of adventure piqued by the stories we had told. We drove for thirty-nine hours straight in order to have some days available for our search.

In the original canyon site, we found a small amount of the stones I was now calling Rosophia (for the Rose of Sophia). I loved the new name, which was inspired by the swirling heart currents the stones emanated—as if a many-petaled rose were opening in one's heart. We searched elsewhere in the area and in other parts of northern New Mexico and Colorado. By the time we headed for home, we had found enough of the salmon-colored stones to offer them in all the forms I hoped to produce—raw, tumbled, spheres, hearts, beads and jewelry. As soon as we returned from our Rocky Mountain journey, we set to work with Rosophia, in both outer and inner ways.

Rosophia is first and foremost a stone of the heart. Its currents quickly and deeply move into and throughout the chest, in and around one's heart, bringing sensations of soothing, calming, loving caresses. Through this stone, it feels as though one is being touched with the loving invisible hands of the Divine Feminine, the Intimate One who is vast enough to fill the world and even the cosmos, and is at the same time fully aware of and cares for each human being. There is a feeling quality engendered by these stones that I can only describe as a delicate yet powerful sweetness. They bring an inner feeling of beauty, a serene sense of centeredness within the heart, a gentle appreciation of each perception and all the beings who make up the world. Holding Rosophia, one softens inwardly with no loss of strength. One sees more truly, because the veils of stress and anxiety are lifted. Compassion is enhanced, because fears have been quieted. The heart-centering engendered by Rosophia encourages one's capacity to meet each moment fresh and free, ready to respond with clarity and creativity.

For self-healing, I recommend Rosophia for almost everything, since this is in essence a stone that draws one into wholeness. It helps one to calm the emotional body, release stress, and dissolve repetitive negative patterns on all levels. It is of special benefit to the heart, and my feeling is that its currents are restorative to the natural, healthy functioning of the heart, both as an organ of the body and as a center of consciousness. For diseases rooted in negative self-image or a fearful attitude toward the world, Rosophia can be a powerful spiritual medicine. The self-affirming qualities of this stone make it an excellent ally in dealing with maladies in which the body turns against itself, as in autoimmune conditions. It feels to me like a stone that can work spiritually to aid in circulation of the blood and perhaps the lymphatic system.

Psycho-spiritually, Rosophia can facilitate the remediation of problems stemming from feelings of low self-worth, fear of the future, mistrust of other people and all kinds of stress-related difficulties. This lovely stone aids in liberating one from negative patterns created by old wounds, in this life or past lives, and it helps with the recall of repressed material, if necessary, in order to release it. It can facilitate insight into the unconscious patterns that lead to similar problems again and again. It encourages a stronger sense of self, based in the heart's truth rather than in egoic pride.

In a more mystical aspect, Rosophia can, I believe, help one awaken to the consciousness present within one's heart. This is its greatest potential gift, because when we meet the self, the "I" residing in our heart, we enter the realm of our wholeness and we have at last found our true home. We realize that our truest self is this heart-dweller, rather than the one we thought we were, and that this heart-dweller knows us in every detail and loves us without any judgment. I feel a resonance between the Rosophia stone and this deeper "I," and I intuit that the stone's heart currents support the growth of a web of ever-stronger and more conscious relationship with this one.

Behind the true Self I have described is the Soul of the World, Sophia. Through deepening into the true Self, we simultaneously reach further into conscious, loving, co-creative partnership with Her. This is, from all I have been learning, our truest destiny, and each step on that path is an entry into joy. Rosophia allows us to touch and be touched by Her.

NEW ATTUNEMENT   All stones on Earth are in some way expressing the qualities of the Soul of the World, even though stones such as Azeztulite seem to carry frequencies that are more attuned to what one might call the Solar Logos, the Divine male energies. Yet even these stones are not without traces of Sophia's harmony and spontaneity of expression. Rosophia seems saturated with the love energies of the Divine Feminine as the Soul of the World. I feel in Rosophia a playfulness as well as this all-nourishing love. The mood with which Rosophia infuses my vibrational field—in addition to the swirling currents of love—is one of a high-spirited playfulness that invites me to wake up and join Her.

I feel that the intimate nourishment which comes though the Rosophia is meant to heal and strengthen the parts of our psyche, energy field and body that have been fragmented or damaged through the many stresses and strains of human life. When we are fully whole and strong once more (or perhaps at last), the Being gesturing through Rosophia seems to say, "Dance with me!" It is certainly my feeling that the Soul of the World wants us as her partners, not only as her children. We are invited into the co-creative dance of the becoming of the world, and for all of her capacity to nourish us, my heart tells me that Sophia must have advocates, defenders and lovers who wish to serve her after having seen who She is. All of these things are available through meditative work with the stone Rosophia.

When one meditates with Rosophia, the first sense is likely to be an infusion of gentle, swirling currents in the area of one's heart, engendering a feeling of receiving love and being gently invited into loving relationship. As attention is focused on these heart currents, one's entire being "curls around the heart," and heart awareness fills one's consciousness. There is a perception not only of one's own known self. but an echo of the "other" self existing in the center of the heart. Rosophia can help us awaken the "I" that dwells in the cave of the heart, and that "I" is our truest self. Many mystic traditions have maintained for untold years that there are two selves within each person. Our culture of superficiality and materialism has all but annihilated our memory of the Other who lives in the heart's core.

Because this being is the spark of Sophia in us, and because Sophia in her essence is love, neither she nor our "I" self will ever force their way into us. Both will wait for us to turn toward them, toward her. When we make the invitation, we must mean it and we must stay attentive and listen, for the heart's voice is a soft voice, especially at the beginning. Only in circumstances of dire need or overwhelming feeling does the heart speak loudly and forcefully within us. This is why it's crucial to develop a dynamic relationship in which one's everyday self turns toward the heart self, which Robert Sardello has called our Perfect Nature. By our doing this, She is encouraged, and our own deepest Self is encouraged to speak to us. Often the messages are not words but images, and these images must be felt. Yet if we give patience and attention to the currents of the heart, a treasure greater than any other we could gain dwells there. Rosophia stone offers, in many ways, this gift that dwells in the center of our heart. Its currents encourage our heart into activity. When the heart awakens and we feel its selfhood, an additional unfolding flows through us the way our blood flows, reaching every part of our being. In this flowing we become the Grail, the holy cup of renewal, and our very bodies hold the nourishing spiritual elixir that can heal the world.

All of these things were spoken as I held the Rosophia to my heart and listened to the words that arose. In her feminine attributes, her resonance with our hearts, and her affinity for Earth, Rosophia is, of all stones, the most resonate with Sophia. Sophia is the one in myth who imbued the universe with the qualities of beauty and wisdom. This occurred through her sacrifice, which caused some of her Divine nature to remain "fallen"—as the gnostics have said—in the material world. In this mythos, which pervades many gnostic teachings and those of other spiritual streams, the descent of the Christ was intended to free Sophia from her bondage to the Earth. Some of these tales say that Sophia chose to remain here, out of her love for the world.

The mythic pattern of Sophia as the feminine, the Soul of the World, and Christ as the embodiment of the heavenly Light, or the Solar Logos, is reflected, rather astonishingly, in the resonance of Rosophia and Azeztulite. As I described, the stone Rosophia emanates qualities like those one might associate with Sophia—dark, intimate, undulating currents which are gentle, comforting, nurturing and loving. Azeztulite displays some of the qualities one could associate with the pattern of Christ—its mode is Light, its energies have "descended" from the Great Central Sun, and its purpose is to fill the world with Light and awaken humanity. There is much more that I could say here, but I only want to sketch this picture. (I do not mean to take any sort of religious position, except to say that I believe the primal mythic patterns manifest again and again, on all levels of reality. Prior myths reflect the patterns of both Christ and Sophia. The leap I am making here is to say that the stones can also reflect these patterns.)

When I first encountered Rosophia, I began wearing two strands of tumbled nuggets—one of Rosophia and one of my other favorite, Azeztulite. After a couple of days, I noticed that I was feeling some amazing and powerful energies while wearing these two stones together. At odd times, even when I was eating dinner or watching a movie, I felt sudden infusions of strong currents pouring down through the top of my head and coming up from below as well. They seemed to be reaching for one another, and they sometimes did link at the heart. I sensed feelings of intense longing between these two streams. When they both entered my heart, I experienced a great sense of joy and fulfillment.

For some years I have noticed the parallels between the story and currents of Azeztulite and the mythos of Christ as the Son of the Sun. (Chapter Ten, "The Tale of the Azez," I present an excerpt from one of the gnostic gospels in which a figure identified as Christ is speaking. He is giving initiation instructions for souls ascending through the spiritual realms, and he appears to mention the Azez [!] as protective spirits who help the ascending soul.) It is clear that the purpose of Azeztulite parallels the mission of Christ—to bring Light to the Earth and teach humanity how to overcome the forces of limitation and death.

Rosophia embodies and emanates the types of currents we associate with Sophia—love, generosity, wisdom, harmony, beauty, tenderness, grief, creativity and courage.

When one holds or wears Rosophia and Azeztulite at the same time, their currents combine in an amazing way. I sense the currents of Azeztulite as the Light reaching down into matter, as the spiritual realms extending themselves in a gesture of love and blessing. I see these currents inwardly as golden Light descending into the body from the crown chakra, pouring Light into and through the Liquid Crystal Body Matrix. Emotionally, Azeztulite feels like utter benevolence and love from the vastness of the luminous Divine.

I feel Rosophia as the feminine counterpart to Azeztulite's rather masculine radiance. Rosophia's currents arise from within matter. They feel dark, nourishing and intimate. Her longing reaches "upward," from matter toward the Light of Spirit. When these two streams meet in the heart, there is an astonishing alchemical transformation. One can feel the two long-separated beings uniting in the vessel we have offered them—the Grail of our heart. I see inwardly that this meeting gives birth to a new spiritual being. It is related to the "I" that we carry in our heart, although it is much greater than I have ever known it to be.

Seeing such visions, and feeling them bodily, inspires devotion to the realization of the great potential of what can be. I have become convinced that these two spiritual streams, or beings (we can call them Christ/Sophia or Masculine/Feminine or Heaven/Earth), long for union within the realm of matter. In spirit they may already be united, but their opportunity for incarnation depends on us, upon our free choice. If we offer ourselves as the vessel for their union, they can fulfill their longing. Their marriage within us transfigures us into the fulfillment of our destiny—free and awakened spiritual human beings, co-creating in union with the Divine, transforming ourselves into beings of Light, and the Earth into a Planet of Light. These Divine beings have entered into the stones Azeztulite and Rosophia. As with the other spiritual beings or streams embodied in the stones, their potential is frozen until we come into relationship with them and free them into expression in the world. Spiritually, they become the Divine parents and we become the Holy Child. In a sense, we all create one another—just as in human life, in which there are no actual "parents" until the child is born.

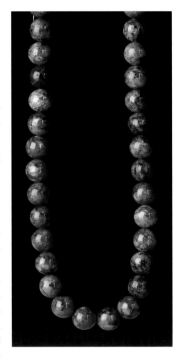

When one wears or meditates with Rosophia and Azeztulite together it is common to feel the penetration of the crown chakra by high-frequency Light currents, and to feel that the Earth's invisible currents of love are reaching upward through one's body to meet the Light currents entering from above.

I hesitate to begin speaking of the more superficial benefits or potential of Rosophia because my heart is so ardently supportive of what I see to be Rosophia's deepest purpose, as well as Azeztulite's. However, I will offer a few words. I feel that Rosophia would benefit the heart in every possible way, from the most deeply spiritual to the physical. Certainly Rosophia's influence helps one to let go of stress quite readily. (I have found that holding a Rosophia stone near the heart when I am ready to sleep works to dispel stress, relax the mind and emotions, and usher me into a deep and restful sleep. It can also facilitate dreams of Sophia.) Rosophia's influence encourages us toward self-love—to experience oneself *as* love. Rosophia allows us to feel close to the Divine Feminine. It helps us remember that we are not alone in the world, that we are every moment within her embrace. All of these things work psychospiritually to engender peace throughout one's being, and when peace is present, disharmony is gone. Thus, as a stone for spiritual healing, Rosophia encompasses our bodies—physical, astral, etheric and all other levels—and it brings harmony, which is her essence, into them all.

Like the Philosopher's Stone of alchemy, Rosophia is rather humble-looking and might be easily missed as one passes by. However, if one notices her and turns to her with the heart's attention, her touch is unmistakable and is immediately treasured. Rosophia is a reddish stone, and the Philosopher's Stone appears in alchemical texts as both red and white, depending upon its stage of transformation. (I liken the white aspect of the Philosopher's Stone to Azeztulite.) A great many references are made in alchemical texts—most notably the *Aurora Consurgens*— that identify Sophia with the Philosopher's Stone. The fact that Rosophia resembles the Philosopher's Stone in both its appearance and its qualities is an exciting discovery. In alchemy, creating, achieving and receiving the Philosopher's Stone was said to bring the alchemist the gifts of enlightenment, healing, wisdom, rejuvenation and even immortality. Whether this was meant as physical immortality or something purely spiritual is not known, and the alchemist had to do much inner work to reach the stage of union with the Stone. My sense is that alchemy itself was inspired by visionary experiences of the coming *potential* for human and Divine transformation, which is beginning to ripen in these times. This may account for the discovery, at least in our era, of physical stones such as Rosophia and Azeztulite (and Moldavite) with qualities resembling those of the fabled Philosopher's Stone. My own intention is to pursue the path of inner alchemy, in conjunction with my stone work, and to see for myself what is possible. I encourage interested readers to join in this endeavor.

Rosophia works in a special harmonic resonance with the stone called Master Shamanite, which deepens Rosophia's link to the interior of the Earth and to the worlds in the depths of consciousness. These are the domains of dreams, the realms of shamanic journeys, the dwelling places of the Black Madonna and of Kali, which are faces of Sophia (and Rosophia) as much as are the beings Kwan Yin and Mary. Yet all of these are human masks covering the invisible ever-becoming evanescent dancing beauty which is Sophia and which gestures to us through this, her stone.

The combination of Azeztulite, Rosophia and Master Shamanite is energetically resonant with the Tree of Life. Master Shamanite works in unity with Rosophia and Azeztulite in a way that creates the Tree of Life pattern and energy state within one's body. The grounded and protective, purifying energies of Master Shamanite stimulate the "roots" of our body-tree. The Rosophia, centering as it does in the heart, fulfills the function of the tree's trunk—bridging the Below and the Above, providing stability and circulation of life currents. Azeztulite awakens the "leaves" of our energetic Tree of Life, stimulating the upper chakras and bringing in the Light of the Great Central Sun, which gives Life to the entire tree and provides the energy for growth.

Human beings are destined to be the living bridge between the realms of matter and spirit, just as a tree literally bridges heaven and Earth, drawing nourishment from below and the Light of life from above. The image of the Tree of Life as our own divine template helps us bring our conscious will into alignment with this purpose. Combining the three stones—Azeztulite, Rosophia and Master Shamanite—invites and awakens this pattern into manifestation within each of us and the world.

ROSOPHIA SPEAKS "I am Wisdom, love and intimacy. I am the strength of the Earth, and the power of tenderness. I am your Beloved, as you are mine. I am the all-giving, and I need your gift. Our Love is a circle and a spiral, ever-living and always becoming."

SATYA MANI QUARTZ™

KEY WORDS Spiritual truth and enlightenment

ELEMENT Wind

CHAKRAS Third Eye (6th), Crown (7th)

Satya Mani Quartz is the name given to a group of translucent to transparent Quartz specimens found in southern India. It is a silicon dioxide mineral with a hardness of 7. Its crystal system is hexagonal (trigonal). It is found almost exclusively in massive form. The name refers to the spiritual qualities of the stone. *Satya Mani* is a Sanskrit phrase meaning "Truth Stone," or "Gem of Truth."

BACKGROUND Satya Mani Quartz is, as its name implies, a stone of spiritual truth and initiation. It attunes one to hear the inner call of one's path of destiny. It brings the joy that comes from recognizing that the appearances of the solid-seeming material world are simply the manifestations of deeper, living currents from the spiritual realms. Satya Mani Quartz can help one awaken to the truth of one's existence as soul and spirit, and the deeper truth of the interrelatedness of all beings. Satya Mani Quartz is a stone of enlightenment, bringing the light of Truth into one's mind, by virtue of its connection to the heart. It inspires the expression of truth, and the commitment to kindness, clear awareness, non-judgement and compassion. The currents of Satya Mani Quartz intensify the circuit of consciousness between the heart and the high brain.

Satya Mani Quartz also works harmoniously with Phenacite, Natrolite, Danburite, Brookite, Herderite, Tibetan Tektite, Azeztulite, Petalite, Scolecite and other high-vibration stones. It has a special affinity for Moldavite, and enhances that stones powers of spiritual transformation. It intensifies the potential benefits of all other silica-based minerals, especially those in the Quartz family.

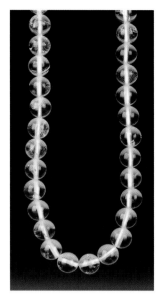

NEW ATTUNEMENT Meditating with Satya Mani Quartz, I began by holding an unpolished piece over my heart and pulsing my heart chakra open to meet the stone in the in-between space. Soon the area between the heart and the stone "caught fire" in a very tangible way—there was a potent sense of burning between my heart and the stone. I liken this to the spiritual fire—the *agni* of the Vedic *rishis* who said that the inner fire is the Fire of Truth, and the source of bodily transformation into the New Human Being. The future of the body is in this burning, for this is not a burning of destruction but the burning of the Fire of Life itself.

Satya Mani means "gem of truth," and this stone is strongly resonant with the heart, particularly in its quality of knowing and expressing truth. The resonance of Satya Mani Quartz beyond the heart chakra is with the throat more than with the higher centers in the brain. It is appropriate to say that Satya Mani Quartz will initiate speaking the truth of the heart, without reference to what the brain might wish to edit or shape into more convenient terms. The brain is always "imagining ahead" to what others may think and trying to steer situations to its own perceived benefit. But the heart cares nothing for this. The heart speaks only the truth it knows from the center of its being. When Satya Mani Quartz is worn or carried or utilized in meditation, the heart is encouraged to give voice to what it knows. The throat chakra becomes so harmonically resonant with Satya Mani Quartz that if one relaxes into it, one can speak without knowing what one is going to say, and yet always there will be an eloquent expression of what is true.

This kind of speaking from the heart—without attempting to edit or control what will be said or heard by others—is essential for true spiritual teaching, as well as for inner exploration and writing. Those who are attuning to and channeling spiritual truth cannot hold back. They must allow whatever expressions the heart engenders in them to come out in a way that is unknown ahead of time. One hears the voice of the heart and follows it, often beginning a sentence without knowing how it will end. Satya Mani Quartz helps us open and attune to the frequencies of the heart's inner wisdom and truth. If we trust those currents, they can guide us to an enlightened destiny.

Satya Mani Quartz is a stone of Light. In engenders Light in the heart, a pure White Light that is like that of a shaft of sun piercing a cloud and reaching the Earth. This shaft is straight, clear and true and gives no concern to anything outside its own pure expression. Imbued with South India's tradition of spiritual enlightenment, the energies of Satya Mani Quartz—if they are given free reign to travel through the body—will spread the pure White Light of enlightened awareness throughout the Liquid Crystal Body Matrix. Surprisingly, the brain may be the last part of us to receive the illumination. This is the strange method of this stone from the land of the great teachers. It is as though the Being behind this stone knows well that the mind has a thousand ways of dodging the confrontation with any truth that might seem to threaten its authority, its position of control. Displaying a kind of spiritual cunning, Satya Mani Quartz's truth travels through the body, filling the Liquid Crystal Body Matrix—all the cells, organs and chakras—with its pure Light. It leaves the brain until last. My intuitive sense tells me that this is a wonderful strategy because by the time this Light of awareness has permeated all of the physical body, the etheric body and the astral body, and worked its way up the chakras, there is no opportunity for the mind to dodge any further. It must recognize the Light and fall into the joy of surrender.

Satya Mani Quartz, in this sense, carries the tradition of the ancient Kundalini path. The Kundalini energy works much like the currents of Satya Mani Quartz in that it raises the Light upward from the lowest chakra—from the base—filling the body until, as with Satya Mani Quartz, there is no choice left for the mind but recognition and ecstatic awakening. It is a great blessing to humanity that a stone such as this, which can carry these frequencies into the world, has been discovered for this value and is being disseminated among those who wish to drink of its Light.

SATYA MANI QUARTZ SPEAKS   "I offer the Light that dispels all shadows. I offer the Light that accepts all shadows. I offer the Light that knows the truth hidden within shadows. My compassion is all-seeing and all-forgiving. My truth makes no compromises. If you will open to me, you will be cleansed of your falsehood and discover that you have nothing to hide from the inner Light of Truth."

SCOLECITE

KEY WORDS   Inner peace, relaxation, tranquility, interdimensional travel, awakening the heart, entering the White Light

ELEMENTS   Wind, Water

CHAKRAS   Third Eye (6th), Crown (7th)

Scolecite is a hydrous calcium aluminum silicate, a zeolite mineral with a hardness of 5 to 5.5. Its crystal system is monoclinic. It occurs as thin, vertically striated prismatic crystals, and also in radiating fibrous masses. It can be colorless, white or yellowish, and it has a vitreous to silky luster. Scolecite forms in cavities in basaltic lavas, as well as cavities in syenites and granites. Fine Scolecite crystals have been found in Teigarhorn, Iceland, and in Poona, India.

BACKGROUND   The phrase that best summarizes the energy of Scolecite is "inner peace." For those who wish to enhance meditation, sleep more restfully or dream more sweetly, Scolecite is highly recommended. Holding a piece of Scolecite to the third eye, one may experience a slow, rolling pulsation of energy. A sense of calm descends, and with it comes a feeling of serenity that can gently lift one to higher planes of awareness. The uplifting, relaxed state brought about by Scolecite is ideal for healing sessions, meditations, lucid dreaming or restful sleep. It offers protection from the intrusion of negative astral energies or entities, as it lifts one to the higher vibrational planes.

Scolecite is an interdimensional stone. Contact with intelligences from far-flung inner and outer domains is possible when Scolecite is used for journeying. It assists travel through time as well as space, allowing one to access knowledge from ancient and even future civilizations.

Emotionally, Scolecite enhances the heart-chakra energies, making the spontaneous expression of love a more frequent experience. It is a good stone to be exchanged between lovers, helping to establish a constant invisible connection between their hearts.

Scolecite is one of the Synergy Twelve stones, and it harmonizes especially well with Phenacite, Herderite, Azeztulite, Danburite, Satyaloka Azeztulite and Apophyllite. Perhaps its best ally is Natrolite, which is nearly identical to Scolecite in its molecular structure.

NEW ATTUNEMENT   Scolecite is a cousin of the stone Natrolite, which is also discussed in this book. The crystalline structure of these two stones has only one molecule of difference, and there are many commonalities in the way these stones interact with us. For instance, the upper chakras, in particular the crown and third eye, are stimulated and moved into higher levels of activity by both Scolecite and Natrolite. Yet there are also contrasts. In the case of Natrolite, its power moves fast and is extremely intense. It is a stone of very high energy that can be exciting, enjoyable and transformative, but it is sometimes a bit overwhelming. Scolecite takes one into the same levels of consciousness and many of the same inner spiritual domains as Natrolite. However, Scolecite's signature is gentleness and peace. When I began meditating with this stone, my first felt sense was of a wave of white, peaceful Light energy moving through my body. The entire meditation with Scolecite was permeated by this quality of soft White Light and very gentle, peaceful currents of feeling.

My intuition was aware of the being of Scolecite as one of great power, and a gentleness that was even greater. To meditate with Scolecite is to feel almost as though one is held in great arms of Light and cradled there, protected like a precious child. There is an ascent of consciousness to higher levels of awareness. This can engender the expansion of one's mind and capacities for insight. Awareness of the Light realms is widely expanded, yet this expansion is not like flying up in a skyrocket with a great explosion of light and color. It is much more like the gradual, floating ascent one might experience in a hot-air balloon. One reaches the same altitude as the rocket, arriving there at a pace and with a softness that lend the experience a very different quality.

Scolecite is a healing balm for anyone whose awareness is tainted with fear or anxiety, or even unconsciously held tension or stress. As we undergo the process of awakening to our unknown dimensions and capacities, we sometimes need this sort of gentle, non-threatening awakening. This helps certain parts of ourselves traumatized by difficult past experiences to enter the unknown without debilitating fear. Scolecite's influence broadens our field of consciousness—I see images of vast celestial prairies of white clouds. I can see and feel some amazing beings through Scolecite; they appear as spheres of radiant silver-white light. In meditative experience, the approach of such beings is coupled with the infusion of a vast compassionate blessing that goes beyond the usual experience of love.

Like Phenacite, Scolecite can be a key to what I call interdimensional travel, which is characterized by a sense of one's consciousness moving through corridors of geometric light patterns, into scenes that depict activities and beings in other dimensions. Scolecite facilitates access to such corridors, but the travel is slower, more stately; and one has a greater opportunity to examine and assimilate the qualities of the Light pattern geometries.

Scolecite encloses one's auric field and physical body within a white envelope of protection and healing Light. It helps to remove the tension from one's mind and bring on a quiet state of serenity. Meditating with Scolecite is helpful for entering the realms of silence and slowly ascending to the level of Source. Some who have experienced it have called this level or realm the Vastness.

Within the evolutionary process of Light Body awakening, Scolecite shows me that it serves the purpose of healing the snags, holes and other disharmonies of the auric field. It cleanses the field with its healing radiance, charging it with its pure White Light. In many traditions, the mystical White Light awakening is one of the prized experiences of meditation. Scolecite is so much a stone of the White Light that one can readily slip into this realm simply by holding a Scolecite with one's eyes closed. This is an echo of mystic awakening, not the full-blown experience. Deeper levels of union with the White Light can occur when one dwells within this space for a while, resting within undulating soft currents of White Light—which is a consciousness of love. Dwelling in the experience of this relationship with the Light is so sweet and holy that one might wish to remain there always. However, this experience is one of initiation, showing us that such a place is a part of us. It also is a restorative experience that heals us so we may continue in our life journey, fortified with love and Light.

SCOLECITE SPEAKS "I am the Light you seek and I am the Light you carry. I am the guardian who reminds you of your essence. Visit me when you need to remember your home and to heal the little wounds of your adventure in time and space."

SELENITE

KEY WORDS Spiritual activation, communion with the Higher Self, attuning to the Universal Mind Lattice, integration of heart awareness with the brain/mind

ELEMENT Wind

CHAKRAS Third Eye (6th), Crown (7th), Transpersona and Etheric (8th through 14th, above the head)

Selenite is a hydrous calcium sulfate mineral with a hardness of 2. It is a form of Gypsum that is called Selenite if it is relatively clear and well formed. Selenite is closely related to fibrous gypsum, also known as Satin Spar, and the massive, fine-grained variety known as Alabaster. Its crystals are typically tabular, with striations running along the length. Selenite is formed as an evaporate in clay beds and around hot springs. Enhydro crystals containing inclusions of water and gas bubbles are found relatively frequently. Some Selenite crystals have the startling property of being soft and flexible enough to be bent in one's hands. Selenite can be colorless, gray, white, green or golden brown. Selenite is found in many countries, including Australia, Greece, Mexico and the U.S. The best-known and most popular Selenite crystals for metaphysical use are the long, clear crystals from Mexico. Semi-transparent Selenites from Morocco are used to make spheres, wands, lamps and a variety of metaphysical talismans and tools.

BACKGROUND Selenite quickly opens and activates the third eye, crown chakra and the Soul Star chakra above the head. Its intensity is remarkable. A Selenite wand pointed at the third eye sends energy that can feel like a gust of wind going through the forehead and out the top of the head. Selenite is fast and effective at cleansing the auric field, and it can clear congested energies or negativity from one's physical and etheric body. When one attaches other stones to Selenite wands, their energies are magnified. When one combines several stones and attaches them to a Selenite wand, the energies of the group are blended and amplified, emanating from the wand as a harmonious whole. Placing a Selenite wand upon one's back, along the length of the spine, can achieve an energetic alignment of the vertebrae and the chakras.

Selenite can lift one's awareness to higher planes of inner experience, making it possible to consciously meet one's spirit guides and guardian angels. It is an excellent stone for building energy grids in the home or outdoors. A group of six or more wands of at least eight inches can be arranged to create a miniature energy vortex, which can be disassembled or reassembled as one wishes. Lying down in the center of such a grid can bring about experiences of spiritual ascension.

Selenite combines synergistically with almost any stone or combination of stones. It works fantastically well with the Synergy Twelve stones. Combining all these stones can raise one's vibration to the highest, fullest and most harmonious possible frequency. Attaching healing stones such as Seraphinite and Rosophia to Selenite is an excellent way to make vibrational tools for any healing application. Selenite can also lend a great deal of power to body layouts and energy grids.

NEW ATTUNEMENT   In meditating with a piece of clear Selenite, I experienced the image of its energetic signature or spiritual essence as a kind of column-shaped fountain of blue-white light, flowing up from the bottom and out through the top. It appeared a bit like the roots and branches of a tree, although more fluid and more symmetrically arranged.

Upon holding the Selenite wand in front of my face with my eyes closed, I experienced a column of energy moving both up and down in my body—up through the crown and down into the body—simultaneously, in a pulsing motion. The energy column Selenite generated felt like the same form I had inwardly seen. I suddenly recalled an Alex Grey painting called "The Universal Mind Lattice." It depicts an interlaced field of torus-shaped patterns of blue-white Light. The currents of Light I had seen and felt were in the same torus form, and the column in the center was the core of the toric field. The pattern of magnetic fields also reflects the torus form. (See image at: http://www.sacredmirrors.org/html/mirrors.cgi?m=16)

In meditation, Selenite stimulates the flow of spiritual energies throughout one's Liquid Crystal Body Matrix, as well as the astral and etheric bodies. One way of visualizing the human energy field is to view it as a torus. The chakra column that runs along the spine is the location in us of the central column of our torus field. There are resonant levels of this field such that smaller torus fields exist within shells of larger ones. The heart generates three such torus fields, with the first (in healthy individuals) extending approximately three feet from the center of the heart. The second shell has a diameter of about fifteen feet, and the third is about fifty-five feet. These dimensions can vary considerably, depending on one's vitality and level of consciousness. I have worked with a master dowser who maintained that many people's vital fields extend not much beyond their skin, while exceptional individuals can generate fields extending out a kilometer or more. (He measured my wife Kathy's field at several hundred yards, while mine went out the basic fifty-five feet!) The torus-field stimulation engendered by Selenite is nearly instantaneous and quite powerful. People who can see or feel auras can often sense a dramatic shift as soon as the person they are observing picks up a Selenite wand.

By amplifying the flow of spiritual currents through the human energy field, Selenite also charges, stimulates and awakens the fourth torus shell of one's energy field. The fourth shell is centered in the heart, and it can extend indefinitely. It may be that the dowser measuring the kilometer-wide field was attuning to the individual's activated fourth shell. With the aid of Selenite, the energized fourth shell stimulates the quantum connection—one's link, through quantum waves, with all other beings, objects and activities in the universe. The extension of the fourth toric field initiates the extension of consciousness as a sort of great torus-shaped cloud of awareness, through which one can potentially experience direct knowing at far distances and throughout multiple dimensions.

Selenite, especially the clear Selenite that occurs in wand form, is deeply attuned to the Water element. In fact, water occurs in the interior of many Selenite wands, and water is key in the growth of Selenite. The mineral Gypsum, of which Selenite is the most refined form, is carried by water in the formation of Selenite crystals. The huge Selenite crystals from Naica, in Chihuahua, Mexico, were formed in a water-saturated cave. The speed of Selenite's infusion of energy into the body reminds me of the capacity of Selenite to form considerably more rapidly than other crystals. These traits of rapid formation and fast-moving

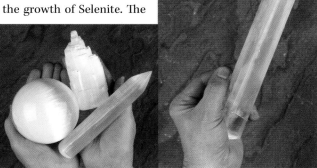

energy make Selenite a prime stone for the acceleration and evolution of consciousness in human beings at this transformational time.

Selenite links easily with the Soul Star chakra above the crown, drawing one's Higher Self or higher awareness into the consciousness of the everyday self in a way that is almost effortless. The feeling when this attunement occurs is of White Light streaming through the core column of the body, accompanied by a sense of peaceful knowing. This creates a powerful calming effect in the emotional body and a pleasurable sense of Light around the crown. In fact, Selenite can readily facilitate the full opening of the crown chakra, known in the Hindu tradition as the Thousand-Petaled Lotus. When this chakra is dramatically activated by Selenite, these names are easily understood, for the opening of the crown feels as if the skull has sprouted a Flower of Light, which rests upon it like a crown upon a queen or king. The "thousand petals" are, as I see them, the multiple streams of energy currents linking one with the Universal Mind Lattice. The "crown" signifies the experience of the expanded awareness generated by Selenite creating a feeling of spiritual sovereignty and authority, of the kind one might associate with a spiritual King or Queen.

Selenite, when used in meditation, can assist in facilitating the integration of the left and right sides of the brain. The estrangement and disconnection of the two brain hemispheres is one of the serious fragmentations humanity has experienced (see Julian Jaynes' book, *The Origin of Consciousness in the Breakdown of the Bicameral Mind*). Yet this wound is not to be condemned, for it has been a spur to a certain necessary aspect of our evolution. Our individualization involved our coming into a kind of self that feels separate from other people, from the world and the spiritual realms. The development of the egoic self was actually facilitated by the estrangement of the brain hemispheres. In most people, the left hemisphere is dominant. This hemisphere is the most neuronally isolated, with the fewest connections to the rest of the brain. The right brain, which is more directly linked to the limbic brain and the heart, tends toward a more holistic consciousness. If the two brains had remained well integrated, we might never have known the sense of separateness now so pervasive in humanity. This separation, this individualization, has generated both geniuses and tyrants, lovers and loneliness. Now evolution calls us toward the reintegration of the two hemispheres, as well as their full engagement with and service to the heart. The great myth of human destiny portrays these two brains as if they were two beings—which we might whimsically personify as a pair of warring princes—the rational/materialist left and the idealist right hemisphere. They have struggled with one another for control of the human being. The resolution to their seemingly insoluble conflict arises with their finding that neither of them is the rightful ruler of the human being. The sovereign throne of the human being is in the heart, where one's true self, the "I" of the heart, dwells. When this is recognized and integrated as a bodily fact, there can be a great healing, beginning in the individual and spreading out to the world.

Selenite can accentuate the felt sense of the column of Light that connects the heart and the brain. This column of Light is the veritable road to heaven, for heaven is in our hearts. Therefore, Selenite's role in human evolution includes the stimulation and strengthening of the neurological structures connecting the heart and the brain, as well as the spiritual conduits of energy flowing between them. Through resonance with the columnar flow of spiritual energies

offered through the crystalline angelic being of Selenite, the physical, astral and etheric bodies begin to recognize their essential unity. They are able to feel and to echo the pattern of Selenite—a pattern of connection and fluid communication, integration and loving engagement between the brain and the heart.

In most or all of us, the brain is only partially awake, and its spiritual capacities are barely developed. Using

a Selenite wand, directing its energy flow into the head through the third eye chakra, the currents of the stone move through the forehead, filling the cranium and moving out through the back the head. My intuitive sense is that through immersion in the toric field amplified by Selenite, the brain begins to move toward an awakening of unknown capabilities and activities for which we do not yet have words.

Placing a Selenite wand at the back of the skull, pointing forward, creates a current that feels highly pleasurable and seems to be something for which one's body has longed. I cannot discern the function of this current, only that it is something welcomed in the body. (As previously mentioned, the little-noticed chakra point at the back of the head, where the spine and skull join, is known esoterically as the Mouth of God.) This current, entering from the back, emerges from the top of the crown and pours out over the forehead in the shape of a cobra. As I experienced this, I was quite amazed. I remembered that the ancient Sphinx has a cobra rising out of the head, displaying the exact shape of the energy flow generated by the Selenite. The Sphinx was regarded as an entity of vast wisdom, and my intuition suggests that working with Selenite in this way could awaken one to direct knowing of World Wisdom. I encourage experimenting with this application of Selenite, and I intend to do so myself.

SELENITE SPEAKS   "Although my pattern is ancient, I am young. I am alive with the vibrancy you equate with youth and with living attunement to the promise of the future. My service—my offer—is an awakening of all that you are as a Being of Light. The Light of the *pleroma*—the worlds of Light—pours through me. This Light is dormant in you, yet present. I can reveal to you the means to kindle your light. This radiance, which you may imagine is coming from me, is in truth your own as well as mine, for all are born of one Light."

SERAPHINITE

KEY WORDS   Self-healing, regeneration, wholeness, angelic connection, attunement to the Divine Feminine
ELEMENTS   Storm, Earth
CHAKRAS   All

Seraphinite is a variety of Clinochlore, a hydrous magnesium iron aluminum silicate with a hardness of about 4. Its crystal system is monoclinic. Seraphinite is found only in the Lake Baikal region of Siberia. It is characterized by its deep green color, laced with shimmering patterns of silver that move with changing angles of light reflection. Seraphinite derives its name from its perceived link to the Seraphim, the highest order of angels.

BACKGROUND   Seraphinite is among the most powerful stones for bringing all the elements of the nonphysical bodies into alignment along the I Am column of the spinal cord. It is both centering and energizing at the same time, and its beautiful green shades show how well it is suited to the heart chakra. Furthermore, this stone can be beneficially utilized on any chakra or any other part of the body where enhanced and harmonized energies are desired. It can move

259

blocked energies in the meridians and can be used alone or combined with acupuncture for this purpose.

Seraphinite is very evolved and will bring the user along rapidly in his or her own evolution. These stones resonate strongly with all levels of the angelic domain, even the highest. Those who wish to meet the angels in meditation or dreaming can use this stone to facilitate the necessary attunements. Seraphinite is also one of the best overall healing stones in the mineral kingdom.

Seraphinite easily harmonizes with the vibrations of other high-energy gemstones such as Moldavite, Phenacite, Scolecite, Petalite, Tanzanite, Danburite, Azeztulite, Herkimer "Diamonds," Tibetan Tektite, Strontianite and Charoite. It has a powerful and important connection with Rosophia, which amplifies its healing qualities and its connection to Sophia.

NEW ATTUNEMENT   Meditating with Seraphinite I initially experienced strong feelings of loving currents moving into the heart and resonating also at the crown chakra. This indicates two aspects of Seraphinite's qualities. It is a stone of healing and regeneration of the physical and etheric bodies. It is also attuned to the angelic realm and the higher frequencies associated with the crown chakra.

A green healing ray pours into the body when one invites Seraphinite to enter. It comes most readily through the heart, and its influence permeates one's entire being. Seraphinite emanates currents of wholeness and well-being that I experience as a kind of calm, inner smile throughout the body. To resonate with Seraphinite is to feel in touch with one's highest angelic protectors and guides. Seraphinite is very feminine and is attuned to the Divine Feminine in her love aspect.

My intuition, as I attuned to this stone, confirmed that Seraphinite's healing currents penetrate all the way through the Liquid Crystal Body Matrix, into the very nucleus of the cells. In fact, I was given a vision that Seraphinite's wholesome emanations benefit the alignment of the DNA within the cell nuclei. I saw, in this image, the ray of Seraphinite's green healing flow wrapping around the cell nuclei and bringing light forth from the DNA. This image suggests that Seraphinite aids one's activation of the Light Body through generation of light in the cells. Seraphinite's welcoming energies draw spiritual Light into the world through the DNA itself. I felt that the DNA acted as a corridor, linking the spiritual side of one's being—through each cell—with the material world. I sensed the welcoming currents of Seraphinite resonating through the DNA, carrying the love and Light that long to pour into the world through us. Seraphinite generates an opening that gives spiritual Light the key to the corridor into this world. As this activity occurs within the cellular matrix of the body, our organs and body processes are spiritually rejuvenated and restored. (This is a helpful picture of the activity of Seraphinite, and I recommend that those working with this stone for self-healing use this image for visualization.)

Seraphinite gently reminds the body, as well as the soul, of its pattern of perfection. We live in a milieu within which great forces of destruction, disease, fear, contraction and isolation have their sway. All of these forces work to the detriment of the harmony and well-being of one's heart, soul, spirit and body, upon every level. We have, in many cases, entered the world with the mission or purpose of healing these disharmonious forces and patterns. The human world exhibits pervasive violence, destruction, harshness, isolation and fear, but these are not laws. They are habit patterns created by fragmented beings reflecting their fragmentation. There is no judgment about this, only the wish to heal. Seraphinite's mission, in partnership with us, is to heal all those who turn toward it and to help each being become a radiant source of healing.

Seraphinite is part of the great Healing Conspiracy of Sophia (if I may say this in a joking way). She is, in many cosmologies, one of the highest angels (or the feminine aspect of the

Divine itself). She is described as having given herself to the material realm out of compassion and a desire to heal the world and bring it to its highest destiny. The activity of Seraphinite is essentially the drawing of beneficial spiritual currents of Light into the world. Seraphinite unites the heart and the crown in a way that crowns the heart as the sovereign center and true source of our wholeness. When we work with Seraphinite and receive her healing gifts, we can also pass them on. This can be initiated by holding the image of another person—in his or her most radiant, healthy state—in one's heart while meditating with Seraphinite. The practice of doing this is one aspect of the New Consciousness as an activity of blessing. Seraphinite's core purpose is to facilitate this activity of blessing as a constant flow through one's heart, into all moments of life. It is also our highest destiny.

SERAPHINITE SPEAKS   "Like all angels of my kinship, I am a messenger of love, light, truth, compassion, healing, wholeness and well-being. I am an emanation of Divine harmony, and I bring my harmony into relationship with all those who invite me. I rejoice in your choice to love and I honor it, for to find the strength to love within the harshness of your sphere takes courage. I encourage you and your hearts to do so. We will bring much Light to the Earth together."

SERIPHOS GREEN QUARTZ

KEY WORDS   Awareness of the Earth as Paradise, joyful acceptance of physical life, healing, connecting with nature spirits

ELEMENT   Earth

CHAKRA   Heart (4th)

Seriphos Green Quartz is a special type of Quartz crystal, a silicon dioxide mineral with a hardness of 7. Its crystal system is hexagonal (trigonal). It is found only on the tiny Greek island of Seriphos, in the Aegean Sea about one hundred kilometers southeast of Athens. The leaf-green color of these blade-shaped crystals comes from inclusions of the fibrous mineral Hedenbergite. The formation of the crystals happened in two stages—first the fibrous green Hedenbergite was formed, followed by the Quartz, which encompassed the Hedenbergite during a later period of growth. Seriphos Green Quartz is deposited in irregular cavities in marble and is often found in association with Hematite "iron roses."

Seriphos Green Quartz is unique not only for its coloring, which ranges from pale lettuce green to a deep spinach color, but also for its growth in odd and unusual shapes which suggest plant life more than crystals. Some specimens are like long, slender leaves, tapered at each end, while others are clustered like a spray of flowers. A few are carpeted with tiny druzy crystallizations, looking as if they are coated with dew. They seldom grow bigger than two inches long, and large clusters are extremely rare.

BACKGROUND   Synchronicity must have been at work when the island where these stones are found was named after angels. Seriphos Green Quartz crystals emanate a most heavenly energy, and one can imagine the flower beds of the higher realms budding with just such as these. They emanate a sweet, strong vibration that evokes the state of wholesome enjoyment of physical life and facilitates the attainment of vibrant good health. Seriphos Green Quartz helps the user or wearer be grounded in the best possible way—through love for the material world and one's place within it. It reminds us that we too are blooms brought forth from the womb of the fertile Earth, and our experience of life can be exquisite when we bring our attention to its beauty and pleasure.

Seriphos Green Quartz harmonizes with Green Apophyllite, Staurolite and Moldavite. Rosophia is particularly resonant with Seriphos Green Quartz, in regard to the recognition of the Divine qualities of the material world. Combining Seriphos Green Quartz with Phenacite or Azeztulite brings awareness of the higher dimensional aspect of oneself into alignment with one's earthly life. Golden Azeztulite crystals are the type of Azeztulite with the most synergistic connection with Seriphos Green Quartz.

NEW ATTUNEMENT In sitting to meditate with Seriphos Green Quartz, I first held the stone to my heart. The space between the outside of my chest and the interior of my heart was soon filled with energy. In this case, the immediate feeling was one of healing. Seriphos Green Quartz's currents generate well-being and balance in the Liquid Crystal Body Matrix. They tend to flow into areas within the body where imbalances exist, and to correct the difficulty through their strong and harmonious vibrations. As I asked to be shown the qualities of these stones, I saw images of ocean and sunshine, and scenes of people relaxed and at ease. They were taking in the warm sun and experiencing the pleasant, comfortable, invigorating qualities of nature. Usually such inner images come to me in order to display the feeling of a stone's qualities. I believe that Seriphos Green Quartz evokes the pleasurable sense of nature's health-giving qualities.

I was pleasantly surprised when, shortly after I placed the crystal on my chest, the heart itself responded. There was a kind of leap, an exuberant palpitation that was not uncomfortable, but rather seemed to me to signify that my heart was in a state of joy to find itself near the Seriphos Quartz. This continued for some minutes, feeling almost as one might imagine or remember seeing a dog greeting a person whom it loves—with a great deal of tail-wagging and shaking of the body. That is the sort of beating that my heart did in the encounter with Seriphos Green Quartz.

After some time, this heart experience began to shift slowly from the greeting exuberance to a kind of aching longing. My felt sense is that the body and my heart sense the Seriphos Green Quartz as an aspect of the World Soul. It seems to so strongly resemble Her that it rekindles the longing for the Beloved of the Soul that exists deep in every human heart. The Soul of the World, with whom we seek union, and for whom all of our work with the stones is dedicated, smiles to us through Seriphos Green Quartz. Here we can feel Sophia's playful qualities. Here we can almost see her face in its ever-beautiful radiance. The "almost" is what triggers the deep longing, for there is nothing our hearts more deeply wish for than this union with Sophia.

Seriphos Green Quartz is resonant with the Earth element, and with the spirits of living things. It is attuned to the realm of the plant and animal spirits. Those who work with Seriphos Green Quartz may find themselves drawn to meditate with it outdoors, the better to experience its gift of communion with nature. If one imagines the sensual experience of sitting in the grass on a sunny day, smelling and feeling the breeze, hearing the sounds of the natural world, one has a glimpse of the feeling engendered by meditation with Seriphos Green Quartz.

Seriphos Green Quartz is a pure stone of the Green Ray—the ray most closely aligned with the heart and the living world. It is also associated with healing. One can experience deep healing through wearing, carrying or working meditatively with Seriphos Green Quartz.

At the end of one meditation, Seriphos Green Quartz expressed a feeling of kinship with Moldavite, and a kind of wish to be combined with Moldavite for our work. It called Moldavite its "heavenly sister."

SERIPHOS GREEN QUARTZ SPEAKS "I am a being of the living world. I am the tree that smiles down upon the sea, and I am the breeze that links the tree with the water. I am the leaves more than I am the roots, for my resonance partakes of the Sun. I am of the Earth, yet I live lightly upon it. My heart is a dancing heart that does not consider any fear. You can hear how I sound if you listen to the bird cries in the wind. I am like a young heart that will never age. I can teach your heart to feel as I do."

STAUROLITE

KEY WORDS   Grounding and physical well-being, linking with the near realms of fairies, devas, animal and plant consciousness

ELEMENT   Earth

CHAKRAS   Root (1st), Heart (4th), Third Eye (6th), Crown (7th)

S taurolite is a complex mineral containing iron, magnesium, zinc, aluminum and silicon. Its hardness is 7 to 7.5 and its crystal system is monoclinic. It forms in prismatic crystals, often in cruciform (cross-shaped) twins. The color is reddish brown, dark brown or brownish black. The name comes from the Greek word *stauros,* meaning "cross," and the twinned crystals have been given the nickname "fairy crosses." Localities for Staurolite crystals include Fannin County, Georgia (U.S.); Rubelita in Minas Gerais, Brazil; and Monte Campione, Switzerland. Numerous good specimens have recently come from Russia.

BACKGROUND   Staurolite vibrates to the frequencies of the other dimensions closest to our own. As such, it can act as a key to the astral plane, the devic realm and the domain of the fairies. It can be used to communicate with plant and animal spirits as well. Keeping the vibration of Staurolite in one's energy field helps to open one's eyes to the closely connected worlds that exist in symbiosis with the physical Earth. One is thereby inspired to treat the beings and environment of this plane with the same reverence one would have for the higher worlds. Also, the love and sweetness that permeate the fairy realm resonate deeply in the human, recalling the forgotten parts of the soul. For making this reconnection, Staurolite is a beneficial ally.

Staurolite is a helpful aid for those seeking to give up self-destructive habits and can assist one in going through cleansing regimens. It can even instigate spontaneous natural purgings of negative energies and parasitic organisms. Staurolite also helps one pick up healthy habits, reducing resistance to positive changes in diet and exercise, and the establishment of meditation and stress-relief programs.

Those who wish to learn the practice of "animal communication," in which one can psychically converse with pets or other animals, will find in Staurolite a tool for achieving the inner attunement that opens the door for such work.

As a crystal echoing the symbol of the four directions, Staurolite also contains the invisible link to the "fifth direction," the vertical inner direction by which one experiences and navigates other worlds. Staurolite's energy increases one's ability to attune to the frequencies of whatever domain one wishes to visit or explore. For instance, sleeping with a Staurolite crystal in the pillowcase can initiate astral travel or lucid dreaming.

Staurolite's power can be increased by pairing it with Crimson Cuprite. Rosophia provides intimate conection with the living world. Phenacite, Herderite and Strontianite can help with the enhancement of the psychic senses. Seriphos Green Quartz and Green Apophyllite will assist in attuning to the planes of the fairies and devas. Prophecy Stone will help one to stay grounded and centered while linking one's awareness to multiple worlds.

NEW ATTUNEMENT   In my meditation with Staurolite, I was drawn to place pieces of these cross-shaped crystals at my heart and third eye. I felt immediately that Staurolite is a stone we can work with for both the broadening of awareness and the deepening of consciousness. Its very form suggests the *axis mundi,* center of the spinning world. The cross has always been a symbol of the intersection of the physical and spiritual realms—the physical realm of the four directions and the vertical dimension, extending from the highest heavens to the deepest of the Underworlds. This has been one of the meanings of the cross in myth.

In my meditation, after placing the Staurolite over my third eye, I saw internally an echo-image of the equal-armed cross. My felt sense was that of Staurolite as a stone of the crossroads between the spiritual and physical realms. It is very important as a stone of the New Consciousness, because we will not move out of the physical world as we develop this consciousness. On the contrary, we will become more fully physical by drawing our spiritual energies "down" into full integration with our physical bodies. No more, in the time of the New Consciousness, will we speak of body and soul, or of spirit and matter, as separate domains. Although their qualities will still retain the resonance of identity we have known, they are destined to merge into what will be a species of whole spiritual human beings. In order for this to occur, our spiritual side must come in from its exile in the realm of the unknown, or the disbelieved. When our daily activity, moment by moment, is both physical and spiritual, we will have become whole—so says Staurolite.

As I meditated further with Staurolite, I was strongly drawn to place one crystal beneath the base chakra and another at the crown chakra. Having never done this with Staurolite before, I felt surprised at the inner insistence to do so. Yet moments later, after placing the stones in this position, I sensed why. I could feel a current of aligning force extending from the crown to the base and from the base up to the crown, drawing all the chakras into line. All of my energies seemed to align themselves along this polar axis between the base and crown. Then more currents, unlike any I had ever felt before from Staurolite, began descending down the chakra column. Their movement took more time than I usually experience with most of the high-frequency stones. However, the felt sense was that this slow descent, almost like honey dripping down inside me, was a deeper and more penetrating experience of the entrance of Supramental currents.

The Supramental Force—so named by Sri Aurobindo—has been experienced as an ambrosial dripping descent, and as intensely pulsating currents that seem to pound their way down through the crown and all the way through the body. With Staurolite, one experiences these currents gently and gradually. It took perhaps five minutes or more for the current to flow from the crown to the throat. As this occurred, it seemed that my entire head and upper throat were saturated with slowly undulating sensations of nourishment and pleasure. The slowness of Staurolite's currents does not mean that they are less profound than those of "faster" stones. In fact, the depth of their permeating quality is so remarkable that they could easily become a highly favored type of crystal for those working to attune and awaken the Light Body. This honey of deep amber-colored light—for that is what it had become—eventually reached the heart chakra, and I experienced the feeling of a wide expansion horizontally from the heart. Indeed the heart became the center point of the vertical/horizontal axis, thus echoing Staurolite's cross-shaped pattern.

Staurolite is resonant with the deep past, and it can aid one in meditatively reaching into the Akashic records of the spiritual history of the Earth. It also helps one attune to the records of past civilizations, held in the morphogenic fields of the Earth and in our cellular memory. The holographic consciousness of the biosphere—the mind of all life—is something shamanic explorers have encountered. Staurolite indicates to my intuitive sense that it has a way of helping us attune to this frequency. The spiritual being of Staurolite expresses a great delight for the encounter with life, and it wishes life to do well in its process of evolution.

Staurolite's slow energy continued descending in my body as I meditated, and it eventually reached the solar plexus. Its currents continued to descend, filling all of the body with its dark honey of amber Light. Staurolite is a helpful stone for communing with devas and nature spirits. I could feel them in the land, and the living plants around the room, as I meditated with Staurolite. Staurolite stimulates the vision centers in the brain, giving rise to a multiplicity of meaningful images. Images seem to be Staurolite's means of communication, in addition to the slowly descending energy it emanates.

Staurolite helps one find the membranes of dimensional boundaries, and to cross them at will. Staurolite can be helpful for perceiving the spiritual stream of the archetypal Cross all the way back through time. The cross is much more than a Christian symbol. It has always been an image of the way that the inner and outer worlds intersect. Thus Staurolite's physical appearance is a symbolic diagram of its qualities.

STAUROLITE SPEAKS "You are deeper beings than you have yet discovered. You are called to descend, and to ascend from the depths to the heights. You are called to stretch your awakened awareness across the entire expanse of all that is, and I will help you. I will, if you wish it, show you the way of increasing your spirit's length and breadth, beyond all limits."

STRONTIANITE

KEY WORDS Strength and confidence, enthusiasm for life, increased vitality and sexuality, decisiveness and self-control, awakening the human Light Body

ELEMENT Storm

CHAKRAS Sexual/Creative (2nd), Solar Plexus (3rd), Third Eye (6th)

Strontianite is a strontium carbonate mineral with a hardness of 3.5. Its crystal system is orthorhombic. It forms in prismatic, frequently needle-shaped crystals, occurring in low-temperature hydrothermal veins in marbles and limestones, often is association with Celestite, Barite and/or Calcite. Occasionally it forms as concretions in clay or limestone. Strontianite's colors include white, yellowish, greenish, gray, brownish, reddish and colorless. The finest specimens are from Strontian, Scotland, and Munster, Germany.

BACKGROUND Strontianite is a stone of strength and confidence. It clears and opens the third chakra, allowing for the full expression of one's personal power. It channels spiritual energy into the physical body, giving one increased vitality and endurance, as well as a supply of reserve energy to be called upon for high-intensity activities. It recharges the auric field, creating a palpable sense of one's personal space—an energy that can actually repel those who do not align with one's highest good. It assists in knowing oneself deeply, thus allowing for certainty in one's choices and commitment in one's activities.

Strontianite initiates a positive attitude toward life. It eliminates doubt and hesitation, encouraging one to leap into an experience and enjoy it. It helps one overcome fears by facing and accepting the facts. It enhances the senses, making it possible for one to discharge feelings of numbness and isolation. It increases one's receptivity to pleasure, stimulating the pleasure

centers of the brain and attenuating the connections to stored memories of guilt and shame. It also enhances one's receptivity to and enjoyment of others. It opens one's eyes to the common humanity we all share and encourages friendship.

Strontianite promotes healthy sexuality. It supports the optimal functioning of the sexual organs while stimulating the psychological programming that brings lovers together. It helps one appreciate one's partner, opening one's eyes to what attracted one to him or her in the first place. It encourages the enjoyment of romance and reminds us that love has no need to hurry.

Strontianite harmonizes with Celestite, which softens its willfulness and emphasizes compassion. It also works well with Merkabite Calcite and Lemurian Aquatine Calcite, as well as Spanish Aragonite. Libyan Gold Tektite can increase its capacity to energize the third chakra.

NEW ATTUNEMENT As soon as I sat down to meditate with two Strontianites in my hands and a third around my neck, there were immediate pulsations in the third eye and the head. The currents traveled quickly up to the crown chakra and down the spine—all the way down. This strong pulsation marked Strontianite's intense and powerful vibrational signature. I believe that the initial feeling we receive from a crystal or stone is the energetic signature—its way of saying "Hello, this is who I am." Strontianite is a very dynamic, powerful stone with a strong quality of purpose. After a few moments, as I centered my attention in the heart and opened to a relationship with the being of Strontianite, the pulsations quieted and the energy of the stone became more steady and harmonious. It began to circulate in the space between the stone and my heart.

At my invitation, the currents of Strontianite went through my body rapidly. Its powerful vibrations brought a wave of resonance through the Liquid Crystal Body Matrix. The first images that arose in meditation with Strontianite were radiant sunbursts of patterns that appeared rather like Strontianite's growth structure—radiating intergrown crystals going in all directions. My felt sense was that Strontianite's primary purpose is awakening the radiance of the human Light Body.

As I mentioned, the pulsating energies of Strontianite were very strong in the head, beginning in the third eye and moving upward to the crown. Strontianite's natural place of resonance is with the higher chakras. This is because of its high frequencies, which stimulate the Light Body, as well as its impulse to organize and focus the mind in order that one's purpose may be realized.

Strontianite stimulates tingling sensations throughout the body. I feel this signifies that the cells are vibrating at a higher frequency. Strontianite's currents infuse the cells with spiritual Light, beginning the activation of the Light Body.

The human body is a liquid crystal structure with liquid crystal information patterning distributed both between and within the cells. Human DNA emits light. Strontianite stimulates the cells with the purpose of increasing the frequency and intensity of light moving through the human being. This process is integral to Light Body activation. Strontianite showed me the image of the human Light Body as our evolutionary destiny.

The spiritual history of humanity is a descent into ever-increasing density and materiality. This densification process has resulted in cultural forms of materialism that deny or ignore our innermost connection with the spiritual realms. Through its strong and immediate quickening of vibrations within the body, Strontianite reminds us of our potential, and of our purpose to develop and become the Body of Light. When the spiritual and physical worlds are estranged, as they have become through the focus of consciousness on matter and mental constructions that limit spiritual resonance, there has been a disconnection from the Light of the Source.

Strontianite powerfully brings the Light of Source into resonance with the body, showing us the destination toward which we are working. However, it is not a visual display—it is an experience, a feeling, the first stirrings of the Light Body.

As I looked to my heart, and to the space between my heart and the Strontianite stone on my chest, an image arose. I saw a living pair of pine branches formed in the shape of a cross, with a bright blue sky behind them. My understanding of this image was that I was being shown the pattern suggested by Strontianite for our work together. The branches were completely covered with long green pine needles. I recognized the pattern of the needles as one of a similar radiant form to Strontianite's crystallization. It also reminded me once again of the images of radiating lines that arose at the beginning of the meditation. The cross signifies the crossroads between the spiritual world of verticality and the horizontal physical world. Strontianite suggested through this image that we have the opportunity to become the living cross, the living crossroads between the worlds. The bright blue sky behind the branches was there to remind me that the light of the world comes from the sun, and that the Light of the spiritual realms comes from the Great Central Sun. We are offered the opportunity to receive, through relationship with Strontianite, the Light of the spiritual realms. We are to use that Light to nourish our spirits, and to help the Earth become a Planet of Light.

Strontianite enters into connection with the human being with a powerful force of purpose and will. This stone is so focused that it enters the auric field with great intensity, even at the slightest invitation. To pick up and hold the stone for a moment is all the invitation Strontianite needs to enter one's energy field. If one allows inner and outer habits to be changed by the new resonance offered through Strontianite, the capacity to focus on one's purpose and to fulfill one's destiny through exercising strength and will is enhanced.

The reason Strontianite feels as if it has a strong will is because what it awakens within us is our own strength of will and clarity of purpose. As a stone of initiation into the Light Body, Strontianite helps us to glimpse the goal, and to inspire our will to guide us to our goal's fruition. The feeling of Strontianite's relationship with us is somewhat like the relationship one might have with a dedicated spiritual teacher. Although one might wish for the teacher to pay attention to one's ego or personality, the teacher, who is focused on the enlightenment of all beings, cares less about one's personality than about the fruition of one's capacity for enlightenment. Strontianite seems to brush past cordial greetings and set right to work bringing Light into all levels of one's being.

Strontianite's influence encourages us to develop through the exertion of focused will and complete dedication to our highest purpose. It offers a kind of clarity that illuminates the steps that fulfillment of our purpose requires.

Interestingly, Strontianite's encouragement of the development of an intensely focused will includes the release of any specific idea of how one's focused will should manifest. Strontianite encourages us to move toward fulfillment of the Divine blueprint—our evolutionary impulse to become Beings of Light. However, to achieve this we must totally commit to this intention, while releasing all preconceived notions of how the results will come about or even what they will be. When we feel the currents of Strontianite, we first experience its focused will, followed by a relaxation or surrender. Through this gesture, Strontianite teaches us how we are to follow our path of destiny.

Strontianite is excellent for people who do not usually sense stone energies. Its currents are so strong that almost everyone can feel them, and in doing so, the fantasies of what working with a stone ought to feel like dissolve in the presence of the actual vibration of the stone. The Liquid Crystal Body Matrix easily and enjoyably assimilates the vibrations of Strontianite. When these vibrations are welcomed, they feel quite pleasurable throughout the body. It is also true that the increase of one's capacity for focused intention generated by resonance with Strontianite feels like a kind of effortless resolve. Perhaps "effortless" is not the right word, because certainly effort is involved, but the feeling of resistive counter-forces within us dissipates. This allows much greater focus and effectiveness in regard to staying with a new pattern one has chosen. The strength of habit to pull us back into old ways is very much diminished.

Strontianite resonates very well with all forms of Azeztulite, for Azeztulite is also a powerful stone of Light Body awakening. Golden Azeztulite from North Carolina, Himalaya Gold Azeztulite from North India, and the original white Azeztulites from North Carolina and Vermont all work well with Strontianite. When Pink Azeztulite is used in combination with Strontianite, the impersonal quality of Strontianite is softened, and softer, more loving currents come into the body. Using Sanda Rosa Azeztulite in combination with Strontianite encourages healing of the physical body and helps focus Strontianite's powerful currents on repairing dysfunctional patterns in the body, as well as activating the Body of Light.

Other stones that resonate with Strontianite include Herderite, which carries a great tendency for expansion of consciousness beyond the physical form. One's awareness of and within the Light Body is broadened when Strontianite is combined with Herderite.

If one uses Strontianite in combination with Phenacite, there is a strong enhancement of the visionary aspect of this stone's influence, as well as a redoubled stimulation of the third eye and crown chakras. This combination opens the portal of the crown such that one may move awareness upward into the etheric chakras above the body, and into resonance with beings of the angelic domain.

Strontianite aligns most readily with the upper chakras, although through focused attention and intention it will resonate with the heart, solar plexus and even the first and second chakras. If one wishes increased grounding beyond what a stone such as Sanda Rosa Azeztulite can provide, stones like Black Tourmaline and Master Shamanite can be helpful.

Rosophia imparts a loving gentleness to Strontianite's powerful resolve. The two stones work together in a dynamic balance that is healthy for the body and nourishing to the soul.

STRONTIANITE SPEAKS   "I awaken the heart to service of your purpose; I illuminate the mind with awareness of your destiny. I enliven the body for fulfillment of the human being—of your purpose as living embodiment of matter and Spirit as one."

SUNSET GOLD SELENITE

KEY WORDS   Creating through the will, integration of the brain hemispheres, unification of brain/mind and heart/wisdom

ELEMENTS   Fire, Wind

CHAKRAS   Solar Plexus (3rd), Heart (4th), Third Eye (6th), Crown (7th)

One of the most unusual and rare forms of Selenite is a material called Sunset Gold Selenite, so named because of its color and radiance. These crystals are found in Texas and are a recent discovery. Selenite is a hydrous calcium sulfate mineral with a hardness of 2. Selenite is closely related to fibrous gypsum, also known as Satin Spar, and the massive, fine-grained variety known as Alabaster. Sunset Gold Selenite crystals are irregular and rather convoluted, although with many of them, two of their four sides are flat and shiny. Most crystals of Sunset Gold Selenite have a high degree of translucence and range from two to four inches in length.

BACKGROUND   Sunset Gold Selenite quickly opens and activates the third eye and solar plexus chakras. When it is held to the third eye, its currents move up also to the crown, stimulating its opening. Like Himalaya Gold Azeztulite, Sunset Gold Selenite aids in developing the creating activity of the will. As we move more and more into the birth of what certain myths refer to as the New Heaven and the New Earth—the spiritual and physical realms united as one—the creating capacities of will become vitally important. Through partnership with the realms of spirit, we will learn to manifest whatever is needed or desired, in alignment with the wisdom and harmony of the World. Sunset Gold Selenite aids in these transition times by stimulating our vision and our will to create. This creating activity is first and foremost an activity of trust. Through trusting the unknown while holding the essence of our heartfelt intention, we can play an essential role in creating a world more wonderful than we can yet imagine.

Sunset Gold Selenite aids in developing the strength of intention and trust, through its enhancement of the power of the third chakra and its way of linking the solar plexus to the third eye. It helps us feel the energy of trust and intention going out into the future through our solar plexus. It helps us develop a feeling/seeing sensitivity via which we can recognize the movement of our creating forces, joining with the World Soul's creating forces, forming the stream of the unfolding future. Working meditatively with Sunset Gold Selenite, placing one piece on the solar plexus and another on the third eye, we receive the aid of this ally in reawakening and strengthening these long-dormant capacities. Adding one or two pieces of Himalaya Gold Azeztulite and/or North Carolina Golden Azeztulite crystals on these same chakras redoubles the effectiveness of the Sunset Gold Selenite crystals.

Sunset Gold Selenite can aid in self-healing in these areas: digestive difficulties, bowel sluggishness, impaired vision and hearing, muscle weakness and addictive behaviors. Addictions and other sorts of bad habits are, from a certain perspective, diseases of the will. The enhancement of will forces offered by Sunset Gold Selenite can help one break through all sorts of old stuck patterns.

Sunset Gold Selenite also resonates powerfully with Agni Gold Danburite, Golden Labradorite, Phenacite, Herderite and a number of other high-vibration stones. I suggest experimenting with gluing other stones onto these crystals in order to make power wands, meditation enhancers and tools for healing.

NEW ATTUNEMENT   In meditating with Sunset Gold Selenite, I am first impressed by the intensity and power of the currents, which immediately resonate through my body upon holding the stone. Sunset Gold Selenite transmits a current that may be even more powerful than that of clear Selenite. Interestingly, this stone seems not to carry a Blue-White ray. It has a ray of intense energy that does not give rise to a visible interior light, yet the felt sense is that it transmits an invisible or transparent ray. When I work with Sunset Gold Selenite, placing a crystal in front of the third eye, the energy that enters and spreads throughout the brain area is quite amazing. It feels both pleasurable and expansive, and its currents move deeply into the brain. It also seems that a special purpose of this crystal involves the stimulation of the corpus callosum—the connection area between the two brain hemispheres.

In discussing clear Selenite, I mentioned that Selenite's activity involves the reintegration of the brain hemispheres. The relative disconnection between these halves of the brain is illustrated by the fact that connective nerve fiber bundles between them are considerably less dense in right-handed men than they are in women and left-handed men. This suggests that women and left-handed men have greater brain integration. It also underlies the idea I expressed earlier that the spiritual pathology of separation of self from others and from the world is reflected in the relative separation of the left and right hemispheres. Since the majority of males are right-handed, in a general way one might say that right-handed males have dominated human culture for some centuries, during which hierarchical patriarchal civilizations have prevailed. Such societies have as an underlying premise the separation of the individual from the world. Individually, this gives rise to what we know as the egoic sense.

I am talking about the underlying sense of separation that comes from seeing the world as "out there" and oneself as "in here." One of the greatest gifts of our experience of the currents of the stones is that an object from "out there" can generate inner experiences. The stones show us that there is a mysterious and important overlap between the world and our inner life. Thus, a more accurate premise for our experience of life is one of relationship—we are intimately woven in with the whole fabric of the world. This is one good reason to re-imagine our work with the stones as one of co-creative partnership, and from my perspective, that is the way it really is.

We need not harshly judge or condemn the egoic sense. In fact, judgment and condemnation can only occur from the position of the (illusory) isolated ego self. I mention it to support the assertion that in human evolution, the time of isolated individuality is passing. A great theme of evolution's movement now is the theme of reintegration—the reconnection of individual consciousness with the consciousness of other people, other beings and that of the spiritual and physical worlds. This movement dissolves the feeling of isolation (with its underlying fear of the world) and takes us ultimately into shared consciousness with all that is.

I have gone into all of this here because I feel that the separate sense of self has neural underpinnings in the brain structure. In his book *The Origin of Consciousness in the Breakdown of the Bicameral Mind* (mentioned also in the section on Selenite), Julian Jaynes argued that in a time of upheaval about five thousand years ago, the capacity for feeling oneself to be a *separate* individual had survival value. For example, if one encountered potentially hostile members of another tribe, the separated ego self could tell a lie in order to survive. The unseparated "bicameral" person had no concept of untruth and could not even imagine a lie. (A number of provocative ideas spring from this, but they will take us too far from our focus here.) Persons with less well-connected brain hemispheres had an easier time developing ego consciousness. Over a few thousand years, this trait became more and more pronounced, and the contents of its Pandora's Box of difficulties spread everywhere.

We tend to lose abilities we do not use, and the forgotten ones have the worst of it. I believe that it is possible to rediscover one's capacity to function as a whole self, integrated within the brain as well as with the world. Certain crystals, such as clear Selenite and Sunset Gold Selenite, seem able to stimulate the brain in ways that increase the bilateral hemispheric integration (as well as encouraging synergistic unification of heart/brain awareness), helping us to feel more whole and more entwined with the world. Whether this reunion entails a change in the neuronal activity, a repatterning of the Liquid Crystal Body Matrix or both is as yet unknown.

Selenite, in all its forms, is a great ally for those who seek to discover the lost or unknown potentials of an integrated whole-brain consciousness. The felt sense of Sunset Gold Selenite's currents is of a laser-like flow of positive healing and awakening vibrations, moving precisely to their correct linkages within the brain and etheric systems. While meditating with a Sunset Gold Selenite crystal, one can point the crystal toward the head, focusing upon different chakra points and brain areas. When I do this, I can feel the currents deep inside the head. Working with Sunset Gold Selenite in this way is something of an experiment, but remember that we are working with a helpful *being,* not a blind object. All the currents feel beneficial and pleasurable, and I trust the process. I feel we are safe in taking this approach, and that doing so is another part of our gesture of trust, entering into co-creative relationship with the beings of the stones, and with the world.

Sunset Gold Selenite, pointed toward the heart, generates currents of golden light, reminding the "I" within the heart of its sovereignty and encouraging the heart's consciousness to wake up. We have, as a consequence of our descent into separation, experienced a great turning away from the "I" of the heart. This "I" of the heart seems to be more than a neurological phenomenon—the second self in the heart is experienced as something divine, as if the heart is where the Divine "I AM" is "wired" into the human being. Whatever the reality of this may be, the "I" of the heart is a being that loves unconditionally—loving even the separated self which turns away from it. It will wait lifetimes for the chance of reunification of the self, which we are now beginning to experience throughout humanity. Yet the many ages of waiting have left the heart vulnerable to dormancy and sleep. We must turn toward the heart with full consciousness, encouragement and love, and we must feed the heart with our attention in order to inspire it to become conscious once again, and to remain in a wakeful state. When the heart is awake and takes its seat of sovereignty as governor of mind/body and all the layers of our being, we come into wholeness, and the Kingdom is once again healthy and thriving. Balance is achieved naturally when the heart is honored as the seat of wisdom, seat of the true "I."

This awakening takes persistence, patience and faith. One cannot turn toward the heart for a moment and away from it the next, expecting that the heart will remain awake. Sunset Gold Selenite offers an aid to heart awareness by providing its intense, energetic, exuberant current-flow to the heart. As we develop the new way of being in which the brain/mind and heart/wisdom are in communion, Sunset Gold Selenite is capable of assisting by generating precise resonant current flows that can help bring integration to the brain/mind and synergistic communion between the brain and the heart.

SUNSET GOLD SELENITE SPEAKS "I embody the golden flow of the Time of Turning, the rediscovery of unity and wholeness. My intensity is a reflection of the urgency of the need for your transformation into a being of resplendent wholeness. Those who turn to me, holding the wish for spiritual metamorphosis, will find a friend."

TANZANITE

KEY WORDS Linkage of the mind and heart, enhanced spiritual perception, compassionate self-expression, adherence to truth

ELEMENT Wind

CHAKRAS Heart (4th), Throat (5th), Third Eye (6th), Crown (7th), Soul Star (8th)

Tanzanite is a member of the Zoisite family, a calcium aluminum silicate mineral with a hardness of 6.5 to 7. Its crystal system is orthorhombic, and it forms prismatic, usually striated crystals. The color ranges from blue to blue-violet, although some crystals are golden to brownish yellow. When heated to around 900 degrees Fahrenheit, the crystals with yellow tones turn to blue or blue-violet.

Tanzanite was first discovered in 1967 in Tanzania, Africa. The name Tanzanite, obviously derived from the country where the stone is found, was introduced by Tiffany and Co., the New York jewelers. This has become the name accepted around the world, though scientists refer to it as blue Zoisite.

BACKGROUND Tanzanite is the stone that most effectively integrates the energies of the mind and heart, helping one to remained centered in the heart's wisdom while evaluating the ideas of the activated mind. It opens a cascade of thoughts and insights, but it keeps one calmly anchored upon the inner throne of compassionate humanity, thereby ensuring that one not be carried away on mental tangents of little true value.

The integration of mind and heart offered by Tanzanite takes place through the linkage and attunement of the heart and third eye chakras. The importance of this development in one's spiritual life cannot be over-emphasized. The need to bring the heart into cooperation and communion with the mind is in part what is meant by the search for wholeness. Once the mind understands what the neglected heart has to offer, there is no going back. The mind reflects its

pleasure to the heart, which releases greater joy, causing the mind to reflect greater pleasure, and so on.

Another effect of Tanzanite's linkage of mind and heart takes place at the throat chakra. Under Tanzanite's influence, one finds it far easier to speak the heart's truth with all the resourcefulness and eloquence the mind can conjure. In fact, Tanzanite makes it difficult to conceal or deny what one knows in one's heart.

Tanzanite is one of the Synergy Twelve stones, along with Moldavite, Phenacite, Danburite, Azeztulite, Herderite, Tibetan Tektite, Petalite, Brookite, Natrolite, Scolecite and Satyaloka Azeztulite. This is the most powerful combination of stones yet discovered for evolutionary quickening and raising one's vibrational level. Other stones that harmonize well with Tanzanite include Rosophia, Agni Gold Danburite, Pink Azeztulite, Sanda Rosa Azeztulite, Morganite, Satya Mani Quartz and Nirvana Quartz.

NEW ATTUNEMENT When I sat down to work with Tanzanite meditatively, I first placed a stone over my heart chakra. I felt a gradually building resonance between the stone and my heart, which created a kind of comfortable ache in the heart. From this I recognized Tanzanite as a stone of emotional healing. For those who are burdened by loss, grief, depression or unreasonable fear, Tanzanite makes an ideal companion to carry or wear. Tanzanite's currents are very nourishing to the emotional body. They aid anyone who works with this stone in freeing areas of the auric field that are blocked as a result of past negative experience. Fixations on past events that disturbed the emotional body are among the most common spiritual ailments, and many stones are helpful in undoing them. Tanzanite works its very powerful spiritual magic in this realm, with a great deal of gentleness. Tanzanite invites the heart to release its pain. It then moves throughout the energy field with its own current, flowing through darkened areas in the etheric and astral bodies, bringing clarity and smoothness to what were previously jagged or knotted places.

Tanzanite resonates best with the heart, throat, third eye and crown chakras. When I was working with the stones for this meditative attunement, I placed one Tanzanite in each of these four areas. Inwardly I saw a column of blue-violet light extending through these exact areas of the body. There was an accompanying sense of clarification, straightening and aligning of these four chakras with one another. This is in keeping with Tanzanite's well-known property of aligning the mind and the heart. Further, it prepares and attunes the mind to receive the knowing of the Higher Self through the spiritual portal of the crown. When the Higher Self energy enters through the crown, it is transduced next by the third eye chakra. Tanzanite awakens the spiritual organ of receptivity at the crown and fills it with Light patterns offered from above. Then the third eye begins to correlate these patterns with ideas and other meaningful structures or forms derived from receiving the geometries of Light. Thus Tanzanite is an aid to channeling all kinds of spiritual information from higher sources. The capacity of its currents to descend from the crown through the third eye and throat all the way to the heart displays Tanzanite's tendency to bring these four centers into correct alignment. Tanzanite engages the mental processes of the third eye in ways that allow us to see, understand and express the Divine information received. It also stimulates the neural connectivity that gives rise to various kinds of intelligence—mathematical, linguistic, abstract, intuitive, telepathic, prophetic, clairaudient and clairsentient.

Tanzanite at the throat chakra activates this area to a high degree. When it is used in conjunction with Tanzanites at the third eye and crown, it allows one to (almost without conscious thought) give clear vocal expression to the impulses and images received from the spiritual realms. It is ideal for those who are engaged in intuitive practices such as channeling, offering readings and using oracles or other tools for divining the flow patterns of the unfolding universe. Tanzanite's descent through the top three chakras into the heart brings one's mental understanding into resonance with one's true center in the heart. The heart is the barometer or compass of truth within us, because the heart perceives reality in a direct manner, and the heart is the impulse of the Divine in us. Therefore the heart's resonance with reality is true in the deepest sense, and it can be a wonderful guide to one's thinking and expression. Tanzanite can serve as an unsurpassed ally in delving into the spiritual realms. It can awaken spiritual receptivity, mental resonance and understanding, verbal and written expression, and one's inner compass of truth.

As one of the Synergy Twelve stones, Tanzanite provides strong anchoring in the heart. It accentuates the ability to express the truth of the fullness of one's being, which is awakened by the combination of the Synergy Twelve stones. Through its heart connection, Tanzanite lifts compassion to the top of one's hierarchy of essential priorities. It deters detachment from the feeling dimensions of life.

Tanzanite teaches, through infusion, the vibration of spiritual love. Its connection with the heart opens us to deep intimacy with other people. It enhances intuitive vision, so we see through the outer facade of personality, into the deep patterns of soul and spirit within partners, friends, or any other human being. Thus Tanzanite can be a powerful ally for those seeking spiritual relationships. People wishing to attract or attune with their spiritual mates or partners—even what is called the Twin Flame—can be greatly assisted by assimilating the vibrational spectrum of Tanzanite. Tanzanite's love resonance tends always upward, toward the spiritual much more than the sexual, and thereby attunes one to those beings—physical and non-physical—with whom one has a spiritual love-resonance.

Tanzanite's currents are an aid to what one might call "higher grounding." Such stones as Black Tourmaline, Master Shamanite, Jet and others help one to ground through the lowest portal of the body at the root chakra. Tanzanite does not descend this far, yet it permeates the physical body with its cords of connection from the brain to the heart. Therefore, one does not easily stray from the body and lose connection with matter when working with Tanzanite, yet one is primarily attuned to the highest and most evolved centers of consciousness within the human being. Thus Tanzanite is an excellent ally for grounding oneself sufficiently when working with extremely high-vibration stones such as Azeztulite, Phenacite, Scolecite, Herderite, Diamond and others (most notably the Ascension Seven).

TANZANITE SPEAKS   "I am a keeper of the Violet Flame and a purifier of all that you aspire to spiritually. My service is to pour through your upper gates, offering a cleansing absolution. I am a teacher and healer to those who wish Ascension into higher awareness. I assist all beings, in their seeking, to remember their truth and their identification with Source."

TIBETAN BLACK QUARTZ

KEY WORDS   Spiritual protection and purification, enhancement of meditation, balancing the chakras and meridians, clearing and energizing the aura, purification of desire

ELEMENT   Storm

CHAKRAS   All

Tibetan Black Quartz is a member of the Quartz family, a silicon dioxide mineral with a hardness of 7. Its crystal system is hexagonal (trigonal). The crystals are nearly all double-terminated, and many contain black inclusions of carbon or manganese. The word "black" in the name is not a literal description of all crystals in this group. The majority of stones, all of which contain black material, are not completely black, and some are nearly clear. Tibetan Black Quartz is found in the Himalaya Mountains of Tibet and Nepal.

BACKGROUND   The Himalaya mountain range of Tibet, where these crystals are found, is among the most sacred areas of the Earth; and Tibetan Black Quartz double-terminated crystals are among the most powerful stones of spiritual protection ever found. Carrying or wearing one creates a "bubble of Light" around the body, allowing only positive vibrations to penetrate the auric field. Sleeping with or near Tibetan Black Quartz protects one from lower astral energies and can help eliminate disturbing dreams. Keeping one or more of these stones in a living space can purify and cleanse the area of any negative influences. I even recommend putting one on top of the television or computer screen to counteract the disharmonies these might emanate.

Meditation with Tibetan Black Quartz can be most beneficial, especially to those who feel an affinity for Tibetan Buddhism. The stones seem to emanate a silent "Om" at all times, and they can be powerful activators of the third eye. They also resonate with the state of silent alertness that is essential to meditation.

In addition to offering protection and purification, Tibetan Black Quartz crystals can activate and balance the chakras and meridian system. If one of the chakras or nodal points is blocked or sluggish, touching that point with one of these crystals can quickly alleviate the problem. For full-body crystal treatments, place double-terminated points at each of the seven chakras, aligning them so the crystals lie lengthwise along the chakric column. This allows an energetic linkage among all the crystals and a resonant strengthening of the connections between all the points in one's energy body.

Tibetan Black Quartz harmonizes with Moldavite, Lithium Quartz, Aegirine, Black Tourmaline, Nuummite and Master Shamanite. Combining these stones with all varieties of Azeztulite will bring in angelic energies, and using them with Phenacite can enhance visionary experiences.

NEW ATTUNEMENT   In the awakening or, one might also say, in the creating of the Body of Light—which is one way of looking at the birth of the New Consciousness—we need stones capable of aiding us in grounding, cleansing and purification. Tibetan Black Quartz is one of the most potent and wholesome allies for this work.

In beginning my meditation with Tibetan Black Quartz crystals, I had just finished meditating with the stone Natrolite, which is an extremely high-vibration stone of Light. After working with Natrolite, I felt so highly stimulated in my energy body that it was quite difficult to focus

myself and become centered for the next meditation. However, I picked up the four pieces of Tibetan Black Quartz that I planned to work with, and in a matter of moments I was much more grounded, more clear-headed, and very clear in the body as well.

Continuing the experiment, I placed one of the crystals under my base chakra, two of them over my heart and one at the crown. The resulting sensations were unlike any others I have experienced. I would describe them as a vibrant, slender energy cord that dropped repeatedly from the crown to the base chakra, in a very unobtrusive yet helpful way. By unobtrusive, I mean that the cord was thin and the energy not overly intense. By helpful, I mean that each downward sensation felt like a clarifying wave.

After a few minutes I noticed that the root chakra was experiencing sensations of opening, and it was extending a connection down into the Earth. I try to do this purposely when I begin to meditate. After working with the high-frequency Natrolites, I was not easily able to re-link through the base chakra until I placed the Black Tibetan Quartz below the root. Then after just a few minutes there was a sense of my "grounding cord" dropping down through the base chakra into the earth. There was also the feeling of a flow of excess energy out of my body and down into the earth. My intuitive sense was that with the Natrolite I had temporarily taken in more Light than my cellular and energetic structures could hold. I sensed that it was beneficial to have brought in so much Light, and again beneficial to be able to release the excess into the earth.

I heard inwardly, as this was occurring, that the energy flowing out of my body into the ground was nourishing for the Earth. This is in accord with many other insights I have had regarding high-frequency stones such as Azeztulite. The Earth needs the incarnating breath of the Light as much as we do, and we can serve the Earth as points of infusion of spiritual Light. Therefore it is helpful to purposely release whatever Light goes beyond our assimilation capacity and drop it into the Earth's depths. I might even suggest that in some meditations we hold the intention that *all* of the Light entering us goes to the Earth. This is a way of offering healing to the planet. My wife Kathy, who is a healer, has told me that when she acts as a conduit for the healing of others, she always receives healing as well—so we need not worry about depleting ourselves.

Tibetan Black Quartz is a great aid in this kind of cleansing and beneficial energy release. It does not cause us to release more than the excess Light. (Or perhaps it works as I said above—in releasing Light we also receive Light. It may be that the rebalancing we experience with the release is the felt sense of the Light fully integrating into us.)

Tibetan Black Quartz is an excellent stone for the enhancement of meditation. It helps us enter the realms of silence, and its currents encourage the silence to permeate the mind, so mental activity does not become a barrier to entering the meditative depths. Tibetan Black Quartz's quieting effect on the mental body is most helpful for releasing stress and finding a place of inner peace. At the same time, Tibetan Black Quartz acts as a guardian. Its cleansing influence purifies the auric field of any negative cords or attachments, or any holes in the fabric of the aura, as well as the astral and/or etheric bodies. It simply smooths out these imperfections and brings a gentle state of quiet, comfortable, purified alertness of mind.

Tibetan Black Quartz can also be a deeply relaxing stone. It is recommended for those wishing to find ways of more readily entering the sleep state, even in times of stress or intense activity. The relaxing influence of Tibetan Black Quartz tends to lead one to the threshold of sleep and the dream realm. Those wishing to experience lucid dreaming are encouraged to use this stone.

Tibetan Black Quartz is involved in the activity of purification in a deeper way—through the purification of desire. Our desires are not to be washed away, yet they are to be purified. For example, one may desire love in a manner that is impure, and in this impure desire the feeling of neediness may cause one to look for love relationships in inappropriate ways—such as obsession with a celebrity or a fascination with pornography. Such patterns stem from the wholesome desire for love, but in an impure form.

Tibetan Black Quartz, with its cleansing influence and its way of soothing and smoothing the astral body, helps to dissolve all such impure patterns. One can facilitate this process by consciously, during meditation with Tibetan Black Quartz, offering one's impure desires to the Earth or the Soul of the Earth. I suggest imagining that one's impure desires are cupped (along with a Tibetan Black Quartz crystal) within one's extended hands; one then reaches the hands outward in a gesture of offering. Another practice might involve holding one of these stones while imagining washing one's hands in a pool of clear water, seeing the fixations dissolve as they are accepted by the water, and through the water by the Mother. One can create other images and processes that will work just as well. After the process, I suggest cleansing the Tibetan Black Quartz by holding it under cool running water and asking for the stone to be cleansed. At the end, one is left with a sense of clarity and gratitude, and what remains of the desire when this work is accomplished is pure and unencumbered by distortion.

TIBETAN BLACK QUARTZ SPEAKS   "I am a guardian at the gate of the world of dreams. I am a protector in the unseen realm. I offer my nourishing darkness, my invisible cleansing hands to wash your soul body. When you ascend too quickly or too far, I will help you rejoin the Earth."

TIBETAN TEKTITE

KEY WORDS   Opening the chakra column, attunement
to the Supramental Force, accelerated evolution,
Light Body awakening

ELEMENT   Storm

CHAKRAS   All

Tibetan Tektite is the name given to a family of black or brown-black Tektites found in Tibet and southern China. Tektites are glassy objects associated with meteoric impacts. Their hardness ranges from 5.5 to 6.5, and their crystal system is amorphous. Tektites are rich in silica, with silicon dioxide content ranging from sixty-eight to eighty-two percent. The name "tektite" comes from the Greek word *tektos,* meaning "molten." The classic forms of Tektites—teardrops, smooth rounded "buttons" and dumbbells—suggest that these stones were, at the time of the associated meteoric impact, heated to the liquid state and flung through the atmosphere. Scientists have long debated whether Tektites were themselves meteorites, terrestrial rocks melted by meteoric impacts, or some fusion of terrestrial and extraterrestrial material. Most Tektites are black or brown-black, with bottle-green Moldavite a notable exception.

Tektites have been found in North America, Australia, Africa, China and Southeast Asia. The most abundant Tektites are those found strewn in the vast fields of China and Indochina. It is to these Tektites that the metaphysical information below primarily refers. (See also the sections on Moldavite and Libyan Gold Tektite.)

Tektites have a long history in lore and legend. More than two thousand years ago, the Chinese writer Liu Sun gave Tektites the name *Lei-gong-mo,* meaning "Inkstone of the Thunder-god." Australian Aborigines refer to them as *Maban,* which means "magic," and they believe that finding a Tektite brings good luck. In India the stones have been known as *Saimantakimani,* the "sacred gem of Krishna." The Sanskrit name for Tektites, *agni mani,* can be translated into English as "fire pearl" or "teardrops from the moon." Natives of the island of Billiton in the Java Sea, where teardrop-shaped Tektites are plentiful, call them "magic black seeds," which they believe can be planted to grow tin, an important material for sale and export.

Tektites range from several hundred thousand years to more than a billion years old. Tibetan Tektites are believed to be among the older varieties. Tibetan monks are said to have revered these Tektites, calling them the "Stone of Shambhala," referring to the legendary realm upon which the stories of "Shangri La, Land of the Immortals," were based. The Tibetan prophecy of the Kalichakra predicts that the powerful Lords of Shambhala, at a time of the world's dire need, will issue from their mysterious realm and banish evil from the Earth. Tibetan Tektites, as talismans of Shambhala, are thus considered to be sacred stones.

BACKGROUND   When we were first introduced to these stones in 1992, our supplier told us that they had long been collected and gathered by the Drokma, a tribe of nomads living on the Chang Tang or Great Plateau in central and northern Tibet near Motsobuhna Lake. It was said that these Tektites were worn in ceremonial garb by monks and lamas, and that their Sanskrit name was *agni mani,* meaning "fire pearl." Energetically they are indeed "pearls of fire." I have used them for years to clear and open the chakra columns of people, as an initial exercise for working with stones in meditations and/or body layouts. In these exercises, everyone works with a partner, standing in profile while the partner rotates a Tibetan Tektite above the crown chakra and simultaneously slowly slides another one down along the spine from the back of the head to the sacrum. This practice produces a predictable and strong sensation of warmth and opening of the whole spinal column, which can culminate with the opening of the crown chakra. It is often accompanied by energy surges where blockages are cleared, and sensations of mild warmth to intense heat.

Early in our acquaintance with Tibetan Tektites, these words came through in meditative work: "These highly energetic, intensely vibrating stones are truly a gift from beyond the Earth, having been psychically directed here as an evolutionary seed. The beings of these domains, who have directed these seed-stones to Earth, are available for communication through psychometric meditation with these Tibetan Tektites. They are benign beings who desire to bring about a minded cosmos through the telepathic interconnection of all intelligent species and planets through the universe. They are already in contact with beings on the higher etheric levels of the Earth realm, and are attempting with them to reach down into our sphere for the awakening of humanity and the completion of their goal of interconnected intelligences."

The placement of seven of the Tibetan Tektites on the body, one at each chakra point, is optimal for stimulating and activating the Light Body. For lucid dreaming one is advised to sleep with two Tibetan Tektites, at the head and foot of the bed. To enhance the visionary capacity of dreams, add a Phenacite. For conscious out-of-body experiences, Herderite is a recommended ally. Natrolite, Cryolite, Merkabite Calcite, Satya Mani Quartz and all varieties of Azeztulite are helpful in facilitating the conscious link to universal intelligence that these stones offer. Tibetan Tektite is also one of the Synergy Twelve stones.

NEW ATTUNEMENT   For years I have introduced Tibetan Tektites into groups where I am teaching and invited people to pair up as partners and work with these stones to open the chakra column—the spinal energy channel. I have more recently worked with two stones in the hands of the person whose channel is being opened and two stones in the hands of the person doing the treatment. The person receiving the treatment is asked to turn profile to the facilitator and to close his or her eyes while standing. The person doing the treatment takes one Tibetan Tektite and rotates it slowly above the head of the individual, while carefully touching or holding the second Tibetan Tektite an inch or two away from the back of the recipient's head. Then the person doing the treatment is asked to slowly draw the Tibetan Tektite at the back of the head downward along the spinal column, stopping at any spots where intuition suggested there might be a block or something to be worked through. Invariably in these groups more than ninety-eight percent of those working in this process can feel the flow of energies down

the chakra column. Many feel blockages dissolve and open. Many feel warm, tingling, electrical currents moving down the spine in a pleasurable manner. Some become light-headed, and others experience infusions and even slight "explosions" of energy where the chakras are located. Often these occur at the crown chakra or the heart—sometimes both. The effect after this process is that people feel much more open to the currents of the other crystals with which we work that day. It is definitely a way of demonstrating to people that stone energies are very real.

In the work suggested by this book, Tibetan Tektites serve this function and more. They are highly recommended to be used in the very way I have taught it, with two people working together to open up the chakra column so that each can be more receptive to and aware of the stones' energies. One also can use the same practice to draw down the currents of what is called the Supramental Force.

For this attunement I held two Tibetan Tektites in front of me and gazed upon them with a diffuse focus.

As I looked at them with my half-closed eyes, I perceived around them a dark fog filling my cupped hands. After a few minutes of doing this, I placed the two stones at my forehead with my eyes closed. Immediately there were two outlines of brilliant light corresponding to the form of the two stones. I was surprised, having seen them visually as being so dark. As I was considering this, I experienced the intuition that Tibetan Tektite is an embodied form of what may be called the Light within the Darkness. This is one of the ways of describing the Transparent Ray. I believe this Light is the same as what is called the Supramental Force. It is what the Vedic *rishis* five thousand years ago called the *saura agni,* or the "solar fire" (as discussed earlier in these pages). It is the Light that is the radiance of the spiritual Sun "behind" the sun we know.

Saura agni (aka the Supramental Force or the Transparent Ray), when it permeates our bodies through the DNA gateway and becomes the infusing consciousness of our liquid crystallinity, creates the human Light Body and the spiritual human being who lives the New Consciousness. That is a large and portentous sentence! As mentioned, the Tibetan Tektites have long been revered by monks in Tibet, who recognized them as spiritual talismans of great importance and power. And we've noted that they were called *agni mani,* or "fire pearl." This fire is the same *saura agni* that we feel pouring into the body with the aid of Tibetan Tektite. In fact, the whole array of the crystalline allies discussed in this book is part of a great benevolent conspiracy to intervene and aid in our evolution. This has been going on longer than history, and the fragments of history show us that stones such as these Tibetan Tektites and others have been recognized as Divine for thousands of years.

I repeat, for the sake of emphasis, that Tibetan Tektite, the *agni mani,* the gem of fire, emanates the currents of the Supramental Force, the Transparent Ray, the Light in darkness, the *saura agni* or solar fire of the Sun behind the sun. In working with these stones mainly for the opening of the chakra column, I feel I have only scratched the surface of their awesome potential and what they can engender in us. I hope my recognition of them here will lead me and others to explore deeply the gifts of Tibetan Tektites.

TIBETAN TEKTITE SPEAKS "I am the Black Pearl of the Holy Fire, glowing at the bottom of the great ocean of the fertile darkness. I radiate the invisible Light of the Midnight Sun. I need only your turning of attention to me, and your invitation to my invisible ray, to infuse your body with my transforming Light."

AFTERWORD

"We have in our short lives only two choices: to be safe or astonished."

—MARY SOJOURNER

As I look back upon all that has been presented in this book, I am struck by how many times the implications of the ideas with which I was working brought me beyond the brink of what I had always considered to be the "safe" ideas about the nature of life. Those boundaries that only "material" things are real, that only "organic" entities are alive, that only human beings are conscious, that angels and spiritual beings are probably "just our imagination," and other such assertions that define the limits of how we view ourselves and our world offer us the promise of security. However, the price we pay is our capacity to be astonished. Yet when we consider even the things that consensus reality purports to accept as true, we are drawn inevitably into the realm of wonder.

We are told by consensus science that we exist in an unimaginably gigantic universe, within which our entire planet is comparable to a single grain of sand amid all the beaches and mountains of the world. Our most accepted theory about the origin of this vast and fiery array of stars, floating amid an even greater and incredibly frigid void, is that it emerged spontaneously, fifteen billion or more years ago, from a single point much, much smaller than a grain of sand. Somehow or other, life and consciousness arose on this little blue gem of a planet, and now the universe has billions of eyes looking back at itself from our vantage point at the edge of the Milky Way. Compared to these articles of scientific faith, believing in our personal experiences of the energies of stones and the consciousness we seem to perceive within them seems easy. Yet simply believing in either or both of these propositions is not the goal to which I am trying to point. The goal is to live in an ongoing awareness of the astounding, magical and mystical unknowns that surround us on every side, within and without. The goal is to stay with the unknown, moment after moment, in a state of astonishment, trust and love that makes its way through the world without attempting to be "safe."

Infants enter the world in this sort of state. Everything they have ever known as they grew within the womb is suddenly overturned by the monumental event of birth. How much greater their world is now than the one which was previously their All! When we observe babies, we can often catch a glimpse of their total openness, while at other times we see them crying out for the nurturing security of Mother. Yet openness is as crucial for them to develop and grow into whole human beings as physical safety is necessary for their survival. The tension between our desire for safety and the bare fact that reality is utterly astonishing is a fundamental quality of being, and one that we should embrace. It is not that we can ever be safe in the sense in which we usually think of safety. It is that in surrendering to the overwhelming mystery of existence, in affirming it and offering ourselves to it without reservation, we discover that we have always been at one with the whole thing. When this surrender really occurs, we experience a second birth, perhaps more astonishing than our first.

How can we move into this moment, our birth into the New Consciousness? As I have said throughout this book, we have the power, through our imagination and our will, to engage the world through the activity of blessing. This is as simple as taking each moment, each object and each being into our heart with an inner gesture of appreciation. Related qualities such as forgiveness, gratitude and love are all implied within the generosity of our blessing gesture. And the miracle beyond all others is the discovery that we are met by another consciousness, the Soul of the World, when we practice offering ourselves to the world in this way. The stones are a part of it, and the discovery of their life opens our eyes to the ocean of consciousness within which we all swim and entangle in the ever-changing dance of being, which is eternal. The crystals, so I affirm, are angels, holding open the door to the Paradise we are called to discover and to co-create. Our stresses and anxieties amount to the contractions of our birth canal. It is time to be born.

—Robert Simmons
East Montpelier, Vermont

BIBLIOGRAPHY

Blavatsky, H.P. *Isis Unveiled: A Master-Key to the Mysteries of Ancient and Modern Science and Theology.* Pasadena, CA: Theosophical University Press, 1877.

Blavatsky, H.P. *The Secret Doctrine: The Synthesis of Science, Religion and Philosophy.* Pasadena, CA: Theosophical University Press, 1888. Electronic version, ISBN 1-55700-124-3.

Bly, Robert. *Eating the Honey of Words: New and Selected Poems.* New York, NY: Harper Collins, 2000.

H.H. Dalai Lama. "OM MANI PADME HUM." Online article: http://www.tibet.com/Buddhism/om-mantra.html.

Denton, Michael J., Legge, Michael, Marshall, Craig J., Department of Biochemistry, University of Otago, Dunedin, New Zealand. "The Protein Folds as Platonic Forms: New Support for the Pre-Darwinian Conception of Evolution by Natural Law." Online article: http://www.sciencedirect.com/science?_ob=ArticleURL&_udi=B6WMD-473VN67-5&_user=10&_rdoc=1&_fmt=&_orig=search&_sort=d&view=c&_acct=C000050221&_version=1&_urlVersion=0&_userid=10&md5=b8eadc965e2f5818aeeb70a5deed7d6b.

Emoto, Masaru. *Messages from Water.* Vol. 1. Kyoikusha, Japan: Hado Kyoiku Sha Company, 1999.

Fideler, David. *Jesus Christ, Sun of God: Ancient Cosmology and Early Christian Symbolism.* Adyar, India: Quest Books, 1993.

Heartmath articles, source for all: http://www.heartmath.org/ and http://www.heartmath.org/research/overview.html.

Ho, Mae Wan. *The Rainbow and the Worm: The Physics of Organisms,* 1st edition. Singapore: World Scientific Publishing Company, 1993.

——. "Coherent Energy, Liquid Crystallinity and Acupuncture." Online article: http://www.i-sis.org.uk/acupunc.php.

Narby, Jeremy. *The Cosmic Serpent: DNA and the Origins of Knowledge.* New York: Tarcher, 1997.

Norbu, Namkhai. *The Crystal and the Way of Light: Sutra, Tantra and Dzogchen.* Ithaca, NY: Snow Lion Publications, 2000.

Oschman, James L. *Energy Medicine, The Scientific Basis.* Edinburgh, UK: Churchill Livingston, 2000.

Pavitra (transcriber). "A Talk with Sri Aurobindo." Online article: http://www.mirroroftomorrow.org/blog/_archives/2009/1/2/4042583.html.

Pearce, Joseph Chilton. *The Biology of Transcendence: A Blueprint of the Human Spirit.* Rochester, VT: Park Street Press, 2002.

Pinkham, Mark Amaru. "Nicholas Roerich and the Chintamani Stone," *Four Corners* Magazine. Online address: http://www.bibliotecapleyades.net/sociopolitica/sociopol_shambahla11.htm.

Pitkanen, Matti. "Biosystems as Conscious Holograms. J of Non-Locality and Remote Mental Interactions II[1]," 2003. www.emergentmind.org/PDF_files.htm/conschol00302.PDF.

Raff, Jeffrey, PhD. *The Wedding of Sophia: The Divine Feminine in Psychoidal Alchemy.* Berwick, ME: Nicolas-Hays, Inc. 2003.

Sardello, Robert. *Love and the Soul: Creating a Future for Earth.* Berkeley, CA: North Atlantic Books and Goldenstone Press, 2008.

Satprem. *On the Way to Supermanhood.* New York, NY: Institute for Evolutionary Research, 1985.

Satprem. *The Mind of the Cells.* New York, NY: Institute for Evolutionary Research, 1982.

Sheldrake, Rupert. *The Presence of the Past: Morphic Resonance and the Habits of Nature.* Rochester, VT: Inner Traditions International, 1995.

Sidirov, Lian. "Control Systems, Transduction Arrays and Psi Healing: An Experimental Basis for Human Potential Science." Online article: www.emergentmind.org/Sidorov02.htm.

Simmons, Robert, and Ahsian, Naisha. *The Book of Stones: Who They Are and What They Teach.* Berkeley, CA and Montpelier, VT: North Atlantic Books and Heaven and Earth Publishing, 2007.

Simmons, Robert, and Warner, Kathy Helen. *Moldavite: Starborn Stone of Transformation.* Montpelier, VT: Heaven and Earth Publishing, 1988.

Schirber, Michael. "Diamonds May Be Life's Birthstone." *Astrobiology Magazine.* [Posted 09/25/08] Online article: http://astrobio.net/news/index.php?name=News&file=article&sid=2883.

Stavish, Mark. Institute for Hermetic Studies. "The Body of Light in the Western Esoteric Tradition." Online article: http://www.hermetics.org/stavish/BodyOfLight.html.

Stephenson, MaAnna "The Body's Crystal Matrix—Part Two." January 18, 2009. EzineArticles.com. Accessed June 15, 2009 <http://ezinearticles.com/?The-Bodys-Crystal-Matrix—Part-Two&id=1894834.

The Mother. *Collected Works.* Pondicherry, India: Sri Aurobindo Ashram Trust, 1972.

Trismegistus, Hermes. *The Emerald Tablet of Hermes and The Kybalion: Two Classic Books on Hermetic Philosophy.* Raleigh, NC: Lulu Press, 2005.

Web site about Sri Aurobindo: www.gurusoftware.com/GuruNet/AurobindoMother/Aurobindo.htm.

Witcombe, Christopher L.C.E. "Water and the Sacred." Online article: http://witcombe.sbc.edu/sacredplaces/water.html.

INDEX

ABOUT THE AUTHOR

Robert Simmons has been a student and investigator of many spiritual paths since a spontaneous mystical experience during his first year at Yale changed the course of his life. Fifteen years later, his encounter with Moldavite shifted and expanded his horizons yet again. In 1986 he married Kathy Helen Warner, and together they established their company, Heaven and Earth, which began as a crystal shop specializing in Moldavite, then expanded into a mail-order company offering more than two thousand stone, gem and jewelry items to both individuals and stores. Robert and Kathy are co-authors of *Moldavite: Starborn Stone of Transformation.*

Robert has been writing and teaching about the metaphysical properties of stones for more than twenty-three years. He co-authored *The Book of Stones* with Naisha Ahsian. He is also author of the award-winning visionary novel *Earthfire: A Tale of Transformation.* He collects stories of individuals who have undergone profound spiritual experiences with Moldavite and Azeztulite, with other crystals and minerals, or with no stones at all. He is co-founder of The Crystal Conference (www.thecrystalconference.com), a biennial four-day weekend of seminars in which teachers and students from around the world gather to explore the energies of the mineral realm.

As an Atlantis alumnus, Robert enjoys working with minerals and crystals to create stone synergies in jewelry, tools and meditation environments. He is exploring the incorporation of high-vibration stones into labyrinths and healing spaces. He enjoys working on home improvements and is thus actively engaged in helping to transform the Earth into a Planet of Light. He welcomes all volunteers to join in this group activity.

Robert sometimes travels to present workshops and talks on stone energies, spiritual evolution and other topics he enjoys. To contact him regarding a workshop or to share your story of spiritual awakening, send an e-mail to heavenandearth@earthlink.net.

Companion volume to *Stones of the New Consciousness,* featuring over 320 different minerals, crystals and gemstones. The book includes vivid color photos, scientific data, and essays by both authors on the spiritual properties of each stone.

RESOURCES

As we discover more stones and write about their spiritual and energetic properties, we'll post these new articles on our Web site: www.heavenandearthjewelry.com. We encourage readers to visit the site, and to write us with comments and suggestions. The mailing address is:

Heaven and Earth Publishing LCC
P.O.BOX 249
East Montpelier, VT 05651

Or you can e-mail us at: heavenandearth@earthlink.net

Readers interested in inviting Robert Simmons to come to your shop or organization to present a talk, workshop and/or crystal and jewelry trunk show are encouraged to contact him through Heaven and Earth Publishing. Robert is always collecting stories of people's spiritual and healing experiences with stones. If you have one you would like to share, please write to him at one of the addresses above.

The Heaven and Earth Publishing Web site is *heavenandearthpubl.com*. This Web site contains information on *Stones of the New Consciousness, The Book of Stones, The Crystal Ally Cards, Moldavite: Starborn Stone of Transformation* and *Earthfire,* as well as other titles offered by Heaven and Earth Publishing.

Heaven and Earth LLC publishes an extensive catalog of crystals, minerals, gemstones and jewelry. Readers interested in obtaining a copy can send a request by post or e-mail. Phone requests can be made by calling 802-476-4775.

The Crystal Conference is a biennial seminar where a number of teachers, including the author of this book, come together to offer a four-day series of workshops featuring a variety of modalities for working with stones and their energies. For information regarding dates, locations and featured speakers at upcoming Crystal Conference events, contact Heaven and Earth Publishing or visit the Conference Web site: www.thecrystalconference.com.

Robert and Cheryl Sardello offer courses in Heart Initiation, Spirit Healing, Caritas (caring for those who have died) and other areas of soul growth through their School of Spiritual Psychology. For information, contact:
The School of Spiritual Psychology
Robert Sardello, PhD, and Cheryl Sanders-Sardello, PhD, Co-directors
www.spiritualschool.org